Prussians, Nazis and Peaceniks

Manchester University Press

Prussians, Nazis and Peaceniks

Changing images of Germany in International Relations

Edited by
Jens Steffek and **Leonie Holthaus**

Manchester University Press

Published by Manchester University Press
Oxford Road, Manchester M13 9PL
www.manchesteruniversitypress.co.uk

British Library Cataloguing-in-Publication Data
A catalogue record for this book is available from the British Library

ISBN 978 1 5261 3571 1 hardback
ISBN 978 1 5261 9569 2 paperback

First published 2020
Paperback published 2026

The publisher has no responsibility for the persistence or accuracy of URLs for any external or third-party internet websites referred to in this book, and does not guarantee that any content on such websites is, or will remain, accurate or appropriate.

EU authorised representative for GPSR:
Easy Access System Europe – Mustamäe tee 50, 10621 Tallinn, Estonia
gpsr.requests@easproject.com

Typeset by Newgen Publishing UK

Contents

List of figures and tables   vii

Notes on contributors   viii

Foreword by Roland Bleiker   ix

1   Introduction: changing images of Germany   1
Jens Steffek and Leonie Holthaus

2   Power as a German problem: a historical survey   17
Andreas Osiander

3   The liberal internationalist self and the construction of
an undemocratic German other at the beginning of the
twentieth century   40
Leonie Holthaus

4   From emulation to enmity: the changing view of Germany
in Anglo-American geopolitics   64
Lucian M. Ashworth

5   Federalism versus sovereignty: the Weimar Republic in the
eyes of American political science   82
Paul Petzschmann

6   Germany's fight against Versailles and the rise of American
realism: Edwin Borchard between New Haven and Berlin   100
Jens Steffek and Tobias Heinze

7   The tale of the 'two Germanies': twentieth-century Germany
in the debates of Anglo-American international lawyers and
transitional justice experts   123
Annette Weinke

8   The silent presence: Germany in American post-war
    International Relations   145
    Felix Rösch

9   *Deutschtum* and Americanism: memory and identity in
    Cold War America   167
    Brian C. Etheridge

10 'Civilian power' seen from abroad: the external image of
    Germany's foreign policy   184
    Siegfried Schieder

11 Conclusion: International Relations theory and Germany   211
    Richard Ned Lebow

Select bibliography   226

Index   231

Figures and tables

Figure

11.1 Total index pages of the top nine countries   218

Tables

10.1 Views of Germany's influence in selected countries   194
11.1 Authors and books   215
11.2 Number and percentage of index entries per country   219

Notes on contributors

Lucian M. Ashworth is Professor in the Department of Political Science at the Memorial University of Newfoundland.

Roland Bleiker is Professor of International Relations at the University of Queensland.

Brian C. Etheridge is Director of the University Honors Program and Professor of History at Kennesaw State University.

Tobias Heinze holds a master's degree in Political Theory from Goethe-Universität Frankfurt and Technische Universität Darmstadt.

Leonie Holthaus is Senior Research Fellow at Technische Universität Darmstadt.

Richard Ned Lebow is Professor of International Political Theory at King's College London and Bye-Fellow of Pembroke College, University of Cambridge.

Andreas Osiander teaches International Relations at Humboldt Universität Berlin.

Paul Petzschmann is Lecturer in European Studies at Carleton College.

Felix Rösch is Associate Professor in International Relations at Coventry University.

Siegfried Schieder is Assistant Professor in International Relations and European Politics at Ruprecht-Karls-Universität Heidelberg.

Jens Steffek is Professor of Transnational Governance at Technische Universität Darmstadt.

Annette Weinke is Senior Lecturer in Modern History at Friedrich-Schiller-Universität Jena.

Foreword

Roland Bleiker

Germany looms large in international politics, far larger than its size and population would suggest. The Second World War and the battle against Nazi Germany is one of the defining moments of the twentieth century. The Holocaust has become a global symbol of the horror of genocides. The Nuremberg trials were a founding precedent for war crimes tribunals and transitional justice. The Berlin Wall turned into a symbol for both the global ideological confrontation during the Cold War and the successful struggle to overcome it. It is not by accident that US President John F. Kennedy's 'Ich bin ein Berliner' speech (1961) was a defining metaphor for international politics at the time. Today, unified Germany is a crucial force of peaceful European integration and economic development. All this and much more took place against the background of a long history of German literary, artistic and scientific achievements. Many of them have shaped International Relations (IR) scholarship, from the writings of Immanuel Kant, Alexander von Humboldt and Karl von Clausewitz to more recent contributions of German émigré scholars, such as Hannah Arendt, Albert O. Hirschman and Hans Morgenthau.

This volume offers a compelling and highly sophisticated account of the complexities associated with these changing images of Germany in IR. The volume is characterised not only by its conceptual contribution but also, and primarily, by exceptionally detailed and thorough historical and contemporary case studies.

Germany as a contestable and constantly contested concept

One of the key insights that emerge from the contributions to *Prussians, Nazis and Peaceniks: Changing Images of Germany in International Relations* is that analysing the political role of Germany is never just about political facts and phenomena, but also, and primarily, about how we make sense of them and how we integrate these interpretations into both collective consciousness and concrete political positions and actions. When discussing the negative and positive international perceptions of Germany, Lucian M. Ashworth (in Chapter 4) stresses that they were 'caricatures that often bore little relation to the reality of the German situation'. Likewise, Leonie Holthaus (in Chapter 3) points out how liberal internationalist views of Germany at the beginning of the twentieth century had as much to do with preconceived liberal values as with the actual empirical phenomena being observed and addressed. The same is the case in more recent periods. For Brian C. Etheridge (in Chapter 9), US narratives of Germany during the post-war period had a lot to do with America's understanding of itself: to fit into and support this narrative, certain notions of Germany and Germanness were suppressed, while others were promoted.

Germany, then, is not – or at least not only – the nation-state we usually perceive it to be. It is and should also be seen as a contestable and constantly contested concept: a political construct that is both contingent and in constant flux. This is as much the case with the evolution of German politics and ideas as it is with how this evolution shaped international perceptions. What we can observe here is a constantly shifting idea that contains numerous dimensions: a nation, a state, a historical legacy, a cultural sphere, an intellectual tradition and much more. These dimensions overlap and shift, and are all part of what Germany is and is seen as. To understand the politics of these contested concepts is one of the core objectives of this book, and the authors manage to bring out the associated complexities and their relevance for understanding both Germany and its role in international relations.

Shifting images of Germany in IR

Shifting images of Germany are evident when we examine how political events and developments in and around Germany shaped international thought. Andreas Osiander (in Chapter 2) stresses the need to discuss what 'Germany' actually was at different stages of its historical trajectory. Doing so starts with the seemingly straightforward but in reality highly unstable issue of territorial delineation. Borders kept changing, from the creation of a German state during a wave of nineteenth-century nationalism to the expansion under the Third Reich, the subsequent contraction, followed by national division during the Cold War and then reunification. Some territories, like the Elsass or the Südtirol, were being moved back and forth between different political-ideological-cultural-linguistic spheres.

The same is the case with how the international community has perceived Germany over the past century and a half. Ashworth (in Chapter 4) points out how, between 1900 and 1945, these perceptions changed from great admiration and emulation of German scholarship and ideas to a deep-seated hostility towards raising militarism. There was a rapid move 'from exemplar to threat'. The so-called great debate in international theory, waged in the interwar period between realists and liberal internationalist, was all about how to best deal with the threat of Nazi Germany. The shift was just as swift and dramatic at the end of the Second World War, Etheridge (in Chapter 9) stresses. Occupation forces divided Germany into West and East, and each of them turned from arch-enemy into a strong ally and friend of the respective protective superpower, the US and the Soviet Union. The unified Germany today is again an exemplar of successfully dealing with the problematic legacy of a violent past, so much so that the German word for this process – *Vergangenheitsbewältigung* – has become a widely used term. A new 'tamed' and 'civilian' Germany is a model of a peaceful, stable and tolerant state, and an important engine of European integration and economic development. But the ensuing increase in responsibility and power does, as Siegfried Schieder (in Chapter 10) points out, inevitably also lead to mixed reactions – and increased anxiety – from the international community.

The constructed and constantly shifting concept of Germany becomes even more obvious when we follow Richard Ned Lebow (in Chapter 11) and look at Germany not just as a political actor but also as a *Sprachraum* – a linguistic and cultural sphere. Where, for instance, should we place the Nobel Prize winner Herta Müller, who grew up in the German-speaking part of Romania, or the Czech writer Franz Kafka, or the Austrian Robert Musil, or the Swiss Max Frisch?

Among the most widely discussed transnational German influences on IR scholarship are those from so-called émigré scholars, particularly those who left Nazi Germany for the US. Hans Morgenthau and John H. Herz are widely recognised for their contribution to realist thought; Hannah Arendt marked key discussions in international ethics; Henry Kissinger shaped both the theory and practice of US foreign policy; Albert O. Hirschman was central to the development of international political economy; Gerda Lerner made key contributors to feminist international history; and Karl Deutsch influenced writings on nationalism and security. These are just a few examples and there are many more that are explored in this book, such as Edwin Borchard's influence on realism (Jens Steffek and Tobias Heinze in Chapter 6), Friedrich Ratzels' on human geography (Ashworth in Chapter 4) and Carl Schmitt's on constitutional politics (Paul Petzschmann in Chapter 5). One could also trace more indirect German influences on IR theory, such as those of Kant on liberal internationalism and cosmopolitanism; Hegel and Marx on dependency and world system theories; von Clausewitz on strategy and defence; Nietzsche and Heidegger on post-structuralism; and Habermas on critical theory.

Towards a critical engagement with the role of Germany in IR

Because images of Germany in IR are in constant flux, they also need to be submitted to regular and critical scrutiny. The purpose of this book is not to do so, but I hope that it opens up debates that scrutinise both the potentials and problems entailed in the role that Germany, in all its complex and contested dimensions, plays in international relations. The traditions of thought that this book engages are – perhaps inevitably – dominated by men. Few of them question the gendered nature of both German contributions and international perceptions of Germany. The same is the case with the Eurocentric nature of the respective exchange of ideas. Awareness of the level of privilege, power and subjugation associated with these positions is only just emerging. We need more self-critical and reflective engagements to further explore and question them.

The German tradition of thought is very much implicated in establishing and entrenching dominant modes of thinking, including those that rely on problematic gender- and race-related systems of exclusion. But Germany's intellectual legacy also offers numerous inspiring ideas for critical engagement. I think, in particular, of ideas that emerged in the broad wake of Nietzsche's critical engagement with the nature and legacy of modernity. Here we find innovative inquiries into the links between knowledge and power. We can see how these links frame the political in particular ways. Here we find, for instance, Max Horkheimer and Theodor Adorno's problematisation of the violent logic of Enlightenment thought in *Dialektik der Auflkärung*; Paul Celan's poetic rethinking and rewriting of the Holocaust legacy; and Käthe Kollwitz's visual depiction of hunger and poverty. It is this German tradition and spirit of critique that can make particularly powerful contributions to broader discussions about the key dilemmas we face in global politics today. May this book, through its sophisticated empirical and conceptual investigations, provide the impetus for more critical reflections about the role of Germany in IR.

1

Introduction: changing images of Germany

Jens Steffek and Leonie Holthaus

> Just because Germany remains in the middle of Europe, and is again more powerful (but *not* in all dimensions) than its neighbors, is there really no difference between the revisionist imperial Germany in clumsy search of a world role, the rabid revolutionary Germany of Hitler, and the satisfied, cooperative and world-shy new united republic?[1]

In November 2016, the *New York Times* contended that under the leadership of Angela Merkel, Germany had become the ultimate bastion of liberal democracy in the world, a bulwark against right-wing populism and autocracy.[2] That assessment might have been somewhat premature and formulated under the impression of Donald Trump's victory in the presidential election, which had raised fresh doubts over the health of American democracy. Nevertheless, it testifies to a remarkable shift in the external image of Germany. Few countries of the world, if any, have seen their image change as radically throughout the twentieth century. Germany was at least co-responsible for the outbreak of the First World War and unambiguously responsible for the Second World War. It produced one of the most brutal dictatorships in human history that committed a genocide of unprecedented dimensions. Until 1945, German foreign policy was associated chiefly with militarism, territorial expansion and a pronouncedly anti-liberal political culture. Today, the country is widely perceived as a 'civilian power' – an economic giant but military dwarf that is firmly committed to multilateralism, European integration and the peaceful settlement of disputes.[3]

Situated at the intersection of International Relations (IR) and history, this book has two objectives. One is to analyse and compare external perceptions of Germany during the twentieth century. The second is to use the German case as a prism to refract Western conceptions of international affairs more generally. Images of Germany not only determined the way in which Germans were seen or treated by others in IR; as the chapters that follow will demonstrate, such images even influenced the very concepts used to describe and theorise IR in the English-speaking world. At crucial moments in the twentieth century, international theorists used the case of Germany as example, contrast foil or cautionary tale when making more general points about the nature and regularities of IR.[4] According to figures compiled by Richard Ned Lebow (see Chapter 11), only references to the US have been more frequent than references to Germany in IR theory books since 1939. The case of Germany has been of interest to IR scholars in every decade and across theoretical paradigms. Our ambition in conceiving this book was to shed more light on this connection and to interweave two stories that are usually told separately.

Over the past two decades, historical IR scholarship has considerably improved our understanding of the origins of the discipline and its prominent theories.[5] German intellectual influences and the role of German (émigré) scholars in the formulation of IR theories have been uncovered in the process, in particular regarding the genesis of 'classical' realism.[6] However, changing images and conceptions of Germany in IR theorising have not been studied systematically. IR as an academic discipline was established when its English-speaking founders distinguished their vision of cooperative IR from an inherently aggressive and militarised 'Prussian' foreign policy. Western observers described the country as the uncivilised other, a rogue that thwarted attempts at a peaceful organisation of IR.[7] In that sense, one particular image of Germany was almost constitutive for the nascent discipline of IR. In the interwar years, the German fight against the Treaty of Versailles allowed liberal internationalist to distinguish the West, multilateralism and the international rule of law from Germany's revanchism and aggression.

As German resistance against the Versailles order became ever more militant in the 1930s and breaches of international law frequent, the German case posed another question to IR that early realists in particular addressed. It epitomised, with great political urgency, the problem of how an international order, imposed by some states in a particular situation and for particular purposes, would be able to accommodate subsequent changes in power relations. Although to different degrees, E. H. Carr and other early IR realists 'normalised' the ruthless power politics that the liberal internationalists had castigated as uncivilised behaviour.[8] What Germany did, trying to regain its lost status as a great power by all means available, was natural and not an aberration.

On the other hand, during roughly the same period, German intellectual influences became increasingly visible in IR theorising. The allegedly illiberal science of geopolitics, which relied on German sources and the example given by Germany in history, became an accepted part of English-speaking IR.[9] Many of these influences were carried overseas by German-speaking emigrants who brought with them Max Weber's sociology of power, the sociological approach to the study of law and Carl Schmitt's ideas about the nature of the political.[10] Regardless of the conflicts and tensions at the political level, Germany's universities and intellectual achievements were still held in high esteem abroad. The rise of the Nazis and the question of how to confront them again brought Germany into the limelight of Western international theory. Was appeasement the right strategy to deal with a nation of discontents whose revisionism was essentially rational and understandable? Or had a bunch of violent madmen and ideologues taken over who could only be deterred from aggression by the threat of war?[11]

During the Second World War, the German question still loomed large in debates over the post-war order.[12] Should the post-war international organisation include Germany?[13] Was it possible to re-educate a people and build, with external assistance, a democratic German state after its military defeat?[14] And how should the atrocities of the Nazis be dealt with? The Nuremberg trials after the Second World War remain exemplary to the paradigm of transitional justice, and the West German state a textbook case of successful democracy promotion.[15] The great experiment of European political integration and German–French reconciliation also opened new horizons for international theory. The peculiar semi-sovereignty of (West) Germany triggered scholarly interest.[16] On the other hand, in the Cold War years the central IR debates shifted elsewhere quite quickly, even if the divided Germany, and particularly Berlin, remained a theatre of the geopolitical standoff. As the future of Germany had ceased to be a pressing problem or a potential threat to the West, academics now debated themes such as great power conflict, nuclear deterrence and the dynamics of decolonialisation.

However, with the re-unification of the country in 1990, fears of a relapse into old patterns resurfaced. Worries mounted especially in France and Poland, where memories of German invasion and occupation were still alive. Chancellor Helmut Kohl tried to counter such fears, successfully in the end, with the promise of continuity in the country's foreign relations. In particular, he showed great commitment to European integration and to the State of Israel. United Germany thus continued a course that the Federal Republic had adopted at its foundation in 1949.[17] In the following years, the united country was often characterised as a civilian power (*Zivilmacht*) with a mighty economy, but reluctant to use force in its foreign relations and deeply committed to international cooperation.[18] Germany thus came to epitomise, together with Japan, a type of state that renounces the use of force in its foreign relations, despite its economic and technological capacities.[19] Politically, such a country may be a beacon of hope rather than a rogue to fear, but still an aberration from what many (realist) IR theorists consider normal state behaviour.[20]

With some regularity, the country's Western allies urge German governments to do more in terms of military engagement abroad. Domestic resistance to such 'adventures', but also to coercion as political strategy more generally, is still solid in Germany. In 2001, Gerhard Schröder's coalition government of Social Democrats and the Greens refused to join the US-led 'coalition of the willing' that invaded Iraq after the 9/11 attacks. Nor did Angela Merkel's more conservative coalition of Christian Democrats and Liberals support the intervention in Libya during the Arab Spring that ousted long-term dictator Muammar al-Gaddafi ten years later.[21] Together with Russia and China, the German delegation abstained from voting in the United Nations Security Council on Resolution 1973 that authorised military action to protect Libyan civilians. This move infuriated many Western observers, but, in the polls, a solid majority of Germans supported the line of the government.[22] The year before, President Horst Köhler had unwittingly violated a taboo when he mused in a radio interview whether safeguarding German economic interests abroad might, in some very exceptional circumstances, require military action. Facing public outrage over that statement, Köhler resigned. The highest representative of a civilian power, it seems, must not even ponder the use of force in pursuit of such mundane ends.

At the same time, the image of Germany as a civilian power is frequently called into question by external and domestic audiences. For left-wing critics, Germany is a highly developed capitalist state whose elite profits from arms export to war-torn regions. In their view, descriptions of Germany as a civilian power are a farce. In particular since 2010, German positions in the financial crisis of the eurozone also triggered much foreign and domestic criticism. Germany is here seen as an irresponsible power because it denies its contributions to the crisis, such as its enormous surplus in trade with Southern Europe. From the critics' point of view, German politicians and central bankers instead impose an austerity regime upon highly indebted countries, thus stifling their economic recovery. The quest for austerity in the eurozone led to a revival of images of 'Nazi Germany', especially in the Greek discourse, along with new fears of German hegemony in Europe.[23]

Intellectual engagements with images of Germany thus allow us to review much of the history of twentieth-century IR, and Western academic reflection about it, through the vicissitudes of one country. Many canonical themes of academic IR will make their appearance along the way, such as the relationship between power and plenty, the possibilities and limits of international organisation, the ambiguities of industrial modernity, the (re)socialisation of countries into the international community, the spread of democracy and the possibility to do justice for crimes against humanity.

Conceptual remarks on the images of states

Images of states are the central concept in this volume and therefore some clarifications are in order. We do not follow Robert Jervis' often-cited approach that relates images of states closely to external expectations about how these states will behave, and thus to strategic decision-making.[24] This definition of images is rather narrow and seems to explore the phenomenon through its consequences. At a very general level, an image is defined as a mental representation, impression or idea.[25] We understand an image as a mental picture of an entity that identifies its typical, maybe even unique characteristics through audio-visual or narrative representations. Images of states certainly have an audio-visual dimension, as states have territories, capitals and inhabitants. Germany is often pictured through images of its cities and landscapes, the Brandenburg Gate or the romantic valley of the Rhine. In caricatures, persons often come to stand for the country, from the *Kaiser* over Adolf Hitler to the post-war chancellors. In popular culture, the darkest episodes of German history are still visually present. Countless novels and movies still feature blond henchmen in Nazi uniforms who represent Germany as the archetypical evil. Visual images of Germany still include tanks, concentration camps and cities reduced to rubble; ecstatic crowds, geometrically aligned and uniformed that are greeting Hitler at the Nuremberg party rallies; or hailing 'total war' in response to Joseph Goebbels' 1943 'Sportpalast' speech. These visual images have spread around the world and, even if shot in black and white, they proved to be sticky.

Yet images of states also have a narrative dimension that contains ordered storylines with clear beginnings and endings. Historical narratives are often organised around some causal claims about what happened to a country and why.[26] Images of states may be created through the aggregation of such narratives, but can also precede more disciplined and coherent story-telling.[27] In any event, images of states convey what cannot be observed directly through our senses, and they represent them in a *pars pro toto* fashion. Images of states or nations are often transmitted through education and public discourses. Their public creditability depends greatly on how they interpret shared experiences and events.

The scholar K. E. Boulding, who inaugurated research on national images in the 1950s, argued that such images are shaped by structural, reciprocal and long-term developments, but also by recent events.

Furthermore, he emphasised how academics seize and elaborate on popular images of other nations. He frequently cited images of Germany, as the rogue state that invaded Belgium, the Nazi state or the ally of the US.[28] However, the latter image documents that scholars do not always distinguish neatly between images of states or nations and foreign policy role conceptions.[29]

Talking about changing images of Germany may invoke the idea of a more or less orderly succession in which new images simply supersede their predecessors. Yet this would be a misconception. As many of the following chapters will illustrate, there never was just one image of Germany, but always several standing next to each other, sometimes compatible, sometimes contradictory. Images are created by an audience and external ascriptions usually matter as much as the actions and intentions of those observed. External re-descriptions tend to highlight and essentialise certain traits and aspects from a far more variegated and ambiguous picture. They reflect, as this book will also show, national experiences, anxieties and domestic political debates of the observers. Images of Germany are thus tainted by the interest and political projects of others. In other words, and in awareness of historiographical debates over the importance of historical events for analytical reconfigurations in the development of IR, we suggest that it is not historical events themselves but their stylised representation in discourse that affect academic theorising.[30]

Even in times when digital texts and pictures flow seamlessly around the globe, local perceptions and interpretations of countries still vary. As new pictures of Germany become available, they will usually find different receptions influenced by national traditions of thinking about the country. For historical reasons, Israel, Poland or Russia may look differently at changing images of Germany than the US, Britain, or France. It is therefore important to underline that this book is limited to discussing Anglo-American perceptions of Germany. This is because the academic discipline of IR, whose transformations over time we also study in this book, is largely an English-language phenomenon. We thus concentrate on the writings of Anglo-American scholars and public intellectuals who had an impact on academic thinking about IR. Some chapters of this book also address the views of political decision-makers and the results of public opinion surveys, but these are not the main focus.

We are aware that the conception of this book does not allow for a truly global perspective on images of Germany. Due to our interest in the history of IR theorising, it is a Eurocentric endeavour and we do not cover perspectives on Germany from its former colonies, from Israel or Eastern Europe. Having said this, we are still confident that this volume can contribute to the decentring and globalisation of IR. It exposes the mechanisms of othering and exclusion, of Western self-assurance to be standing on the side of civilisation and moral progress, while at the same time distancing itself from the backwardness of others. As Robbie Shilliam has argued, it was precisely this perceived 'backwardness' of Germany that became a long-term driver of German thought on IR.[31]

An overview of the chapters

In the next chapter, Andreas Osiander starts discussing the connection between images of Germany and the notion of power as a key concept of IR. In the eyes of many observers, Germany always had a peculiar and unusual relationship with power politics and, more specifically, power abuses. This was undoubtedly true of the Nazi regime, but there is a body of opinion that sees a tradition of German power being mishandled reaching further back, to the 1871 Empire or even beyond, with the foundations of what is seen as 'Prussian militarism'. To trace the origins of that line of thought, Osiander puts this issue into a historical perspective that is longer still, beginning with the founding of the German kingdom in the tenth century and then taking the story to the early twentieth century. Necessarily, his approach entails discussing what 'Germany' actually was at different stages of its historical trajectory. Its successive incarnations involved much change that necessarily also meant that power played a different and variable role for each of them. At the same time, 'power' is a notoriously multi-faceted concept, which of course complicates the matter further. The Nazi era and its impact on post-Second World War Germany is deliberately left out, not with any view to downplaying its importance, but in an attempt to avoid any temptation of either a teleo-logical or a relativising, exculpatory interpretation of the subject matter at hand.

Chapter 3 takes issue with the rise of liberal internationalism as one of the original theories of IR and shows how it was constructed, at the beginning of the twentieth century, in distinction from a German other. Leonie Holthaus here seeks to reconstruct and contextualise lib-eral internationalism's image of an autocratic and militarist German adversary. Germany thus became part of the category of 'less civilised societies', which existed in Europe and beyond. The construction of the German other helped liberal internationalists accentuate their own (and Great Britain's) imagined political virtues. L. T. Hobhouse and other intellectuals, who were otherwise rather critical commentators of British foreign relations, strongly supported the official wartime propaganda and the othering of Germany during the First World War. In different social roles as academics or journalists, they distinguished between a Western and, by definition, liberal civilisation, led by Britain and a backward and militarist Germany. Unable to deny Germany's capacity for economic modernisation, which was all too obvious at the time, they nevertheless contended that Germany was unable to allow for meaningful political self-government. Like later theorists of the *Sonderweg*, they identified Germany's rampant nationalism as the cause of its departure from the Western model.[32]

To balance this view, Chapter 4 shows that despite all the othering of Germany, there were also notable German influences on international theory. Lucian M. Ashworth demonstrates that for most political geographers in pre-1914 Britain and America, Germany was a major source of inspiration. The home of Friedrich Ratzel and boasting excellent universities that took geography seriously, Germany was the place to go for lessons in the formulation of geography as a university subject. The early innovators in Anglo-American human and political geography, such as Ellen Churchill Semple, Ellsworth Huntington, Halford J. Mackinder and Isaiah Bowman, all looked to Germany and its universities for inspiration. The outbreak of the First World War was to change all that. The chapter traces how rapidly Germany went from exemplar to threat, but also that there was a period of overlap between these two contrasting views. Mackinder, for example, remained impressed with Germany's advances in geography and spatial literacy, while increasingly seeing that superior knowledge as part of the political and military threat posed by an insurgent Wilhelmine Empire. By the 1940s, though, German geography, through the popular image of Karl Haushofer, had been re-interpreted as a pathological throwback. All of these images of Germany, both positive and negative, were to some extent caricatures that bore little relation to the reality of the German situation. That said, the creation of Germany, first as exemplar and finally as warning, acted as the 'other' against which people like Bowman and Derwent Whittlesey created a contrasting Anglo-American geopolitics that would heavily influence the post-1945 construction of a new global order. In this sense, the vision of Germany and its geopolitics was the foil against which the post-war settlement was framed.

With the same keen sense for ambiguities and latent contradictions, Paul Petzschmann in Chapter 5 explores competing American accounts of the Weimar Republic and their significance for IR during the interwar period. At the centre of his account are two interpretations of the Weimar Republic in the context of German sovereignty and regime change. Johannes Mattern, America's foremost authority on matters concerning German constitutional history and jurisprudence, argued that the Weimar Constitution put an end to the legal debate about the location of sovereignty in the German polity. In his view, destabilising activities of radical political movements that contested the sovereignty of the Weimar republic were nothing but a temporary aberration from a political history steadily evolving towards undivided sovereignty. Rupert Emerson, on the other hand, regarded the revival of German Federalism as part of an international trend towards fragmented sovereignty and as a potentially positive step into the direction of a new, 'post-sovereign' international order. Both interpretations show in an exemplary fashion how domestic concerns and debates shaped the observers' perceptions of Germany. Petzschmann highlights the importance of the American experience of the state, of contested sovereignty and of the Civil War for shaping academic discourses on sovereignty and IR. The rift between the ideal of legal sovereignty and its political reality prefigures diagnoses made by early realists such as Morgenthau.

In Chapter 6, Jens Steffek and Tobias Heinze continue this discussion. They show how Germany's fight against the Versailles peace settlement left a mark on early American IR realism. Studying transatlantic connections between German and American scholars in the interwar years, they show how an early version of political realism was used to discredit international law and organisations. Realist arguments about the ever-conflictual nature of IR and the inborn weakness of international law naturalised and legitimated German revisionism and the fight against the Treaty of Versailles. The discussion is focused on the international lawyer Edwin M. Borchard, one of the major advocates of neutrality in the US and one of the first American scholars promoting a realist approach to IR. He argued that international treaties, and in particular collective security schemes, were unable to accommodate change. Interwar Germany was his case in point to illustrate this theoretical claim. He developed this argument in a relentless political campaign against the Versailles peace settlement, the Kellogg Pact and military action against Nazi Germany. The chapter also documents how German international lawyers who were busy legitimating breaches of the Treaty of Versailles and trying to discredit American involvement in the Second World War profited from personal relations with Borchard and happily cited his ideas.

Transitional justice and the punishment of war crimes are the focus of Chapter 7, in which Annette Weinke shows how, since the 1990s, a worldwide community of transitional justice (TJ) scholars have taken the case of contemporary German history as a universal model for dealing with perpetrators and victims of state-sponsored violence. She argues that throughout the twentieth century, Germany was at the heart of transatlantic debates about international law, international criminal law and human rights. This discourse entailed a dualistic image of 'two Germanies', one peaceful and civilised, the other militarist and expansionist. The TJ discussions setting in immediately after the fall of the Berlin Wall should be seen as part of a long trajectory that started with the First World War. In this chapter, Weinke disentangles these debates in a *longue durée* perspective and analyses their underlying political, ideological and historical assumptions. Given that punitive international legalism is deeply coloured by a dichotomous view on twentieth-century

German history, the chapter also raises the question of how this might have impacted on the evolution of international criminal law and on the emergence of a more robust international human rights regime, setting in immediately after the end of the Cold War.

Chapter 8 takes issue with the impact that German émigré scholars had on the development of IR in the US. This story has been told well in recent years, especially with regard to the classical realism of Hans J. Morgenthau and others. In this chapter, Felix Rösch addresses a puzzle that has received less attention so far. He shows how a distinctively German intellectual socialisation and a German style of argument continued to inform the political thought of the émigré scholars and how that fact became increasingly overlooked. As Rösch argues, it has to be acknowledged that émigré scholars at least partly caused this silencing themselves. After their forced emigration, they were at pains to adjust their research and teaching to the different intellectual and historical backgrounds of their American colleagues and students. They did so not only in order to find employment in the higher education sector, but also to avoid being perceived as enemy aliens. However, Rösch urges us to reverse the perspective and to explore the social spaces in which the immigrants acted and which they, to some degree, also transformed.

In Chapter 9, Brian C. Etheridge studies the nexus of memory, identity and public diplomacy in Cold War America. One of the remarkable phenomena of the Cold War is the rapid reversal of (West) Germany from enemy to ally in American political discourse. Often this reversal has been viewed as a necessary or inevitable expediency of the post-war conflict with the Soviet Union. Etheridge's chapter, and the larger work from which it draws, demonstrates that this process was much more complicated, and incomplete, than typically recognised. Using a framework called memory diplomacy, Etheridge highlights how both American and (West) German actors, both public and private, were involved in the production and reception of images of Germany. This process was messy and contentious as different groups fought over the shaping of American understanding of *Deutschtum* (or Germanness) through the mass media. Another equally important part is how the fruits of these efforts (articles, books, films, television programs, etc.) were interpreted by those Americans who consumed them. When taken together, they illustrate how narratives of Germany were more about the American understanding of self than the American understanding of Germanness.

In Chapter 10, Siegfried Schieder explores the external image of Germany's foreign policy. His starting point is the notion of a 'civilian power' – a state that pursues its foreign policy through multilateral diplomatic channels and economic cooperation rather than military force and that seeks to 'civilise' world politics by strengthening international institutions. According to dominant domestic self-understanding,

Germany is such a profoundly 'tamed' and 'civilian' power. However, since the 1990s, and especially in the recent crisis-ridden years, Germany has modified its role in light of far-reaching changes in its foreign policy environment. Against this backdrop, this chapter explores how Germany's foreign policy is perceived from abroad. Is Germany still seen as a 'civilian power' from the outside or is the image of Germany's foreign policy changing in times of crisis? The chapter builds on a constructivist reading of German foreign policy and reconstructs the political, historical and intellectual context in which Germany's role conception as a 'civilian power' has evolved after the Second World War. It also explores whether Germany is still seen as a 'civilian power' by using surveys, opinion polls and other data. The evidence reveals a marked dissonance between Germany's self-perception and outside views, which threatens the country's credibility both at home and abroad.

In the concluding chapter, Richard Ned Lebow reconsiders the German influence on the development of IR theory. He shows that from the early years of the discipline onwards, the interchange of IR scholars between the Anglosphere and the *deutsche Sprachraum* has been nearly continuous and important for the intellectual growth of those involved, the development of the discipline and the view of Germany in the discipline. To gauge the importance of references to Germany for IR theory, Lebow uses a sample of twenty-one well-known theory books, representative of diverse traditions in the field and analyses the references to countries made in them. Germany's central role in IR is, in Lebow's judgement, attributable to several reinforcing factors. Germany was Europe's dominant power from 1870 to 1945 and for much of that period sought to advance its interests through the exercise of military and economic power. German political and historical thought greatly influenced the realist tradition, and many first-generation realist IR scholars emigrated from continental Europe to the US. Will Germany remain such a central reference point for the future development of IR? In his conclusion, Lebow argues that this is rather unlikely. In recent decades, American economic and political interests have shifted away from Europe and have become increasingly focused on Asia. Academic theorising has also begun to move in this direction, spurred on by the evolution of a discipline that globalises and leaves its traditional focus on the Western world behind.

Notes

1 S. Hoffmann, *European Sisyphus: Essays on Europe 1964–1994* (Boulder, CO: Westview Press, 1995), p. 284, emphasis in original.
2 A. Smale and S. Erlanger, 'As Obama exits world stage, Angela Merkel may be the liberal West's last defender', *New York Times*, 12 November 2016, www.nytimes.com/2016/11/13/world/europe/germany-merkel-trump-election.html.

3 H. W. Maull, 'Germany and Japan: the new civilian powers', *Foreign Affairs* 69 (1990), pp. 91–106; H. Haftendorn, *Deutsche Außenpolitik zwischen Selbstbeschränkung und Selbstbehauptung 1945–2000* (Stuttgart: Deutsche Verlagsanstalt, 2001); R. Baumann and G. Hellmann, 'Germany and the use of military force: "total war", the "culture of restraint" and the quest for normality' *German Politics*, 10:1 (2001), pp. 61–82.

4 We use the term 'international theorist' to include a wide range of intellectuals who made abstract and generalising claims about the nature and regularities of social and political relations across borders. They were not necessarily affiliated with universities or IR as an academic discipline.

5 B. Schmidt and N. Guilhot (eds), *Historiographical Investigations in International Relations* (London: Palgrave Macmillan, 2018); D. Armitage, *Foundations of Modern International Thought* (Cambridge: Cambridge University Press, 2013); C. Sylvest, *British Liberal Internationalism, 1880–1930: Making Progress?* (Manchester: Manchester University Press, 2009); B. Schmidt, *The Political Discourse of Anarchy: A Disciplinary History of International Relations* (Albany, NY: State University of New York Press, 1998); D. Long and P. Wilson (eds), *Thinkers of the Twenty Years' Crisis: Interwar Idealism Reassessed* (Oxford: Clarendon, 1995); A. Osiander, 'Rereading early twentieth-century IR theory: idealism revisited', *International Studies Quarterly*, 42:3 (1998), pp. 409–32; P. Wilson, 'The myth of the "First Great Debate"', *Review of International Studies*, 24 (1998), pp. 1–15; D. Long and B. C. Schmidt, *Imperialism and Internationalism in the Discipline of International Relations* (Albany, NY: State University of New York Press, 2005); L. M. Ashworth, *A History of International Thought. From the Origins of the Modern State to Academic International Relations* (London: Routledge, 2014); D. Bell (ed.), *Political Thought and International Relations: Variations on a Realist Theme* (Oxford: Oxford University Press, 2009); R. Vitalis, *White World Order, Black Power Politics: The Birth of American International Relations* (Ithaca: Cornell University Press, 2015).

6 A. Söllner, 'German conservatism in America: Morgenthau's political realism', *Telos*, 72 (1987), pp. 161–72; R. N. Lebow, 'German Jews and American realism', *Constellations*, 18:4 (2011), pp. 545–66; F. Rösch 'Introduction. Breaking the silence: European émigré scholars and the genesis of an American discipline', in F. Rösch (ed.), *Émigré Scholars and the Genesis of International Relations: A European Discipline in America?* (Basingstoke: Palgrave Macmillan, 2014), pp. 1–20; O. Jütersonke, *Morgenthau, Law and Realism* (Cambridge: Cambridge University Press, 2010); R. N. Lebow (ed.), *Max Weber and International Relations* (Cambridge: Cambridge University Press, 2017).

7 On the role of the German other in the genesis of conceptions of the West, see R. Bavay and M. Steber (eds), *Germany and 'the West': The History of a Modern Concept* (New York: Berghahn Books, 2015); G. Hellmann and B. Herborth (eds), *Uses of 'the West': Security and the Politics of Order* (Cambridge: Cambridge University Press, 2016).

8 P. Wilson, 'Carr and his early critics: responses to the Twenty Years' Crisis, 1939–46', in M. Cox (ed.) *E.H. Carr: A Critical Appraisal* (Basingstoke: Palgrave, 2004), pp. 165–97.

9 L.M. Ashworth, 'Mapping a new world: geography and the interwar study of International Relations', *International Studies Quarterly*, 57:1 (2013), pp. 138–49; N. Guilhot, 'Introduction: One discipline, many histories', in N. Guilhot (ed.), *The Invention of International Relations Theory: Realism, the Rockefeller Foundation, and the 1954 Conference on Theory* (New York: Columbia University Press, 2011), pp. 1–32, at p. 2; N. Spykman, 'Geography and foreign policy, I', *American Political Science Review*, 32:1 (1938), pp. 28–50; N. Spykman, 'Geography and Foreign Policy, II', *American Political Science Review* 32:2 (1938), pp. 213–36; H. W. Weigert, *Generals and Geographers: The Twilight of Geopolitics* (Freeport, NY: Books for Libraries, 1972 [reprint of 1942 edition]).

10 Rösch, *Émigré Scholars and the Genesis of International Relations*; G. Steinmetz, 'Ideas in exile: refugees from Nazi Germany and the failure to transplant historical sociology into the United States', *International Journal of Politics, Culture, and Sociology*, 23 (2010), pp. 1–27; M. Ash and A. Söllner (eds), *Forced Migration and Scientific Change: Émigré German-Speaking Scientists and Scholars after 1933* (Cambridge: Cambridge University Press, 1996); U. Greenberg, *The Weimar Century: German Émigrés and the Ideological Foundations of the Cold War* (Princeton: Princeton University Press, 2014).

11 On the legacy of the so-called Munich analogy and the problem of uncertainty in foreign policy decision-making, see F. V. Kratochwil, *International Order and Foreign Policy: A Theoretical Sketch of Post-war International Politics* (Boulder, CO: Westview Press, 1978), pp. 89–100; J. Record, *The Specter of Munich: Reconsidering the Lessons of Appeasing Hitler* (Washington DC: Potomac Books, 2006); Y. F. Khong, *Analogies at War: Korea, Munich, Dien Bien Phu, and the Vietnam Decisions of 1965* (Princeton: Princeton University Press, 1992).

12 D. Plesch and T. G. Weiss, '1945's lesson: "Good enough" global governance ain't good enough', *Global Governance*, 21:2 (2015), pp. 197–204, at p. 199; A. Salter, *Dumbarton Oaks Conference* (London: Chatham House Archives, 1944).

13 W. Krieger, 'Die Amerikanische Deutschlandplanung. Hypotheken und Chancen für einen Neuanfang', in H. E. Volkmann (ed.), *Ende des Dritten Reiches – Ende des zweiten Weltkriegs. Eine perspektivische Rückschau* (Munich: Piper, 1995), pp. 25–50; J. Ikenberry, *After Victory* (Princeton: Princeton University Press, 2001), p. 165.

14 M. Intrator, 'Educators across borders: the Conference of Allied Ministers of Education, 1942–1945', in D. Plesch and T. Weiss (eds), *Wartime Origins and the Future of the United Nations* (New York: Routledge, 2015), pp. 56–76, at p. 57.

15 For the legacy of the Nuremberg trials, see R. Teitel (1999) 'Nuremberg and its legacy, fifty years later', in B. Cooper (ed.), *War Crimes: The Legacy of Nuremberg* (New York: TV Books, 1999), pp. 44–54; P. de Greiff, 'International courts and transitions to democracy', *Public Affairs Quarterly*, 12:1 (1998), pp. 79–99. For recent references to Germany as a success story of US-led democracy promotion, see C. Rice, *Democracy: Stories from the*

Long Road to Freedom (New York: Twelve, 2017), pp. 25–6. For contestations of this narrative, see P. Fritz, 'Imposing democracy to ensure the peace: the role of coercive socialization', *Foreign Policy Analysis*, 11:4 (2015), pp. 377–96; A. J. Enterline and J. M. Greig, 'Against all odds?: The history of imposed democracy and the future of Iraq and Afghanistan', *Foreign Policy Analysis*, 4:4 (2015), pp. 321–47; J. L. Payne, 'Did the United States create democracy in Germany?', *Independent Review* 11:2 (2006), pp. 209–21; T. Carothers, J. Cavanagh et al., *Multilateral Strategies to Promote Democracy. First Report of the Empire and Democracy Project* (New York: Carnegie Council on Ethics and International Affairs, 2004), p. 39.

16 P. J. Katzenstein, *Policy and Politics in West Germany: The Growth of a Semi-sovereign State* (Philadelphia: Temple University Press, 1987); H. P. Schwarz, *Die gezähmten Deutschen. Von der Machtbesessenheit zur Machtvergessenheit* (Stuttgart: Deutsche Verlagsanstalt, 1985); W. E. Paterson, 'Beyond semi-sovereignty: the new Germany in the new Europe', *German Politics* 5:2 (1996), pp. 167–84.

17 P. J. Katzenstein (ed.), *Tamed Power: Germany in Europe* (Ithaca: Cornell University Press, 1997), pp. 1–48; J. S. Duffield, *World Power Forsaken: Political Culture, International Institutions and German Security Policy after Unification* (Stanford: Stanford University Press, 1999); T. Banchoff, *The German Problem Transformed: Institutions, Politics and Foreign Policy, 1945–1995* (Ann Arbor: University of Michigan Press, 1999); S. Harnisch, 'Change and continuity in post-unification German foreign policy', *German Politics* 10:1 (2001), pp. 35–60. P. Létourneau and M.-E. Räkel, 'Germany: to be or not be normal?', in P. G. Le Prestre (ed.), *Role Quests in the Post-Cold War Era: Foreign Policies in Transition* (Montreal: McGill-Queen's University Press, 1997), pp. 111–30; S. Bulmer and W. Paterson, 'Germany in the European Union: gentle giant or emergent leader?', *International Affairs*, 72:1 (1996), pp. 9–32.

18 Hanns W. Maull formulated the civilian power concept with regard to Germany, as explained in detail in Schieder's chapter. In such a view, national role conceptions emerge from specific political cultures and describe patterns of attitudes and behaviour, which state representatives display in their international conduct. See H. W. Maull and K. Kirste, 'Zivilmacht und Rollentheorie', *Zeitschrift für Internationale Beziehungen*, 3:2 (1996), pp. 283–312, at p. 289. Maull's seizure of the civilian power concept reflects an interest in the provision of foreign policy advice and definition of national interests in an interdependent world. On this, see H. Tewes, 'Das Zivilmachtkonzept in der Theorie der Internationalen Beziehungen. Anmerkungen zu K. Kirste und H.W. Maull', *Zeitschrift für Internationale Beziehungen*, 4:2 (1997), pp. 347–59, at p. 347. On conflicts in the definition of a civilian power's interest, see J. Wolff and H.-J. Spanger, 'The interaction of interests and norms in democracy promotion', *Journal of International Relations and Development*, 20:1 (2017), pp. 80–107.

19 S. Harnisch and H. W. Maull (eds), *Germany as a Civilian Power? The Foreign Policy of the Berlin Republic* (Manchester: Manchester University Press, 2001). H. Tewes, *Germany, Civilian Power and the New Europe: Enlarging NATO and the European Union* (Basingstoke: Palgrave Macmillan), pp. 9–32.

20 G. Hellmann, 'Fatal attraction? German foreign policy and IR/foreign policy theory', *Journal of International Relations and Development*, 12:3 (2009), pp. 257–92; J.S. Duffield, 'Political culture and state behaviour: why Germany confounds neorealism', *International Organization* 53:4 (1999), pp. 765–803; R. Baumann, V. Rittberger and W. Wagner, 'Macht und Machtpolitik. Neorealistische Außenpolitiktheorie und Prognosen über die deutsche Außenpolitik nach der Vereinigung', *Zeitschrift für Internationale Beziehungen*, 6:2 (1999), pp. 245–86.

21 For the foreign policy debate that the 2001 decision triggered, see Bundeszentrale für Politische Bildung (ed.), *Aus Politik und Zeitgeschichte*, B11 (2004); P. Katzenstein, 'Same war, different views: Germany, Japan, and the war on terrorism', *Current History*, 101:659 (2002), pp. 427–35; S. Brockmeier, 'Germany and the intervention in Libya', *Survival*, 55:6 (2013), pp. 63–90; K. Oppermann, 'National role conceptions, domestic constraints and the new "normalcy" in German foreign policy: the Eurozone crisis, Libya and beyond', *German Politics*, 21:4 (2012), pp. 502–19.

22 On 20 March 2011, the *Bild* tabloid presented the results of a nationwide ad hoc survey that it had commissioned. It showed that 62 per cent of respondents supported military action against Ghaddafi while 65 per cent militated against German participation in it (source: www.bild.de/politik/2011/libyen-krise/aber-mehrheit-lehnt-beteiligung-ab-16933388.bild.html). See also J. Bucher et al., 'Domestic politics, news media and humanitarian intervention: why France and Germany diverged over Libya', *European Security*, 22:4 (2013), pp. 524–39.

23 C. Sternberg, K. Gartzou-Katsouyanni and K. Nicolaïdis, *The Greco-German Affair in the Euro-crisis: Mutual Recognition Lost?* (London: Palgrave Macmillan, 2017). R. Adler-Nissen, 'Are we all "lazy Greeks" or "Nazi Germans"? Negotiating international hierarchies in the Euro crisis', in A. Zarakol (ed.), *Hierarchies in World Politics* (Cambridge: Cambridge University Press, 2017), pp. 198–218; S. Bulmer and W. E. Paterson, 'Germany as the EU's reluctant hegemon? Of economic strength and political constraints', *Journal of European Public Policy*, 20:10 (2013), pp. 1387–405; M. Matthijs, 'The three faces of German leadership', *Survival*, 58:2 (2016), pp. 135–54; C. J. Schneider and B. L. Slantchev, 'The domestic politics of international cooperation: Germany and the European debt crisis', *International Organization*, 72:1 (2017), pp. 1–31.

24 R. Jervis, *The Logic of Images in International Relations* (Princeton: Princeton University Press, 1970), p. 5.

25 P. Hanks (ed.), *Collins Dictionary of the English Language* (London: Collins, 1984), p. 731.

26 G. Roberts, 'History, theory and the narrative turn in IR', *Review of International Studies* 32:4 (2006), pp. 703–14.

27 On images and narratives, see R. Scully, *British Images of Germany: Admiration, Antagonism, and Ambivalence, 1860–1914* (New York: Palgrave Macmillan, 2012). Some genres such as comics combine images and textual comments. On their relevance in IR, see L. Hansen, 'Reading comics for the field of International Relations: theory, method and the Bosnian war', *European Journal of International Relations*, 23:3 (2017), pp. 581–608.

28 K.E. Boulding, 'National images and international systems', *Journal of Conflict Resolution*, 3:2 (1959), pp. 120–31; for references to Germany, see pp. 122, 125, 128.

29 For a classical study of role conceptions, see K. J. Holsti, 'National role conceptions in the study of foreign policy', *International Studies Quarterly*, 14:3 (1970), pp. 233–309.

30 For the claim that analytical reconfigurations are more important than historical events, see Schmidt, *The Political Discourse of Anarchy*. Objections to this view can be found in I. Hall, 'The history of international thought and International Relations theory: from context to interpretation', *International Relations* 31:3 (2017), pp. 241–60; I. Hall and M. Bevir, 'Traditions of British international thought', *International History Review*, 36:5 (2014), pp. 832–4.

31 R. Shilliam, *German Thought and International Relations: The Rise and Fall of a Liberal Project* (Basingstoke: Palgrave Macmillan, 2009), p. 20.

32 Historians such as Heinrich August Winkler and Ralf Dahrendorf have focused on Germany's late Industrial Revolution, top-down reforms in imperial Germany or the incomplete character of the German revolution (1918/19) to argue that Germany democratisation has always remained fragile and incomplete. See www.zeit.de/zeit-geschichte/2010/03/Text-Interview. However, the wider historical community started to debate the different claims of the *Sonderweg* thesis in the 1980s. See K. D. Bracher, *Deutscher Sonderweg – Mythos oder Realität?* (Munich: Oldenbourg, 1982); H. W. Smith, 'When the Sonderweg debate left us', *German Studies Review*, 31:2 (2008), pp. 225–40; S. E. Berman, 'Modernization in historical perspective: the case of imperial Germany', *World Politics*, 53:3 (2001), pp. 431–62. Today, the *Sonderweg* thesis is largely discredited among historians.

2

Power as a German problem: a historical survey

Andreas Osiander

Germany, historically, seems to have or have had a 'problem' with power because its recent history has clearly been shaped by German political power being abused. This was undoubtedly true of the Nazi regime, but there is a body of opinion that sees a tradition of German power being mishandled reaching further back, to the 1871 Empire or even beyond, with the foundations of what is seen as 'Prussian militarism' having perhaps been laid early on in the development of the Prussian state (see Leonie Holthaus' and Annette Weinke's chapters on early *Sonderwegstheorien*). This chapter seeks to put this issue into a historical perspective that is longer still, beginning with the founding of the German kingdom in the tenth century and then taking the story to the early twentieth century and (briefly) the present. Necessarily such an approach entails discussing what 'Germany' actually was at different stages of its historical trajectory. Its successive iterations involved much change that necessarily also meant that power played a different and variable role for each of them. At the same time, 'power' is a notoriously multi-faceted concept, which of course complicates the matter further.[1]

If we look at the history of the various European countries, it is readily apparent that their power – using the term here simply as a ballpark reference to their importance relative to other, similar entities – has waxed and waned. For extended periods of time, the Spanish crown, the French crown or the British crown played a key role in European politics. Of the three, Spanish power was the earliest to reach its climax. By the eighteenth century, it had declined dramatically compared to the period before the War of the Spanish Succession, which began in 1701. When the Congress of Vienna inaugurated the concept of 'great powers', the Spanish crown was not among them. The expression 'great powers', almost never used before the early nineteenth century, begins to appear in official documents in the run-up to the Congress of Vienna. At the Congress itself, unlike earlier peace conferences, decision-making was solely in

17

the hands of the five actors subsequently recognised as belonging to that select group: France, Britain, Russia, Austria and Prussia.[2] The fate of Spain was shared by other actors. The rulers of Portugal, Sweden and the Netherlands had, in the past, founded empires in distant corners of the globe, or shaped the destiny of the European system, or both. At Vienna they found themselves relegated to the second tier, obliged to follow the lead of the Big Five. The case of Poland is more extreme still: from being a kingdom both vast and militarily effective in the sixteenth century, by the beginning of the nineteenth century it had declined and shrunk to the point of ceasing to exist as an independent entity, its very core area annexed by its neighbours.

History has not been altogether kind to the great powers of 1815 either. Two hundred years on, both France and Britain look back on a period in which they too have seen their importance in world politics dwindle. In the twentieth century, both were eclipsed by the advent of the 'superpowers', a term applied to the US and Soviet Russia from 1945 (and coined by W. T. R. Fox).[3] Yet, at the time of writing, the word 'superpower' has itself almost disappeared from current discourse. After the collapse of the Soviet Union, Russia, it seemed, had lost its 'superpower' status, whereas, by the same token, the status of the US seemed to have increased. Indeed, in the 1990s, the US was lionised as 'the sole remaining superpower'. Even then, the frequency with which that notion was invoked might have suggested a certain hollowness of the position thus described.[4] In the early years of the twenty-first century, US power and prestige have also declined. Far from demonstrating the superiority implied by the superpower epithet, the US interventions in Afghanistan and Iraq have yielded embarrassing results. Both of these countries have become highly volatile. Destabilisation has spread to Libya, Syria and other areas. US power seems no longer to count for much in the eyes of adversaries like Russia and Iran or even supposed allies like Saudi Arabia and Israel. As the time of writing, the advent to the US presidency of Donald Trump would appear to presage a further fall in US prestige and leverage abroad.

This waxing and waning of 'power' seems to be regarded as a fairly normal phenomenon (with the concept of 'power' itself often left undefined or vague in the relevant narratives, though broadly under-stood as being essentially military and economic).[5] However, Germany looks different from this pattern. Here is quite a large entity: large both geographically and demographically (no less so than Britain, France or Spain) and an entity because it has, since the early tenth century, con-tinuously been perceived as such, not only in geographical but also in political and cultural terms, both by those belonging to it and those on the outside. Moreover, this entity occupies a strategic location in the middle of the European continent. Yet somehow this entity always seems to have had a strange relationship with power, however conceived.[6]

What, politically, the term 'Germany' has meant in successive historical periods has been different both from one period to the next and in comparison with the history of other countries – one reason for this 'strange' relationship with power, which is different from that of the countries mentioned earlier. 'Germany' did not become a unitary actor in world politics until quite late (1871), but then went on to play a major role in two conflicts – the First and Second World Wars – that were turning points in world history. The Second World War left Germany split in two (three if, adopting a view prevalent both before 1871 and in the interwar period, you count Austria) and unable to go on playing an independent role in the international sphere. Issues deriving from its demographic weight, its central and thus strategically important position in Europe and the fact that, among the countries of Europe, it is the one with the most neighbours lost much of their importance as a result of the country's division.

When the collapse of the Soviet influence in Eastern Europe led to the merger of the Federal Republic of Germany with its smaller eastern counterpart, the expectation was that these issues would revive in the context of Germany once more becoming a 'normal' player on the international scene. But predictions along these lines have not so far been fulfilled. It is a tempting hypothesis that part of the reason for this may be that a 'normal' player is not something that Germany has ever been, save, possibly, for a few decades after 1871. Perhaps more importantly, its ultimately traumatic experience with being a 'power' (between 1871 and 1945) continues to shape the political culture of the Federal Republic to a greater extent than many foreign observers anticipated or than they may realise even now; to a greater extent, too, than some within Germany may wish.

In what follows, I will discuss, first, the importance of power in the Germany of the Holy Roman Empire – the longest period by far in the history of the country. Or, rather, I will emphasise the relative nonimportance of power in the Holy Roman Empire. I will show that the pre-eminent role of the emperor never depended on his coercive abilities, and that what held the empire together, throughout the many centuries of its existence and right up to about 1800, was not coercion in any form, or the threat of it, but the self-interest of the participating players and issues of political legitimacy. Though the peculiar set-up of the Holy Roman Empire meant that it never wielded power outside its borders, this was not true of all the princes participating in it. I will therefore also discuss the way in which power (meaning, at that time, essentially military power) was wielded, or not wielded, by the two foremost players in the early modern empire: Habsburg and Brandenburg-Prussia. I will then trace the rise to preponderance of post-Napoleonic Prussia, which culminated in the founding of the Wilhelmine German Empire in 1871.

Unlike the Holy Roman Empire, this new empire was very much capable of participating in power-political rivalries in Europe or even the world as a whole; indeed, it could hardly avoid it. Was there something distinctively German in the way it did so? Finally, even though this will also be the subject of other chapters in this book, the chapter would not be complete without at least a brief look at the period since the end of the First World War. This saw the most egregious abuse of power on the part of Nazi Germany and then a new Germany, the Federal Republic, resolutely turning its back on anything that might look like an open, let alone self-seeking exercise of power and clinging to this attitude even after the reunification of Germany in 1989.

Germany and its princes in the *ancien régime*

It may serve our purpose best if we assume 'power' to mean, very generally, the ability of a political entity to assert itself against competitors. If we ignore the Carolingians and begin our survey with the establishment of a separate German crown in the early tenth century, we may say that that crown as such never had a strong position in its dealings with the non-German world, let alone a hegemonial one. This was despite the prestige resulting from being not only German but also 'Roman', representing a Roman Empire that even in the late pre-Reformation period was regarded throughout Europe as having had a continuous existence since the time of Augustus. In the cosmology of the period, based on the biblical prophecy of Daniel, the Roman Empire was the last of the four great empires that would succeed each other in the history of the world. When this last empire fell, this would mean the end of the world as people knew it, heralding the coming of the Antichrist. Few people ever thought that the end of the world was actually close; hence, the Roman Empire was, necessarily, still there.[7]

The claim of the German crown to the Roman imperial dignity was inherited from Charlemagne and was made somewhat more plausible by geographical contiguity: it must not be overlooked that northern Italy (though not Rome itself) formed part of the dominions of the German crown as inherited from the Carolingians. Nor, on average, were the German rulers of the pre-Reformation period weak (or weaker than was, in fact, normal for all supralocal rulers of the period): they did not look ridiculous in asserting their 'Roman' claim. But they were never that strong either. They were busy enough consolidating their position within the German realm, a position forever threatened by powerful and unruly princes, and they were busy consolidating the dynastic position of their own family. This left no resources to try to project power elsewhere in Europe, unless they inherited additional thrones there – as did the

Hohenstaufen dynasty in southern Italy and Sicily following the marriage in 1186 of the future Emperor Henry VI to Constance of Sicily or, more durably, the Habsburg dynasty in Spain following the marriage in 1496 of Philip of Habsburg with Joanna, heiress of Aragon, Castile and León with their overseas territories (which in the case of Aragón included the former Hohenstaufen possessions in southern Italy). Further to that, the marriage of Ferdinand of Habsburg, the future Emperor Ferdinand I, with the heiress of Bohemia and Hungary, Anna, in 1521 led to the Habsburg dynasty acquiring both of those thrones as well.[8]

Despite being unruly, until the early 1800s none of the German princes, not even the most powerful like the King of Prussia (in his capacity as Elector of Brandenburg) or the British king (in his capacity as Elector of Hanover) ever tried to leave the empire. Even the supposed 'secession' from the empire of the Swiss and the Dutch in 1648 turns out on closer inspection to have been no such thing; rather, their ties with the empire loosened gradually and almost without their wanting to.[9] In their case, this was possible not least because they were no princes. I would contend that the chief reason why German princes never questioned their adherence to the empire was the importance of the feudal nexus with the emperor as the foundation of their legitimacy. Their position as princes was based on feudal law (a major ingredient of the 'public law' taught assiduously at German universities, written about by countless German jurists especially in the seventeenth and eighteenth centuries, and forming an important part, not least, in the education of future princes themselves). Feudal law was the basis on which the princes of the empire recognised each other and were recognised by their subjects as well as by foreign princes. Until the very end of the empire, therefore, all German princes sent representatives to the emperor to do homage for their possessions every time either they or a new emperor mounted their thrones. Interestingly, right up to the early 1800s, the imperial court was able to charge them substantial sums for this, a fact that underlines how valuable (even in a literal sense) the feudal nexus was for them. To call this basis of their legitimacy into question would have been an invitation to challenge their position. Competing hereditary claims to a principality, or parts of it, could be extremely difficult to adjudicate. Within the empire, this fell to the emperor (or the two supreme courts that spoke in his name) and this arbitration was, until the end of the eighteenth century, normally accepted by all concerned. Outside the empire, the likelihood was that a contested succession meant war.[10]

Removing the emperor as arbiter of such conflicts, and as protector of those who held their dominions as imperial fiefs, would have exposed many princes to revived claims by rival contenders, who in turn would almost certainly have gained the self-interested support of powerful foreign princes. Even a King of Prussia or Britain would have found it hard to defend outlying possessions militarily. An unravelling of the empire would thus have involved incalculable risks even for powerful players. Nor was the empire really a hindrance when it came to opportunities for expansion. The preferred method for this, in the Europe of the *ancien régime*, was not conquest (which was banned in the empire in any case), but marriage and inheritance.[11] This worked both within the empire and outside it (thus, for example, the Elector of Hanover gained the British crown because of his Stuart ancestry). The common institutions in which the princes and free cities of the Holy Roman Empire shared might well be resented as an irritant in given instances, but in other instances they might also turn out to be useful – most notably as an agency providing for the peaceful arbitration of disputes as well as a degree of common defence. It is my impression that even in the late eighteenth century, there was a wide consensus in the empire that these institutions should be retained and perhaps even made more efficient.

The complete lack of attempts by individual princes to leave the empire was matched by a complete lack of collective attempts to abolish it, at least until the early years of the nineteenth century. Critics of the empire called for its reform (in ways that would have strengthened it, but without changing its fundamental nature), not its removal. It is probably correct to state that until the very end of the eighteenth century, no one in Germany was unhappy with the empire (though they might wish for it to be stronger), and while some were disdainful, many more people were deeply attached to it.[12] From the point of view of this chapter, this is important because it meant that, until the French Revolution and Napoleon turned Europe upside down, nothing was ever likely to replace the empire: neither a unitary state nor a division of Germany between several medium-sized players who would have gobbled up the plethora of small and weak entities whose survival depended on the empire's protection.

This also meant that no power (in any sense in which the word is used in everyday parlance or by social scientists) was exercised by anything that could be called 'Germany'. By common, universally shared admission both among German speakers and in the rest of Europe, 'Germany' before 1800 was the empire. And the empire was not unitary; it was not a 'state'. It was a *legal order*[13] and it did not wield, or strive for, any form of power – least of all with regard to those not part of it. To have power (whatever that might have meant) was not a goal held by the empire as such. The empire did not act as a maximiser. It did not seek to maximise power, or even anything more tangible such as, in particular, economic advantage. Within the empire, individual actors did strive to increase their wealth. Among princes, establishing manufactures was fashionable in the late *ancien régime* and sometimes produced the hoped-for profits. Renting out troops or, in the case of a couple of the more enterprising

German princes (the Count of Hanau in the late 1660s and the Elector of Brandenburg in the 1680s), trying to gain overseas trading posts in Africa or the Caribbean were likewise attempted. Subsidies by foreign princes (such as the French king) might be available. Income thus gained was, on the whole, not invested in power-political activities, but rather in cultural display (such as new palaces). Princes who invested seriously in their military were rare. A standing army was not much use to them unless they had stakes in the politics of Europe at large or feared attack.

Duke Carl Eugen of Württemberg (ruled 1737–93) was one of the few German princes who did try to maintain a substantial standing army. This made sense in that the duchy needed to be on guard against French incursions, from which it had suffered badly in the past. However, his estates fought him tooth and nail, refusing to accept the requisite taxation – one reason for the duke to rent out his troops to Venice. In the end the duke had to submit to them following a decision in favour of the estates by the Imperial Aulic Council (one of the empire's two supreme courts) in Vienna.[14] A better-known case is King Friedrich Wilhelm I of Prussia (ruled 1713–40). Known as the 'soldier king', he doted on his troops and, in order to fund them, took the very unusual step of cutting down brutally on expenditure for new buildings or a lavish court life as soon as he mounted the throne. But – and in this respect he was typical of eighteenth-century German princes – he never fought a war. It was his son Friedrich II who did use the troops he inherited when he came to the throne in 1740 to annex Silesia. It should be underlined that this sort of behaviour was utterly exceptional. Brandenburg-Prussia, like the dominions of all the more important German princes, was a conglomerate of discrete provinces and lordships that the ruling house had accumulated over many centuries. During all those centuries, not one of the component entities that made up the territory of Brandenburg-Prussia had been acquired by force. All of them had been gained through inheritance, purchase or the secularisation of ecclesiastical principalities after the Reformation.[15] Silesia was the first province of the Prussian crown to be gained through conquest and it remained the only one until the nineteenth century.

During the Seven Years' War, Friedrich came within a hair's breadth of receiving his comeuppance and was saved from the loss not only of the recently gained Silesia, but of rather more territory only by the death of the Empress Elizabeth of Russia and the fact that her successor Peter III was a Prussophile eccentric: Peter immediately ceased hostilities, without demanding anything of Friedrich, and indeed offered conditions as if he had lost the war rather than won it. This astonishing manoeuvre was soon followed by his assassination, but the anti-Prussian coalition had already fallen apart and Peter's widow and successor, Catherine II, as yet had too insecure a hold on the throne to allow her to embark on foreign adventures. Though chastened, Friedrich remained alive to power-political issues as well as ambitious; he was a driving force behind the first partition of Poland of 1772. I am not counting this as acquisition of territory by force since no fighting took place, but it is a borderline case.

Poland was partitioned twice more and vanished from the political map, but this happened in the 1790s in a climate of general upheaval. If this was a Hobbesian climate, it nevertheless cannot be said that the rulers of Prussia who succeeded Friedrich II – none of them great luminaries – or their advisers were more Hobbesian than others in Europe.

Habsburg Austria and the imperial tradition

Still less could this be said of the rulers of the other great German power, the Archdukes of Austria, who until 1806 also wore the crown of the Holy Roman Empire. What this imperial dignity really meant is something that has been chronically and perhaps increasingly misunderstood at least since the empire came to an end in 1806. As pointed out earlier, the pre-eminence of the Roman-German imperial dignity in pre-Reformation Latin Christendom was not based on power-political preponderance. Rather, it tied in with a cosmology in which everything, in heaven as on earth, was part of a hierarchy – a hierarchy that, though it was regarded as enormously important and questions of rank loomed large, at the same time always remained essentially nominal. The Roman emperor ranked highest among the rulers of Christendom, but this did not mean that he laid down the law to anyone beyond the dominions – those of the German crown – of which he was king. This posed no problem at all in a world (Latin Christendom) where rulers generally had little power even *within* their own dominions (let alone outside them) and normally did not legislate anyway, at least not in the sense of making rules that all of their subjects would then be expected to follow. Instead, in the pre-Reformation period, general law was overwhelmingly based on local custom, and what rulers, at every level of the feudal pyramid, issued was not general rules for all, but specific privileges for discrete individuals or collectives.

The erroneous and anachronistic modern expectation that an 'emperor', someone of a rank above that of 'mere' king, ought also to have been more powerful than any king has presumably contributed to a perception of the rulers of the Holy Roman Empire as weaker than they actually were. Both before and after the Reformation, and as late as the end of the eighteenth century, their position in the empire was neither particularly strong nor merely nominal, and for all the other change that of course took place during such a long period, I would suggest that whether you look at the fourteenth century, the sixteenth century or the eighteenth century, the power of the emperor *qua* emperor did not actually vary very much. Yet there seems to be a perception as common as it is vague that somehow the emperor must once have had 'real' power – presumably conceived in conformity with present-day notions as supreme and effective power over territory and anyone it contains. According to this view, it was in order to take this power from him or to prevent him from regaining it that the Thirty Years' War was fought, after which the Holy Roman Empire became meaningless, though somehow it dragged on for another century and a half. Contrary to a widespread perception, the Peace of Westphalia of 1648 is silent on the emperor's prerogatives – proposals to curtail them were unsuccessful. I have shown elsewhere that before, during and of course after the Thirty Years' War, no threat to the autonomy of any rulers emanated from the emperor and that this is not only true of rulers outside the empire, but even of those within the empire.[16]

If, during the Thirty Years' War, the Swedish crown attacked the emperor, it was not because it feared Vienna, but because it saw an opportunity. And the real enemy, during the same war, of the French crown and the Dutch States General was not the emperor, but the Spanish crown. The emperor came into it because he belonged to the same dynasty – the House of Habsburg – as the rather more powerful Spanish king. It was the Spanish crown, which ruled not only all of the Iberian Peninsula (including, at that time, Portugal) but also much of Italy and what is now eastern France and Belgium (the old Duchy of Burgundy), that the French crown wanted to diminish. As to the Dutch, their independence from the Spanish crown had been essentially won by 1607, when a twelve-year truce was signed by the parties. This expired as the Thirty Years' War got under way. Had the Dutch been prepared to renew it or even turn it into a permanent peace, the Spanish crown would almost certainly have consented so as to prevent another Franco-Dutch alliance. The Dutch, for their part, felt that they had much to gain from such an alliance, which they expected to wring still greater concessions from Madrid than they might have obtained anyway. Therefore, they too opted for war not due to any fear of Habsburg power, but because they saw an opportunity.

Vast as they were, the possessions of the Habsburg dynasty, both of the Spanish branch and of the German branch, were not the result of conquest, but, famously, of marrying the right people to each other ('tu felix Austria nube'). By contrast, expansion through the piecemeal annexation of contiguous territory had been the strategy of the French crown at least since Philip the Fair in the early fourteenth century – at the expense mostly of the Holy Roman Empire, the only other neighbour of France being Spain in the south. The French crown of course tried marriage too, but was not as successful or lucky in this respect as the Habsburgs, with one rather important exception: when the Spanish branch of the

Habsburg dynasty became extinct in 1700, the hereditary claim of the French crown to the Spanish succession was as good as the claim of the German branch. This stalemate resulted in the War of the Spanish Succession, which the French crown (or to be more precise the Bourbon dynasty) managed not to lose, though with difficulty and without being able to hold on to the Habsburg inheritance in its entirety.[17]

In his capacity as emperor, the head of the German branch of the House of Habsburg followed no expansionist policy with regard to the rest of Christian Europe, other than by trying to marry or inherit yet another crown for himself or a junior member of the dynasty (or, in the case of the Polish crown, trying to have that junior member elected to it). A major reason why it could hardly have been otherwise was the Ottoman Empire, which until the end of the seventeenth century continually either expanded at the expense of the Habsburg dominions or at least threatened to do so, with Ottoman troops laying siege even to Vienna in 1529 and again in 1683. After that latter siege, the tide turned, with the Habsburg dominions expanding again at the expense of the Turks in the eighteenth century. But precisely because this was happening, there was little reason to fight elsewhere in Europe except in response to attacks.

Apart from the somewhat special case of Habsburg–Ottoman relations (special not least because it involved a power outside Christendom), in the continental Europe of the *ancien régime* it was the French crown that routinely made its will prevail against the resistance of others (in other words, exerted power) through the forcible appropriation of territory and more often than not at the expense of the Holy Roman Empire. Given the situation in which the French crown found itself, anything else would have been surprising. Its subjects formed the largest population of any kingdom in Europe by far and the king's domestic position was strong. Conversely, owing to the lack of a central power (which even the emperor was not), the Holy Roman Empire was ill-equipped to defend itself against the French crown. The latter's continual nibbling away at territory belonging to the empire was still somewhat tolerable as long as the territory in question was both French-speaking rather than German-speaking and owned by the Spanish king in his capacity as heir to the Dukes of Burgundy. But in the seventeenth century, more and more German-speaking territory held by German princes (Alsace and, for a while, parts of the Palatinate and of the Saar area) fell under French rule.

The spectre of French hegemony and the rise of nineteenth-century Prussia

During the Napoleonic era, the demographic and economic weight of France, combined with an unprecedented mobilisation of the population through the revolutionary instrument of the *levée en masse*, enabled an explosion of French dominance that brought most of continental Europe under French control. This phenomenon was out of all proportion with the dominance exercised by the French crown of the *ancien régime* and it did not last long – half a generation or so. Yet in retrospect, it was nevertheless easy to see continuity here, a circumstance that, in the German collective memory of the nineteenth century, helped a perception of France as an enemy so dangerous that it could never be weakened enough:

> Today [21 August 1870] we are fighting a war against the 12th or 15th assault or war of conquest that France has carried out against Germany in the past 200 years. In 1814 and 1815 guarantees against these disturbances of the peace were sought in the mild treatment of France. But the danger lies in the incurable imperiousness and arrogance inherent in the French national character and which any ruler of the country may mischievously exploit in order to attack peaceful neighbouring states. Sterile attempts temporarily to alleviate French sensitivities can afford no protection against this evil; gaining well-fortified borders can. We need to end the pressure that for two centuries France has exerted on southern Germany, defenceless against it, and which has become an essential lever for disrupting the affairs of Germany. Through the continuous and methodical appropriation of German land and of all the natural bulwarks sheltering it, France has placed itself in a situation where even with a comparatively small army it may at any time penetrate into the heart of southern Germany, before help can be made available … In such circumstances the only correct policy is to render an enemy that you *cannot* turn into a sincere friend at least a little less harmful, and that means not the demolition of the fortresses with which he threatens us, but the cession of some of them.[18]

Thus, in 1870, wrote Otto von Bismarck to the Prussian envoy in London to justify the annexation not only of (German-speaking) Alsace but also of (largely French-speaking) Lorraine. On its own terms, this sounds reasonable, yet – somewhat ironically it was to turn out – the policy towards France advocated and implemented by Bismarck would later feed a reputation for aggressiveness on the part of Prussia and Germany rather than France.

The easy defeat and territorial amputation of Prussia by Napoleon made a nonsense of the assumption prevailing until then that despite its modest size, Prussia had to be reckoned with in the politics of Europe because of its military. It left the Berlin elite in turmoil and gave rise to a determination, once Napoleon had been removed, to make Prussia so strong that its future as a major European player was assured. At the Congress of Vienna, the insistence with which the Prussian leadership put forward its demands irritated the other negotiators. But as the smallest by far of what came to be known as the 'great powers' and the one with the least defensible territory, Prussia was not in a position where its leaders felt that they could or should be more accommodating than was absolutely necessary to prevent the negotiations from collapsing. They were only partially successful. They wanted Saxony – wealthy, contiguous and Protestant; instead, they got Westphalia and the Rhineland – non-contiguous and Catholic. The fact that the new western provinces of Prussia were territorially separate from the rest of the kingdom made them almost impossible to defend and likely hostages in any war in which the French took the other side. This anomaly did not fit in well with being one of the 'great powers'.

Bismarck was born at that time (in 1815) and grew up in a climate where people of his background could not feel especially secure. The Prussian gentry to which he belonged was privileged, but had never been particularly rich. In the first half of the nineteenth century, its social pre-eminence was under threat from progressive and even radical political ideas. Its (always somewhat precarious) economic position as agrarian producers was under threat – in both domestic and export markets – from foreign and even domestic competitors (for example, in the Polish territories annexed in the eighteenth century) and it was under threat from the growing importance of industrial venture capital.

In the 1848 revolution, the Prussian king was offered the position as head of a new German empire, but declined to receive its crown from the hands of the liberals dominating the Frankfurt National Assembly. Not the least of his reasons was that he did not wish to be disloyal to the Emperor of Austria, who headed the German Confederation that had replaced the old empire at the Congress of Vienna, nor could he afford to alienate Vienna in light of the fact that, unlike the Russian-backed Habsburg emperor, he had little support among the powers of Europe.[19] Bismarck, who started his political career as a Christian conservative in the Prussian Diet before evolving into an adherent of the concept, made famous by himself, of *Realpolitik*, came to feel that the mixture of loyalty and lack of determined ambition that characterised the royal house was wrong. For him, the way to save Prussia lay in the opposite direction: the traditional deference towards the emperor in Vienna had to be abandoned and the German national movement should be made the ally of Prussia that much of it wanted to be in any case. As the second most-important member of the German Confederation but much less encumbered by non-German-speaking dominions, Prussia seemed predestined to become the leading power in Germany, a role that Bismarck felt it should seek rather than shirk, but which might well necessitate strengthening Prussia by whatever means available.

I dwell on the role of Bismarck because I do believe that without this exceptional individual, the course of German history would have been completely different (and, to be frank, probably happier). In the famous budgetary crisis of 1862 – caused by the refusal of the liberals in the Prussian Diet to contemplate a reform of the army, which was in no great shape – Bismarck managed against the odds to solve the problem. This prevented the ageing king, Wilhelm I, from abdicating in favour of the crown prince, whose sympathies lay with the liberals. In the next few years, on more than one occasion it was Bismarck who threatened to resign in order to get what he wanted against the hesitancy of the king and the opposition of the crown prince. This included not so much the war against Denmark in 1864, but the war against Austria in 1866 and the annexation, by Prussia, of Hanover and parts of Hesse in its wake, which finally linked up the two parts of the kingdom territorially. If the war against Austria was an enormity, the annexation was perhaps an even greater one, making a mockery of conservative legitimist principles.[20] The victorious war of 1870 against France, which Bismarck wanted but contrived to get the French to start, allowed him to propel the king (unenthusiastic as ever) to accept the crown of the new German Empire. Its government was to be headed by Bismarck as Chancellor. Within that empire, Prussia would henceforth be both dominant as it had never been before and secure – at least that was the idea.[21]

'It is not easy to be emperor under a chancellor like that', Wilhelm I is supposed to have said; the quote may be apocryphal, but, as an author citing it only just over a decade after his death observes, it sounds credible.[22] Having become emperor, Wilhelm stayed on the throne for another seventeen years. During that time, Bismarck pursued no further expansionist aims. When, in 1888, Wilhelm died at the age of ninety, he probably had no reason to feel that he had been untrue to what he wrote to King Johann of Saxony in January 1871 in a programmatic letter that must have been inspired or indeed dictated by Bismarck:

> Germany, strong on account of the unity of its princes and tribes, has regained its position in the council of nations, and the German people has neither need nor inclination to strive for anything beyond its borders save the friendly intercourse of nations founded on the mutual recognition of their independence and the joint promotion of their welfare. I trust that, secure in its own strength and satisfied, the German empire, after the victorious termination of a war in which an unjust attack has embroiled us and with its borders with France made safe, will be an empire of peace and happiness, in which the German people will find and enjoy what for centuries they have striven and longed for.[23]

After an extremely brief reign by the liberal crown prince Friedrich, already moribund at his accession, Wilhelm II succeeded his grandfather in 1888. He let Bismarck go. His time on the throne coincides with the peak of what is now generally known as the age of imperialism. In Germany as in other countries, there was a movement clamouring for a more assertive, muscular foreign policy in general, and more and better overseas possessions in particular, that the government had to humour. The new emperor was himself rather given to grandiloquence and bluster. But the four people who held the German chancellorship between the departure of Bismarck in 1890 and the outbreak of the First World War were hardly more expansionist than their predecessor. Out of the four, only Chancellor Bernhard von Bülow (in office 1900–9) had any sympathy for imperialism and allowed himself to be talked into a programme of naval armaments that was understood as a challenge to Great Britain (which had also massively reinforced its navy after the Naval Defence Act of 1889, and in 1909 launched a further programme of naval armaments in response to the German programme).

Towards the end of his tenure, Bülow would have liked to abandon this naval policy. By that time, he felt that it needlessly aggravated relations with Britain without offering any chance even of denting British domination of the seas in the foreseeable future. His successor Theobald von Bethmann-Hollweg shared that opinion. However, the emperor supported the naval programme, which was also popular with parts of the electorate. That was important. It is true that under the Constitution of the 1871 Empire, the chancellor was appointed by the emperor, not elected by the Reichstag. However, since the Reichstag, elected by universal male suffrage, had to pass the budget as well as all legislation, it was difficult to ignore – indeed, it was much more powerful than is often assumed. Wilhelm II liked to interfere with the politics of the government, but did so in such a haphazard and inconsistent manner that his influence did not actually amount to much. He could, theoretically, replace the chancellor and other ministers at will, but since he needed a cabinet both willing to work together and capable of delivering majorities in the Reichstag, he soon found that his freedom in this respect was in fact severely constrained.[24]

Bülow thought that in order to be successful, the naval programme (which its instigator Admiral Tirpitz expected to take twenty years to complete) required abstention from foreign-political conflicts for its duration. Bethmann-Hollweg for his part thought that while Germany would never be taken seriously as a naval power, its army should be strengthened, but this too would take time. He too abstained from allowing foreign-political friction to escalate and attracted heavy criticism from the jingoists for supposedly not standing up to France in the Moroccan crisis of 1911.[25]

In light of this, it seems ironic that when, at the Paris Peace Conference of 1919, the German delegation complained that the proposed Treaty of Versailles was unfairly punitive, the victors, in their official reply, retorted that it was merely what, given its record, Germany deserved. Their reply echoes the accusations directed at France in the passage by Bismarck quoted earlier. Indeed, the French Prime Minister Georges Clemenceau in 1919 followed the same logic as Bismarck in seeking to weaken Germany and to strengthen France by obtaining as many cessions of German territory as possible (though the logic of his demands was not only strategic but also economic, reflecting the heightened importance that had come to be attached to economic aspects of world politics).

A German *leyenda negra*?[26]

'For many years', declared the 'Allied and Associated Powers' whose representatives had drafted the proposed treaty:

> the rulers of Germany, true to the Prussian tradition, strove for a position of dominance in Europe. They were not satisfied with that growing prosperity and influence to which Germany was entitled, and which all other nations were willing to accord her, in the society of free and equal peoples. They required that they should be able to dictate and tyrannise to a subservient Europe, as they dictated and tyrannised over a subservient Germany. In order to attain their ends they used every channel in their power through which to educate their own subjects in the doctrine that might was right in international affairs. They never ceased to expand German armaments by land and sea, and to propagate the falsehood that this was necessary because Germany's neighbours were jealous of her prosperity and power. They sought to sow hostility and suspicion instead of friendship between nations. They developed a system of espionage and intrigue which enabled them to stir up internal rebellion and unrest and even to make secret offensive preparations within the territory of their neighbours whereby they might, when the moment came, strike them down with greater certainty and ease. They kept Europe in a ferment by threats of violence and when they found that their neighbours were resolved to resist their arrogant will, they determined to assert their predominance in Europe by force.[27]

The document goes on to re-affirm that Germany must bear sole responsibility for the outbreak of war in 1914. It is interesting to note that the *Reply* does not cite any actual German aggression prior to the attack on Belgium in August 1914, after the war had broken out. It does cite domestic propaganda (which certainly existed, but came from pressure groups and publicists rather than the government), armaments, a 'system of espionage and intrigue.' Given that, both before and during the war, such were the means employed by every government in Europe – certainly by those with a major share in the war – the indictment seems somewhat hypocritical. That an official document of major importance could stoop to this kind of polemic is an illustration of how heated the climate of the period was and how little chance facts had to prevail over perception.

Did Wilhelmine Germany abuse its military or economic power? Germany was no more aggressive, in the decades leading up the First World War, than the other major players in Europe – which is not to say that it lacked aggressive impulses. However, it is true that on the German side the war itself was fought brutally; the blame for this must be laid in the first instance at the door of the military. That for all his love of bluster Wilhelm II was really a weak and irresolute character did not help and hampered efforts by the civilian government to rein in the generals. Wilhelm was, in theory, supreme commander of the German forces, but, during the war, abdicated all actual decision-making power to career officers. His sole contribution was in hanging on, as long as he could, to the comparatively moderate Erich von Falkenhayn as chief of the general staff before being forced to drop him in favour of Paul von Hindenburg and his ruthlessly hawkish advisor Erich Ludendorff in 1916. To what extent did this reflect a difference in the 'deep culture' of Germany from that of other European countries, a special tendency to exercise power ruthlessly, and to what extent was it rather attributable to an unfortunate concatenation of circumstances?

There was, in Germany and elsewhere in Europe, a culture of extreme nationalism and militarism with strong racist overtones. Its representatives were vociferous even though it is doubtful if they ever constituted a majority in any country. However, their voice is also echoed by the tone of the *Reply*. It was this culture that was largely responsible for the failure to make any effort to conciliate Germany after the First World War. This in turn strengthened that culture further in Germany too. The Nazi regime ultimately did every bad thing that Germany had ever been accused of (and more), and literally did it with a vengeance. In the light of that horror, it could appear as if every previous criticism of Germany had, as it were, been validated retrospectively. And it could appear that indeed there must be a tradition of German abuse of power of which the period 1933–45 was merely the logical culmination.

With the Treaty of Versailles attributing sole responsibility for the war to Germany, this kind of contention was naturally an object of heated debate in the aftermath of that war. It became so again, at least in Germany, when in the 1960s German historian Fritz Fischer likewise put forward the thesis that the German leadership in 1914 had not stumbled into the war, but had been working towards it.[28] Fifty years after Fischer, it seems fair to say that his defenders are now few. In time for the centenary of the outbreak of war in 2014, the historian Christopher Clark published a much-noted study[29] of the antecedents of the war that tends to exonerate the German leadership and to place rather more blame on other participants, like the Serbian leadership, the Russian cabinet, the French President Raymond Poincaré and the British Foreign Secretary Lord Grey. Clark does so on the basis of, to my mind, rather more solid evidence and arguments than was the case with Fischer. Reviewers in Germany mostly hailed the book, but felt obliged to wonder if it was not too 'pro-German.'[30] It is interesting that Clark – prudently it would appear – refrains from spelling out his conclusions in the same combative manner as Fischer, or indeed at all.

If Fischer was so successful and if his critics are even now wary of saying anything in defence of the German leadership of 1914, it is obviously because the traumatic experience of the Third Reich has left much of the German public with a willingness, even an eagerness to credit just about any bad thing to the 'old' Germany of before 1945, extending that perception to the Wilhelmine period or even beyond. As the egregious abuse of power is very much seen as a main characteristic of this 'old' Germany, this attitude is bound up with a deep-seated distrust of any exercise, on the part of German politicians, of power in whatever visible form, certainly if it is not clearly inspired by pure and indeed altruistic motives – *sacro egoismo* in reverse, as it were. After the founding of the Federal Republic in 1949, the West German leadership has been consistently keen to dispel any fear that it might not have learned its historical lesson and to prove itself a cooperative, fair-minded and well-meaning partner in its external dealings. Importantly, this attitude was backed, indeed expected, by much of the electorate.

Under its first chancellor Konrad Adenauer (in office from 1949 to 1963) and his immediate successors, the new West Germany strove to prove itself a loyal member of the US-led 'free world', immune to the temptation of neutralism, let alone defection to the communist East. From at least the early 1970s onwards, the leadership of the Federal Republic also sought to conciliate the Eastern Bloc. The *Ostpolitik* of the Brandt government was designed to allay any fears harboured by the Soviet leadership or its satellites that West Germany might seek to force a revision of the boundaries drawn after the Second World War, involving the partition of Germany and the loss of German territory to Poland. During his long tenure as Foreign Minister from 1972 to 1994, Hans-Dietrich Genscher symbolised the benevolent, non-nationalistic, anti-power-political attitude cultivated by the West German political establishment to such a degree that it became known as 'Genscherism'. Throughout the second half of the twentieth century, the foreign policy of the Federal Republic consistently advocated goals that did not serve Germany alone, but something larger, such as the Western alliance, European integration or the developing world – this being a defining feature of the 'civilian power' (*Zivilmacht*) as which (West) Germany re-invented itself (on this concept, see also Siegfried Schieder in Chapter 10 in this volume).[31]

Following reunification, the pattern has continued. Twenty-five years after reunification, it remains the case that politicians, political commentators and the electorate in Germany show little or no interest in any kind of aggressive defence of the 'national interest'. Predictions that the end of the Cold War and the reunification of Germany would result in the German leadership abandoning this attitude in favour of great power ambitions[32] have not so far been borne out. The spectre of a possible future 'Fourth Reich' has been variously evoked by journalists, publicists and historians since 1990.[33] It is easy to dismiss the notion of a 'Fourth Reich' as sensationalist nonsense. On the other hand, its lingering if modest popularity serves as a reminder that the memory of Nazism remains very much part of the global folklore and influences how Germany is perceived in many, often quite subtle ways. It is an ever-present backdrop, whether explicitly referred to or not.

As a result, if the German government is seen as wielding excessive pressure in its external relations, concern about this will be tinged with more or less open warnings about the country reverting to evil old ways. Remarkably, even the right-wing populists who currently enjoy the favour of an increasing segment of the German electorate have so far failed to call for any kind of aggressive foreign policy. They appear to be content to demand less permeable borders and to regard the world beyond those borders as something that it is necessary to keep at bay rather than as something that offers opportunities. It is worth pointing out that at present, this seems to be the case not just in Germany but also across Europe. As far as I am aware, nobody in (non-Russian) Europe is calling for a return to power politics or the kind of great power rivalry that was fashionable around the turn of the twentieth century.

Already during the Cold War, the West German insistence on being a 'civilian power' working for the greater good of humanity has, with a certain regularity, invited criticism. An early example, relatively well known in Germany, is Hans-Peter Schwarz, who in a book published in 1985 accused his compatriots of having veered from being obsessed with power to being oblivious to it.[34] But while the German political establishment is keen to obviate this kind of criticism, it also knows how dangerous it is to be seen to go too far in the other direction. When the then President of the Federal Republic Horst Köhler said in an interview in May 2010 that the German military ought perhaps to be deployed to protect trade routes important to Germany, the media echo was extremely negative, leaving Köhler, who unexpectedly resigned shortly afterwards, visibly shaken. When his successor Joachim Gauck opened the Munich

Security Conference in January 2014, he offered a fascinating testimony to the ambivalence that his speechwriter clearly thought necessary in addressing the question of the role that Germany should play in the world.[35] '[T]he key question', Gauck said, was if Germany had 'already adequately recognised the new threats and the changing structure of the international order', and reacted to it in accordance with its weight. 'Some people at home and abroad have a quick and somewhat simplistic answer: they regard Germany as the shirker in the international community.'

After reiterating the trope that for a long time the problematic recent history of Germany induced understandable caution in politicians both in Germany and elsewhere, Gauck went on to assert that Germany had redeemed itself. Throughout the speech, Gauck implied that 'Germany' could and would 'do more' in the future, but remained eminently vague as to how. The speech dwelled at some length on the then fashionable concept of humanitarian intervention, both affirming that it is an option that needs to be considered and that it is not easy to put into practice and often cannot be put into practice. This was as concrete as it gets – no other scenarios for using the German military were discussed – and was embedded in a review of the many non-military ways in which 'Germany' has exerted itself to make the world a better and safer place ('development cooperation', 'tak[ing] the world into a resource efficient future' and 'promot[ing] international institutions').

Indubitably we are still about as far removed here from 'Prussian militarism' or indeed any form of 'great power' behaviour as could be imagined. But, as this chapter has sought to remind readers, 'Germany' did not begin with and was never identical with 'Prussia' – nor of course should 'Prussia' be reduced to any single aspect of its history. If the historical review attempted in this chapter shows anything, to me it would appear to be this: that while 'Germany' (whatever this has meant in different centuries) and 'power' have often had an odd relationship, compared to what is popularly considered 'normal', there is no continuity here – except, conceivably, a tendency to go to extremes in either direction, whether in striving for and exercising power or in ignoring or even shunning it. However, this seems explicable in terms of historical constellations and path-dependent contingency rather than anything that might be regarded as specifically 'German'.

Notes

1   The most thorough treatment of the concept of power probably is S. R. Clegg and M. Haugaard (eds), *The SAGE Handbook of Power* (London: SAGE Publications, 2009) and S. R. Clegg and M. Haugaard (eds), *Power and Politics*, 4 vols (Los Angeles: SAGE Publications, 2012). At rather less length,

a useful introduction to the complexity of the subject is also provided by K. W. Deutsch, *The Analysis of International Relations*, 3rd ed. (Englewood Cliffs, NJ: Prentice Hall, 1988), chs. 3, 4.

2 A. Osiander, *The States System of Europe 1640–1990: Peacemaking and the Conditions of International Stability* (Oxford: Oxford University Press, 1994), pp. 232–47.

3 W. T. R. Fox, *The Super-Powers: The United States, Britain, and the Soviet Union – Their Responsibility for Peace* (New York: Harcourt Brace, 1944).

4 'What is going on with The World's Only Superpower? This label, or sometimes the tautological The World's Only Remaining Superpower, now seems to follow "the United States" or "America" almost automatically in the articles appearing in your paper [the *New York Times*] … If this is to continue, may I suggest that you could save space and ink by using the acronym TWOSP instead of the whole phrase: D. H. McKay, 'The Superpower and Ink', *New York Times and International Herald Tribune* (29 December 1998), letter to the editor of the *New York Times*.

5 Perhaps the best-known and most influential contribution to this subject is P. Kennedy, *The Rise and Fall of the Great Powers: Economic Change and Military Conflict from 1500 to 2000* (London: Unwin Hyman, 1988).

6 An urban legend popular not least in Germany itself has it that Germany discovered its national identity only around the turn of the nineteenth century. In fact, throughout its history, the Holy Roman Empire 'of German Nation' was very much a national enterprise, and the discourse of its politics was not just conscious of a common nationality, but was given to nationalist ardour, no matter which century of its history you look at. No doubt the routine invocations, from at least the early sixteenth century onwards, of the 'geliebtes Vaterland deutscher Nation' or 'beloved fatherland of German nation' were not always sincere, but the important point is that they were expected. Still further back in time, the perception of Germany as a cohesive if federal entity (federal in that at the time, it was seen as made up of five 'tribes' which, however, shared a common or at least mutually intelligible language) underlay the establishment of a separate German crown in the early tenth century and formed the background to German history throughout the High Middle Ages. Here too, this is easily perceived if one bothers to read the sources of the period; cf. Osiander, *The States System of Europe 1640–1990*, pp. 30–9, 74; A. Osiander, *Before the State: Systemic Political Change in the West from the Greeks to the French Revolution* (Oxford: Oxford University Press 2007), pp. 258–68, 419.

7 Osiander, *Before the State*, sec. 3.4.

8 It is true that even before 1186, southern Italy (the Kingdom of Sicily) was regarded by the Hohenstaufen dynasty and its adherents in both Germany and Italy as forming part of the empire. According to this view, the Hauteville dynasty established at Palermo were usurpers, though that did not prevent the Emperor Friedrich I from marrying his son to the Hauteville heiress anyway.

9 A. Osiander, 'Sovereignty, international relations, and the Westphalian myth', *International Organization*, 55:2 (2001), pp. 251–87, at pp. 267–8.

10 J. S. Pütter, *Historische Entwickelung der heutigen Staatsverfassung des deutschen Reichs* (Göttingen: Vandenhoeck, 1787), pp. 221 ff. gives a detailed account of the enfeoffment ceremony regularly and routinely performed by

the emperor in Vienna, as well as examples of the charges levied. The only exception to the duty to do homage to the emperor, and only in the second half of the eighteenth century, were those few princes who held electoral rank, and it was understood that not having to do homage to the emperor did not mean that they denied his role as their feudal overlord. Italian nobles were, it seems, not normally expected to do homage. Interestingly, however, when the Emperor Leopold, in 1697, requested all holders of imperial fiefs in northern Italy to present the relevant charters for confirmation, he was surprised to learn that he had many more vassals there than his chancery even knew of, anecdotal yet powerful further evidence of how seriously the feudal nexus was taken (K.-O. von Aretin, 'Reichsitalien von Karl V. bis zum Ende des Alten Reiches. Die Lehensordnungen in Italien und ihre Auswirkungen auf die europäische Politik', in K. O. von Aretin, *Das Reich. Friedensordnung und europäisches Gleichgewicht 1648–1806* (Stuttgart: Klett-Cotta, 1992), pp. 76–163, at pp. 123–4.

11 The Ewiger Landfrieden (Perpetual Peace of the Land) of 1495 banned all feuds in the empire and made the peaceful settlement of disputes mandatory. Until 1806, it counted as one of the so-called Fundamental Laws of the Empire (Reichs-Grundgesetze), which collectively made up the empire's constitution. Indeed, after about the middle of the sixteenth century, military clashes between princes or cities of the empire almost never occurred, except during the Thirty Years' War and the Seven Years' War.

12 B. Braun, 'Das Reich blieb nicht stumm und kalt. Der Untergang des Alten Reiches in der Sicht der Zeitgenossen', in C. Roll and M. Schnetger (eds), *Epochenjahr 1806? Das Ende des Alten Reichs in zeitgenössischen Perspektiven und Deutungen* (Mainz: Philipp von Zabern, 2008), pp. 7–29.

13 A. Osiander, 'Legal order without sovereignty: local lordships and the legal-political system of the Holy Roman Empire', in E. J. M. F. C. Broers and B. C. M. Jacobs (eds), *Interactie tussen wetgever en rechter vóór de Trias Politica* (The Hague: Boom, 2003), pp. 63–84.

14 G. Haug-Moritz, *Württembergischer Ständekonflikt und deutscher Dualismus. Ein Beitrag zur Geschichte des Reichsverbands in der Mitte des 18. Jahrhunderts* (Stuttgart: Kohlhammer, 1992).

15 Osiander, *Before the State*, pp. 452–4.

16 Those who at this suggestion will immediately feel tempted to cite the Edict of Restitution or the Peace of Prague are asked to read the article in question first: Osiander, 'Sovereignty, international relations, and the Westphalian myth'.

17 Osiander, *The States System of Europe 1640–1990*, ch. 3.

18 G. A. Rein, W. Schüssler, E. Scheler, A. Milatz and R. Buchner (eds), *Otto von Bismarck, Werke in Auswahl* (Stuttgart: Kohlhammer 1968), pp. 515 ff.; my translation, emphasis in original.

19 C. Clark, *Iron Kingdom: The Rise and Downfall of Prussia 1600–1947* (London: Penguin, 2007), pp. 397, 488 ff.; W. Neugebauer, *Die Geschichte Preußens. Von den Anfängen bis 1947* (Munich: Piper, 2006), pp. 104–5.

20 It is true that though they had opposed the war against Austria, once it had been won, both the king and the crown prince felt that now was the time to annex Saxony, allied to Austria, after all. Bismarck vetoed this.

21 'I cannot tell you', Wilhelm wrote to his wife on 18 January 1871, the day after his proclamation as 'German Emperor', 'in how morose a mood I have been during these last few days, in part because of the great responsibility that I now have to assume, in part and above all because of my pain at seeing the Prussian title displaced.' He went on to say that he had once more been on the point of abdicating in favour of the crown prince; H. Kohl (ed.), *Die Begründung des Deutschen Reichs in Briefen und Berichten der führenden Männer* (Leipzig: Voigtländer, 1912), p. 94, my translation.

22 L. Bamberger, *Bismarck Posthumus* (Berlin: 'Harmonie' Verlagsgesellschaft für Literatur und Kunst, 1899), p. 8.

23 Wilhelm I of Prussia to King Johann of Saxony, 14 January 1871, in Kohl, *Die Begründung des Deutschen Reichs*, p. 90; my translation.

24 This is masterfully shown by C. Clark, *Kaiser Wilhelm II. A Life in Power*, revised ed. (London: Penguin, 2009). Not the least merit of this book is the careful manner in which it engages with the influential work of John Roehl, who in many publications has argued forcefully that Wilhelm II pulled all the strings in German politics and is personally responsible not least for what Roehl regards as an eminently nefarious German foreign policy.

25 A. Osiander, 'A forgotten theorist of international relations: Kurt Riezler and his fundamentals of world politics of 1914', in I. Hall (ed.), *Radicals and Reactionaries in Twentieth-Century International Thought* (New York: Palgrave Macmillan, 2014), pp. 43–74, at p. 51.

26 The 'Black Legend' – a term popularised by the historian Julián Juderías in J. Juderías, *La leyenda negra y la verdad histórica. Contribución al estudio del concepto de España en Europa, de las causas de este concepto y de la tolerancia política y religiosa en los países civilizados* (Madrid: Tip. de la 'Rev. de Arch., Bibl. y Museos', 1914) – is a type of discourse found throughout Europe from the sixteenth century onwards that depicted the Spaniards as uniquely cruel and ruthless in their desire to subjugate and dominate others. It played a large role in anti-Spanish propaganda during the Wars of Religion and the Thirty Years' War.

27 Multiple authors, *Reply of the Allied and Associated Powers to the Observations of the German Delegation on the Conditions of Peace* (London: H.M. Stationery Office, 1919), pp. 2–3, www.babel.hathitrust.org/cgi/pt?id=uc1.$c180735;view=1up;seq=5.

28 F. Fischer, *Griff nach der Weltmacht. Die Kriegszielpolitik des kaiserlichen Deutschland 1914/1918* (Düsseldorf: Droste, 1961); F. Fischer, *Krieg der Illusionen. Die deutsche Politik von 1911 bis 1914* (Düsseldorf: Droste, 1969).

29 C. Clark, *The Sleepwalkers: How Europe Went to War in 1914* (London: Allen Lane, 2012).

30 Cf., for example, G. Krumeich, 'Unter Schlafwandlern', *Süddeutsche Zeitung* (30 November 2012); L. Machtan, 'Over-sophisticated. Anmerkungen zu Christopher Clarks Bestseller', *sehepunkte*, 14:1 (2014); V. Ullrich, 'Zündschnur und Pulverfass', *Die Zeit* (17 September 2013).

31 S. Harnisch and H. W. Maull (eds), *Germany as a Civilian Power? The Foreign Policy of the Berlin Republic* (Manchester: Manchester University Press, 2001).

32 This is an expectation expressed, for example, by so prominent an analyst of international relations as Kenneth Waltz: K. Waltz, 'The emerging structure of international politics', *International Security*, 18:1 (1993), pp. 44–79. Waltz even thought it likely that the new Germany would seek nuclear armaments – a prediction that anyone familiar with the political culture of post-war Germany probably would not have made.

33 See e.g. P. Béhar, *Du Ier au IVe Reich. Permanence d'une nation, renaissances d'un État* (Paris: Desjonquères, 1990); C. Coker, 'At the birth of a Fourth Reich? The British reaction', *Political Quarterly*, 61:3 (1990), pp. 278–85; M. Walker, 'Overstretching Teutonia: making the best of the Fourth Reich', *World Policy Journal*, 12:1 (1995), pp. 1–18; G. Sangiuliano and V. Feltri, *Il Quarto Reich. Come la Germania ha sottomesso l'Europa* (Milan: Mondadori, 2014); N. Blome et al., '"The Fourth Reich": what some Europeans see when they look at Germany', *Der Spiegel* (21 March 2015), 13, English translation of an article originally published at: www.spiegel.de/international/germany/german-power-in-the-age-of-the-euro-crisis-a-1024714.html; B. Reading, *The Fourth Reich* (London: Weidenfeld & Nicolson, 1995).

34 H. P. Schwarz, *Die gezähmten Deutschen. Von der Machtbesessenheit zur Machtvergessenheit* (Stuttgart: Deutsche Verlagsanstalt, 1985).

35 I quote the official translation made available by the Bundespräsidialamt: www.bundespraesident.de/SharedDocs/Downloads/DE/Reden/2014/01/140131-Muenchner-Sicherheitskonferenz-Englisch.pdf;jsessionid=4F1DFEC65C9FF7813F4CFF22115D360A.2_cid285?__blob=publicationFile.

3

The liberal internationalist self and the construction of an undemocratic German other at the beginning of the twentieth century

Leonie Holthaus

This chapter seeks to reconstruct and contextualise liberal internationalism's creation of an autocratic and militarist German adversary at the beginning of the twentieth century.[1] Therewith, it turns to one example par excellence of othering within the European spectrum. Others have seminally discussed liberal internationalism's Eurocentric and self-conscious discrimination of a different, less civilised, traditional or undemocratic counterpart along the lines of West–East divisions.[2] However, liberal images of Germany have hardly received attention. This is a severe lacuna because liberal internationalism has a complicated relationship with German thought and politics. When tensions between liberalism and democratisation became evident within Britain and when British imperial power declined, liberal internationalist views of less civilised societies as well as of a militarist German state involved the accentuation of their own British virtues and recollection of liberal beliefs.

Liberal internationalism originated in Victorian Britain, and many Victorians much appreciated German high culture, thought and progress towards (social) reform. Like American students of political science, many British intellectuals spent time in Germany, especially during their academic education.[3] However, in view of the German rise to power, admiration of Germany's culture and uneasiness with the dubious German politics became entangled. In 'Representative Government' (1861), John Stuart Mill still provided a balanced comparison of the American federal constitutions and the German confederation.[4] But the tone altered after German unification in 1871 and in view of increasing imperial rivalry.[5] Liberal internationalist philosophers such as Henry Sidgwick contributed to this change of mood when they shifted the focus from 'the men of practice', and thus British politicians and officials, to German thought as liberal internationalism's ideological adversary.[6] The international lawyer Lassa Oppenheim, a German émigré to Britain, argued similarly.[7] British liberalism is then identical to humanitarianism, whereas German thought celebrates the state as an end in itself.[8] Hence, I observe in this chapter, as do Annette Weinke and Felix Rösch in their chapters in this volume, the exclusion of Germany from the community of civilised states, debates about its possible re-integration, and the role of International Relations (IR) scholars in the creation of respective images of Germany in the US and Britain.

The famous British new liberal L. T. Hobhouse, who temporarily moved to a more conservative point of view during the First World War, and other liberal internationalists such as A. Zimmern, who was of German origin and who became the first chair of International Relations (1919) in Aberystwyth in Wales, developed the commenced line into easy dichotomies. In their different social roles as academics or journalists, intellectuals, who were otherwise critical and apt commentators, gave strong support to the official wartime propaganda. Even prior to the American entry into the war (1917), British intellectuals and the official propaganda machine spoke of a war against autocratic Prussianism and for democracy.[9] Prussianism functioned as an umbrella term and often paved the way for attacks on German nationalism, and in particular intellectuals who focused on German nationalism without distinguishing between the German people and their militaristic elites constructed a strikingly simplistic image of Germany.

Like later *Sonderwegstheoretiker* (theorists of Germany's special path), Hobhouse identified German nationalism during the war as the cause of Germany's departure from the Western model and distinguished between a Western and, by definition, liberal civilisation, led by Britain and later the US, and a backward and militarist Germany.[10] Intellectuals could not ignore Germany's capacity for economic modernisation as Germany passed through a late but rapid and state-directed economic modernisation process in the nineteenth century.[11] However, liberal internationalists denied that the state of Germany allowed for meaningful political self-government, and the question as to whether democracy could auto-develop in Germany distinguished between more conservative liberal sceptics and British radicals.[12]

Debates about German democracy, or rather the absence of it, strongly interrelated academic, political and ideological arguments. The questions discussed concerned liberal and democratic development, war guilt, British and American responsibility to adopt an active policy of democracy promotion towards the Weimar Republic, and the construction of the post-war order. Within these overlapping debates, the vocabulary for the nascent discipline of IR was formed. While other disciplines have reconstructed and deconstructed British and American intellectuals' othering of Germany and its legacy, IR remained reluctant to further challenge its 'noble identity myth', the standing of liberal internationalism, and the problematic origins of democratic peace theory and democracy.[13]

This chapter is structured as follows. The second section will define and contextualise liberal internationalist principles. The third section will then turn to liberal internationalists' constructions of an image of Germany as an inherently illiberal state during the First World War. They proceeded in a remarkably similar, tripartite manner and almost always began with postulating a causal connection between German philosophy and the unfolding of German militarism, which was then furthered by the illustration of the illiberal nature of the German state and finalised by the exposure of the unprecedented character of German nationalism. After the reconstruction of this image of Germany, the fourth section argues that the discursive regime served different ends, such as hiding tensions within liberal internationalism or fears that some German developments were not an exception, but rather a model. The conclusion sums up and makes an argument for the historical contextualisation of German democratisation and the origins of the democratic peace thesis.

Contextualising liberal internationalism

Liberal internationalism is often defined in distinction to realism and by its attempt to domesticate international relations.[14] Accordingly, liberal internationalism embraces domestic analogies which derive international theories and reform proposals from the political and legal relations of individuals in the domestic sphere. However, this way of defining liberalism is problematic because it suggests that classical liberals drew clear domestic-international distinctions or conceived of states as corporate actors with equal rights. In particular, the proposals of liberal imperialists rather looked like homologies, speaking of a world as of a British state, but still embraced internally racist hierarchies.[15]

For those who try to avoid invoking the domestic analogy, it has become conventional to begin definitions of liberalism, and correspondingly of liberal internationalism, with the acknowledgement of their fuzzy natures. Only three principles remain unambiguously liberal, and these are the belief in the individual as the sole unit of moral concern, faith in a free market and commitment to representative democracy.[16] However, classics such as John Stuart Mill already noted that the logics underlying a free capitalist market (competition) and democracy (equality) were normatively and empirically incomprehensible.[17] Hence, classical liberal internationalism, as later neo-liberalism, evolved in a polyvocal manner.[18] I thus share the view that it is best to conceive of liberal internationalism as a discourse that is constructed in manifold, contradicting ways and that steadily changes its shape so that its boundaries are only defined by what other self-identified liberal internationalists accept as liberal or not.[19] In the following, I contextualise the origins of classical liberal internationalism and its core debates in order to identify its most important discursive traits at the turn of the twentieth century.

Many liberal principles can be traced back to the second half of the nineteenth century when the emergence of self-conscious liberal reasoning coincided with Great Britain's 'golden' Victorian age.[20] Britain then possessed the first truly global empire and the Industrial Revolution promised increasing prosperity. Intellectuals had good reason to assume that the present constellation would endure.[21] Based on the British example, the philosopher and sociologist Herbert Spencer argued that industrialised societies are more peaceful than pre-modern, militaristic societies and that they are forces of orderly international cooperation.[22] He allowed that other races might auto-develop, but still assumed that their developmental path could only repeat British experiences.[23] The liberal *Weltanschauung* welcomed and universalised social transformations towards modernity while liberalism, as a political ideology, advanced in Britain because it served the representation of extending middle-class interests. Patriotic themes were central in the Victorian liberal party and the discourse pivoted around constitutionalism, tolerance and Christian humanitarianism.[24] The special conditions of the international dominance of Britain's naval power, which facilitated free trade as well as a trend towards liberal politics in Europe until the late 1870s, allowed liberal patriotism to flourish.

Victorian liberalism gave rise to liberal internationalism when a portion of liberal intellectuals, especially those who worked in colonial administration, reformulated ideas of human morality and rationality in view of a spectrum ranging from 'civilised' to 'non-civilised' societies.[25] Evolutionary philosophy made it possible to conceive of humanity as one progressing community moving towards orderly conduct and ruled by international law, while simultaneously drawing distinctions between different degrees of civilisation.[26] Classical liberal internationalism involved substantial British self-aggrandisement, varying degrees of paternalism, and internal liberal disagreement. Although many liberal internationalists, such as Gladstone, were popular politicians, some liberal internationalists identified the 'men of practice' and diplomats involved in European affairs as their ideological adversary.[27] Overall, however, there was a widely shared faith that the British elite was more rational than other national elites and therefore capable of governing the British Empire.[28] Besides liberal internationalists who turned to imperialism, the British public devoted comparably little attention to the colonies and rather assumed that they were moving towards independence.[29]

For Mill, who revisited liberal beliefs in view of the state of the empire and socialist demands for democracy, nationality was a precondition for representative government and he believed that a nation exists when a portion of mankind is united by mutual sympathies, developed from race, descent and language, attachment to a particular geographical space, and a common historical memory.[30] In analogy to a person's character and capacity for self-determination, Mill assumed that some nations are ready for the institutions of representative government, while others have yet to civilise. He further assumed that, as virtues, nationalism and liberal internationalism were compatible and that nationalism was a first step towards a self-conscious and enlightened internationalism.[31] In debates about Italian or German unification, he supported the trend towards larger political units. However, the terminology discriminated between nationality, Mazzinian nationalism and vulgar nationalism, and, as we will see, German nationalism had to be theorised into another manifestation.

Towards the end of nineteenth century, the British public shifted the focus from Europe to themes of empire, and the overall optimism declined. Liberal constitutionalism appeared increasingly unsuited for binding the nation in national and global purposes, and disillusion with Britain's political system under the stress of democratisation became the defining intellectual feature.[32] While liberalism had previously hosted an impulse to put limits on the powers of the monarch, liberal internationalists like Spencer then asked whether liberal and democratic trends could fall apart.[33] They followed the path first opened by Jeremy Bentham (1843), whose universal peace thinking had been driven by the desire to correct popular misconceptions and to advance enlightened understandings of Britain's interests. By the same token, Mill worried about the British parliament's epistemic capacities, parliamentarian oversight over colonial administration, and about what the rule of the less educated working class might mean for democracy.[34] In spite of the 1884 suffrage reform, women and up to 40 per cent of the men had no right to vote, and many of those eligible to vote did not make use of their rights, but liberals acted as if Britain was a full democracy facing an uncertain future.[35]

At the same time, Britain's commercial dominance was challenged by Germany and the US, and in the public and intellectual imaginary, imperial unity became a necessity in times of global competition.[36] Sceptical reflections about British democracy went hand in hand with the perceived need of imperial unity. Many liberal internationalists flirted with the idea of an imperial federation in one way or another, and the respective debates can be viewed as an instance for an overall turn from philosophical to more institutional patterns of arguments. This change occurred gradually from the middle of the eighteenth century onwards, but I assume that imperialists have always been more institutionally minded than other liberals.[37] However, the turn to institutional arguments added internal tensions to liberal internationalism because it raised questions about the relationship between universal and particular rights and the role of the state.[38] Meanwhile, the German case illustrated distinctions between a virtuous sense of nationality and aggressive nationalism, and nationalism's challenge of internationalism. German historians such as Leopold von Ranke and Heinrich von Treitschke advanced a self-conscious intellectual tradition that praised a German *Machtstaat* and *Realpolitik*.[39]

Another turning point was prompted by the South African wars (1898–1902) in which white settlers of Dutch origin fought for independence from the British Empire. The wars attracted much public attention because they were costly for both sides and because they occurred between white peoples.[40] The British newspaper the *Manchester Guardian*, a meeting point for liberal internationalists and socialists, inaugurated and led the public opposition to the war, which further polarised British liberals.[41] L. T. Hobhouse, John A. Hobson and Emily Hobhouse, a peace and welfare activist, Hobhouse's beloved sister and one of the *Manchester Guardian*'s South African correspondents, all linked liberal auto-criticism to contemporary anti-war arguments. Emily Hobhouse testified about the British concentration camps from a feminist perspective and was among the best-informed people on the subject.[42] Yet, her contributions are marginalised in IR while the male philosophers gain sole credit for launching the opposition to war and for distinguishing theories of 'old' and their own 'new' liberal internationalism.[43]

The discursive construction of a German other

The declaration of a 'new liberalism' already involved the making of anti-German arguments that were later seized and re-structured in the 'war of ideas' 1914. According to L. T. Hobhouse's narrative, the success of the old liberalism had provoked an anti-liberal counter-reaction, which was internationally evident in the German rise to power and which was domestically evident, in Spencer's terms, in the British society's 're-barbarisation' and in popular support for the war.

Hobhouse intended to dissociate sober liberalism from violent imperialism. Although his main ideological adversaries were still overpaid, incompetent and cruel colonial officials, he tried to formulate an especially devastating criticism of British imperialism by identifying it with German thought.[44] Accordingly, German thought led the anti-humanitarian backlash, while Bismarck's foreign policy embodied Hegel's principle that the state is an end in itself. He continued to repudiate British imperialism as an incarnation of the German theory of the omnipotent state.[45] Hence, Hobson and Hobhouse did not provide full-fledged rejections of British imperialism because, despite their critique of imperialism, they did not call into question the superior qualities of British rule or the idea of empire. Hobson continued to suggest a sane imperialism and a techno-cratic administration for the colonies.[46] Hobhouse hesitated to endorse Hobson's paternalist proposal, but offered the reader two different explanations for British liberalism's moral crisis, namely, Britain's demo-cratic degeneration or German thought. Anglo-German relations further deteriorated after the South African wars because the German press had criticised British policy – a fact downplayed by Hobhouse.[47]

The early twentieth century was marked by rising Anglo-German antagonism, but at first Hobhouse and other liberal intellectuals tried to moderate the political tensions. Kaiser Wilhelm II ordered a naval build-up to catch up with Britain and France, and challenged the French rule of Morocco during the Second Morocco Crisis (1912–14), which also worsened German relations with Britain.[48] Only a brief period of improvement preceded the outbreak of the First World War. Through the initiation of a Foreign Policy Committee and participation in the British Neutrality Committee, Hobhouse pressured the British government to seek better relations with Germany in order to avoid war, but eventually he supported the British war cause.[49]

Hobhouse exerted much influence on public debates. He became the first Professor of Sociology at the London School of Economics in 1907 and continued a close friendship with the *Manchester Guardian*'s sem-inal editor, C. P. Scott. Hobhouse served as a political correspondent (1910–12), and informally replaced Scott and functioned as a managing editor when Scott was on leave. Because of staff shortages, Scott and Hobhouse contributed most of the *Manchester Guardian*'s leaders and thus shaped the agenda of one of the most important British newspapers during the war.[50]

Furthermore, liberal internationalists, such as Norman Angell, J. A. Hobson, Alfred Zimmern and John Dewey, contributed to the creation of a so-called German theory of the state and to the ideology of German power politics as liberal internationalism's 'other'.[51] Zimmern was among those British intellectuals who already declared in 1914 that Britain was fighting for the democratic cause and thus anticipated the rise of an ideo-logical key concept, being 'Western democracy'.[52] As an expert working for the Political Intelligence Department, he tended to view victory over Germany as a necessity and spurred scepticism about Germany's cap-acity to develop a democratic government on its own.[53]

Like other liberals, Hobhouse began to support the war after the pub-lication of 'the manifesto of the ninety-three'[54] (1914), in which many German professors declared their support for the government's decision to go to war. He was perturbed by the fact that well-known colleagues with socialist sympathies and many international contacts, such as the German philosopher and psychologist Wilhelm Wundt, had signed the manifesto.[55] Another reason for his change of mind was probably the choice of the Social Democratic Party of Germany (SPD) to support the war, in spite of earlier pacifist and anti-capitalist declarations.[56] Hobhouse was not, like Gilbert Murray, among the British professors who signed a response that blamed only Germany for the outbreak of war. However, he used the manifesto as a piece of evidence for the fact that the war was a conflict between divergent civilisations – a war between the liberal, humanitarian civilisation and the German *Kultur* that glorified power, militarism and the state.[57] In doing so, Hobhouse seized, intensified and re-structured nineteenth-century liberal internationalists' anti-German themes. He then dropped Spencer's vocabulary of re-barbarisation and called any illiberal policy a 'Germanisation'.[58] Only the variation of available arguments can explain the quick emergence of liberals' discursive 'othering' of German thought in response to the outbreak of the war. British and American philosophers almost always began their elaborations with the postulate that German philosophy caused the German aggression.[59]

The causal impact(s) of German philosophy

Hobhouse soon suggested a causal relationship between German philosophy and German aggression without referring to the manifesto. Hobhouse targeted Hegel and argued that: 'You will find all the essentials of a brutal, autocratic, militant, unscrupulous nationalism tricked out with the finest phrases in the Hegelian philosophy.'[60] However, instead of studying this nationalism and Germany's mass politics, Hobhouse steadily attacked Hegel, as in the opening of his widely read philosophical polemic *The Metaphysical Theory of the State* (1918), which was reprinted in 1938, 1951 and 1960.[61] He starts with his war experiences:

> As I went back to my Hegel my mood was one of self-satire. Was this a time for theorising or for destroying theories, when the world was tumbling about ears? My second thoughts run otherwise. To each man the tools and weapons he can best use. In the bombing of London I had just witnessed the visible and tangible outcome of a false and wicked doctrine, the foundations of which lay, as I believe, in the book before me.[62]

Hobhouse linked the causal claim to an exaggeration of the much-needed role of British philosophers, who appeared to have been the only agents qualified to fight the roots of the war. Such arguments proved valuable for H. G. Wells or Arnold Toynbee, who gained employment in British and American propaganda institutions.[63]

Another prominent advocate of German philosophy's causal impact was the respected intellectual and internationalist, supporter of the League of Nations, and erstwhile ambassador to the US, James Bryce. Bryce equally supported the view that '[i]t is, more than anything else, the German theory of the State – the doctrine of the omnipotence of the State, of its right to absorb and override the individual, to prevail against morality, indeed practically to deny the existence of international morality where State power is concerned – it is this deadly theory which is at the bottom of the German aggression'.[64]

Bryce also headed a committee which was ordered by the British War Propaganda Bureau to write a report (1915) on German war crimes in Belgium. The report was translated into thirty languages and clearly served as a means of wartime propaganda, since it used questionable sources to demonstrate the need to fight a violent and international-law-breaking Germany.[65] Like many British publications published prior to 1917, it also addressed an American public to raise the impression that Britain was fighting for common democratic values.[66]

Bryce's account and Toynbee's work for both American and British propaganda institutions rightly indicate that American intellectuals shared in the British liberals' case against German philosophy. A prominent example is John Dewey's *German Philosophy and Politics* (1915),[67] even if Dewey feels a need to explain how philosophy can lead to war. Accordingly, the modern German state had many facilities that guaranteed that ideas can have effects, especially since education was under statist control: 'In spite of freedom of academic instruction when a professor is installed in office, political authorities have something to say.'[68] Given that the universities' chief function was the education of state officials and that philosophy was part of that training, Germany's educational and administrative agencies channelled Hegelian ideas into the minds of state officials and practical life.

Norman Angell varied the argument and conceived of German philosophy-informed Prussianism not as a unique phenomenon, but as an exemplification of any nationalism that ought to be overcome. He was a freelancer who became an internationalist icon after the publication of his bestseller *The Great Illusion: A Study of the Relation of Military Power in Nations to Their Economic and Social Advantage* (1910).[69] Angell argued in his classic work that military victories did not promise economic gains, and he asserted that this lesson had to be learned first and foremost by Germany. Although Angell was not particularly anti-German, he used the option to gain wider publicity and, at the beginning of the war, he re-published parts of this classic under the title *Prussianism and its Destruction* (1914).[70] Here, he argued that Prussian philosophy had contributed to the war through 'ambitions and attitude of mind which have been responsible for the aggression of the German State, and will inevitably in the future prompt like aggression by other States, unless such a philosophy is radically discredited among the people concerned.[71] The distinction is critical because it indicates that Angell was not fully persuaded of German war guilt, though he supported the defence of Britain.[72]

However, among more conservative liberals, the oversimplified postulate of German philosophy's causation of military aggression quickly became a conventional opening for the othering of Germany, and the American liberal internationalist, politician and advocate of Anglo-Saxon union Elihu Root seized and further popularised the vocabulary. He urged for American entry into the war as a necessity in order to fight the forces of autocracy.[73] In the 1930s, the liberal internationalist philosopher Bertrand Russell resumed the pattern that can be traced back to Hobhouse when he argued that Gottlieb Fichte and Friedrich Nietzsche had been part of a philosophical movement that culminated in Hitler's fascist foreign policy.[74]

The anti-canon and the illiberal other

After stating German philosophy's causal impacts, liberal internationalists led a surrogate discussion about which German philosophers can be made responsible for the war. It had become socially unacceptable to distribute stereotypical images or cartoons of Germany after the beginning of the war, but the verbal drawing of an image of Germany as the inherently militaristic other by the use of selective philosophical references remained possible and may be seen as a substitute.[75] Eventually, liberal internationalists largely blamed the same German philosophers for the outbreak of the First and later the Second World Wars.

John Dewey's anti-canon of German philosophy encompasses the historian Friedrich von Bernhardi as well as Friedrich Nietzsche and Johann Gottlieb Fichte because of their glorification of war, nihilism and nationalism.[76] Additionally, Dewey used the anti-German *Zeitgeist* to make a case against Kant's metaphysics and for his own pragmatist philosophy. Dewey could not deny that Immanuel Kant was the author of 'Perpetual Peace' (1795),[77] but still characterised him by a set of distorting traits of character. Dewey used Kant's postulate of *a priori* truths to exhibit Kant's stubbornness, dogmatism and unwillingness to re-think postulates once he had made them.[78] For Dewey, later German philosophers merely developed Kant's unpragmatic attitude into fanatic political principles. Put simply, militarist Wilhelmine Germany had its roots in Kant's transcendental philosophy. Kant's overly formalistic gospel of duty had allowed the autocratic German state to define duty in terms of an overall obligation to serve the historical role of the German nation.[79]

Hobhouse did Kant more justice and presented a fairly conventional anti-canon. In his gloss of Hegel, Treitschke and Nietzsche, Hobhouse simplified the thought of quite different German thinkers, philosophers and historians until they all appeared as advocates of a doctrine. Nietzsche and Treitschke, Hobhouse argued, glorified the state, while Hegel's nationalistic philosophy praised the state as the 'highest good' standing above human morality. Hobhouse steadily repeated that Hegel's praise of the state as intrinsic good and as the highest human community effectively mandated a never-ending war in international relations.[80] In the aftermath of Hegel, Germans conceived of the state in a manner which was not 'natural' for the liberal and humanitarian British people.[81] In his logic, Anglo-Saxons pursued happiness in individual manners whereas Germans were all the same and sought to be martyred for the national cause.[82]

For Angell, prototypical Prussian philosophers were Treitschke, Bernhardi and Nietzsche. They had all nursed a fanatical belief in one's country ('my country right or wrong') and in the use of military force to express its power. He left Hegel out of his canon of Prussianism and focused instead on Bernhardi and Nietzsche. Bernhardi, Angell argued, had popularised the belief that military superiority is an intrinsic good, that war furthers culture and that a nation must dominate others or in turn will be dominated.[83] Yet, Angell devoted most of his attention to Nietzsche's anthropological arguments. In his reading, Nietzsche is about the will to gain power, which he thought Nietzsche believed was an inherent part of human nature. By extension, the desire to see one's nation as superior to other nations only parallels this drive for power. Together, these desires resulted in a Darwinian struggle of all against all. For his part, Angell criticised Nietzsche's doctrine as meaningless, unable to adequately explain why the dominance of other nations is a real asset. Angell argued that the philosophy was self-defeating, since it could only end in 'the slavery of all to dead matter'.[84] Like Hobhouse[85] and Dewey,[86] Angell contrasted British utilitarianism and desire for happiness with German nihilism. He continued these patterns during the interwar period, as did Harold Laski in his attacks on Hegel and Treitschke.[87] Again, Russell continued a conventional anti-canon and relied mainly on Fichte and Nietzsche in his warnings of Hitler, although he first supported the appeasement policy.[88]

Western civilisation and the German *Sonderweg*

Historians have already acknowledged the similarities between liberal internationalists' wartime arguments and the theories of a German *Sonderweg*, which later attempted to explain German fascism.[89] As the term *Sonderweg* indicates, both accounts assume that there is a conventional development towards liberal democracy, and that the German path exemplifies an aberration. Prior to the war, British images of Germany already included narrative structures ('from Bismarck to Bülow') and especially towards the end of the war, liberal internationalists advanced the narrative parts of their arguments.[90] In doing so, they departed from earlier criticism of Britain's oligarchy and justified a leading role for Britain as a power of democracy in the coming post-war order.

Hobhouse was among the first British intellectuals who started nursing a British equivalent of a *Sonderwegstheorie* when he began to exclude Germany from the realm of Western civilisation. According to his narrative, the German revolutions of 1848 did not effectively challenge the feudal order and instead marked the beginning of the moral degeneration that led to aggressive German nationalism.[91] Hobhouse hence offered two accounts of the malady of modern nationalism: a temporal and a cultural or even racist one. According to his temporal distinctions, nineteenth-century nationalism was linked to a democratic impulse until most Western nationalities could identify with the political institutions of the modern states.[92] Then, jingoism, an aggressive exaggeration, became likely, so that any modern nationalism appeared to be Janus-faced. However, following his second account, only Anglo-Saxon nationalism had involved positive communal sentiments.[93] German nationalism did not move from a peace-promoting to an aggressive stage, but was inherently aggressive.

The key to Dewey's diagnosis of Germany's abnormal development is a contrast between Germany's capacity to bring about unusual technical efficiency and its incapacity to allow for meaningful political self-government. He differentiated between Western civilisation, which people were unconsciously a part of, and the self-conscious celebration of a German *Kultur*. A distinctive German trait, he explained, was the combination of self-conscious idealism, evident in the celebration of German culture, with technical efficiency.[94] In other words, whereas Britain had moved from militarism to modernity, Germany was modernly militarist. The problematic combination, in contrast to liberal experiences, resulted in the 'relative impotency of German Volk en masse for real political self-direction'.[95] A public opinion comparable to the British one never existed in Germany.[96] Dewey's image of Germany includes a disciplined state, a *Volk* but no society.

Zimmern likewise assumed that the politicisation of *Kultur* had changed the nature of German nationalism.[97] In Germany, cultural sentiments had entered into a strange relationship with militarism. The Prussian system organised everything in a top-down manner and suppressed social groups and the development of modern society. The statist system of education and training embraced the individual and nursed the development of militarist sentiments. In 1914, Zimmern had already defined democracy as 'a spirit' in order to praise British democracy and to downplay the fact that Germany had universal male suffrage while Britain had not, and he continued the commenced line.[98] Dewey and Zimmern hence relied heavily on cultural explanations and finally assumed that, in the German case, an embracing state had preceded a modern society.

Hobson, on the other side, provided an economic explanation. Towards the end of the war, he varied his theory of imperialism and identified German militarism as an opponent of democracy, instead of the British oligarchy. He opened his book *Democracy after the War* (1917) with a Hegel quote saying that the people are that part of a state which does not know what it really wants, and argued that German democratisation had been unable to question the power of the German capitalist bourgeoisie.[99] This class voted for war to settle socialist unrests, to gain lucrative foreign markets and to make profits out of armaments, but their decision immediately gained general public support.[100]

According to Hobson's narrative, Germany's industrialisation had benefited first of all the Krupps and the armament trade. Even if similar links between industrialisation and militarism could be observed in Britain and France, the whole philosophy of militarism was only celebrated and glorified in Germany. Objections to liberalism in German thought resulted in immorality and a 'literal anarchy' unknown in Britain.[101] Hobhouse wrote a friendly review of Hobson's book and added references to Fichte's *Der geschlossene Handelsstaat* (1846) to theorise the inherent relationship between German militarism and protectionism.[102] In the 1930s, many liberal internationalists, including David Mitrany (1933), continued the line created by Hobson and Hobhouse and argued on the basis of Fichte that protectionism is a potential for war.[103] However, the original argument was designed to (re-)establish Britain as an international agent of democracy.

Towards the end of the war, the arguments changed and the new liberals shortly assumed contending spheres of influence in the coming post-war order. Hobson supposed that advocates of the German *Kultur* wished to impose their way of feeling and thinking upon the rest of the world.[104] Angell contrasted British and German patriotism, and called for a league of democracies to fight German militarism, but proposed that, once the aim was achieved, Germany ought to be re-included in the society of nations.[105] Angell thus did not make a harsh argument against Germany and tackled the new pressing questions which included support for absolute victory over Germany or a negotiated peace as a starting point for German democratisation, and German inclusion in a post-war international organisation.

Hobhouse temporarily supported an absolute victory and thus the conservative war aims.[106] He only changed his position and supported a negotiated peace when an absolute victory became unlikely, but still proposed a league of democracies as the ideal post-war organisation.[107] Unlike the holy alliance, the 'league of peace' ought to have included only democracies defined by their respect for national self-determination in order to resist possible attacks from autocracy or a militant empire.[108] At other times, he was less interested in the establishment of international organisation to extend the civilised democratic zone of peace if necessary by military means and more in both the formal and informal assimilation of illiberal or transforming societies vis-à-vis autocratic states.

Hobhouse's advocacy of a league of democracies to assist the democratisation of non-Western states shows that Eurocentric and intra-Western practices of othering can overlap. Eurocentrism can be defined as the belief in European pre-eminence and Europe's unique and independent modernisation. A dividing line then separates the West from the East, which lacks pioneering agency and which can, at best, develop along Western lines. However, it is imperative to conceive of Eurocentrism in the plural and so to ask how the Western bias unfolds.[109] In Hobhouse's case, it is evident that he worked with two distinctions in order to differentiate between liberal Britain and illiberal Germany, and between these Western states and rather passive spheres of influence.[110] Even if he was not as enthusiastic about the Russian Revolution as Scott or some British progressives, he opposed the isolation of revolutionary Russia.[111]

To make his argument, Hobhouse invoked a self-congratulatory vocabulary which he otherwise avoided. Accordingly, he believed that Britain, a 'more experienced' democracy, ought to provide guidance to the Russians because 'the people who sit in the political darkness look upon us in the great light'.[112] His historical case in point was the British reluctance to support the Young Turk Revolution (1908), which opened the door for German influence and the spread of militant nationalism in the Ottoman Empire. Accordingly, liberal trends elsewhere depended on British assistance to flourish and to replicate the British model. Like Root, Hobhouse's argument seized and intensified the identification of the realm of civilisation with democracy which had already begun in the nineteenth century.[113] More narrowly defined, democracy was an achievement of 'the West'.[114] Hobhouse thus supposed that the Americans, as Anglo-Saxons and members of the democratic community, would support the British decision to maintain contact with Russia.[115] He predicted that Germany would never recover from its moral crisis and that it was up to Britain to advance democracy and a liberal internationalism which, like modern science, transcended the boundaries of sex, culture and colour.[116] However, Hobhouse's calls for an anti-racist internationalism and for a league of democracies are themselves biased.

In a more polemical manner, Elihu Root[117] divided the world into peace-loving democracies and militarist autocracies in order to argue the need for democratic alliances: 'To be safe democracy must kill its enemy when it can and where it can. The world cannot be half democratic and half autocratic. It must be all democratic or all Prussian. There can be no compromise. If it is all Prussian, there can be no real international law.'[118] Root equally derived from the conflict between Anglo-Saxon democracies and Prussia the argument that democratic peace had to be achieved by military means, while reducing the rest of the world to a venue of this core conflict.

The functions of the discursive regime

The previous section outlined how it quickly became conventional for British and American liberal internationalists to attack the German ideology of power politics and that most authors, in doing so, stated the causal impact of German philosophy, created an anti-canon and introduced narratives about Germany's abnormal political development. While I do not want to imply that all internationalists endorsed these patterns – Leonard Woolf[119] maintained ordinary diplomats who think in inherited nationalist terms as ideological adversaries – they were still widely used and constituted a part of the discourse of the evolving discipline of IR.[120]

A common assumption says that each self-constitution necessitates othering, and this implies that British and American authors identified themselves as liberals through their response to a common enemy.[121] However, this basic truth hardly explains the shape of the social and argumentative patterns involved. Although they were linked to aesthetic and political representations of Germany, and sometimes substituted them, liberal internationalist practices of othering still developed a logic of their own. Based on my understanding of Hobhouse, a chief architect of anti-German arguments, I propose allowing a mix of ideological, political, aesthetic and personal reasons for why liberal internationalists wrote about Germany in the way they did.[122]

Liberal internationalists had begun to turn German thought into an ideological adversary at a time when the simultaneous decline of Britain's global power and materialisation of democracy called liberal assumptions and the domestic popularity of the liberal ideology into question. Liberal intellectuals worried greatly about the rationality of an extending demos and socialist claims. Othering German thought made it possible to distract attention from the ambiguous positions towards the modern state with an expanding bureaucracy in Europe. Hobhouse promised a welfare bureaucracy compatible with democratic principles, unlike the Bismarckian example, but remained vague on institutional questions. He and other internationalists flirted with pluralist criticism of the state, which ironically evolved from the British reading of Otto von Gierke, when they attacked Hegel.[123] Hobhouse hence tried to reconcile the tensions between his appreciations of the liberal state and criticism of state economic intervention. He also attempted to find a method of the provision of social welfare that did not enhance nationalist identifications with the state, as in Germany.

The most simplistic images of Germany were produced in response to German intellectuals' support for the war and a new German nationalism. References to Hegel then began substituting debate on the conundrum of why formerly admired intellectuals could be mobilised for a militaristic nationalism that they had opposed earlier. Indeed, among scholars, the earlier admiration of Germany perhaps contributed to the force of their arguments. Furthermore, censorship during the war and new ideological lines within the British public furthered the creation of simplistic accounts of Prussian philosophy and German militarism. Positions towards German militarism, the chances of democratisation, and the war aims reflected the conservative ignorance of democracy as an irrelevance, the radicals' demand to assist the democratic forces in Germany, and liberals' negotiation of critique and support of the government, plus their interest in both German democratisation and international stabilisation.[124]

In the heyday of the war, when war losses made visual representations and cartoons unacceptable, the employment of philosophical terms offered aesthetic advantages because selective references to and quotations from mainly nineteenth-century German philosophy allowed for the attribution of illiberal traits of choice to the political enemy. What emerged was a verbally created image of a top-down-controlled German *Einheitsstaat* that embraced a militarist community.[125] This suited Hobhouse's half-philosophical, half-scientific and obviously political style, and allowed philosophers such as Dewey to make a case against metaphysics and for pragmatism. Diverse personal motifs and attempts to use intelligible tools to make sense of political events for lay people hence play into the production of apparently similar images. IR intellectuals such as G. L. Dickinson[126] began changing the available academic-journalistic discourse when they generalised German thinking as a characteristic of an anarchic state system. In doing so, Dickinson questioned German war guilt and the uniqueness of German nationalism, and instead argued that widely evident modern European nationalism could only be overcome by a system of supranational law.[127]

The main function of *Sonderwegstheorien*, which often come along with images of undemocratic Germany, is the identification of the German example as an abnormal development and the idealisation of Britain's path to democracy; when Hobhouse was writing, Britain was still an incomplete, partly oligarchic democracy. Later, German émigrés in the US and German post-war historians resumed narratives about Germany's abnormal development.[128] For Ralf Dahrendorf: 'Industrialization in Germany failed to produce a self-conscious bourgeoise with its own political aspirations [...] As a result, German society lacked the stratum that in England and America, and to a lesser extent even in France, had been the moving force of development in the direction of greater modernity and liberalism.'[129] Besides, as the writings of the British historian A. J. P. Taylor show, essentialist accounts of the German people have managed to re-occur in the British context.[130] For Taylor, German nationalism was the antithesis of Mazzinian and liberal hopes, and he argued that only the Germans had been unable to maintain a perfect democratic constitution, referring to that of the Weimar Republic. German history was 'distasteful' and 'mysterious' and had been a history of unimaginable extremes for a thousand years.[131]

Here and elsewhere, the *Sonderweg* narrative downplays the fact that Britain introduced universal male suffrage only reluctantly during the war (1918) and overstates differences in the degree of democratisation between Britain and Germany prior to 1914. Germany acquired universal male suffrage before Britain, had modern parties such as the SPD and a (though largely conservative) civil society.[132] The problem was rather the dominance of Prussia, that Germany's parliament was not sufficiently democratic, and that the state and military apparatus remained responsive to the monarchical elites rather than the people.[133] The narrative equally neglects that the English developmental path emerged under the very special conditions of Britain's position as an early industrialiser and global power.[134]

Conclusion

In this chapter, I have sketched liberal internationalism's creation of images of Germany at the beginning of the twentieth century. I first contextualised liberal internationalism's origins in a polyvocal philosophical, political, ideological and partly racist discourse. This discourse emerged along with Britain's acquisition of a global empire. Ideas about Britain's distinctive liberal nationalism, representative democracy and orderly international cooperation were definitive, but, after a very short timespan and real-world developments, implied conflicting trends. Liberal internationalists self-consciously addressed some contradictions, but, following the turn of the twentieth century, increasingly offered two interpretations. Readers could choose to view illiberal developments as results of liberal failures or manifestations of German influence.

To analyse discursive patterns of liberal internationalist's othering of the German ideology of power politics, I focused on the era of the First World War. Key IR pioneers including Hobhouse and Zimmern developed a homogeneous image of Germany as the disciplined, militaristic, autocratic other, while conversely maintaining Britain as the realm of liberalism, civilisation, democracy and Christianity. The discourse also involved racist ideas of Anglo-Saxon unity and allowed twofold practices of othering, discriminating between Western democracies and Germany, and non-Western states. These intellectuals supported the official wartime propaganda, but also used the anti-German vocabulary in order to distract from liberal internationalism's internal tensions, their own political shifts or the notorious tensions between democratisation and nationalism that were all too common. Furthermore, they translated the questions of German war guilt into debates about international anarchy or order.

To conclude, I join J. M. Hobson in arguing that both positivist conceptions, which assume that IR theories emerge in a political vacuum, and the 'noble identity myth' do not hold. Liberal internationalists' involvement in timely political debates clearly impacted their theories of political development and democratic peace, and stigmatisations of Germany.[135] Bruce Russett rightly traces democratic peace theory's political origins back to the othering of Germany during the First World War.[136] However, he quickly normalises the wartime rhetoric in order to gain lessons about democracies' external relations. Instead, I propose that historical contextualisation is one means to deconstruct earlier simplifications, to detect politically motivated oblivions within theoretical developments and to counter essentialist images of an allegedly democracy-favouring or democracy-opposing people.

Notes

1 I would like to thank Casper Sylvest, Jens Steffek, Luke Ashworth and all participants of the workshop (2016) for their comments on earlier versions of this chapter. Financial support by the DFG through the cluster of excellence 'Formation of Normative Orders' is gratefully acknowledged.

2 J. Hobson, *The Eurocentric Conception of World Politics: Western International Theory, 1760–2010* (Cambridge: Cambridge University Press, 2012).

3 I. Oren, 'The subjectivity of the "democratic" peace: changing U.S. perceptions of imperial Germany', *International Security*, 20 (1995), pp. 147–85.

4 J. S. Mill, *Considerations on Representative Government* (New York: Cosimo, 2008[1861]), p. 437.

5 J. Parry, *The Politics of Patriotism: English Liberalism, National Identity and Europe, 1830–1886* (Cambridge: Cambridge University Press, 2006), p. 397.

6 C. Sylvest, *British Liberal Internationalism, 1880–1930: Making Progress?* (Manchester: Manchester University Press, 2009), p. 46.

7 Sylvest, *British Liberal Internationalism*, pp. 200–6.

8 D. Bell and C. Sylvest, 'International society in Victorian political thought: T.H. Green, Herbert Spencer, and Henry Sidgwick', *Modern Intellectual History*, 3:2 (2006), pp. 207–38, at p. 230.

9 C. Hobson, *The Rise of Democracy: Revolution, War, and Transformations in International Politics since 1776* (Edinburgh: Edinburgh University Press, 2015), pp. 140–3.

10 H. W. Smith, 'When the Sonderweg debate left us', *German Studies Review*, 31:2 (2008), pp. 225–40, at p. 232.

11 P. Gourevitch, 'The second image reversed: the international sources of domestic politics', *International Organization*, 32:4 (1978), pp. 881–912, at p. 886.

12 D. Newton, *British Policy and the Weimar Republic 1918–1919* (Oxford: Clarendon Press, 1997), p. 80.

13 P. Hoeres, *Krieg der Philosophen* (Paderborn: Ferdinand Schöningh, 2004); T. L. Akehurst, *The Cultural Politics of Analytical Philosophy: Britishness and the Spectre of Europe* (London: Continuum, 2010); R. Scully, *British Images of Germany: Admiration, Antagonism, and Ambivalence 1860–1914* (New York: Palgrave Macmillan, 2012).

14 B. Jahn, *Liberal Internationalism: Theory, History, Practice* (New York: Palgrave Macmillan, 2013), p. 30.

15 P. Owens, *Economy of Force. Counterinsurgency and the Historical Rise of the Social* (Cambridge: Cambridge University Press, 2015), p. 1; D. Long and B. C. Schmidt (eds), *Imperialism and Internationalism in the Discipline of International Relations* (New York: State University of New York Press, 2005); L. Curtis, *The Commonwealth of Nations: An Inquiry into the Nature of Citizenship in the British Empire, and into the Mutual Relations of the Several Communities Thereof* (London: Macmillan, 1916).

16 B. Buzan and G. Lawson, *The Global Transformation: History, Modernity and the Making of International Relations* (Cambridge: Cambridge University Press, 2015), p. 103.

17 S. E. Berman, *The Primacy of Politics: Social Democracy and the Making of Europe's Twentieth Century* (Cambridge: Cambridge University Press, 2010), p. 1.

18 C. Jönsson, 'Classical liberal internationalism', in T. Veiss and R. Wilkinson (eds), *International Organization and Global Governance* (London: Routledge, 2014), pp. 105–17.

19 D. Bell, 'What is liberalism?', *Political Theory*, 42:6 (2014), pp. 682–715.

20 Buzan and Lawson, *The Global Transformation*, pp. 102–5.

21 Bell, *The Idea of Greater Britain: Empire and the Future of World Order, 1860–1900* (Princeton: Princeton University Press, 2007), p. 3.

22 Bell and Sylvest, 'International society in Victorian political thought'.

23 Hobson, *The Eurocentric Conception of World Politics*, p. 93.

24 Parry, *The Politics of Patriotism*, p. 387.

25 J. Pitts, *A Turn to Empire* (Princeton: Princeton University Press, 2005), p. 2.

26 C. Sylvest, '"Our passion for legality": international law and imperialism in late nineteenth-century Britain', *Review of International Studies*, 34:3 (2008),

pp. 403–23; L. T. Hobhouse, 'The ethical basis of collectivism', *International Journal of Ethics*, 8:2 (1898), pp. 137–56.

27 Sylvest, *British Liberal Internationalism*, p. 45.

28 Parry, *The Politics of Patriotism*, p. 388.

29 Bell, *The Idea of Greater Britain*, p. 31.

30 Mill, *Considerations on Representative Government*, p. 299.

31 C. Sylvest, 'British liberal historians and the primacy of internationalism', in W. Mulligan and B. Simms (eds), *The Primacy of Foreign Policy in British History, 1660–2000: How Strategic Concerns Shaped Modern Britain* (Basingstoke: Palgrave Macmillan, 2010), pp. 214–31, at p. 217.

32 Bell, *The Idea of Greater Britain*, p. 41.

33 C. Hobson, 'Beyond the end of history', *Millennium – Journal of International Studies*, 37:3 (2009), pp. 631–51, at p. 641.

34 Berman, *The Primacy of Politics*, p. 1; Mill, *Considerations on Representative Government*, p. 462.

35 Bell, *The Idea of Greater Britain*, p. 41; J.L. Halperin, 'Power to the people: nationally embedded development and mass armies in the making of democracy', *Millennium – Journal of International Studies*, 37:3 (2009), pp. 605–30, at p. 608.

36 Parry, *The Politics of Patriotism*, p. 397.

37 Sylvest, *British Liberal Internationalism*.

38 Jönsson, 'Classical liberal internationalism', p. 112; L. Ashworth, *A History of International Thought: From the Origins of the Modern State to Academic International Relations* (London: Routledge, 2014), p. 113.

39 Sylvest, 'British liberal historians and the primacy of internationalism'.

40 Sylvest, '"Our passion for legality"'.

41 J. L. Hammond, *C. P. Scott of the Manchester Guardian* (London: G. Bell and Sons, 1934), p. 77.

42 E. Hobhouse, *The Brunt of War and Where it Fell* (London: Methuen, 1902).

43 D. Ayerst, *Guardian: Biography of a Newspaper* (London: Collins, 1971), p. 285.

44 L. T. Hobhouse, *Democracy and Reaction* (Brighton: Harvester Press, 1972), p. 83.

45 L. T. Hobhouse, 'The omnipotent state', *Manchester Guardian* (30 September 1916), p. 5.

46 Hobson, *The Eurocentric Conception of World Politics*, p. 51.

47 S. Wallace, *War and the Image of Germany: British Academics 1914–1918* (Edinburgh: John Donald Publishers, 1988), pp. 14–15.

48 Scully, *British Images of Germany*, p. 297.

49 H. Smith, 'World War I and British left wing intellectuals: the case of Leonard T. Hobhouse', *Albion: A Quarterly Journal Concerned with British Studies*, 5:4 (1973), pp. 261–73, at pp. 262–4.

50 Ayerst, *Guardian*, p. 378.

51 B. C. Schmidt, *The Political Discourse of Anarchy: A Disciplinary History of International Relations* (Albany, NY: State University of New York Press, 1998), p. 162.

52 M. Llanque, 'The First World War and the invention of "Western democracy"', in R. Bavaj and M. Steber (eds), *Germany and 'the West': A History of a Modern Concept* (New York: Berghahn Books, 2015), pp. 69–80, at p. 69;

R. W. Seton-Watson, J. Dover Wilson, A. E. Zimmern and A. Greenwood, 'Introduction', in R. W. Seton-Watson, J. Dover Wilson, A. E. Zimmern and A. Greenwood (eds), *The War and Democracy* (Nabu Press, 2010 [1914]).

53 Newton, *British Policy and the Weimar Republic 1918–1919*, p. 226.

54 Professors of Germany, 'To the civilized world', *North American Review*, 210:765 (1919), pp. 284–7; see also S. Harden, 'Reply to German professors', in *The American Verdict on the War: A Reply to the Manifesto of the German Professors* (Baltimore: Norman Remington, 1915).

55 L. T. Hobhouse, *Questions of War and Peace* (London: T. Fisher Unwin, 1916), p. 25.

56 K. N. Waltz, *Man, the State and War: A Theoretical Analysis* (New York: Columbia University Press, 1968), p. 135.

57 Hobhouse, *Questions of War and Peace*, p. 25.

58 Hobhouse, *Questions of War and Peace*, p. 60.

59 Akehurst, *The Cultural Politics of Analytical Philosophy*, p. 18.

60 Hobhouse, *Questions of War and Peace*, p. 20.

61 Akehurst, *The Cultural Politics of Analytical Philosophy*, p. 24.

62 L. T. Hobhouse, *The Metaphysical Theory of the State: A Criticism* (London: Routledge/Thoemmes Press, 1993), p. x.

63 Wallace, *War and the Image of Germany*, p. 170.

64 J. Bryce, 'Opening address', in N. Widder (ed.), *The International Crisis: The Theory of the State. Lectures Delivered in February and March 1916* (London: Oxford University Press, 1916), pp. 1–8, at p. 2.

65 Wallace, *War and the Image of Germany*, p. 185.

66 Llanque, 'The First World War and the invention of "Western democracy"', p. 71.

67 J. Dewey, *German Philosophy and Politics* (New York: Henry Holt and Company, 1915).

68 Dewey, *German Philosophy and Politics*, p. 15.

69 N. Angell, *The Great Illusion: A Study of the Relation of Military Power in Nations to their Economic and Social Advantage* (New York: Putnam, 1910)

70 N. Angell, *Prussianism and its Destruction* (London: William Heinemann, 1914).

71 Angell, *Prussianism and its Destruction*, p. xiii.

72 M. Ceadel, *Living the Great Illusion: Sir Norman Angell, 1872–1967* (Oxford: Oxford University Press, 2009), p. 108.

73 B. Russett, *Grasping the Democratic Peace: Principles for a Post-war World* (Princeton: Princeton University Press, 1993), p. 33.

74 Akehurst, *The Cultural Politics of Analytical Philosophy*, p. 23; B. Russell, *In Praise of Idleness and Other Essays* (New York: Routledge, 2004), pp. 53–71.

75 Scully, *British Images of Germany*, p. 304.

76 Dewey, *German Philosophy and Politics*, pp. 36, 57.

77 I. Kant, *Zum Ewigen Frieden. Ein philosophischer Entwurf* (Berlin: Reclam, 2004 [1795]).

78 Dewey, *German Philosophy and Politics*, p. 43.

79 J. T. Kloppenberg, 'The reciprocal vision of German and American intellectuals: beneath shifting perceptions', in D. Junker (ed.), *Transatlantic Images and Perceptions: Germany and America since 1776* (Cambridge: Cambridge University Press, 1997), pp. 155–70, at p. 168.

80 L. T. Hobhouse, *The World in Conflict* (London: T. Fisher Unwin, 1915), p. 54.

81 L. T. Hobhouse, 'Science and philosophy as unifying forces', in F. S. Marvin (ed.), *The Unity of Western Civilization* (London: Milford, 1936 [1915]), pp. 162–79, at p. 175.

82 L. T. Hobhouse, 'About happiness', in J. A. Hobson and M. Ginsberg (eds), *L.T. Hobhouse: His Life and Work* (London: Routledge/Thoemmes Press, 1996), pp. 292–5.

83 Angell, *Prussianism and its Destruction*, p. 91.

84 Angell, *Prussianism and its Destruction*, p. 16.

85 Hobhouse, 'About happiness'.

86 Dewey, *German Philosophy and Politics*, p. 58.

87 Schmidt, *The Political Discourse of Anarchy*, p. 164.

88 Akehurst, *The Cultural Politics of Analytical Philosophy*, p. 26.

89 P. Hoeres, 'Die Ursachen der deutschen Gewaltpolitik in britischer Sicht. Eine frühe Sonderwegsdebatte' in F. Becker, T. Großbölting, A. Owzar and R. Schlögl (eds), *Politische Gewalt in der Moderne. Festschrift für Hans-Ulrich Thamer* (Muenster: Aschendorff, 2003), pp. 193–211.

90 Scully, *British Images of Germany*, p. 280.

91 Hobhouse, *Questions of War and Peace*, p. 19.

92 L. Holthaus, 'L.T. Hobhouse and the transformation of liberal internationalism', *Review of International Studies*, 40:4 (2014), pp. 705–27; L. T. Hobhouse, 'The past and the future: the influence of nationalism', in J. A. Hobson and M. Ginsberg (eds), *L.T. Hobhouse: His Life and Work* (London: Routledge/Thommes Press, 1996), pp. 225–330.

93 L. T. Hobhouse, 'Irish nationalism and liberal principle', in J. H. Morgan (ed.), *The New Irish Constitution: An Exposition and Some Arguments* (London: Hodder & Stoughton, 1912), pp. 361–72.

94 Dewey, *German Philosophy and Politics*, p. 27.

95 Dewey, *German Philosophy and Politics*, p. 36.

96 Dewey, *German Philosophy and Politics*, pp. 15–17.

97 A. E. Zimmern, *Nationality & Government with Other War-Time Essays* (London: Chatto & Windos, 1918), p. 7.

98 Seton-Watson, Dover Wilson, Zimmern and Greenwood, 'Introduction', p. 4.

99 J. A. Hobson, *Democracy after the War* (London: George Allen & Unwin, 1917), p. 5.

100 Hobson, *Democracy after the War*, p. 42.

101 Hobson, *Democracy after the War*, p. 201.

102 L. T. Hobhouse, 'The recovery of liberty', *The Manchester Guardian* (1917).

103 D. Mitrany, *Economic Planning and International Relations* (London: Chatham House Archives, No. 8/303, 1933).

104 Hobson, *Democracy after the War*, p. 41.

105 N. Angell, *The Political Conditions of Allied Success: A Plea for the Protective Union of the Democracies* (Charleston: Bibliobazaar, 2009).

106 Smith, 'World War I and British left wing intellectuals', pp. 271–2.

107 Hobhouse, *The Metaphysical Theory of the State*, p. 116; Hobhouse, *Questions of War and Peace*, p. 199.

108 L. T. Hobhouse, 'The future league of peace', in Hobson and Ginsberg (eds), *L.T. Hobhouse*, pp. 309–12.

109 Hobson, *The Eurocentric Conception of World Politics*, p. 1.

110 L. T. Hobhouse, 'Alliance among democracies', *Manchester Guardian* (24 November 1917), p. 6.

111 Ayers, *Guardian*, p. 402.

112 Hobhouse, 'Alliance among democracies'.

113 A. de Tocqueville, *Democracy in America* (Ware: Wordsworth, 1998 [1835/1840]), p. 8; E. Root, *The Effect of Democracy on International Law* (New York: American Association for International Conciliation, 1917), pp. 9–10; C. Hobson, 'Democracy as civilisation', *Global Society* 22:1 (2008), pp. 75–95.

114 Llanque, 'The First World War and the invention of "Western democracy"'.

115 D. Bell, 'The project for a new Anglo century: race, space, and global order', in P. Katzenstein (ed.), *Anglo-America and its Discontents: Civilizational Identities beyond West and East* (London: Routledge, 2012), pp. 33–56.

116 Hobhouse, 'Science and philosophy as unifying forces', p. 179.

117 Root, *The Effect of Democracy on International Law*.

118 Root, *The Effect of Democracy on International Law*, p. 18.

119 L. Woolf, *Memoranda on Work of the International Group*, Mitrany Papers, Box 60 (London, undated).

120 Schmidt, *The Political Discourse of Anarchy*, p. 164; L. T. Holthaus, 'Prussianism, Hitlerism, realism: the German legacy in British international thought', in I. Hall (ed.), *Radicals and Reactionaries in Twentieth-Century International Thought* (New York: Palgrave Macmillan, 2015), pp. 123–44.

121 P. E. Gottfired, *After Liberalism: Mass Democracy in the Managerial State* (Princeton: Princeton University Press, 2001), p. 3.

122 Q. Skinner, *Visions of Politics: Regarding Method* (Cambridge: Cambridge University Press, 2004), p. 3.

123 P. Q. Hirst, *The Pluralist Theory of the State: Selected Writings of G. D. H. Cole, J. N. Figgis, and H. J. Laski* (London: Routledge, 1989), p. 18. L. Holthaus, *Pluralist Democracy in International Relations: L.T. Hobhouse, G.D.H. Cole and David Mitrany* (New York: Palgrave Macmillan, 2018).

124 D. Newton, *British Policy and the Weimar Republic 1918–1919* (Oxford: Clarendon Press, 1997).

125 Sylvest, 'British liberal historians and the primacy of internationalism', p. 219.

126 G. L. Dickinson, *The European Anarchy* (London: George Allen & Unwin, 1916).

127 J. Morefield, 'A democratic critique of the state: G. Lowes Dickinson's *The European Anarchy*', in H. Bliddal C. Sylvest and P. Wilson (eds), *Classics in International Relations: Essays in Criticism and Appreciation* (London: Routledge, 2013), pp. 24–35, at p. 31.

128 N. Guilhot, *Democracy Makers: Human Rights and the Politics of Global Order* (New York: Columbia University Press, 2005), p. 60.

129 G. Eley, *The Pecularities of German History: Bourgeois Society and Politics in Nineteenth-Century Germany* (Oxford: Oxford University Press, 1984), p. 73.

130 A. J. P. Taylor, *The Course of German History: A Survey of the Development of Germany since 1815* (London: Hamish Hamilton, 1945), p. 185.

131 Taylor, *The Course of German History*, p. 13.

132 S. E. Bermann, 'Modernization in historical perspective: the case of imperial Germany', *Third World Quaterly*, 53:3 (2001), pp. 431–62; S. E. Bermann, 'Civil society and the collapse of the Weimar Republic', *World Politics*, 49:3 (1997), pp. 401–29.

133 D. Rüschemeyer, *Capitalist Development and Democracy* (Chicago: University of Chicago Press, 1992), p. 44.

134 Gourevitch, 'The second image reversed', p. 883; Rüschemeyer, *Capitalist Development and Democracy*, p. 62.

135 Hobson, *The Eurocentric Conception of World Politics*, p. 16.

136 Russett, *Grasping the Democratic Peace*, p. 33.

4

From emulation to enmity: the changing view of Germany in Anglo-American geopolitics

Lucian M. Ashworth

On 30 April 1945, American troops entered Munich. Amongst other things, Munich was known to British and American political geographers and strategic studies experts as the home of the *Institut für Geopolitik*. The *Institut* was the publisher of the *Zeitschrift für Geopolitik* that was edited by a professor at the University named Karl Haushofer. For the last four years of the war, Haushofer had come to be seen as the *éminence grise* of the Nazi regime. He even made it into popular culture. The Oscar-nominated American film *Plan for Destruction* (1943) presented Haushofer as the educator and planner who had produced the German plan for world conquest, under the influence of Nietzsche, Clausewitz, Moltke, Scharnhorst and Bismarck. Through Hess, Haushofer is seen advising the Nazis on their next target for conquest.

The role of Haushofer in shaping German grand strategy has long been a question of debate, but his influence as a foil for Anglo-American assessments of German geopolitics cannot be doubted. In the US, a diverse range of academics treated Haushofer and the Munich-based *Institut für Geopolitik* as the exemplar of the intellectual roots of Nazi international thought. These included the historian Andreas Dorpalen, the security studies expert Robert Strausz-Hupé and the geographers Isaiah Bowman, Hans Weigert and Derwent Whittlesey.[1] In the cases of Bowman and Weigert at least, this antipathy for the German tradition of geopolitics came despite an admiration for the earlier German contribution to the science of human geography. Indeed, the history of the four decades between the death of Ratzel in 1904 and the liberation of Munich in 1945 had been one in which Anglo-American international political geography (IPG) had moved from emulation of the 'anthropogeography' found in German universities to antipathy for what seemed to be a culture that had ruined itself through an addiction to intellectual error. Thus, German geopolitics would be constructed as the dark 'other' against which the plans for post-war settlement in the English-speaking world would be judged. Despite this, when American troops finally found the *Institut für Geopolitik*, its physical existence turned out to be no more than a professor's office.[2]

My introduction to the importance of German geographical scholarship to the English-speaking world came at a young age. My professional geographer father had, for as long as I can remember, a framed page over his desk in our study that showed all the famous German geographers from 1900. Pride of place was the founder of political geography (and, amongst Anglos at least, a leading light in the development of human geography) Friedrich Ratzel. In the late 1960s, Ratzel had to compete for wall space with a much larger poster of Che Guevara, demonstrating that for British geographers of the 1960s at least, a picture of Ratzel and his peers was a statement of scientific affinity and not an endorsement of his imperialist and militarist politics. My father's homage to Ratzel is probably no surprise. As a graduate of Cambridge, he had been a student of Harriet Wanklyn, the author of an intellectual and bibliographical sketch of Ratzel that had done much to rescue Ratzel's reputation from an association with Haushofer and the German geopolitical tradition.[3] Thus, the story of the relationship between Anglo-American IPG and its German contemporaries during the first half of the twentieth century is not a simple story. While by the early 1940s the German academy had become a cautionary tale for English-speaking political geographers, this same German tradition had also been instrumental in the development of Anglo geography, and many of the writings on geostrategic questions published in Britain and America in the years leading up to the Second World War owed much of their scholarship to the German academy.

This is the story of this link and in terms of the history of international thought, it is no mere marginal vignette. In the English-speaking world, IPG was an important and influential strain of international thought that often directly influenced foreign policy, especially in the US. Geographers like Isaiah Bowman walked the world stage as advisors to presidents and published popular works on international relations. This chapter will start by examining the way in which German academic life and ideas influenced the development and perceptions of IPG in the years before the First World War. While the War did lead to stinging attacks by some international experts such as the geographer Halford Mackinder, it really was not until the Second World War that attitudes shifted to see German scholarship as a distinct and dangerous alternative to the IPG of the West. The second half of this chapter will look at how this view of German geopolitics developed, and the conclusion will explore how this affected the perception that International Relations (IR) has had of geopolitics and political geography ever since.

Learning lessons from a rising power: anthropogeography before and after the First World War

> Ratzel performed the great service of placing anthropogeography on a secure scientific basis.[4]

American and British emulation of German universities and their scholarship have deep roots. This is especially true of the US, where the view of Germany as a fellow rising power made its educational models often seem more attractive than those of Britain. There is a large literature on the influence of German education on the US before the First World War.[5] At the same time, the German 'Humboldtian' model remained attractive to British higher educational reformers in the nineteenth century.[6] While this emulation can be found across the range of scholarly fields, the German influence on British and American geography was particularly marked in the late nineteenth and early twentieth centuries. 'Geography', wrote the British geographer J. R. Smith in 1902, 'is in much higher regard as a university study in Germany than in England or America.'[7] German society generally was seen as having an advantage in the study of space, and perhaps the most obvious manifestation of this was in the development of tabletop war games for the training of Prussian officers, developed first in the 1810s and 1820s by Georg Leopold von Reiswitz. This *Kriegspiel* was seen as giving Prussian officers an advantage in their wars against Austria (1866) and France (1870–71), leading to attempts in both the US and Britain to copy it.[8] Alongside this superiority in spatial gameplay, the German interest in maps was seen as a major advantage in appreciating the nature of the world, especially in terms of geostrategic issues and international affairs. For British experts in particular, this admiration of German spatial sciences was also tinged with a sense of needing to keep up with a potential rival. However, this British emulation/fear often did not take account of similar attitudes in Germany directed towards Britain. Ratzel himself bemoaned the lack of a 'space perception' in the German population, comparing this unfavourably with the imperial vision of the British.[9]

Nevertheless, it was in the field of human geography that the superiority of German education seemed to be unchallenged, and for British and American geographers it was the figure of Friedrich Ratzel who came to embody that superiority. Yet, translations of Ratzel's works into English came late. Most of them were published after his death in 1904, while a large part of his oeuvre remains untranslated to this day. Indeed, for most British and American geographers without a knowledge of German, the main source of Ratzel's ideas came through the writings of his American student Ellen Churchill Semple.

Semple's interaction with Ratzel has become the stuff of legend in the history of human geography. Going to study under Ratzel in Leipzig, the often-told story is that Semple was barred from enrolling in the University by its rules on the exclusion of women from the student body. Undaunted, the story goes, she listened in to Ratzel's lectures in an adjoining room perched on a stool by the door.[10] During a conference that I attended in Leipzig to mark the centenary of Ratzel's death, the British and American geographers present were particularly interested to be shown where this had taken place. The truth is more prosaic. While it is true that Leipzig did not allow women to matriculate or take exams, they could petition to attend lectures and seminars. Semple successfully petitioned through Ratzel.[11] Sadly for the anecdote, but luckily for Semple, there was no sitting on a stool in an adjoining room.

Semple was not the only Anglophone source for Ratzel's ideas – indeed, Semple herself had been introduced to Ratzel's writings via Duren James Henderson Ward, an American minister who had completed a PhD at Leipzig. Other contemporaries in US geography, such as Albert Perry Brigham, were also aware of Ratzel.[12] Colleagues of Semple, such as the historian Frederick Jackson Turner, admired Ratzel. Indeed, Turner singled out Ratzel as the 'forerunner' showing the path that American historians would have to follow in order to understand 'the evolution of society in the American environment'.[13] However, Semple had the good fortune to be in Leipzig between 1891 and 1892, which 'coincided with the ultimate expression of Ratzel's anthropogeography'.[14] This, coupled with Ratzel's charisma as a lecturer, led Semple to become an avid disciple of Ratzel's approach.[15]

For Semple, the problem with Ratzel's ideas was that they were mostly applied to German and Slavonic examples, and her initial work (starting in 1897) tried to apply Ratzel's methods to specific American examples that would be of more interest to US audiences. This culminated in her first major book, *American History and its Geographic Conditions*, which applied Ratzel's thought to the historical geography of the US.[16] Rapidly adopted as a textbook and added to every US Navy ship's library, the book was a runaway success.[17] Yet, in terms of her longer-term influence on British American geography, and specifically the development of a Ratzel-influenced IPG, it was her even more overtly Ratzelian 1911 book *Influences of Geographic Environment on the Basis of Ratzel's System of Anthropo-geography* that was her key publication.[18]

Influences of Geographic Environment was a bestseller on both sides of the Atlantic. Reviewed both favourably and unfavourably by academic geographers, it even made a splash amongst non-academics, with *The Scotsman* heralding its author as 'one of the ablest geographers of the day' and a reader in Utah proclaiming the book as a potential validation of the Book of Mormon.[19] Its proclaimed intent of bringing Ratzel's 'anthropogeography' to an Anglo audience raised both Ratzel and German geography into a pre-eminent position in the eyes of British and American geographers. This was despite the fact that later analysts would argue that Semple had mistakenly superimposed an American environmental determinist ethos (present in, for example, the earlier writings of the historian Frederick Jackson Turner) onto Ratzel's anthropogeography.[20] Ratzel himself had left room for human agency through his notion of human societies as 'aggregate organisms' of individuals bound together by 'moral and spiritual forces' that could take many forms.[21] Thus, human societies did not necessarily act in a predictable way towards the environment as real organisms did. This important disclaimer was missing from most Anglophone interpretations of Ratzel, including much of Semple's work. The environmental determinist label would continue to be stuck on Ratzel by British and American commentators and would become a source of criticism of Ratzel after German geopolitics became the *bête noire* of Allied propaganda in the early 1940s. Interestingly, the French geographers influenced by Ratzel never made this leap to environmental determinism, and it was the influence of French professors, such as Jean Brunhes, that would help to wean Anglophone human geographers off of Semple's determinist reading.[22]

However, by 1911, Semple was no longer trying to apply Ratzel solely to American examples. The strength of *Influences of Geographic Environment* was that it was a work that tried to understand the ebb and flow of human history on a global scale. In this sense, it formed the basis – along with the work of historians like Turner and political scientists like Paul Reinsch – of a new American appreciation of the nature of international affairs. For Semple, human history and politics could be understood as an interaction with the environment, with the environment playing the dominant role in favouring different societies over time (compare this with Brunhes' view that the relationship between the natural and human factors are always changing and can even reverse over time,[23] a position that would be expanded upon by Semple's student Derwent Whittlesey). This meant that success in international affairs was primarily a product of understanding what actions the environment favours. The parallel with Turner's understanding of how the environment of the frontier created the American character (and the need to continue that 'frontier' through expansion into the Pacific) is instructive.[24]

Semple's work turned Ratzel and German anthropo-geography into something for Americans to emulate, and her successors in American political geography continued her work. Her student Ellsworth Huntington and the rising star of American geography Isaiah Bowman taught a course on anthropo-geography together at Yale. While Bowman's work began in forest physiography and the physical geography of Latin America, his interests would increasingly draw him to world affairs and, by the 1920s, he would become one of the foremost experts in the IS in IR, as a result of his work in the advisory group to President Woodrow Wilson – the

Inquiry – at the Paris Peace Conference. The culmination of his work at the Conference was the publication of his seminal survey of world affairs, *The New World*, first published in 1924. *The New World* brought together both his geographical knowledge and his experience of world affairs.[25]

While the First World War did undermine German influence across the English-speaking world, it did not necessarily end the emulation of German geography amongst experts in IPG. For many of the Americans at the Paris Peace Conference, who went on to found the Council on Foreign Relations directly after the War, the problem of 'Prussianism' in Germany had been solved by the revolution of 1918 and the peace treaties. At a meeting held in Paris between members of the American and British delegations on 30 May 1919, it was made clear to many members of the British delegation that, as far as the Americans were concerned, Germany had been cured of the disease that had caused the War, but it was not clear whether the same cure had happened to Britain. Indeed, Anglo-American relations during the interwar period were soured by the American perception of British and French behaviour at Paris.[26] Isaiah Bowman's own assessment of Germany in the 1920s was that while German philosophy had turned to expansionist ideas of space before the war, much of the ethos now was for peace and trade.[27] Similarly, many in Britain, especially on the left, now saw Germany as the victim of a vindictive France. With some notable exceptions like Hugh Dalton, much of the emerging left-wing opinion on foreign affairs took a decidedly pro-German (and anti-French) view.[28]

However, this did not necessarily translate into an awareness of German scholarship. Interestingly, one of the new works on IR that was to come out of British IPG that did directly refer to German scholarship came from Halford Mackinder, who managed to combine both a call to emulate aspects of German thinking and a warning about the longer-term dangers of German thought. Mackinder's *Democratic Ideas and Reality* represents a halfway house between the emulation of German anthropo-geography found at the beginning of the century, and the vilification of German geopolitics that would occur in the 1940s.

As a geographer, Mackinder admired Germany for its science and its expertise in map-making. He also criticised it for its obsession with, and overreliance on, maps and professional technical education. The US and Britain could learn from Germany, but Germany was also a warning. The basis of Mackinder's approach to international politics was his sketch of two policy-maker ideal types. The idealist ideal type, dominating British and American democratic politics, is a dilettante and amateur knowing a lot about many things, but with no deep technical knowledge. The great advantage that the idealist brought to politics was the ability to think outside of the box. 'Idealists are the salt of the earth; without them to move us, society would soon stagnate and civilisation fade.'[29]

The opposite of the idealists are the organisers. An organiser is an expert in a particular field, knowing a lot within a very narrow band. In state politics the organisers are the strategists who know how to efficiently organise the resources of the state to achieve specific ends. Their strength over the idealists is their professional knowledge, but their weakness is their inability to see outside their narrow field. They also lack the broad liberal education of the idealists and are therefore not naturally democratic. 'The great organizer is the great realist ... his imagination turns to "ways and means" and not to elusive ends ... The organiser inevitably comes to look upon men as tools.'[30]

For Mackinder, the great flaw of British and American statesmen is their lack of an awareness of deep professional and technical information. In grand strategy this was most blatant in their lack of knowledge of maps and spatial relationships. Here Germany was to be emulated. British and American statesmen needed to be informed about the kind of technical skills that Germans had to offer. However, the great flaw in Germany was the lack of a strong idealist strain in statesmanship. Organisers are great technicians as long as they are overseen by idealists, but if they are in charge, they become pitiless conquerors unable to understand alternatives to their strategies, especially those based on an understanding of values and ethics.[31] This difference came out most clearly for Mackinder in education, where the German 'ways and means' education stressed subjects like geography, while the British one stressed values and the moral side of human development.[32]

As an educator and champion of geography, Mackinder wanted Britain and America to adopt the technical education, especially in geography, that could be found in Germany, but he also claimed that Germany lacked the strong idealist education to keep the organisers in their proper place. Thus, for him, Germany managed to be both educator and enemy. Yet, despite Mackinder's high standing in university and policy circles, his 1919 book would remain little read until its American re-publication two decades later in a very different political climate. His advocacy of spatial knowledge in strategic planning, along with his analysis of the flaws in German society, was to find fertile ground in the American academy's own contribution to the war effort: the condemnation of German geopolitics.

German geopolitics and the politics of enmity

Geopolitics is the servant of a morbid German craving for world power.[33]

In his 1968 analysis of the birth of computer simulation in US nuclear strategy, Andrew Wilson singles out the example of the development of the Schlieffen plans before the First World War as an example of where technical competence was able to reach great heights, while simultaneously failing to see the deeper implications of central features of the plan. Thus, the invasion of Belgium made perfect sense in terms of military planners trained in the narrow arts of *Kriegsspiel* and looking for a way to outflank the French Army. But planners seemed oblivious to what a diplomat could have told them: that the invasion would likely bring Britain into the war and eventually doom Germany's chance of victory.[34] A neater example of Mackinder's view of Second Empire German policy-making could not be found.

Yet, when Wilson wrote this, the notion of an almost robotic and one-dimensional German general staff owed less to Mackinder than it did to the stream of publications that had appeared in the US after 1941 (although many of these had been influenced by Mackinder). This stream of academic and quasi-academic writing would inform and supplement the story found in the film *Plan for Destruction* mentioned in the introduction. In one of the many contributions that the American academy would make to the war effort, political geographers would describe, construct and criticise what they saw as the ideological backbone of Nazi Germany: the geopolitics associated with the *Institut für Geopolitik*.

The roots of the conflict between the geopolitics of the *Institut* and American IPG go back to the 1920s. The key American IPG text was Isaiah Bowman's *New World*, which (in Bowman's own view) was intended to chart the realities of the new post-1919 political geography through the presentation of the current state of the world. The inclusion of detailed maps integrated with the text gave force to Bowman's view of it as more akin to an atlas. Its value as a work of reference was reinforced by its reprinting by the US government during the Second World War for its service schools and libraries.[35] The key text emerging from the *Institut* in 1925 – *Macht und Erde*, co-written by Haushofer and Otto Maull – was, according to Maull, written as a German response to Bowman's first edition of *New World*, published in 1924. Bowman's response to *Macht und Erde* came in a 1927 review article that covered three other texts by Walter Vogel and Rudolf Reinhard. Bowman wrote off *Macht und Erde* as failing to be scientific and reducing its analysis to putting 'facts into a series, to invent mnemonic schemes' that bore no relation to learning.[36]

This exchange might give the sense that Bowman and German political geographers were in close academic contact, but actually it took place at a distance. Although Bowman worked throughout the decade and a half after the 1919 peace to integrate German geography, the 1920s boycott of Germany by the leading geographers of Allied countries in the International Geographical Congress (IGC), and the following Nazi boycott of the 1934 Warsaw meeting of the IGC, meant that in the area of political geography, intellectual cooperation between Germany and the US remained limited. This was not helped by the German (and Polish) perception that it had been Bowman who had drawn the new German-Polish boundary in 1919.[37]

American entry into the war gave Bowman a chance to revisit his criticisms of German geopolitics, and indeed his major work in this genre, the tantalising short yet remarkably still rambling 'Geography vs. geopolitics', began with a summary of his opinion of *Macht und Erde* from the 1927 review. Developing his criticism, he concentrated on two lines of attack. The first was that German geopolitics, by emphasising territory and soil as determinants of political action, was blind to the crucial moral forces that gave meaning to territory (here, perhaps we can hear an echo of Mackinder's 1919 argument, as well as those of Brunhes and the French Ratzelians). This also had the effect, Bowman argued, of denying democratic norms, as a state seen to be driven by territorial relations is deaf to the concerns of individuals in society. Geopolitical needs were at odds with moral rights. The second line of attack was to argue that while science aims at general theories applicable to humanity as a whole, German geopolitics was geared only to the interests of Germany and German territorial expansion. Basically, unlike American IPG, geopolitics had nothing to say about international order, only about German action.[38]

In his article Bowman included a claim that would have been anathema to his internationalist spirit two decades before. He argued that this German geopolitical pseudo-science was not a reaction to specific grievances towards the conditions of the Treaty of Versailles, but rather the product of two centuries of German political and philosophical thinking.[39] This argument – that the problem of German geopolitics was a problem of deep-seated German culture and thought – would be the theme of two full monographs also published in the US in 1942. One was written by the future strategic studies expert and ambassador Robert Strausz-Hupé. Strausz-Hupé was a conservative anti-Nazi émigré from a wealthy Austrian family financially ruined by the results of the First World War. Although not a geographer, he had gained the reputation in the pre-Second World War US as a popular pundit and expert on European matters. The fact that he had read much of the source material in the original German helped his expert status. The other was edited and written by Bowman's fellow giant of American IPG, Derwent Whittlesey, under the auspices of an advisory committee of top American geographers. Whittlesey was a friend and student of Semple's who was better known for his scholarly work in historical geography. The popularity of both books meant that they would largely define the British and American interpretation of geopolitics and German political culture for decades to come.

At first glance, Strausz-Hupé's and Whittlesey's works could not be more different. The first was more concerned with the need to develop strategic studies and a form of geopolitics in the US, even while it criticised German geopolitics. Written with access to German-language publications, it gave its reader an intellectual history of German geopolitics, but ended with an analysis that favoured the development of an American geopolitical outlook with little reference to existing works of American IPG (although plenty to Mackinder). In hindsight, Strausz-Hupé's work has the quality of the showman about it and there are frequent inaccuracies. Whittlesey's work was the product of a committee and started from the premise that the knowledge of academic geographers could be used to first describe and refute the German tradition of geopolitics, and second to advance an alternative American IPG. However, what both shared was the premise that the roots of German geopolitics, and the morbidity of German strategies of conquest, had deep roots in the history of German thought and philosophy. Out of this would come a timeline of ideas that would find general acceptance amongst American analyses of geopolitics.

Whittlesey began his dissection of German strategy with a nod in the direction of Semple's interpretation of the primacy of the environmental influences on human politics. The roots of German plans, he and his committee argued, lay initially in 'the ancient soil of Germanic Central Europe, where unfixed boundaries led to haphazard expansions without any sense of natural limits'. Germany's very fluidity as a region and concept came from its ecology, and flowed into its ideas.[40] Yet, Whittlesey was no environmental determinist. The environment was merely permissive. For Strausz-Hupé, on the other hand, the origins lay in a mass psychological pathology. For him, the deep roots were to be found in 'a morbid German craving for world power'.[41] This psychological pathology argument that Strausz-Hupé used to understand German geopolitics would later also form the core of his anti-communist writings during the Cold War. In both cases, the German philosophical development that these causes had set in motion led to a geopolitical mindset that had become the blueprint of Hitler's global strategy of conquering the world bit by bit.[42] In the words of E. J. Coil's introduction to Whittlesey's book, geopolitics was part of 'a gigantic, carefully designed scheme of world conquest, worked out with ruthless precision', and the roots of this geopolitics 'far from being shallow, find the sources of their nourishment deep in the soil of Germany's past'.[43]

While Strausz-Hupé's and Whittlesey's timelines differ, they shared a central core story. Strausz-Hupé traced *Lebensraum* back to Friedrich List's political economy, while seeing Kant as the founder of modern geography. He then traced a line through Baron Dietrich Heinrich von Bülow as the first exponent of geopolitics in 1799, and to Karl Ritter's comparative geography. Organic views of the state were traced to Fichte and Hegel, and all of these ideas came together in the work of Friedrich Ratzel (although Strausz-Hupé's timeline of Ratzel's life and intellectual development is flawed).[44] Whittlesey started with Kant as the originator of the German idea of the state, including the unintended justification of military aggressiveness. This he then traced through Schlegel, Fichte and Hegel. This philosophical current then fed (along lines familiar to readers of Mackinder) into a public mind obsessed with maps and the formulation of a political geography linked to military plans of conquest. As with Strausz-Hupé, Whittlesey's story also focuses on Ratzel.[45]

After this, both writers lay out a history of German geopolitics that first emerges out of the political geography of Ratzel. This, though, is a different Ratzel from the one presented by Semple in 1911. Emphasis shifts from his scientific work as a geographer to his more polemic pamphleteering in favour of a strong German Navy and a colonial empire.[46] Interestingly, Whittlesey, who must have been aware of the irony that Ratzel was also a strong influence on American political geography, quickly moves on to how Ratzel's ideas were used differently in the German context, and Strausz-Hupé soon joined him in tracing the path from Ratzel to Haushofer. While Whittlesey acknowledges the extent to which Haushofer also adapted Mackinder's ideas, it is the Swedish political scientist (and inventor of the term 'geopolitics') Rudolf Kjellén who becomes the key link in the narrative. Kjellén adapted Ratzel's ideas into a full-blown view of the state as a quasi-biological entity struggling for survival over territory with an imperative to either grow or die. In both works, it is Kjellén who gives intellectual form to the geopolitics of conquest associated with Haushofer and the Nazis.[47] After this, both works concentrate on how Haushofer, through Hess, provides the link between geopolitics and Nazi plans for world conquest.

Having established the history and nature of German grand strategy, both works follow Bowman in offering up an alternative American grand strategy based upon free trade and the mobility of labour. These, they suggest, would provide a peaceful alternative to the use of conquest to gain resources and relieve population pressure.[48] The history and form of German geopolitics provides the template for the creation of its perceived opposite: American plans for the post-war political economy. In doing this, the geographers Bowman and Whittlesey also draw a distinction between what they see as the pseudo-science of (German) geopolitics and the scientific study of political geography. The former has led the world to war, but the latter, in the form of IPG, will lead to a peaceful and prosperous world.

Strausz-Hupé's take is similar. Indeed, his *Geopolitics* starts as a criticism of Haushofer's brand of geopolitics, but ends with a call for Americans to understand geopolitical realities. Drawing on Mackinder, as Haushofer had done, Strausz-Hupé sees in the idea of the decline of sea power and the increased role of railroads a longer trend that is changing the relationship between great powers to the detriment of the British Empire.[49] While Haushofer had said this too, the great fault of German geopolitics, according to Strausz-Hupé, was that as a 'mechanistic interpretation of history',[50] it was less a matter of scientific truth than a mere school of strategy.[51] Thus, German geopolitics is reformulated as a pathological warning of a road that should not be taken, while an Americanised alternative becomes the basis for the coming post-war settlement. However, what had not changed from pre-war assessments was the argument that in order to fully understand the world, Americans had to understand the role of space and geographical factors in world politics. In that sense, the lessons of German geopolitics did not completely rule out the lessons from German political geography.

Nevertheless, not all of those interested in geopolitics in 1942 were quick to link Ratzel to the geopolitics of Haushofer and the Nazis. Hans Weigert, a German émigré to the US, is one such example. While acknowledging the links – through Kjellén – between Ratzel and Haushofer, Weigert endeavoured to argue that Ratzel the scientist (along with von Humboldt) would never have embraced Nazism. Indeed, it was the way that Ratzel's conception of the quasi-organic nature of the state had been reformulated by Kjellén and others that had produced Haushofer's geopolitics.[52] Having disconnected 'Haushoferism' from German geographical thought, Weigert went one step further by arguing that Haushofer's ideas are not exclusively German, but in fact a global problem. He illustrated this by singling out three American writers, among them Nicholas Spykman, as representatives of an 'American Haushoferism'. He even went some way towards detaching the ideas of Haushofer from the Nazis, arguing instead that Haushofer's ideas were those of the Army and its partisans, rather than the Nazis per se.[53] Another angle was provided in the same year by Andreas Dorpalen, who traced the *Geopolitik* of Haushofer to Japan and to Haushofer's experiences there. Japan became Haushofer's 'geopolitical school'.[54] Despite this deflection to Japan, Dorpalen does conclude that Ratzel was a major influence on Haushofer, pointing out that Ratzel was a close friend of Haushofer's father.[55]

These major works of 1942 largely framed the English-language perception of the German origins of geopolitics and Nazi grand strategy. *Plan for Destruction* in 1943 clearly followed this script, as did Edmund A. Walsh's 1948 assessment based on his conversations with Haushofer after the War.[56] As the War drew to a close, those, like Strausz-Hupé, whose interests were focused on the likely future form of the global order increasingly gave less time to German geopolitics and grand strategy. If Germany did feature, the concerns frequently related to how to guarantee that the German 'industrial empire' was broken up and also the role that Germany would play in a revived Western Europe.[57] As the Nazi threat faded and the problems of reconstruction emerged, German

Geopolitik rapidly took on the mantle of a problem of history, while the German question now became one of what to do with an emerging power vacuum.

By this stage, a very different form of German influence was emerging in the study of international affairs, based around the classical realism of émigrés such as John Herz, Georg Schwarzenberger, Waldemar Gurian and Hans Morgenthau. None of these had a background in geography and were hostile not just to Haushofer's geopolitics, but also to the very idea of IPG even in its Anglo-American form. Herz in 1942 felt able to dismiss geopolitics in a footnote,[58] while Morgenthau in 1948 gave geopolitics a curt less than two-page dismissal, briefly mentioning only two British geographers (James Fairgreve and Mackinder), and thereby glossing over the distinctions between British-American IPG and German geopolitics.[59] Ratzel and his school of political geography had largely disappeared from the American study of international affairs and where it remained, it did so as a warning.

Conclusion: of straw men and the decline of IPG

The story of British and American IPG's interaction with German anthropo-geography and geopolitics – a narrative that begins with emulation and ends in enmity – is dominated by misunderstandings and misreadings. The very attempt to emulate the anthropo-geography of Ratzel was, from its inception, marred by Semple's attempt to fit Ratzel into an American environmental determinist tradition that had taken hold after Frederick Jackson Turner's discussion of the effects of the American frontier. Yet, Semple's error pales in comparison to how American commentators interpreted the role of geopolitics and Haushofer. Basically, while the ideas of Haushofer were largely accurately reported, the roles of geopolitics in German society, and Haushofer and the *Institut für Geopolitik* in the Nazi elite, were not.

There certainly was an *Institut für Geopolitik*, and in the 1930s it served as a working group for feeding news stories to the press. There was also a *Zeitschrift für Geopolitik* edited by Haushofer himself.[60] That said, though, the story of geopolitics in Germany was much more complex than laid out by Bowman, Whittlesey, Strausz-Hupé and others. Geopolitics existed both before and after the First World War as a vulgar version of the ideas of political geography found in the universities. Geopolitics did not become popular until after the First World War and was more a hallmark of the political discourses of the Weimar Republic than of either Second or Third Reich foreign policy. It was also not necessarily associated with the nationalist right and could be found in liberal and social democratic circles. As an approach that applied geographical principles to foreign policy, it was used to explain series of different problems faced by Germany. While usually nationalist, anti-Versailles and concerned with redrawing German borders so that they would be more 'natural', geopolitics was also used by the proponents of pan-Europa and European federation. In the latter form at least, geopolitics could be about cooperation and the creation of a more peaceful Europe.[61] It was in this last form that geopolitics was applied by some of the early architects of European integration to solve the problem of a violent and war-prone Europe. Interestingly, even the *Zeitschrift für Geopolitik* idea survived the association with the Nazis, being refounded in 1951 and continuing to be published until 1968.

David Murphy has claimed that geopolitics was fundamentally a Weimar phenomenon and that actually geopolitics ossified under Nazi rule.[62] Indeed, Haushofer's son and collaborator Albrecht numbered the right-wing Weimar politician (and architect of reconciliation with France) Gustav Stresemann among his political contacts.[63] This is not to say that Haushofer and his more rightist and anti-democratic version of geopolitics did not play a part in the Nazi story, just that it played a more equivocal role. Hess certainly was influenced by Haushofer – first as Haushofer's adjutant during the war and later as his student. Through Hess, Hitler certainly did become acquainted with Haushofer's views and used them while writing *Mein Kampf*. Via Haushofer, concepts like *Lebensraum* and *Herrenvolk* were used during the Third Reich, and Haushofer was associated with the regime at many points, including the diplomatic overtures to Japan. That he collaborated with the Nazi Party and (later) regime is beyond doubt. However, after the flight of Hess, Haushofer lost his strongest supporter in the Nazi hierarchy, and his advocacy of an alliance with Russia did not survive the German invasion of the Soviet Union. Geopolitics was mined by the Nazis, but was ultimately trumped by racism, anti-Semitism and anti-Bolshevism.

Yet, the American idea of a German geopolitical strategy for world conquest was important due to the role it played in presenting an 'other' against which the US and the West needed to construct a new geostrategic alternative. The ideas of free trade, monetary regulation, mobility of labour and political cooperation that were found in the works of Anglo-American IPG were written as a response to the idea of an expansionist German geopolitics. In turn, their authors, especially the well-connected Isaiah Bowman, influenced the debates around the formation of the US-led international order and international organisations that made up the Allied post-war reconstruction efforts. This order, in turn, was the one that would achieve global reach after the collapse of the Soviet-led Eastern Bloc.

While Anglo-American IPG influenced the 1943–5 planning for the post-war settlement, it did not survive the 1940s within the academic study of IR, and by the 1950s, it had been superseded by a classical realism that had little interest in political geography. It is tempting to see this decline of IPG as a product of the unfortunate association of geopolitics with fascism. Elsewhere I have argued that this is untrue, and that the story of the decline of IPG within IR had little to do with geopolitics and much more to do with matters internal to the discipline of geography.[64] Yet, the story of German geopolitics did, at a more vulgar level, poison the concept of political geography within the English-speaking world. It has only been since the 1990s that geopolitics has crept back into IR via geography, but even then the authors in this group reject the geopolitics and political geography of an earlier generation, and add the word 'critical' to geopolitics – serving the role of both an accurate description and as a means of distancing themselves from unacceptable associations.[65] The result of this long unfamiliarity with the ideas of geopolitics and political geography in IR (and in US intellectual culture more generally) has meant that frequently the term 'geopolitics' (or 'geography') is misused as a mere synonym for *Realpolitik*, power politics and grand strategy.[66] This takes us a long way from the early days of Anglo-American emulation of the new German-dominated studies of human and political geography, and in many ways the story of this emulation that slid into enmity is of mostly historical interest. Yet, at its base, the way in which Semple initially interpreted Ratzel's anthropo-geography helped spark a tradition in the English-speaking world that may yet serve us well in the future. Semple emphasised the connection between humans and their environment, and indeed the opening line of her 1911 book was 'Man is a product of the earth's surface'. Semple's interpretation of Ratzel initiated an interest in British and American geography not only in terms of how the environment moulded people, but also how humanity's interaction with the earth also shaped the environment. This fungible nature of the human–earth relationship reached maturity with the Semple-influenced work of Derwent Whittlesey.[67] At a time when concerns are being raised about the effects of human activity on the earth and with calls for a more planet politics approach in IR,[68] this part of the Ratzelian inheritance within Anglo-IPG may yet serve us well.

Notes

1 I. Bowman, 'Geography vs. geopolitics', *Geographical Review*, 32 (1942), pp. 646–58; D. Whittlesey, *German Strategy of World Conquest* (London: F. E. Robinson, 1942); H. W. Weigert, *Generals and Geographers: The Twilight of Geopolitics* (New York: Oxford University Press, 1942); A. Dorpalen, *The World of General Haushofer: Geopolitics in Action* (New York: Holt, Rinehart and Winston, 1942); R. Strausz-Hupé, *Geopolitics: The Struggle for Space and Power* (New York: G. P. Putnam, 1942). See also E. A. Walsh's post-war assessment based on his conversations with Haushofer in *Total Power: A Footnote to History* (New York: Doubleday, 1948).

2 G. Wolkersdorfer, 'Karl Haushofer and geopolitics: the history of a German mythos', *Geopolitics*, 4:3 (1999), pp. 145–60, at p. 152.

3 H. Wanklyn, *Friedrich Ratzel: A Biographical Memoir and Bibliography* (Cambridge: Cambridge University Press, 1961).

4 E. Churchill Semple, *Influences of Geographic Environment on the Basis of Ratzel's System of Anthropo-geography* (London: Constable, 1911), preface.

5 J. Herbst, *The German Historical School in American Scholarship: A Study in the Transfer of Culture* (Ithaca: Cornell University Press, 1965); H. Geitz, J. Heideking and J. Herbst, *German Influences on Education in the United States to 1917* (Cambridge: Cambridge University Press, 1995); A. Werner, *The Transatlantic World of Higher Education: Americans at German Universities, 1776–1914* (New York: Berghahn Books, 2013).

6 J. R. Davis, 'Higher education reform and the German model: a Victorian discourse', in H. Ellis and U. Kirchberger (eds), *Anglo-German Scholarly Networks in the Long Nineteenth Century* (Leiden: Brill, 2014), pp. 39–62.

7 J. R. Smith, 'Geography in Germany: II. The university', *Journal of Geography*, 10:1 (1902), pp. 448–57, at p. 448.

8 For the story of Kriegspiel,alanet politics: AState.s fault.cited in n 6 see A. Wilson, *The Bomb and the Computer: Wargaming from Ancient Chinese Mapboard to Atomic Computer* (New York: Delacorte Press, 1968), ch. 1.

9 Ratzel's conception of space perception is discussed in Weigert, *Generals and Geographers*, pp. 99–100.

10 For a version of this story, see Wanklyn, *Friedrich Ratzel*, p. 31.

11 I. M. Keighren, *Bringing Geography to Book: Ellen Semple and the Reception of Geographical Knowledge* (New York: I. B.Tauris, 2010), pp. 14–16.

12 Keighren, *Bringing Geography to Book*, pp. 14, 33.

13 F. J. Turner, 'Geographic influences on American history', *Journal of Geography*, 4 (1905), 34–7.

14 Keighren, *Bringing Geography to Book*, p. 23.

15 Ratzel's abilities as a lecturer may have come late in his career, at least according to Wanklyn: *Friedrich Ratzel*, p. 28.

16 E. Churchill Semple, *American History and its Geographical Conditions* (Boston: Houghton Mifflin, 1903).

17 Keighren, *Bringing Geography to Book*, p. 34.

18 Churchill Semple, *Influences of Geographic Environment*.

19 See the discussion in I. M. Keighren, 'Reading the reception of Ellen Churchill Semple's influences of geographic environment (1911)' (unpublished PhD thesis, University of Edinburgh, 2007). For a fuller discussion of its reception see Keighren, *Bringing Geography to Book*, ch. 3.

20 Wanklyn, *Friedrich Ratzel*, p. 32.

21 F. Ratzel, 'Der Lebensraum', in *Politische Geographie* (Munich: Oldenbourg 1897), pp. 11–12; F. Ratzel, *Anthropogeographie* (Stuttgart: J. Engelhorn, 1899), p. 2.

22 See, for example, the English translation of J. Brunhes' Ratzel-influenced *La Géographie humaine*, edited by those two giants of US geography Isaiah Bowman and Richard Elwood Dodge: J. Brunhes, *Human Geography: An Attempt at a Positive Classification. Principles and Examples* (London: George G. Harrap, 1920).

23 Brunhes, *Human Geography*, p. 597.

24 F. J. Turner, 'The significance of the American frontier in American history', in M. Ridge (ed.), *Frederick Jackson Turner: Wisconsin's Historian of the Frontier* (Madison: State Historical Society of Wisconsin, 1986); W. A. Williams, 'The frontier thesis and American foreign policy', *Pacific Historical Review*, 24:4 (1955), 379–95.

25 I. Bowman, *The New World: Problems in Political Geography* (Yonkers-on-Hudson: World Book Company, 1924).

26 See, for example, the discussion in A. Williams, 'Before the special relationship: The Council on Foreign Relations, the Carnegie Foundation and the rumour of an Anglo-American war', *Journal of Transatlantic Studies*, 1:2 (2003), pp. 233–51.

27 I. Bowman, *The New World: Problems in Political Geography*, 4th ed. (Yonkers-on-Hudson: World Book Company, 1928), pp. 264–5, 294–6.

28 See L. M. Ashworth, *International Relations and the Labour Party: Intellectuals and Policymaking from 1918–1945* (London: I. B.Tauris, 2007), ch. 2. For a particularly robust and racist example of this genre of pro-German and anti-French left-wing writing, see E. D. Morel, *The Horror on the Rhine* (London: UDC, 1921).

29 H. J. Mackinder, *Democratic Ideals and Reality: A Study in the Politics of Reconstruction* (London: Constable, 1919), p. 9.

30 Mackinder, *Democratic Ideals and Reality*, p. 18.

31 Mackinder, *Democratic Ideals and Reality*, ch. 2.

32 Mackinder, *Democratic Ideals and Reality*, pp. 26–8.

33 R. Strausz-Hupé, *Geopolitics*, p. x.

34 Wilson, *The Bomb and the Computer*, pp. 21–5.

35 G. J. Martin, *The Life and Thought of Isaiah Bowman* (Hamden, CT: Archon, 1980), pp. 100–4.

36 I. Bowman, 'Some German works on political geography', *Geographical Review*, 17:3 (1927), pp. 511–13.

37 See the discussion in N. Smith, *American Empire: Roosevelt's Geographer and the Prelude to Globalization* (Berkeley: University of California Press, 2003), pp. 279–81. Despite the Nazi boycott of the Warsaw meeting, the perseverance of Bowman and others did manage to attract a large delegation of German geographers. This, though, remained a high watermark of cooperation.

38 Bowman, 'Geography vs. geopolitics'.

39 Bowman, 'Geography vs. geopolitics', p. 648.

40 D. Whittlesey, *German Strategy of World Conquest* (London: F. E. Robinson, 1942), p. 14.

41 Strausz-Hupé, *Geopolitics*, p. x.

42 Whittlesey, *German Strategy*, p. 13; Strausz- Hupé, *Geopolitics*, p. vii.

43 E. J. Coil, 'Introduction', in Whittlesey, *German Strategy*, p. 5.

44 Strausz-Hupé, *Geopolitics*, pp. 11–24.

45 Whittlesey, *German Strategy*, pp. 23–45.

46 Whittlesey, *German Strategy*, pp. 45 ff; Strausz-Hupé, *Geopolitics*, pp. 27–36.

47 Strausz-Hupé, *Geopolitics*, pp. 41–4, 50; Whittlesey, *German Strategy*, pp. 70–6.

48 Whittlesey, *German Strategy*, pp. 190ff; Strausz-Hupé, *Geopolitics*, pp. 98–9, 193–4; Bowman, 'Geography vs. geopolitics', p. 655.
49 Strausz-Hupé, *Geopolitics*, pp. 256–61.
50 R. Strausz-Hupé, 'It's smart to be geopolitical', *Saturday Review of Literature*, 6 February 1943, p. 20, 4.
51 Strausz-Hupé, *Geopolitics*, p. 101.
52 H. W. Weigert, *Generals and Geographers: The Twilight of Geopolitics* (Freeport NY: Books for Libraries, 1972 [reprint of 1942 ed.]), pp. 88–92.
53 Weigert, *Generals and Geographers*, ch. 10.
54 A. Dorpalen, *The World of General Haushofer: Geopolitics in Action* (New York: Holt, Rinehart and Winston, 1942), pp. 7–13.
55 Dorpalen, *General Haushofer*, p. 52.
56 E. A. Walsh, *Total Power: A Footnote to History* (New York: Doubleday, 1948).
57 See R. Strausz-Hupé, *The Balance of Tomorrow: Power and Foreign Policy in the United States* (New York: Putnams, 1945), pp. 161–3.
58 J. Herz, 'Power politics and world organization', *American Political Science Review*, 36:6 (1942), pp.1039–52, at p. 1043 n.2.
59 H. J. Morgenthau, *Politics among Nations: The Struggle for Power and Peace*, 6th ed. (New York: McGraw-Hill, 1985), pp. 178–9.
60 D. T. Murphy, *The Heroic Earth: Geopolitical Thought in Weimar Germany, 1918–1933* (Kent, OH: Kent State University Press, 1997), p. vii.
61 Murphy, *Heroic Earth*, pp. 17–19, 23, ch. 9.
62 Murphy, *Heroic Earth*, p. viii.
63 H. Heske, 'Karl Haushofer: his role in German geopolitics and in Nazi politics', *Political Geography Quarterly*, 6:2 (1987), pp. 135–44, at p. 142.
64 L. M. Ashworth, 'Mapping a new world: geography and the interwar study of international relations', *International Studies Quarterly*, 57:1 (2013), pp. 138–49, at p. 147.
65 See, for example, G. Ó Tuathail, *Introduction: Geo-power: Critical Geopolitics* (London: Routledge, 1996).
66 See, for example, J. J. Mearsheimer, 'Why the Ukraine crisis is the West's fault: the liberal delusions that provoked Putin', *Foreign Affairs* (2014), pp. 441–51. On this confusion with *Realpolitik*, see J. Bew, *Realpolitik: A History* (Oxford: Oxford University Press, 2016).
67 See, for example, D. Whittlesey, *The Earth and the State: A Study in Political Geography* (New York: Henry Holt, 1939).
68 See A. Burke, S. Fishel, A. Mitchell, S. Dalby and D. Levine, 'Planet politics: a manifesto from the end of IR' *Millennium*, 44:3 (2016), pp. 499–523.

5

Federalism versus sovereignty: the Weimar Republic in the eyes of American political science

Paul Petzschmann

The late historian Detlev Peukert once made the case that the history of Weimar Germany 'does not consist of just a beginning and an end',[1] yet I think it is fair to say that political scientists have not heeded his advice. Widely thought of only as a 'prelude to Hitler' and as a brief aberration in Germany's authoritarian *Sonderweg*, the Weimar Republic played an important role in the development of political science and International Relations (IR) in the US. In the 1930s and 1940s, the critique of the Weimar Constitution served as a backdrop for a number of German émigré theorists associated with the realist tradition. Hans J. Morgenthau, Franz L. Neumann and Carl J. Friedrich among others accepted, at least in part, Carl Schmitt's diagnosis of the Weimar Constitution as 'decision-less', lacking a real sovereign as a weak compromise between Germany's competing political forces.[2] The Weimar past of the titans of political science is beginning to be recognised, yet comparatively little attention has been paid to the international reception of the Weimar Republic in its own right.[3] When the refugee intellectuals started arriving in the 1930s, America was hardly a blank slate as far as Germany was concerned. The new arrivals had to contend with existing perceptions of German political thought and institutions.

This chapter will explore the lively interest American political science showed in the Weimar Republic and its Constitution. Perceptions and commentary on Weimar were framed in terms of historical continuity, comparison with the post-bellum US and larger questions about the nature of sovereignty during the interwar period. Positive American views of Germany, as explored by Brian C. Etheridge in his chapter in this volume, reached further back than the Cold War. Rather than preoccupations with anti-communism, political scientists during the interwar period expressed concerns about national unity and with trajectories of political development from decentralised to more centralised polities when discussing German developments. American thinking about

Weimar was decidedly not a mere reaction to the First World War nor a response to Germany's 'conversion' to democracy. I argue that the surprising indifference to the war and to German regime change resulted from a long-standing fascination with Germany on the part of the American political science establishment. While prior to the First World War, John Burgess framed similarities between Germany and the US in racial terms, commentators of the interwar period translated similar assumptions about German-American kinship into more social-scientific and legal terminology. Executive leadership, administrative hierarchies and territorial organisation were thought to fulfil similar functions in both contexts and were indicative of parallel struggles for political unity.

Nor were analyses of Weimar necessarily characterised by a reaction against the 'German' idea of sovereignty. Rather than 'idealist' reactions to the First World War, American debates about sovereignty were concerned with taking the measure of the changing constitutional landscape of interwar Europe, of which the Weimar Republic was seen to be the most important case. These reconceptualisations of sovereignty came at the expense of recognising major regime changes in Germany from monarchy to republic and eventually to dictatorship. However, they are worth excavating as they run counter to some founding myths of modern political science and International Relations.

American political science was not a 'stateless' discipline – the discipline was preoccupied with the state and was struggling with the development of a language that reflected its development during times of political change.[4] Nor were its protagonists parochial or intellectually isolated; their conversations and debates were often motivated by a glance across the Atlantic. This was not only true for the founding years of American political science in the post-reconstruction period, but was also the case during the high tide of American isolationism in the 1920s and 1930s.

The German special path in American political science

The classics of the political science literature in the US written after the Second World War understood political science as the 'science of democracy' and were preoccupied with questions about conditions for and pathways to its realisation. Why was it, they asked, that some countries developed democratic institutions and others did not? Oren has argued that this preoccupation with democracy included a reframing of history that divided the world into friends and enemies in which Germany was accorded a special place defined by its lack of a 'civic culture' or of 'capitalist-democratic development'.[5] While the historical profession has partly re-assessed the 'special path' hypothesis, political scientists still rely heavily on this account.

Almond and Verba famously argued that the presence or absence of a 'civic culture' could explain these different outcomes. Whereas Germany was characterised by a 'bureaucratic-authoritarian' culture that put the freedom of action of the state front and centre, Britain and the US were both representative of a 'participant civic culture' focused on the protection of individual rights.[6] Barrington Moore's materialist analysis of the same question saw the land reform and the structure of property ownership as the most important factor, yet reached very similar conclusions. Germany and Japan had taken a 'capitalist-reactionary' path towards modernity, whereas Britain was a prime example of a more benign, 'capitalist-democratic' development. Whatever the methodologies involved, much of the political science establishment after the Second World War agreed that Germany had followed a 'special path' that made it different from other nation-states in the West. In these long-term historical accounts, the Weimar Republic is barely mentioned except to emphasise the extent to which it showcased the co-existence of high levels of commitment to political movements that contrast sharply with a general lack of trust and confidence in the political process.[7] In Barrington Moore's analysis, the Republic gets one passing mention as an 'unstable democracy' that foundered on its inability to bring about 'fundamental structural changes' and, most importantly, a thorough 'rationalisation of the political order.'[8]

Interestingly, rationalisation and 'flexibility' in dealing with its own institutional legacy were features that American commentators celebrated in their analyses of Weimar Germany during the 1920s and 1930s. The final chapter of Elmer Luehr's *The New German Republic*, to name just one example, was entitled 'The Republic triumphant' and closed with a ringing endorsement of its democratic credentials:

> Through the blistering blasts of Bolshevism, through the degradation of treaty and reparations, through the ferocity of Fascism, German democracy stood as the strongest bulwark of free representative government on the European continent.[9]

Political scientists during the interwar period regarded the Weimar Republic not only as an exemplary democracy but also as a project of rationalising the political order into a more unitary and stable regime where multiple checks and balances bound all stakeholders tightly together. The constitutional convention drew praise as being composed of 'intelligent patriots' capable of resurrecting a 'shattered state' and thus compared 'very favorably with the French National Assembly which met in Bordeaux in 1871'.[10] It was recognised that the framers of the Weimar Constitution sought to combine the advantages of parliamentary and presidential systems, providing for a strong *Reichstag* in combination with an elected presidency located somewhere in between the ceremonial office of the French and the 'presidential absolutism' of the US. As McBain and Rogers noted in their study of Europe's new constitutional landscape:

> In Germany it was no doubt advisable to have a rather powerful chief of state. Not only were the people accustomed to authoritarianism, but during the revolutionary transition a strong executive authority was almost indispensable.[11]

For them, as for others, the most important aspect of a constitution was whether it befitted the political temperament of the nation, which in the German case was even then characterised as inexperienced, if not immature, in terms of democratic governance and therefore in need of 'strong leadership' combined with 'political responsibility'. In this the Weimar Constitution had succeeded admirably when compared to that of the US because rather than relying on fear of impeachment and hope for re-election, it had added indirect control of the president by the *Reichstag* and by a cabinet of strong ministers, representing 'a definite improvement over the almost irresponsible situation of the executive in the United States'.[12] Expert analysts applauded the design of the Weimar Constitution and its provisions for wide-ranging ministerial powers that were in stark contrast to the situation in the US, where the legislative process appeared less cohesive, an aspect that had been criticised strongly by American progressives.[13]

If for Almond and Verba a certain degree of passivity was desirable for the stability of the 'civic culture', American contemporaries of the Weimar Republic held that political enthusiasm for leadership personalities was important for ensuring democratic stability. Whereas the first occupant of the office, the Social Democrat Friedrich Ebert, fell short on that score,[14] the same could not be said of his successor, Paul von Hindenburg, who managed to win over the American public over the course of his presidency.[15] Like the legendary military leaders of American history – George Washington, and Grant and Robert E. Lee were often used as comparisons – the 'hero of Tannenberg' was the right man to save his country from anarchy and to exert strong leadership over the 'yelping of politicians'.[16] These comparisons highlight American dissatisfaction with the state of their own democracy in the wake of the First World War. The rationalising thrust of progressivism had petered out by the early 1920s. Then as now, there was a perception that the American state was being captured by special interests and that only strong leadership combined with a professional bureaucracy could rid the body politic of this evil.[17]

Hindenburg's presidency symbolised something that the American presidency seemingly lacked – the promise of stability based on a comforting blend of conservatism and rationalism backed up by his aristocratic and military background. It promised the reconciliation of Germans with the post-war order, which, importantly, included the stipulations of the Treaty of Versailles. The election of Hindenburg meant eschewing radical experiments, especially of the leftist kind that had featured so prominently in the years immediately following the end of the war.

Together with his counterparts Calvin Coolidge in the US and Stanley Baldwin in Britain, Hindenburg was seen as forming a new conservative Maginot Line against communism and Bolshevism.[18] As James W. Gerard, the American Ambassador to Berlin, wrote in 1925: 'I now think that the election of Hindenburg was a good thing for Germany and the world. It means a bulwark against the Reds in Germany and against Soviet Russia.'[19]

So what had changed for American political science since the interwar period? Ido Oren has argued that changes in the depiction of Germany mirror changes in global politics.[20] The 'special path' hypothesis was consequently the result of Germany turning from friend into enemy, from parliamentary democracy into dictatorship. Yet closer analysis reveals that the perception of the US and Germany as kindred nations continued to persist throughout the interwar period. Whereas the likes of Almond and Verba assumed a moderate degree of pluralism to be a desirable and necessary feature of democracy, interwar commentators put a premium on unitary leadership and its ability to bind citizens together into a cohesive national whole. Their perceptions of the use of emergency powers and of administration were a case in point.

Article 48 and the question of emergency powers

Perceptions of Hindenburg's presidency grew even more positive as the German Republic lurched from one crisis to the next during the early 1930s. This was primarily because presidential rule was regarded as evidence of rationalisation and the creation of a unitary German state, not of authoritarian tendencies. Emergency powers complemented the hierarchical nature of the state bureaucracy and highlighted the military 'chain of command' idea that for many American observers were outstanding – and positive – features of efficient administration, especially so in times of economic and political crisis.

The US was not unaccustomed to emergency rule and commentators frequently pointed out the parallels between Woodrow Wilson's presidential leadership during wartime and that of Hindenburg in the latter stages of the German Republic. Lindsay Rogers did not hesitate to refer to Wilson's presidency as a dictatorship, which demonstrates the extent to which the concept was seen to be part of constitutional normality.[21] The *Political Science Quarterly* published a series of articles entitled 'German political institutions' and devoted one of them exclusively to the discussion of emergency rule. In the comparative discussion of the general utility of such provisions, the authors found those contained in the Weimar Constitution to be superior. Government could disregard contractual obligations to ensure an 'ordered control of the financial life of the country', whereas the Eighth Amendment of the US Constitution effectively sanctified contracts:[22]

> So far as public finance is concerned the German government is all-powerful. In the United States, on the other hand ... constitutions and traditions of autonomy prevent a centrally directed attempt to prevent collapse. One may hope that the future course of American public finance will not be such as to cause regret that the Constitution of the United States does not contain an Article 48.[23]

Such acceptance of rule by decree was an important reason why many commentators – both American and German – missed the significance of Hitler's accession to the chancellorship in 1933. If the continued use of emergency rule by the executive was acceptable, the use of the self-same provisions by a National Socialist government represented only ephemeral change. When the German émigré Karl Loewenstein could argue as late as 1937 that 'the transition of power from the cabinet of von Schleicher to the cabinet of Hitler was in accordance with the actual requirements of the political situation and preserved legal continuity', this was not meant as a criticism of the Weimar Constitution. If the primary function of a constitutional order was to ensure legal continuity and stability, then the Constitution had done its job, even at the price of its own abrogation. What was important was not so much the Constitution itself, but the stability of the technocratic elites manning the state machinery. Even after the passage of the Enabling Law of March 1933, which in effect dissolved the Reichstag, Carl J. Friedrich could argue that Germany would 'remain a constitutional, democratic state with strong socialising tendencies whose backbone will continue to be its professional civil service'.[24]

The territorial administration of Germany

While the focus on the executive and on administrative personnel shows a belief that political elites are really what matters when it comes to political stability, a second aspect was the territorial administration of the

Reich. The focus on what for today's historians of Weimar Germany is a peripheral concern is partly due to a special American interest in federalism and state rights. Just like the German revolution and its protagonists were seen in the light of 1776 and 1783, the struggle over the status of the *Länder* in the new German Constitution was reminiscent of the Civil War and its aftermath. Here, as in discussions of the presidential system, American political science showed a strong preference for a unitary Germany and saw the Weimar Constitution as an important step in that direction. They noted with satisfaction that the powers of the *Reich* had been enormously increased with very little left to the states. At the same time, there was dismay that the framers had not gone further in their quest for a unitary state. The suggestion by Hugo Preuss that foresaw the division of the Reich into sixteen territorial units was greeted with enthusiasm and its defeat at the Constitutional Convention was regarded as the rearguard action of feudal interests, of small-minded particularism and party politics.[25] This measure would have effectively dissolved existing states, most importantly Prussia and Bavaria, and created territorial units of approximately equal size. Opponents feared, not unreasonably, that this would turn German states into administrative departments dominated by a strong central state.

Yet, fortunately, in the eyes of commentators, the new Constitution contained provisions that allowed for changes in the territorial organisation of the *Reich* to be undertaken unilaterally. Like the American Constitution, which had taken many years to strike a suitable balance between federal prerogatives and state rights, its Weimar counterpart remained a work in progress and the hope was that the push towards national unity could be achieved without a bloody civil war, given the high degree of constitutional flexibility on this question. When faced with the 'Lincoln-like'[26] decision about the territorial organisation of the Reich, 'only two possibilities present themselves: Either Prussia in her hitherto existing form will take possession of the state ... or ... if one ... will at least make an effort to erect a unitary state ... then the end of Prussia is a preliminary condition, whether this be accomplished in the way of a self-undertaken decomposition or of a destruction declared by the Reich'.[27] These words should prove prophetic – during the so-called *Preußenschlag*, the Reich government in fact removed the social-democratic government from office, to be replaced by a federal representative. What in today's literature is discussed as a prelude to dictatorship with the Nazi jurist Carl Schmitt in a leading role was seen by American commentators at the time as a hopeful sign.[28] As long as Prussia and Bavaria remained separate states with legal standing separate from that of the Reich, 'the danger of a relapse into the old particularism is not entirely past'.[29]

Nationalism and the legacy of John W. Burgess

The positive reception of the Weimar Constitution alongside its inter-pretation as a rationalising enterprise towards a unitary state run by a streamlined executive did not come out of nowhere. Its origins can be found in the teutonophilia of early American political science that mod-elled itself on German jurisprudential *Staatswissenschaft* and interpreted the American experience along similar lines.[30] One prominent example was the scholarship of John W. Burgess, who regarded Germany and the US as kindred nations. 'If I should designate the entire political fabric organised by the constitution of the German empire as "The United States of Germany", I would give the American mind a much clearer and truer conception of it than the title "German empire" conveys'.[31] As for so many others of his generation, it was his experience of graduate study in Germany that drove him to work towards the creation of a separate institutional home for the study of political science based on the German theory of the state. 'The Germans ... are more exact and scientific in their political and legal nomenclature. ... We shall do well to imitate their example...'[32]

Yet while the German mind was unparalleled in its ability to devise systems of concepts, the American political scientists should not be blinded by the Germanic penchant towards 'realism', i.e. their tendency to equate their current system of government with the idea of the state as such. Whereas the German mind can only comprehend the Prussian state as the 'actuality of the ethical idea', the US has the distinct advan-tage of possessing a 'government that is not the sovereign organisation of the state', because behind it lie the sovereign constitution and the sover-eignty of the people. In the end, this signifies that public law has reached a higher stage of development in the US than in Europe and it is therefore in the US that a critical political science can find its true home.[33]

Part of the reason why Burgess thought this was so was because he identified the American nation-state as exhibiting the highest form of political consciousness. Only in the US was there a clear distinction between the state and the government. It allowed the political scientists to distinguish between the state ideal as constituted by a foundational document or constitution and its institutional realisation. The conscious-ness of this important distinction being so clear and so commonplace conferred upon the American student of political science special powers of discernment in the study of foreign countries where this conscious-ness was not as highly developed.

Underlying this – strongly Hegelian – argument was the idea of the world as structured along hierarchically organised civilisations, chiefly among them the 'Teutonic states' such as Germany and the US. As opposed to 'Latinate' and 'Celtic' civilisations, it was left to the genius of

these 'Teutonic states' to create the modern nation-state, the only guarantee of human progress. 'The teutonic nations are particularly endowed
with the capacity for establishing national states … and are therefore …
intrusted, in general economy of history, with the mission of conducting
the political civilisation of the modern world.'[34] Burgess invested much
energy in demonstrating that the US was a Teutonic rather than a Celtic
civilisation, a claim that struck an odd note in the later years of the
First World War.[35] Yet Burgess' emphasis on the institutional parallels
between Germany and the US, and his distinction between state and
government survived in the deep structure of American political science
beyond the First World War and well into the 1930s.[36] One reason
why this was possible, the experience of the First World War notwithstanding, was the longevity and continued prestige of the juristic theory
of sovereignty. While the theory came under attack, not least because
of its – actual or imagined – Germanic overtones, it continued to be
modified and defended. Unsurprisingly perhaps, it was among analysts
of Germany that it found its most vocal supporters. For one, the study
of Germany through the lens of the juristic theory opened the door to
cross-Atlantic comparison. Such comparative studies of constitutional
jurisprudence allowed for innovative reconceptualisations of sovereignty
in light of interwar political developments and theoretical critiques. Yet,
the continued assumption of Germany and the US as 'kindred nations'
also blinded the followers of Burgess to the radical regime change in
Germany, in 1919 and 1933.

Weimar and the American debate about sovereignty

Johannes Mattern's book *Principles of the Constitutional Jurisprudence
of the German National Republic* appeared in 1928 to positive reviews
from both German and American commentators. At the time, Mattern
was unquestionably America's foremost authority on matters concerning
German constitutional history and jurisprudence. The book was not
only a commentary on the constitution but was also interested in what
the German experience meant for the concept of sovereignty generally.
Mattern was quick to highlight the parallels between the German and
the American political experience, emphasising the similarities between
their revolutions while highlighting the difference especially in comparison with France. While the French Revolution also led to a change
of political regime, the similarities with the German revolution of 1919
were 'merely formal'.[37] The German revolution was a peaceful transition between different forms of government without bloodshed. One
of the main reasons for this was the fact that the Weimar Constitution
continued in the spirit of previous constitutions rather than marking a

radical break from the past. It was in keeping with the spirit of the national unity movement of the nineteenth century that Mattern regarded as a democratic expression of the German *Volk*, a 'spontaneous will of the masses under the enthusiastic leadership of the middle classes'.[38] While the 1919 revolution may have signalled a change in personnel, the project remained the same: the continuation of a popular project of national unity under the preservation of the personality (*Persönlichkeit*) of the German state.

The transition between monarchy and democracy that is today regarded as the main feature of the 1919 revolution was a minor feature in Mattern's discussion. That Germany had been a monarchy or a confederation of monarchies for much of its history was not decisive for Mattern, as the spirit of monarchical government had been by and large democratic. Germany's monarchical principle had been based on merit in the exercise of political leadership marked by 'example and persuasion rather than command and enforcement'[39] as it had been in the presumably more authoritarian 'Latinate' states such as France. In effect, Mattern made a case that Germany was more democratic than France, given the latter's repressive legacy of undiluted popular sovereignty in action. Much like Burgess had argued earlier, the difference between the *Kaiser* and the American president was 'really reduced to the one point of difference in the executive tenure'.[40] Furthermore, the German revolution of 1919 removed even this 'minor' difference between Germany and the US.

What could explain this emphasis on historical continuity where later commentators saw only rupture, crisis and exceptionalism? In addition to the profound influence exerted by teutonophiles like Burgess, American interpretations of Weimar also need to be understood in the context of debates about the concept of sovereignty. German political thought was credited with the invention of the juristic theory of sovereignty. In its original version, German scholars had invested the state with metaphysical and quasi-divine qualities that, some argued, linked the theory of the state to the outbreak of war.[41] The juristic theory of sovereignty espoused by Westel Willoughby and Johannes Mattern sought to free the concept from such mystifications, but retained the emphasis on sovereignty as absolute and indivisible. The revolution of 1919 and its aftermath were seen as an important test case for its validity by both supporters and critics. For at least one reviewer, the 'recent establishment of new states in Europe, the new German republic, and efforts at some sort of superior international organisation are in a degree at least responsible for the reexamination of the whole theory of State, Sovereignty, and international law'.[42]

In the wake of the First World War, the so-called 'pluralists' had elaborated a theory of society that put groups at the centre of political theory and argued that the state could no longer claim supremacy over social groups in the same way that it had over individuals. The organisation of individuals into groups was seen by the likes of Harold Laski and Mary Parker Follett as an empirical fact, a corresponding methodology as well as a normative claim.[43] The membership of individuals in different and often overlapping groups was not only a social fact that the social sciences needed to account for, but it was also desirable, for it lifted powerless and otherwise anomic individuals above the 'shapeless' crowd and into the realm of full citizenship. For both Laski and Follett, the US and its federal constitution was a precondition for its vibrant democracy, and it was pluralism rather than sovereignty that both captured the essence of its constitutional order and pointed the way to the future organisation of life inside and outside the state, a critique that will be further explored in the next section.

The debate between pluralist critics and defenders of the juristic theory of sovereignty dominated American political science during the interwar period. Its echoes can also be traced in commentaries on the Weimar Constitution where critics of the juristic conception of sovereignty focused on the nature and history of German federalism. If the reality of German politics had always been federal, it could be argued that the Weimar Constitution was the first coming to terms with the realities of German history, freeing it from centuries of theoretical obfuscation. Federalism was a necessary and realistic recognition of the pluralist character of the German state.

Johannes Mattern's purpose had been to undermine such interpretations through a commentary on the German Constitution as exemplifying the juristic view of sovereignty. Although the commissary *Reich* government under Ebert had acted illegally in calling for a constitutional convention without explicit authorisation from the princes of the *Reich*, it was only the government and its personnel that had changed, not the nature of the state as such. In this he followed a distinction made by Burgess between state and government that sought to explain how the US could be a sovereign state and yet exercise its sovereignty through multiple and even competing organs. Mattern was able to assert that in spite of the pronouncements that sovereignty 'emanates from the people' (Article 1), 'we must accept … that sovereignty or *Staatsgewalt* is vested neither in the monarch nor in the people as the mere total of unorganised individuals, but in the State itself, i.e. the people as a politically organised unit'.[44] The revolution had not constituted a new German state; it had merely brought about a change in the political form through which the state exercised its sovereignty.[45] Whereas during the time of the Empire, sovereignty was exercised jointly by the monarch and the princes of the *Reich*, the Republican Constitution vested its exercise in the Reichstag, the directly elected president, and the citizens through plebiscites and referendums.

There was an additional complication because of the continued existence of individual states, notably Prussia and Bavaria. Mattern's previous book had dealt explicitly with the conflict between the governments of Bavaria and the Reich, and he saw it as a harbinger of things to come not only in Germany but also globally.[46] All over the world, the slogan of sovereignty was becoming a political weapon in the hands of minorities, be they nationalists in British colonies, Nazis in Germany or Southern secessionists in the US:

> Is it not a fact that the advocates of federalisation in the British Empire and the States' righters in the United States and Germany insist upon the State character of their respective commonwealths not because they consider themselves in actual possession of that degree of legal competence equivalent to independence, but as a method of propaganda in the struggle towards the achievement of that status?[47]

Federalism did not present a satisfactory solution to the problem of sovereignty. In case of conflict, the authorities of the *Reich* had caved in to Bavarian demands rather than remove the state government by force as they were entitled to under Article 106 the Constitution. This set a dangerous precedent in that it encouraged all sorts of opponents of the Republic to exploit the concept of federalism as shared sovereignty for their own political benefit. Mattern worried that 'the German National Union is facing the same prospect of a struggle over States' rights much the same as that confronting the United States in the early decades of its existence'.[48] Just as it was misleading to characterise American states as proper 'states', Mattern argued that the *Länder* could not claim to partake in sovereignty or have sovereignty of their own. Never mind the political context to the American Civil War or the post-revolutionary upheavals in Weimar Germany, Mattern regarded a conceptual confusion about the meaning of sovereignty at the heart of these conflicts. Consequently, conceptual clarification was the first precondition for ensuring domestic tranquillity on both sides of the Atlantic.

Mattern's critique of federalism comes close to that of Carl Schmitt, yet adds a distinctly American twist. Mattern, following American convention, regarded the German state as sovereign and did not regard it as 'decision-less' in the manner Carl Schmitt had done. The *Reich* had all the legal powers to execute its will, but lacked the resolve to do so. For Schmitt, the problem was the opposite – it was because the *Reich* Constitution did not identify a political sovereign that the legal stipulations of the Constitution regarding enforcement were meaningless. Defenders of the juristic conception of the state worried that the mixing of legal and political categories would undermine a vital theoretical concept.

Mattern's defence consisted in excluding such political considerations from a discussion of sovereignty because of its irrelevance:

> A study of the constitutional jurisprudence of the German National Republic has no concern with the question whether the Republican Constitution and the kind of government established under it will be able to maintain themselves or not ... Such an enterprise, however, is totally foreign to the task here undertaken ... the important question is not whether the new Constitution of the German National Republic will be successful or will fail as an experiment ... It is rather what its success or failure will contribute ... to that body of opinion which aims at the elaboration and practical realisation of a theory of the State.[49]

Unsurprisingly, Schmitt-inspired German émigré scholars such as Carl J. Friedrich regarded Mattern's work as part of legal positivist obfuscation. Friedrich, although applauding the overall aim of the book, feared that getting lost in the minutiae of constitutional detail meant losing sight of the fundamental, political contradictions inherent in the constitutional order.[50]

Pluralist critics

American Nationalist Progressives had found the idea of the juristic theory of sovereignty to be indivisible and absolute attractive in the aftermath of the Civil War, as it radically denied earlier theories of hybrid or divided sovereignty that were used to account for the special nature of American federalism. Yet in the context of the interwar period, Mattern's attempt to preserve this conception began to look increasingly outdated. G. H. Robinson argued that the approach adopted by Mattern ran the risk of 'saving theoretical phenomena' at the expense of appreciating what was new, showing that the author, rather than giving expression to timeless principles of jurisprudence, remained caught in a time warp similar to the German positivist jurists of the Empire 'who accept the state as a necessity to their definition of law and who do not ... inquire behind the facts of its existence. This lays [him] open to the charge that he too ... is intellectually a creature of his time and environment.'[51]

At the same time, the original American idea of divided sovereignty based on the works of Tocqueville began to look more attractive. Not only did it seem to capture the political realities of interwar Europe, but it also opened up new ways of thinking about international law that managed to respond to the critiques made by pluralists while preserving the concept of sovereignty in some form. Rupert Emerson, whose book *State and*

Sovereignty in Modern Germany appeared in 1929, argued that theories of sovereignty needed to strike a balance between the requirement of theoretical parsimony and the messy political realities of interwar democracies. Absolute and undivided sovereignty remained a fiction, albeit useful, even in the most streamlined dictatorships while divided sovereignty as in the case of Germany and the United States was becoming the norm. The location of political sovereignty was difficult to determine and the mixed constitutions meant that: 'On Monday, it is in the hands of the parliament, on Tuesday of the executive, and Wednesday sees it slipping into the hands of the statesman who spoke Tuesday night.'[52] For pragmatic reasons, Emerson argued that this did not invalidate the usefulness of sovereignty as a concept, even while acknowledging the differences between normative ideal and political reality: 'practically ... political and juristic thought must keep one eye on what can be while searching for what should be.'[53] This was, according to him, precisely what the framers of the Weimar Constitution had done by leaving open the question of sovereignty to be decided through future legislation and constitutional amendment. Rather than as 'decision-less', the product could also be interpreted as a realistic reflection of Germany's political divisions. While it was impossible to point to 'single determinate superior' or 'highest power' in each instance of a constitutional conflict, the German Republic was not 'anarchical' because there existed a procedure that specified what the superior power was in a given situation. For Emerson, the constitutional federalism of Germany and the US struck compromise between the juristic and the sociological method, as well as marking a pragmatic halfway point between sovereignty and anarchy.

What held true for Germany and the US was also to an extent applicable to International Relations. Just as the constitutional principle of divided sovereignty reflected the political realities in federal states, so it was becoming increasingly relevant in characterising the relationship between states.[54] From a juristic point of view, the Weimar Constitution recognised the validity of international law, while from a sociological standpoint, the emergence of monopoly capitalism and international firms established centres of power that were beyond the reach of sovereign states. For Emerson, the emergence of international actors was modelled on a distinctly federal conception of sovereignty. This type of international federalism was not an expression of 'idealism', but started from the analysis of the constitution of an actual state. The historical horizon of commentators such as Emerson coloured their conceptions of what a state or a federation could be. Given the importance of the American Civil War for American political science, foreign constitutions were seen in the light of the experience with federalism and sub-state nationalism. In this context, sovereignty was a double-edged sword with both unifying but also fragmenting potential. Questions of internal and domestic, and national and international were intertwined in debates about constitutional sovereignty.[55] Rather than the 'science of democracy', as it was for the post-war generation such as Almond and Moore, it was a science of national unification and consolidation. The revolution of 1919 and the political upheaval surrounding the early years of the Republic made the comparison to the US attractive, although there were disagreements about how the German Republic and its constitutional order should be interpreted.

Conclusion

American commentators were able to interpret the Weimar Constitution as a vindication of American experiences and the country's own political trajectory. The story of Weimar could be read as evidence that revolutionary regime change did not disrupt legal continuity and that therefore the political upheavals of the interwar period did not change the deep structure of the state. For Mattern, the personality of the state remained unaffected by the day-to-day politics, including the transformation from monarchy to republic, and it was these static features of the constitutional order in which the political scientist should be interested.

Alternatively, the Weimar Constitution could be seen as a flexible construct that – much like its American counterpart – could weather political change because of what remained unwritten. American political scientists studying the Weimar Republic were not 'idealists' in the sense that they were interested in 'how things ought to be or how they whished them to be'.[56] In their discussion of theoretical concepts and their ability to grasp an evolving and complex political reality of interwar European statehood, they performed a type of critique very similar to that of the Weimar jurists like Carl Schmidt, Franz L. Neumann and Hans Morgenthau. Yet American political scientists like Emerson tended to reach very different conclusions. What remains surprising is that American analysts remained largely unaffected by the experience of the First World War and the widespread anti-German agitation in the American press and the academy. The First World War had discredited the 'Teutonic/Aryan nationalist theory'[57] championed by Burgess, yet the new language of political science had preserved many of its assumptions and prejudices.

Notes

1 D. Peukert, *The Weimar Republic: The Crisis of Classical Modernity* (London: Allen Lane, 1987), p. xii.

2 O. Jütersonke, *Morgenthau, Law and Realism* (Cambridge: Cambridge University Press, 2010); H. Lietzmann, *Politikwissenschaft im Zeitalter der Diktaturen. Die Entwicklung der Totalitarismustheorie Carl Joachim Friedrichs* (Opladen: Leske + Budrich, 1999); D. Kelly, *The State of the Political: Conceptions of Politics and the State in the Thought of Max Weber, Carl Schmitt and Franz Neumann* (Oxford: Oxford University Press, 2003).

3 C. Storer, *Britain and the Weimar Republic: The History of a Cultural Relationship* (London: I. B. Tauris, 2010); A. R. Baldwin, 'British Opinion on the German Constitution, 1918–1934' (PhD dissertation, Oxford University, 2008).

4 B. C. Schmidt, *The Political Discourse of Anarchy: A Disciplinary History of International Relations* (Albany: State University of New York Press, 1998), p. 163.

5 I. Oren, *Our Enemies and US* (Ithaca: Cornell University Press, 2003), pp. 23–4.

6 G.A. Almond and S. Verba, *The Civic Culture: Political Attitudes and Democracy in Five Nations* (London: Sage, 1989), p. 37.

7 Almond and Verba, *The Civic Culture*, p. 362.

8 B. Moore, *Social Origins of Dictatorship and Democracy: Lord and Peasant in the Making of the Modern World* (Harmondsworth: Penguin, 1966), p. 438.

9 E. Luehr, *The New German Republic* (New York: Minton, Balch & Company, 1929), p. 427.

10 R. H. Lutz, *The German Revolution 1918–1919* (Stanford: Stanford University Press, 1922), p. 164.

11 H. L. McBain and L. Rogers, *The New Constitutions of Europe* (New York: Doubleday, 1922), p. 30.

12 F. Blachly and M. E. Oatman, *The Government and Administration of Germany* (Baltimore: Johns Hopkins University Press, 1928), p. 99.

13 See, for example, W. A. MacDonald, *A New Constitution for a New America* (New York: Huebsch, 1921).

14 W. J. Shepard, 'The new government in Germany', *American Political Science Review*, 13:3 (1919), pp. 361–78, at pp. 371–2.

15 R. Faulkner, 'American reaction to Hindenburg of the Weimar Republic, 1925–1934', *The Historian*, 51:3 (1989), pp. 402–22, at p. 402.

16 Faulkner, 'American reaction to Hindenburg', p. 405.

17 M. Stears, *Progressives, Pluralists, and the Problems of the State: Ideologies of Reform in the United States and Britain, 1909–1926* (Oxford: Oxford University Press, 2006), pp. 83–6.

18 H. F. Wright, 'The German presidential election', *Advocate of Peace through Justice*, 87:7 (1925), pp. 411–20, at p. 420.

19 J. W. Gerard, *New York Times* (9 June 1925), p. 13.

20 Oren, *Our Enemies and US*.

21 L. Rogers, 'Presidential dictatorship in the United States', *Quarterly Review*, 231 (1919), pp. 127–48.

22 L. Rogers, S. Schwarz and N. S. Kaltchas, 'German political institutions', *Political Science Quarterly*, 47:4 (1932), pp. 576–601 at p. 600.

23 Rogers, Schwarz and Kaltchas, 'German political institutions', pp. 600–1.

24 C. J. Friedrich, *The Development of the Executive Power in Germany* (Cambridge, MA: Harvard University Press, 1933), p. 203. In the second edition of 1935, Friedrich acknowledged that this statement had made him 'look like a fool'.

25 Shepard, 'The new government in Germany', p. 375.

26 *The Spectator* (21 January 1928), p. 69, in Baldwin, 'British Opinion on the German Constitution', p. 95.

27 McBain and Rogers, *The New Constitutions of Europe*, p. 73.

28 R. H. Wells, 'Reichsreform and Prussian Verwaltungsreform in 1932', *American Political Science Review*, 27:2 (1933), pp. 237–43, at p. 243.

29 P. G. Gleis, 'Review of E. Jaekh, *The New Germany*, *Catholic History Review*, 15:1 (1929), pp. 91–8, at pp. 97–8.

30 Oren, *Our Enemies and US*, pp. 27–33.

31 J. W. Burgess, *The German Emperor and the German Government. An Address Delivered before the Germanistic Society of America* (1909), p. 18.

32 J. W. Burgess, *The Foundations of Political Science* (New Brunswick: Transaction, 1994), p. 3.

33 Burgess, *The Foundations of Political Science*, p. 61.

34 Burgess, *The Foundations of Political Science*, pp. 45–6.

35 J. W. Burgess, *The European War of 1914: Its Causes, Purposes and Probable Results* (Chicago: McClurg & Co., 1915).

36 In his foreword written in 1917 but not published until 1933, Burgess showed himself unwilling to contemplate revising his work in the light of historical developments. The theory of the nation, the state, government and liberty 'represent the subject, both as to fact and theory, as things stood down to July of 1914, and, thus, entirely antedate the influences and prejudices of the great upheaval in the midst of which we now live. The presentations contained in them are, therefore, wholly the product of scientific considerations … It cannot be the result of any bias arising out of the experiences of the last three and a half years, or, as for that, of the last twenty-five years' (Burgess, *The European War of 1914*, p. viii).

37 J. Mattern, *Principles of the Constitutional Jurisprudence of the German National Republic* (Baltimore: Johns Hopkins University Press, 1928), p. 5.

38 Mattern, *Principles of the Constitutional Jurisprudence*, p. 35.

39 Mattern, *Principles of the Constitutional Jurisprudence*, p. 14.

40 Burgess, *Principles of the Constitutional Jurisprudence*, p. 18.

41 Schmidt, *The Political Discourse of Anarchy*, p. 163.

42 J. Schwarz, 'Review of J. Mattern, *Concepts of State, Sovereignty and International Law*, *Social Science*, 4:2 (1929), pp. 249–51, at p. 251.

43 Schmidt, *The Political Discourse of Anarchy*, p. 167.

44 Mattern, *Principles of the Constitutional Jurisprudence*, p. 148.

45 Mattern, *Principles of the Constitutional Jurisprudence*, p. 154.

46 J. Mattern, *Bavaria and the Reich: The Conflict over the Law for the Protection of the Republic* (Baltimore: Johns Hopkins University Press, 1923).

47 J. Mattern, *Concepts of State, Sovereignty and International Law with Special Reference to the Juristic Conception of the State* (Baltimore: Johns Hopkins University Press, 1928), p. 177.

48 Mattern, *Concepts of State*, p. 310.

49 Mattern, *Concepts of State*, p. 648.

50 C. J. Friedrich, 'Review of J. Mattern, *Principles of the Constitutional Jurisprudence of the Weimar Republic*', *American Political Science Review*, 23:1 (1929), 202–5.

51 G. H. Robinson, 'Review of J. Mattern, *Concepts of State, Sovereignty and International Law*', *University of Pennsylvania Law Review and American Law Register*, 77:4 (1929), pp. 652–4, at p. 654.

52 R. Emerson, *State and Sovereignty in Modern Germany* (New Haven: Yale University Press, 1928), p. 259.

53 Emerson, *State and Sovereignty*, p. 256.

54 Emerson, *State and Sovereignty*, p. 273.

55 Emerson, *State and Sovereignty*, p. 75.

56 Schmidt, *The Political Discourse of Anarchy*, p. 187.

57 Oren, *Our Enemies and US*, pp. 44–5.

6

Germany's fight against Versailles and the rise of American realism: Edwin Borchard between New Haven and Berlin

Jens Steffek and Tobias Heinze

In this chapter we show how Germany's fight against the Versailles peace settlement was intertwined with the rise of realism in the US.[1] That early International Relations (IR) realism in North America had a notable German connection is undisputed in the literature. The historiography of IR so far located this connection in the personal history of Jewish émigré scholars, such as Hans J. Morgenthau, John (Hans-Hermann) Herz and Arnold Wolfers. These academics witnessed the collapse of the Weimar Republic and Hitler's rise to power, which instilled in them great scepticism towards all narratives of linear progress and civilisation. Together with the refugees, German ideas travelled across the Atlantic that were congenial to realist attitudes, prominently Max Weber's sociology of domination and Carl Schmitt's agonistic conception of politics. These biographical and intellectual pathways were important, but we contend that they represent just one side of realism's German connection. In this chapter we reveal a somewhat darker legacy. We show how reactionary Americans and German revisionists, in particular law scholars, jointly deployed realist arguments to discredit the League of Nations, the Kellogg-Briand Pact and the Versailles peace settlement.

Our discussion focusses on the American isolationist lawyer Edwin M. Borchard (1884–1951) who already in the early 1930s propagated 'realism' as an approach to the study of IR, semantically opposed to the 'evangelism' of the Wilsonian internationalists.[2] In the historiography of IR and international law, Borchard's work has been almost completely neglected. Only Hidemi Suganami seems to have recognised the importance of Borchard's radical reactionary position in interwar IR discourses and engaged with it at some length.[3] Although a classical realist for all means and purposes, Borchard thus remained in the shadow of more prominent exponents of this tradition, most notably Hans J. Morgenthau, who disembarked in the US in 1937. The towering image of Morgenthau as a founding father obscures the fact that a realist perspective on IR and law was already present in the US by the time he arrived and not only in the writings of Borchard. Frederick L. Schuman, a young disciple of the Chicago school of political science, in 1933 had published a widely read IR textbook that suggested a power-based analysis of international affairs.[4] The theologian Reinhold Niebuhr gained prominence with *Moral Man and Immoral Society*, a scathing critique of what he saw as excessive faith in the possibilities of a rational, scientific organisation of societies. Although not written as an IR book, many scholars understood the implications of Niebuhr's tragic realism for the analysis of international affairs.[5] At Yale University, the Dutchman Nicholas Spykman successfully introduced European geopolitical thought to an American audience.[6]

Even if the academic disciplines of international law and IR seem to have all but forgotten Edwin Borchard, his archived correspondence documents how well connected he was in America's intellectual and political circles. Borchard quite literally flooded the *American Journal of International Law*, which he co-edited for many years, with his political commentary. In its pages he fought against the Versailles peace settlement, the collective security system established by the League of Nations and the 1928 Kellogg-Briand Pact that restricted states' right to go to war. As the offspring of a German-Jewish immigrant family and a regular visitor to Europe, Borchard had many sympathies with Germany. He also cultivated his language skills to the extent that he was able to lecture in German.[7] In his view, the Versailles peace treaty with its sanctions and reparation payments was highly unfair to Germany, a typical example of a peace settlement imposed by the victors on the vanquished. He shared such diffuse sympathies for Germany's case with other prominent revisionists in the US, such as Charles Beard and Harry Elmer Barnes, and he collaborated with them.

What renders Borchard's writings distinctive is that he used the case of Germany systematically in the foundation of a realist approach to IR and law. In Borchard's view, international treaties simply sanctioned and perpetuated a political status quo in an attempt to freeze power relations as they existed at one point in time. They thus prevented the discontents of the international system from (re-)climbing the ladder. The case of Germany, humiliated in Versailles and denied its rightful place in the European concert of powers, seemed to prove that theoretical point. Borchard conjoined his realist critique of international law with an argument for American isolationism. American involvement with international organisations and treaty regimes was hazardous, he argued, because it would drag the US into international conflicts in which it had no stake. The alternative that he promoted was a return to the balance of power politics of the pre-1914 era, with the US intervening abroad only when its vital interests were threatened. Unlike other classical realists, such as Morgenthau, Schuman and Herz, who had proposals for a new world order, Borchard really wanted to 'take the road back'[8] to the nineteenth century.

It is perhaps unsurprising that Borchard's ideas were favourably received among German international lawyers. In the 1920s and 1930s, a sizeable portion of the German international law community sought to develop theoretical positions that could bolster the country's revisionist claims and undermine the legitimacy of the Versailles settlement. As we will show in this chapter, the testimony of an American colleague questioning the validity and durability of the Versailles order while calling for more political 'realism' came in handy. To substantiate this claim, we cite the writings of Fritz Berber and Carl Bilfinger, two eminent German international lawyers who collaborated with the Nazis. We also scrutinise Borchard's relationship with the *Kaiser-Wilhelm-Institut für ausländisches öffentliches Recht und Völkerrecht* (KWI) and its long-term director, Viktor Bruns.

The remainder of this chapter is organised as follows: in the next section we introduce the life and work of Edwin Borchard, as his biography is probably unfamiliar to most readers. In the third section we present his early realist approach to IR and his critique of international law. The fourth section reviews his ideas related to the Versailles peace settlement and their reception in Germany. We pay particular attention to the image of revisionist Germany as a textbook case of a rising power trying to overturn the international status quo. The fifth section briefly concludes.

The isolationist lawyer: Edwin M. Borchard (1884–1951)

Edwin Montefiore Borchard was born into a German-Jewish family in New York City, where he graduated from New York Law School in 1905 with an LLB.[9] He received his PhD degree from Columbia University in 1913. Before his first academic appointment, he was employed by the Library of Congress as its law librarian. Representing the US in the Hague Tribunal's *North Atlantic Fisheries* arbitration, he was able to spend time in Europe and familiarise himself with continental law.[10] This resulted in a first study on German law, published in the *Columbia Law Review*.[11] Travelling to Latin America in 1915, Borchard continued his extensive survey of foreign legal material for the Library of Congress, which resulted in further publications.[12] In 1917 he was appointed to a professorship at Yale Law School in New Haven, where he stayed until his retirement in 1950. He also became a member of the *Academy of International Law* at The Hague, resulting in another visit to Europe, this time as a lecturer, in 1923. His main contact in Germany was Viktor Bruns, a renowned professor of international law in Berlin and as of 1924 founding director of the KWI. The personal ties seem to have been close, as Borchard helped his German friends in Berlin already during the hyperinflation crisis of the 1920s, mailing food packages and mobilising funds for his colleagues.[13]

In 1925 Borchard came to Germany again, this time as visiting professor. Bruns had arranged for an invitation by the University of Berlin, which on the occasion awarded Borchard an honorary doctoral degree. In the respective internal correspondence, Borchard was praised as the 'first and only foreigner who made an effort to rebuild the scientific relations between the United States and Germany that have been severed during the war'.[14] Among Borchard's students in Berlin was the young Hans J. Morgenthau, who recalled this episode when asking Borchard for help after his emigration to the US.[15] Borchard became a member of the Kaiser Wilhelm Society in October 1929[16] and contributed to the first volume of the KWI's international law review, *Zeitschrift für ausländisches öffentliches Recht und Völkerrecht*.[17] Even after Viktor Bruns passed away in 1943, Borchard remained in close contact with members of the Institut and the Bruns family.[18]

When the Nazis seized power in 1933, Borchard stood firm to support his German colleagues and friends. His last documented visit to Germany before the Second World War was in 1937.[19] While Borchard, himself of Jewish descent, was appalled by the anti-intellectual attitude and anti-Semitism of the Nazis, he distinguished categorically between his personal and his public views.[20] This led to some puzzling ambivalences in his behaviour. While campaigning against American intervention in Europe, Borchard generously supported Jewish refugees to the US.[21] In particular, he helped academics forced into emigration find a position in America, including Hans J. Morgenthau and John Herz. At the same time, he maintained that '[a] sovereign nation was the sole judge of its domestic politics'.[22] He refused to revise his view even when faced with the atrocities of the Holocaust. In 1943 he defended the memory of Viktor Bruns against Jewish-German émigrés who denounced his collaboration with the Nazis.[23] Bruns in fact had never become a member of the NSDAP,[24] but had published in *Reich–Volksordnung–Lebensraum*, an elitist journal of leading SS jurists.[25] In a series of writings on the restructuring of the German politico-legal system issued by the *Deutsche Hochschule für Politik*, Bruns cited Hitler approvingly as striving for justice and equality of status in a legal community of peoples.[26] To Borchard, Bruns nevertheless remained 'one of the finest men I have ever met ... He was an outstanding figure in the field of international law and made mighty contributions to keep the world civilised'.[27]

Borchard did not change his mind about American intervention after the war. In the late 1940s he contributed to Charles Beard's revisionist campaign. Beard blamed Roosevelt for the Japanese attack on Pearl

Harbor and the subsequent involvement of the US in the war.[28] As a sign of generosity, Borchard also refused to be acknowledged in detail for his contributions to the book or to charge Beard, who was an independent scholar at the time, for access to his files and research assistants at Yale.[29] Due to his deteriorating health, Borchard largely withdrew from public life at the end of the 1940s, but kept his German connection alive. In 1949 he donated a large number of his law books to close gaps in the library of the KWI, whose collection was scattered across Germany and partly destroyed during the war. Relabelled as a *Max-Planck-Institut*, its work continued in Heidelberg under the auspices of Carl Bilfinger, a scholar even more compromised by collaboration with the Nazis than his predecessor.[30]

Borchard stayed at Yale Law School until his retirement in 1950, 'best known for his unwavering adherence to a legalistic and perhaps anachronistic notion of neutrality'.[31] His rigorous insistence on his opinions and his individualism in everyday organisational tasks were remembered as 'problems of the sort that a vigorous and forthright personality would produce'.[32] Once embarked on a political mission, Borchard fought his battles relentlessly. A good example is his advocacy of declaratory judgments, where Borchard argued that American federal courts should be permitted to establish the rights of parties or express an opinion on questions of law without ordering anything to be done or granting a remedy.[33] This campaign led to the adoption of the Declaratory Judgments Act, passed in 1934.[34] Charles E. Clark, the Dean of Yale Law School at that time, called Borchard's effort 'the greatest one-man job of legal reform to occur in this country'.[35] In a similar vein, Borchard campaigned for the rights of convicted innocents and related calls for legal reform.[36] His book *Convicting the Innocent*, which documented some outrageous episodes, became widely known to the American general public.[37] The book may count as another example of Borchard's fusion of legal theory and political activism, his perseverance and 'penchant for drafting model legislation'.[38] In the next section we turn to the one great political battle that Borchard lost: the quest for neutrality and more 'realism' in American foreign policy.

Borchard's early realist approach to IR

In the field of IR, the term 'realism' refers to a tradition of thought that centres on power relations, threats to territorial security and survival of the state. The label has been in use since the 1930s, when scholars began to describe themselves as realists, in opposition to alternative political attitudes pictured as misguided, such as 'idealism', 'utopianism' and 'liberal internationalism'. Some classic political writers, such as Hobbes,

Machiavelli, Rousseau and Thucydides, were retrospectively included in the canon of realist thinking.[39] Critical observers also pinpointed some less appealing legacies of realism, in particular German *Realpolitik*, Prussian militarism and twentieth-century geopolitics. Realism is often understood as an epistemological position, marked by a willingness to face the brute facts of international political life and to resist unfounded optimism and wishful thinking. However, claims to realism were also used as a weapon in political discourse to explain and justify certain political opinions or to discredit others. E. H. Carr found realist arguments to defend the appeasement of Nazi Germany;[40] George Kennan used them to advocate the containment of the Soviet Union in the Cold War;[41] Hans J. Morgenthau condemned the Vietnam War from realist premises;[42] and John Mearsheimer and Stephen Walt castigated America's intransigent support for Israel.[43] Thus, references to realism can prop up very different political messages.

In reconstructing Borchard's early realism, we start from the political message that he promoted. His political mission, pursued vigorously for more than two decades, was to restore American neutrality: 'It was once the opportunity of the United States to serve itself and the world by promoting the doctrines of neutrality, non-intervention, arbitration, mediation and the recognition of governments in fact. These conservative doctrines helped to bring to the nineteenth century one of the greatest periods of prosperity the world has known.'[44] Neutrality was of course not an American invention, but had been practised consistently by many countries until the First World War. Borchard suggested that this was also the best way forward as it would keep the US out of the troubles in Europe, out of the League and any international treaty regime that would compromise its flexibility in foreign policy. He also crusaded against the Versailles settlement, the Kellogg-Briand Pact and the very concept of collective security.[45]

Borchard's views must be understood in the context of a strand of thought on foreign relations known as traditionalism, whose supporters were scattered and largely unorganised. Traditionalists accepted international cooperation as long as America's sovereignty remained untouched and the cooperation was compatible with political neutrality.[46] The arguably most important traditionalist, and a major influence on Borchard, was John Bassett Moore (1860–1947), his teacher at Columbia and life-long mentor. Moore briefly was Assistant Secretary of State in 1898 and became the first American judge to serve on the Permanent Court of International Justice. He argued that neutrality was the original and, in many ways, natural American foreign policy doctrine, suggested by the isolation of the US and its interest in free commercial relations with all parts of the world.[47] He militated against American intervention in the First World War and opposed the foundation of the

League. Borchard seconded Moore in his campaign for American neutrality and defended him in public when under attack.[48]

Borchard linked his advocacy to an epistemological position that he called realism. As mentioned above, realist positions are usually constructed in opposition to another, allegedly flawed strand of international thought, and Borchard is no exception to that rule. His favourite rhetorical move when denouncing flawed visions of world order was to pitch 'realism' against 'evangelism'. In his parlance, the evangelists were Wilsonian liberals who preached a gospel of peace through law and international organisation, but 'had evidenced weak perception of the facts of international relations and had run away from them.'[49] Interestingly, Borchard even tried to debunk the interdependence narrative that since the nineteenth century had served as a justification for internationalised government. 'Legislation is needed within the state', he wrote, 'because the changing needs and demands of millions of people organised into groups require continuous adjustment. The needs, demands and Inter-State relations of nations are relatively few and more stable and require no constant readjustment.'[50]

Unlike liberals, realists were attentive to the material conditions of international life, to power struggles and to the enduring interests and ambitions of states. Borchard had a taste for Darwinism and drew explicit parallels between the realm of IR and biology. For instance, he considered the balance of power a law of nature[51] and suggested that states were like organisms, born, thriving and decaying.[52] In a private commentary on the United Nations Charter, he stated why international organisation would not bring peace: 'Peace is a by-product of other conditions, psychological, economic, social, political. The disparate nations of the world ... are a product of history in which process, accident and circumstance play an important part. The work of statesmen is to proportion territorial allotment to population, capacity, and other qualifications.'[53] It was hence mistaken to place a permanent international organisation, based on treaty law, at the centre of international politics. Occasional contacts between governments required traditional virtues of diplomacy and statecraft, such as compromising, conciliation and self-restraint. Borchard's ideal was, in short, an enlightened, prudent and responsible intergovernmentalism.

Wilsonian liberals, by contrast, had naively transposed their notion of public law from the domestic to the international context. Such analogies between the international and domestic rule of law were mistaken, Borchard argued, because they ignored the specific conditions of the international system. International treaties were inherently unstable since they reflected transitory constellations of state interests and power. 'Most political treaties', he wrote, 'merely establish a modus vivendi, which is bound in time to be departed from because life generally moves faster than treaties.'[54] It was futile to try and enforce legal duties codified in the past. Borchard nevertheless rejected the view that international 'anarchy' in and of itself would lead to war. Ever since Dickinson had published his seminal argument in 1916, international anarchy had been identified with the situation in pre-1914 Europe, and Borchard clearly referred to that interpretation, even if only to refute it.[55] Rather than anarchy, what led to war was the zeal of over-ambitious statesmen who found fighting more attractive than maintaining peace.[56] Wars resulted from misguided individual agency or the collective desire for excessive national and territorial aggrandisement.[57] Like most early IR realists, Borchard found the ultimate cause of war in defects of human nature.

Even if Borchard was a jurist, his realism implied a profound legal relativism and the absolute primacy of politics in the international realm. Whether a question was of legal or political nature in the end remained a political decision of the sovereign. '[W]hat is known as a political question becomes a legal question solely because there is a willingness, induced by any one of many considerations counselling self-restraint.'[58] When an international issue was treated as a legal one and tackled through legal procedures, it was only because the contending parties decided to frame it that way.[59] Borchard gave this position some new legal-theoretical underpinnings by reviving his ideas about declaratory judgments. As mentioned above, he had advocated this legal instrument in the context of domestic American law for quite some time.[60] He came back to the idea in the 1930s, now discussing in brief the relevance that declaratory judgments might have at the international level for preventing international conflict.[61] When filing a case with an international court for a declaratory judgment, the litigant would ask the court to establish the obligations a treaty placed on its parties at the moment of litigation. In its declaratory judgment, the court would then determine whether the treaty was still in force or if 'time and circumstance justify release from the obligation.'[62] International courts would thus not be required to enforce international treaties, but would have the capacity to annul them.

This profound relativism towards treaty law was justified with a hint to the essentially non-voluntary assent to international agreements. 'The doctrine of *pacta sunt servanda*', he argued, 'is often abused to give a supposed moral sanction to treaties, imposed under political duress, which every party to the treaty is well aware will not be observed beyond the time when the force which imposed it is lifted or diverted.'[63] However, Borchard's main theoretical argument for legal relativism was the problem of accommodating change. Change in material circumstances was already a challenge to the domestic legal order, he argued, but even more so in IR. Systems of collective security like the one constructed under the League essentially prevented necessary adjustments. The almost automatic sanctioning of aggressors, in his eyes, 'has had disastrous effects.

It has diminished appreciation and respect for the less dramatic peaceful processes of effecting change and settling disputes.'[64] Collective security forced states to side with certain countries, by defining them as 'victims', and to confront those defined as 'aggressors', even if this was against their material self-interest.

Framed that way, the Covenant of the League 'sanctioned war' rather than enabling states to avoid it by resorting to traditional diplomatic negotiation and compromise.[65] The rigidity of collective security in the end diminished rather than enlarged the space left for international legal rules and instruments. Writing about the nascent United Nations, Borchard still argued in the 1940s that the practice of collective security 'narrows the domain of law and enlarges the sphere of politics. It necessarily plays havoc with the rules concerning non-intervention, recognition, neutrality, and the relation of States to each other; it substitutes the whim and caprice of certain hegemonial Powers for law'.[66] Borchard's realist punchline was that it was futile, erroneous and dangerous to try and regulate international conflict through treaties and international organisations. The alternative was a return to a pre-1914 great power concert:

> The 'old' system adhered to the facts of life. In spite of war propaganda, it did not indulge the institutional phantasy that wars were begun by malicious 'aggressors' against innocent 'victims'. It recognised that international relations were exceedingly complex, perhaps so complex as to defy complete analysis. Without venturing on the extraordinary assumption that they could, by a stroke of the pen, change human nature or the way of international life, they endeavored to minimise the frictions which international competition necessarily aroused. They therefore developed as highly as possible the instruments of conciliation, mediation, and arbitration, and supported negotiation as a form of bridging differences.[67]

Few early American realists drew such straightforwardly reactionary conclusions from their criticism of the League. Frederick Schuman, for one, agreed with Borchard that accommodating change posed a major challenge to the League, but did not dismiss the possibility that the 'Machiavellian politics', which in his view characterised the Western state system, could be overcome eventually through international organisations.[68] Faced with the rise of fascism and Nazism in Europe, Schuman also reached completely different conclusions than Borchard. It was not American neutrality that was the way forward, but united action against villains who disregarded the international order. Borchard, by contrast, refused to brand the Nazis aggressors and propagated neutrality and non-interference. He did not change his mind during the Second World War, when the strategy of appeasing Hitler had quite obviously failed.[69]

The German connection

When Borchard discussed the scope and function of international law, he often cited the Treaty of Versailles, which was both his political target and his favourite example to illustrate his theory. Germany was Borchard's ultimate case to prove that IR could not be tamed through law. Borchard said in retrospect that he started pondering the German question in the light of international theory at the end of the First World War. The US, he argued, might have been able to mediate between the duelling Europeans, but instead was lured into a war against Germany by French and British propaganda.[70] In the post-war situation he sensed continuing tension between France and Germany, fuelled by French revanchism and desires to subdue the menacing neighbour.[71] A functioning system of arbitration would have offered ways of resolving the simmering conflict between the two countries, Borchard argued, but the Treaty of Versailles precluded that option. In his discussion of the decisions of the Mixed Claims Commission concerning charges of American citizens against Germany after the war, he once again emphasised the capacity of a system of arbitration to deal with the material consequences of international conflict.[72]

In 1921 Borchard predicted that 'the Treaty of Versailles, if permitted to remain the charter of the European settlement, condemns the coming generations to frequent and recurring wars'.[73] 'Germany', he wrote to the revisionist historian and Germanophile Harry Elmer Barnes in 1924, 'will be far more responsible for the next war than she was for the last, if present conditions in Europe continue.'[74] It would only be natural for Germany to wage a war 'of liberation or revenge'. Versailles, in his eyes, foreshadowed what he expected to be the next European war of unprecedented destruction.[75] In a later statement he even argued that the Treaty was 'the continuation of war in other forms'.[76] At the heart of the problem was the way in which Germany was being treated. After Hitler's rise to power, Borchard argued for a 'temporary agreement for theoretical equality between France and Germany'[77] that would have allowed a rebuilding of diplomatic relations. Germany had every right to rebel against an unjust and imposed order that denied it its rightful place in IR. The Treaty of Versailles was not sufficiently flexible in his view, since Article 19 permitted only reconsideration of its provisions, not revision, and required unanimity in the Assembly of the League.[78] 'Thus, change by force is declared immoral and illegal, and change by vote is declared practically impossible.'[79]

Borchard's advocacy for revision of the Treaty and the reparations regime did not imply that he perceived the punishment of Germany at the end of the First World War as completely unjustified. However, he denounced the miscarriages of the victors,[80] using interesting semantics of a 'superstructure' being 'out of harmony with its foundations'[81] as the Treaty did not contain adequate measures either for political re-adjustment or for the recognition of economic dynamics. Discussing the latter, he wrote that he was 'hopeful that some day the world may see a centralised body appointed by the nations with authority to allocate raw materials and capital according to economic needs'.[82] As long as uneven economic development fostered conflict between nations, war remained inevitable.

In any event, Borchard condoned German action against the Treaty of Versailles, including manifest breaches of international law by the Nazis. In 1935, for instance, Borchard defended American exports of aircraft to Germany that supported Hitler's re-armament.[83] The episode requires some explanation. Part V of the Treaty of Versailles strictly limited the size of Germany's military forces, effectively disarming the country. Since the US had not ratified the Treaty of Versailles, it endorsed the provisions of Part V in a bilateral peace treaty with Germany, the Treaty of Berlin, in 1921.[84] After Hitler's rise to power, Germany embarked on a massive re-armament programme, openly violating the provisions of the Treaty of Versailles. Borchard's opinion piece on the matter was occasioned by a statement of the US State Department, which declared American export of military aircraft to Germany unlawful under Article 170 of the Treaty of Versailles, stating that the '[i]mportation into Germany of arms, munitions and war material of every kind shall be strictly prohibited'. Aeroplanes were a particularly sensitive matter because Article 198 stipulated that '[t]he armed forces of Germany must not include any military or naval air forces'.[85]

In his attack on the State Department, Borchard went at pains to show that 'the "rights, privileges, indemnities, reparations or advantages" stipulated for the benefit of the United States in the Treaty of Versailles and incorporated by reference in the Treaty of Berlin, did not include the disarmament of Germany and that hence the re-armament of Germany, whatever one may think of it, does not affect or violate the Treaty of Berlin'.[86] While we are not in a position to discuss the merits of Borchard's interpretation of the respective Treaty clauses, the mere fact that he felt the need to contradict the State Department in an editorial of the *American Journal of International Law* on this matter is noteworthy. He did not dispute that German re-armament was a breach of the Treaty of Versailles (it too evidently was), but tried to convince his readers that 'whatever one may think of it', this was not American business. He re-iterated his line of argument once again in 1938 when the US arms trade with Nazi Germany came under fire in the domestic press.[87] When the Second World War broke out, he continued to defend American neutrality and attacked colleagues who argued that the US had a legal obligation to support its Western allies in the struggle against Germany.[88]

Borchard's legalistic notion of American neutrality was widely perceived (and appreciated) in German discourses on international public law. Borchard contributed two articles to the first volume of the *Zeitschrift für ausländisches öffentliches Recht und Völkerrecht (ZAÖRV)* that appeared in 1929. His work was quoted regularly in articles on the question of neutrality in the late 1930s and the early 1940s – sometimes also in articles dealing with general questions of law and politics in the international sphere.[89] As we will show in the remainder of this section, Borchard's writings were instrumental in delegitimising US policy in three different ways: first and foremost, the legalistic notion of neutrality was put forward to reject arguments for American participation in the war; second, some actions of the US President were repudiated as undemocratic and not compatible with US law; third, Borchard's legal relativism and his crusade against collective security were cited by German critics of the League who disputed that such an organisation could be anything but, to quote Bilfinger, a 'universal camouflage for a particular, egoistic type of power politics'.[90]

Among the more influential German scholars who cited Borchard's realism was Friedrich Berber (1898–1984), who since 1937 had been head of the *Deutsches Institut für außenpolitische Forschung* in Berlin and legal advisor to Nazi Foreign Minister Joachim von Ribbentrop. Berber was not an ardent National Socialist or anti-Semite, but rather an opportunistic handyman, ready to deliver legal justification for each and every breach of international treaties that the regime devised. Berber had been a revisionist long before his involvement with the Nazis. Already his early writings 'fused resentment against the Versailles Diktat with calls for solidarity among those oppressed by the "West"'.[91] Berber searched for an argumentative strategy to undermine the obligations that the country grudgingly accepted at Versailles. In this revisionist enterprise, his and Borchard's interests certainly met.

In 1934 Berber presented a theory of international law as politics that was in many aspects quite similar to Borchard's ideas, which he cited approvingly. Berber argued that the study of international law was a 'political science' and international law a peculiar 'compromise' between law and politics.[92] As a consequence, the enforcement of international legal duties was always problematic. International law needed to rely on other grounds than its formal status as law to secure compliance. Berber went on to argue that the 'justice' of international treaties was the only effective guarantee of compliance with international law.[93] As the Versailles settlement was inherently unjust, it was unstable and bound to be violated, and a revolt against it would be legitimate. Berber thus defended and naturalised German resistance to a treaty that formally was law but deserved to be ignored.

Berber also criticised American participation in the Second World War, claiming that the formerly neutral country did not formally declare the end of its neutrality.[94] He proposed a legalistic understanding of the topic and listed in his articles on US neutrality dozens of alleged breaches of (domestic) neutrality legislation. He referred in this context to Borchard's critique of the exchange of old destroyers for the right to use naval bases between the US and Great Britain.[95] He counted such American statements as evidence that US participation in the war was illegitimate. The restrictions imposed by American neutrality legislation were often discussed in *ZAÖRV* as reaching further than the norms of international law.[96] The Kellogg-Briand Pact, for instance, was criticised zealously by Ferdinand Schlüter, who denied precedence of this international treaty to domestic legislation on neutrality.[97] Schlüter also picked up Borchard's critique of 'non-belligerency' or 'measures short of war' as legal terms and used this as an argument to deny any impact of the Kellogg-Briand Pact on sovereign American legislation.[98]

The legislation on neutrality in the second half of the 1930s was interpreted as a defeat for President Roosevelt by Angèle Auburtin, a lawyer at the *KWI* in Berlin and a participant in the German American Student Exchange 1926 and 1927, an institution that Borchard supported financially and as member of the advisory board.[99] The US Congress fought continuously to restrain the president's power to decide individually on whether trading with a country was permissible with regard to non-participation in interstate conflicts. Such questions of neutrality were, for instance, pressing when it came to trade in armaments, ammunition or mineral oil. Whereas Roosevelt sought possibilities to support Britain and France, Congress and public opinion were concerned with remaining neutral in a broader sense.[100] Auburtin understood the president's position as a desire to 'free himself from the chains that prohibited uncompromising combat on the Axis'.[101]

These chains were the shackles of democracy that Congress was supposed to be able to utilise in restricting the foreign policy powers of the president in deciding on war and peace. The praxis of executive agreements, allowing the president to take certain matters of foreign power in his own hands without consulting Congress, went hand in hand with the custom of the Representatives recognising the state of war only after the president already declared it. Whether the president was supposed to be able to have the US military join non-neutral collective action was already debated in the preparations for the 1936 resolution on neutrality.[102] One of the executive agreements Auburtin pointed out as problematic in terms of its democratic qualities and compliance with US law was again the case of the destroyer exchange that was concluded without consulting the Senate.[103] She referred to Edwin Borchard as a prominent critic of this agreement,[104] who disputed the legal powers of the president to put parts of the US

Navy under foreign control and warned against weakening the treaty making powers of the Senate.[105] Reference to Borchard was probably not indispensable here, but helped Auburtin to sell her argument as a seemingly neutral and well-balanced position that was shared by a reputable international lawyer in the US.

Carl Bilfinger's writings offer another clear example of how a German revisionist position on matters of international law profited from Borchard's realism.[106] Borchard and Bilfinger had first met in 1925.[107] Bilfinger was a law professor, colleague and friend of Carl Schmitt.[108] He had joined the NSDAP right after Hitler's rise to power in 1933, intending to, as he wrote in a letter to Schmitt, draw inspiration from the speeches of Hitler and Goebbels, as well as Hitler's *Mein Kampf* ('a lot of good and independent thinking').[109] Bilfinger contended that the Western Bloc alone was responsible for the Second World War, as it did not follow the rules imposed by the League of Nations, concerning for instance the necessity to first seek mediation of a conflict.[110] He pointed out that these rules were set by the very nations that allegedly breached them as they searched for a possibility to enforce the Kellogg-Briand Pact, a treaty that lacked means for coercion.[111] As in Bilfinger's eyes, the state was an irreducibly sovereign entity, there was no space left for international organisations. The wartime project of the United Nations organisation was based on the 'fallacy that those post war plans are consistent with the principles of international law'.[112]

The Kellogg-Briand Pact in general and the Moscow Declarations in particular triggered Bilfinger's sharp criticism, as their designation of Germany as a belligerent nation led to what he described as 'outdoing the form of discrimination already found in the Versailles diktat and the system of Geneva'.[113] Since Borchard had argued for the equality of nations in terms of unrestricted sovereignty, Bilfinger cited him at length when warning against any kind of international organisation that might attain public power.[114] Like Borchard, Bilfinger also favoured a decentralised system of international arbitration instead of an 'universal political organisation of international law', also leaving some space for the *Großraum* ideas that Carl Schmitt developed (and that Borchard would not necessarily have agreed with).[115]

Elements of Schmittian thought are not only present in Bilfinger's critique of a global organisation of sovereign states; Schmitt's much more fundamental ideas about the nature of *the political* can be detected in Bilfinger's writings as well. In an obscure, devious article published in 1950/51, Bilfinger still dismissed the idea that international law could restrict national sovereignty, presenting himself as a modest and responsible man of a world who, every now and then, must 'walk the rocky road of the political'.[116] This *political* could leave no space for conceptions such as a just war. Any kind of armed action, for Bilfinger as well as Borchard, stood in conjunction with the 'special and vital interest' of nations.[117] Consequently, Great Britain, for instance, had special privileges when resorting to war as it was able to claim such special and vital interests anywhere, without geographical limits.[118] This was yet another 'realist' argument Bilfinger found in Borchard's writings and used it to undermine international organisations and law.

Conclusion

In this chapter we have taken issue with interlinks between German revisionism and American isolationism in the 1920s and 1930s. We approached this neglected type of transatlantic intellectual cooperation by focusing on the life and work of Edwin Borchard between New Haven and Berlin. Although he was among the first American academics to openly identify with 'realism' as an approach to international affairs, Borchard remains a marginal figure in the historiography of IR theory. Deeply pessimistic about the prospects of international organisation and collective security, he pitched his realism against what he called the 'evangelism' of Wilsonian liberals. West of the Atlantic, he militated against the Treaty of Versailles, the League and American intervention in the Second World War. In doing so, he collaborated with prominent isolationists and revisionists, most notably Harry Elmer Barnes, Charles Beard and John Bassett Moore. In Germany he kept close ties with international lawyers who sought to reverse the Versailles settlement and justified breaches of international law by the Nazis. It is unsurprising that Borchard's ideas were warmly received and cited in Germany as they gave credit to those who disputed the legitimacy of international law and organisations. His remarkable indulgence of German breaches of treaty law and his staunch defence of American neutrality came in handy. There is nothing to suggest that he actively supported the Nazis or their ideology. However, the fact remains that his realism delivered arguments that were congenial to their revisionist cause, legitimated German re-armament and naturalised the regime's aggressiveness.

The IR realism that Borchard formulated thus cannot be reduced to a scientific statement, but needs to be seen in this rather unpleasant political context. He promoted the idea that international law was not really law because of its eminently political nature and that breaching it was justified whenever circumstances and national interests changed. Treaties among states were valid only as long as they reflected the power relations at the time they were concluded. Trying to enforce them was an act of aggression, agreements like the Kellogg-Briand Pact a mere pretence for going to war. The whole idea of collective security was a smokescreen of the victors to keep down the vanquished at the end of the First World War, which had no other function than preserving the status quo of 1918. All these arguments discredited the League of Nations and the project of peace through international organisations, and, as we have shown, revisionist German scholars were happy to enlist them.

The grim picture of IR and the polemical opposition against world order utopias make Borchard's version of realism similar to those that Carr, Morgenthau, Schuman and Herz formulated in the 1930s and 1940s. However, what renders Borchard's realism distinctive is the isolationism derived from the diagnosis. The alternative to the League of Nations that he promoted was a return to the balance of power politics of the pre-1914 era, with the US intervening abroad only when its vital interests were at stake. Borchard really wanted to turn back time and this may explain why his influence was not lasting. In the interwar years, his political thought, characterised by 'consistency, completeness, and an abiding sense of certainty',[119] still found followers. After America's victory in the Second World War, his stubborn isolationism appeared increasingly anachronistic.

Even if Borchard's backward-looking IR realism did not leave much of a mark on intellectual history, it testifies to the political uses of realist thought. Like E. H. Carr in Britain, Borchard came to argue that a realist approach to the challenge of Nazi Germany (but also fascist Italy and imperialist Japan) suggested appeasement.[120] Both authors had much sympathy for the discontents of the international system and especially for Germany, which was denied its rightful place in the concert of European powers despite its economic recovery. In Britain, the tides turned against appeasement during the war and the realism of the 1930s was soon discredited.[121] However, Borchard did not revise his views even when all the horrors of the Holocaust and the war crimes of Nazi Germany were unveiled. His stubbornness is unsettling. When faced with genocide and unprecedented atrocities, how could one continue to opine that interventions abroad were illegitimate unless mandated by a country's vital interests? How could Borchard, who helped so many Jewish émigrés still claim that fighting the Nazis was the wrong thing to do for the US? How could he still maintain that it was impossible to identify aggressors? In his view, the culprit was always misguided internationalism: 'It has long occurred to me that collective security has been given about all the opportunity to which it is entitled', he wrote to Charles Beard in 1946. 'It has brought us nothing but immense debts and universal misery, with the atomic bomb in the offing.'[122]

Notes

1 The authors would like to thank Lewis Wyman from the Library of Congress, Washington DC and Brian Keough from the M. E. Grenander Department of Special Collections and Archives at the State University of New York, Albany, for their help in tracing and making available correspondence of Edwin Borchard. Katie O'Connell from the New York Public Library, Auste Wolff from the Archives of the Humboldt University, Berlin and Simon Nobis from the Archive of the Max-Planck-Gesellschaft, Berlin have been helpful in preparing visits to their archives. Special thanks go to Stephen Ross, his team at the Manuscript and Archives Section of the Sterling Memorial Library and the staff of the Beinecke Rare Book & Manuscript Library at Yale University, New Haven. An earlier version of this chapter was presented at the 59th Convention of the International Studies Association in April 2018. We would like to thank Leonie Holthaus and Peter Wilson for their comments. Financial support by the DFG through the cluster of excellence 'Formation of Normative Orders' is gratefully acknowledged.

2 E. M. Borchard, 'Realism v. evangelism', *American Journal of International Law*, 28:1 (1934), pp. 108–17.

3 H. Suganami, *The Domestic Analogy and World Order Proposals* (Cambridge: Cambridge University Press, 1989), pp. 111–13.

4 F. L. Schuman, *International Politics: An Introduction to the Western State System* (New York: McGraw-Hill, 1933).

5 R. Niebuhr, *Moral Man and Immoral Society: A Study in Ethics and Politics* (New York: Charles Scribner, 1932).

6 N. Spykman, 'Geography and foreign policy I', *American Political Science Review*, 32:1 (1938), pp. 28–50; N. Spykman, 'Geography and foreign policy II', *American Political Science Review*, 32:2 (1938), pp. 213–36. On geography, see also Lucian M. Ashworth in Chapter 4 in this volume.

7 Letter from V. Bruns to E. Tigges, Humboldt Universität Berlin (HUB), UA, Juristische Fakultät Nr. 37, Bl. 29–31.

8 E. M. Borchard, 'The "enforcement" of peace by "sanctions"', *American Journal of International Law*, 27:3 (1933), pp. 518–25, at p. 525.

9 There is not much literature on Borchard's life and work, but see R. H. Kendall, 'Edwin M. Borchard and the defense of traditional American neutrality, 1931–1941' (PhD dissertation, Yale University, 1964); and J. D. Doenecke, 'Edwin M. Borchard, John Bassett Moore, and opposition to American intervention in World War II', *Journal of Libertarian Studies*, 6:1 (1982), pp. 1–34. Lengthy obituaries were published in the *New York Times*, 23 July 1951; *Yale Law Journal* 60 (1951), p. 1071; and *American Journal of International Law* 45 (1951), p. 708. His Jewish decent is mentioned in S. H. Ludington, 'The dogs that did not bark: the silence of the legal academy during World War II', *Journal of Legal Education*, 60:3 (2011), pp. 397–432.

10 J. D. Doenecke, 'Borchard, Edwin M.', in R. K. Newman (ed.), *The Yale Biographical Dictionary of American Law* (New Haven: Yale University Press, 2009) pp. 61–2.

11 E. M. Borchard, 'Jurisprudence in Germany', *Columbia Law Review*, 12:4 (1912), pp. 301–20.

12 E. M. Borchard, *Guide to the Law and Legal Literature of Argentina, Brazil and Chile* (Washington DC: Government Printing Office, 1917); T. E. Obregón and E. M. Borchard, *Latin-American Commercial Law* (New York: Banks Law Publishing Company, 1921).

13 For evidence of his continuing support to his German colleagues, see letter from E. Borchard to V. Bruns, 21 November 1923, Edwin M. Borchard Papers, Box 15, File 199; letter from E. Borchard to V. Bruns, 28 June 1924, Edwin M. Borchard Papers, Box 16, File 206; letters from M. Wolff to E. Borchard, 18 February 1926, Edwin M. Borchard Papers, Box 19, File 234; 15 December 1926, Box 21, File 248.

14 HUB, UA, Juristische Fakultät, Nr. 481, Bl. 217 – our translation.

15 In 1937, Borchard tried to assist Hans Morgenthau in finding work in the US, also asking Henry Morgenthau, at that time Secretary of the Treasury, for help in this matter (see letter of E. Borchard to Hans J. Morgenthau, 13 November 1937, Box 8, Hans J. Morgenthau papers, Manuscript Division, Library of Congress, Washington DC). In 1941 Borchard also commented on a short report Hans J. Morgenthau provided for the *Yearbook of the American Philosophical Society* that supported him with a research grant. Borchard praised not only Morgenthau's general intentions, but also the specific critique of liberalism and the refusal of the idea that law could operate internationally in analogy to democratic states (see letter of E. Borchard to Hans J. Morgenthau, 25 June 1941, and Morgenthau's answer, 10 July 1941, both Box 8, Hans J. Morgenthau papers). The study discussed was published later as H. J. Morgenthau, *Scientific Man vs. Power Politics* (Chicago: University of Chicago Press, 1946).

16 Membership file, Archive of the Max-Planck-Gesellschaft, Section I, Repositur 1A, File 2985–7.

17 E. M. Borchard, 'The Kellogg Treaties sanction war', *Zeitschrift für ausländisches öffentliches Recht und Völkerrecht*, 1 (1929), pp. 126–31.

18 Receipt, 22 July 1946, Edwin M. Borchard Papers, Box 53, File 594; letter from E. Borchard to V. Bruns, 21 November 1923, Edwin M. Borchard Papers, Box 15, File 199; letter from E. Borchard to V. Bruns, 28 June 1924, Edwin M. Borchard Papers, Box 16, File 206.

19 Letter from E. Borchard to A. Nussbaum, 5 October 1943, Edwin M. Borchard Papers, Box 49, File 548.

20 Kendall, 'Edwin M. Borchard and the defense of traditional American neutrality', p. 158.

21 Kendall, 'Edwin M. Borchard and the defense of traditional American neutrality', p. 160.

22 Kendall, 'Edwin M. Borchard and the defense of traditional American neutrality', p. 161.

23 Letter from E. Borchard to A. Nussbaum, 5 October 1943, Edwin M. Borchard Papers, Box 49, File 548.

24 M. Stolleis, *A History of Public Law in Germany 1914–1945* (Oxford: Oxford University Press, 2004), p. 426.

25 Stolleis, *A History of Public Law in Germany*, p. 323.

26 V. Bruns, *Völkerrecht und Politik* (Berlin: Junker und Dünnhaupt 1934), p. 19.

27 Letter of E. Borchard to E. Aeschbacher-Bruns, 22 August 1945, Edwin M. Borchard Papers, Box 52, File 578.

28 C. A. Beard, *President Roosevelt and the Coming of the War 1941: A Study in Appearances and Realities* (New Haven, CT: Yale University Press 1948).

29 Letter from E. Borchard to Ch. Beard, 3 April 1945, Edwin M. Borchard Papers, Box 1, File 15.

30 Letter from E. Borchard to C. Bilfinger, 25 November 1949, Archive of the Max-Planck-Gesellschaft, Section III, Repositur 44, File 3.

31 M. S. Mayer, '*Borchard, Edwin Montefiore*' (American National Biography Online, 2000), www.anb.org/articles/11/11–00081.html.

32 C. E. Clark, 'Edwin Borchard', *Yale Law Journal*, 60:7 (1951), pp. 1071–72, at p. 1071.

33 E. M. Borchard, 'The declaratory judgment: a needed procedural reform', *Yale Law Journal*, 28:1 (1918), pp. 1–32; E. M. Borchard, 'The declaratory judgment: a needed procedural reform II', *Yale Law Journal*, 28: 2 (1918), pp. 105–50.

34 28 U.S.C.A. § 2201 et seq.

35 Doenecke, 'Borchard, Edwin M.'.

36 Borchard received the pen as a present, which President Franklin D. Roosevelt had used to sign the bill that granted relief for wrongfully convicted (Mayer, 'Borchard, Edwin Montefiore').

37 E. M. Borchard, *Convicting the Innocent: Sixty-Five Actual Errors of Criminal Justice* (Garden City, NY: Garden City Publishing Company, 1932).

38 M. Zalman, 'Edwin Borchard and the limits of innocence reform', in R. C. Huff and M. Kilias (eds), *Wrongful Convictions and Miscarriages of Justice: Causes and Remedies in North American and European Criminal Justice Systems* (New York: Routledge, 2013), pp. 329–55, at p. 336.

39 B. Buzan, 'The timeless wisdom of realism?', in S. Smith, K. Booth and M. Zalewski (eds), *International Theory: Positivism and Beyond* (Cambridge: Cambridge University Press, 1996), pp. 149–85.

40 E. H. Carr, *The Twenty Years' Crisis, 1919–1939: An Introduction to the Study of International Relations* (London: Macmillan, 1939).

41 G. F. Kennan (Mr. X), 'The sources of Soviet conduct', *Foreign Affairs*, 25 (1947), pp. 566–82.

42 H. J. Morgenthau, *Vietnam and the United States* (Washington DC: Public Affairs Press, 1965).

43 J. J. Mearsheimer and S. M. Walt, 'The Israel lobby and U.S. foreign policy', *Middle East Policy*, 13:3 (2006), pp. 29–87.

44 E. M. Borchard, 'Dragging America into war', *Current History*, 40:4 (1934), pp. 392–401, at p. 401.

45 E. M. Borchard, 'The opinions of the Mixed Claims Commission, United States and Germany', *American Journal of International Law*, 19:1 (1925), pp. 133–43; Borchard, 'The "enforcement" of peace by "sanctions"'; E. M. Borchard, 'Sanctions versus neutrality', *The Hungarian Quarterly*, 1 (1936), pp. 254–70; E. M. Borchard, 'Sanctions v. neutrality', *American Journal of International Law*, 30:1 (1936), pp. 91–4; E. M. Borchard, 'Neutrality', *Yale Law Journal*, 48:1 (1938), pp. 37–53; E. M. Borchard, 'Neutrality and

unneutrality', *American Journal of International Law*, 32:4 (1938), pp. 778–82.

46 Kendall, 'Edwin M. Borchard and the defense of traditional American neutrality', pp. 3 ff.

47 J. B. Moore, *American Diplomacy, its Spirit and Achievements* (New York: Harper & Brothers, 1905), pp. 35–7.

48 Borchard, 'Realism v. evangelism', p. 117.

49 Borchard, 'Realism v. evangelism', p. 109.

50 E. M. Borchard, 'The place of law and courts in International Relations', *American Journal of International Law*, 37:1 (1943), pp. 46–57, at p. 52.

51 Letter from E. Borchard to K.F. Geiser, 6 February1943, Edwin M. Borchard Papers, Box 48, File 539.

52 Borchard, 'Neutrality', p. 40; Borchard, 'Neutrality and unneutrality', p. 781.

53 Edwin M. Borchard Papers, Box 51, File 576.

54 Borchard, 'Sanctions v. neutrality', p. 94.

55 G. L. Dickinson, *The European Anarchy* (London: Allen & Unwin, 1916).

56 Borchard, 'Dragging America into War', p. 399.

57 In a letter to the Peruvian lawyer and diplomat Alberto Ulloa, Borchard argued that 'the Nazi philosophy is not one that finds favour in this country and probably in any other American country, for it is a philosophy of over-populated, military, and highly regimented countries' (letter from E. Borchard to A. Ulloa, 17 November 1941, Edwin M. Borchard Papers, Box 47, File 523).

58 E. M. Borchard, 'The distinction between political and legal questions', *Proceedings of the American Society of International Law at Its Annual Meeting 1924*, 18 (1924), pp. 44–57, at p. 53.

59 It should be mentioned that his legal relativism was limited to the international legal order, and even there to questions of high politics. Borchard dealt extensively with international legal issues of lower salience, such as the diplomatic protection of citizens abroad, without doubting the force of the prescriptions; E. M. Borchard, *The Diplomatic Protection of Citizens Abroad* (New York: Banks Law Publishing Company, 1915).

60 Borchard, 'The declaratory judement: a needed procedural reform'.

61 E. M. Borchard, 'Declaratory judgments in international law', *American Journal of International Law*, 29:3 (1935), 488–92.

62 Borchard, 'Declaratory judgments in international law', p. 490.

63 Borchard, 'Neutrality', p. 43.

64 Borchard, 'The distinction between political and legal questions', p. 38.

65 Borchard, 'The Kellogg Treaties sanction war'; see also Borchard, 'The "enforcement" of peace by "sanctions"'.

66 E. M. Borchard, *American Foreign Policy* (Indianapolis: National Foundation Press, 1946), p. 61.

67 Borchard, 'The "enforcement" of peace by "sanctions"', p. 523.

68 F.L. Schuman, *International Politics: An Introduction to the Western State System*, 2nd ed. (New York: Mac Graw-Hill 1937), pp. 36–7.

69 Borchard, 'The place of law and courts in International Relations'.

70 Borchard, 'Dragging America into war'.

71 E. M. Borchard, 'Limitations on the functions of international courts', *Annals of the American Academy of Political and Social Science: The Place of the United States in a World Organization for the Maintenance of Peace*, 96 (1921), pp. 132–7, at p. 132.

72 Borchard, 'The opinions of the Mixed Claims Commission'; E. M. Borchard,: 'Opinions of the Mixed Claims Commission, United Stated and Germany (Part II)', *American Journal of International Law*, 20:1 (1926), pp. 69–80.

73 Borchard, 'Limitations on the functions of international courts', p. 135.

74 Letter from E. Borchard to H. E. Barnes, 24 November 1924, Edwin M. Borchard Papers, Box 1, File 12.

75 Letter from E. Borchard to H. E. Barnes, 30 October 1931, Edwin M. Borchard Papers, Box 1, File 12.

76 E. M. Borchard, 'International law of war since the war', *Iowa Law Review: Yale Faculty Scholarship Series*, Paper 3463 (1934), p. 168.

77 Borchard, 'International law of war since the war', p. 168.

78 Treaty of Versailles, Art. 19: 'The Assembly may from time to time advise the reconsideration by Members of the League of treaties which have become inapplicable and the consideration of international conditions whose continuance might endanger the peace of the world.'

79 Borchard, 'The "enforcement" of peace by "sanctions"', p. 520.

80 E. M. Borchard, 'Common sense in foreign policy', *Journal of International Relations*, 11:1 (1920), pp. 27–44, at p. 39.

81 Borchard, 'Common sense in foreign policy', p. 37.

82 Borchard, 'Common sense in foreign policy', p. 44.

83 Borchard, 'Declaratory judgments in international law'.

84 US Peace Treaty with Germany, 25 August 1921, Art. II(1).

85 Treaty of Peace with Germany (Treaty of Versailles), 28 June 1919, www.loc.gov/rr/program/bib/ourdocs/versailles.html.

86 Borchard, 'Declaratory judgments in international law', 290.

87 E. M. Borchard, 'The export of arms to Germany and the Treaty of Berlin', *American Journal of International Law*, 32:3 (1938), pp. 547–9.

88 E. M. Borchard, 'War, neutrality and non-belligerency', *American Journal of International Law*, 35:4 (1941), pp. 618–25.

89 C. Bilfinger, 'Streit um das Völkerrecht', *Zeitschrift für ausländisches öffentliches Recht und Völkerrecht*, 12 (1944), pp. 1–33.

90 Bilfinger, 'Streit um das Völkerrecht', p. 14, our translation.

91 K. Rietzler, 'Counter-imperial orientalism: Friedrich Berber and the politics of international law in Germany and India, 1920s–1960s', *Journal of Global History*, 11:1 (2016), pp. 113–34, at p. 117.

92 F. Berber, *Sicherheit und Gerechtigkeit. Eine gemeinverständliche Einführung in die Hauptprobleme der Völkerrechtspolitik* (Berlin: Carl Heymanns, 1934), p. 11.

93 Berber, *Sicherheit und Gerechtigkeit*, p. 158.

94 F. Berber, 'Die Amerikanische Neutralität im Kriege 1939/1941', *Zeitschrift für ausländisches öffentliches Recht und Völkerrecht*, 11 (1942/3), pp. 445–76.

95 Berber, 'Die Amerikanische Neutralität im Kriege', p. 458.

96 W. Friede, 'Das Amerikanische Neutralitätsgesetz von 1937', *Zeitschrift für ausländisches öffentliches Recht und Völkerrecht*, 7 (1937), pp. 769–92, at p. 769.

97 F. Schlüter, Ferdinand 'Kelloggpakt und Neutralitätsrecht', *Zeitschrift für ausländisches öffentliches Recht und Völkerrecht*, 11 (1942/43), pp. 24–32, at p. 32.

98 E. M. Borchard, 'The Attorney General's opinion on the exchange of destroyers for naval bases', *American Journal of International Law*, 34:4 (1940), pp. 690–7, at p. 697.

99 Letter from S. Duggan to E. Borchard, 14 November 925, Edwin M. Borchard Papers, Box 19, File 229; Letter from C. Friedrich to E. Borchard, 22 January 1927, Edwin M. Borchard Papers, Box 21, File 250.

100 See, for instance, E. M. Borchard, '"Neutrality" and civil wars', *American Journal of International Law*, 31:2 (1937), pp. 304–6, at p. 306.

101 A. Auburtin, 'Zur Frage der auswärtigen Gewalt des Präsidenten der Vereinigten Staaten', *Zeitschrift für ausländisches öffentliches Recht und Völkerrecht*, 11 (1942/3), pp. 51–88, at p. 73, our translation.

102 W. Friede, 'Die Neutralitätsresolution vom 29. Februar 1936', *Zeitschrift für ausländisches öffentliches Recht und Völkerrecht*, 6 (1936), pp. 423–30, at p. 427.

103 Auburtin, 'Zur Frage der auswärtigen Gewalt des Präsidenten der Vereinigten Staaten', pp. 74 f.

104 Auburtin, 'Zur Frage der auswärtigen Gewalt des Präsidenten der Vereinigten Staaten', p. 76.

105 Auburtin, 'Zur Frage der auswärtigen Gewalt des Präsidenten der Vereinigten Staaten', p. 78.

106 C. Bilfinger, 'Die Kriegserklärungen der Westmächte und der Kelloggpakt', *Zeitschrift für ausländisches öffentliches Recht und Völkerrecht*, 10 (1940), pp. 1–23. See also Bilfinger, 'Streit um das Völkerrecht'.

107 Letter from C. Bilfinger to E. Borchard, 17 November 1945, Edwin M. Borchard Papers, Box 52, File 582.

108 F. Lange, 'Carl Bilfingers Entnazifizierung und die Entscheidung für Heidelberg. Die Gründungsgeschichte des völkerrechtlichen Max-Planck-Instituts nach dem Zweiten Weltkrieg', *Zeitschrift für ausländisches öffentliches Recht und Völkerrecht*, 74 (2014), pp. 697–731, at p. 705, 722.

109 Letter from C. Bilfinger to C. Schmitt, 5 July, 1933, Archive of the Max-Planck-Gesellschaft, Section III, Repositur 44, File 2, our translation.

110 Bilfinger, 'Die Kriegserklärungen der Westmächte und der Kelloggpakt', pp. 2 ff.

111 Bilfinger, 'Die Kriegserklärungen der Westmächte und der Kelloggpakt', p. 7.

112 Bilfinger, 'Streit um das Völkerrecht', p. 8, our translation.

113 Bilfinger, 'Streit um das Völkerrecht', p. 7, our translation.

114 Bilfinger, 'Streit um das Völkerrecht', p. 9.

115 Bilfinger, 'Streit um das Völkerrecht', p. 32, our translation.

116 C. Bilfinger, 'Friede durch Gleichgewicht der Macht?', *Zeitschrift für ausländisches öffentliches Recht und Völkerrecht*, 13 (1950/1), pp. 27–57, at p. 48, our translation.

117 E. M. Borchard and W.P. Lage, *Neutrality for the United States. Second Edition with New Material Covering 1937–1940* (New Haven, CT: Yale University Press, 1940), p. 293.
118 Borchard and Lage, *Neutrality for the United States*; Bilfinger, 'Die Kriegserklärungen der Westmächte und der Kelloggpakt', p. 14.
119 Kendall, 'Edwin M. Borchard and the defense of traditional American neutrality', p. 13.
120 Carr, *The Twenty Years' Crisis*.
121 I. Hall (2006): 'Power politics and appeasement: political realism in British international thought, c. 1935–1955', *British Journal of Politics and International Relations*, 8:2 (2006), pp. 174–92.
122 Letter from E. Borchard to C. Beard, 28 February 1946, Edwin M. Borchard Papers, Box 1, File 15.

7

The tale of the 'two Germanies': twentieth-century Germany in the debates of Anglo-American international lawyers and transitional justice experts

Annette Weinke

Recounting the history of twentieth-century international law as an antagonistic struggle between Germany and the 'West' will inevitably provoke well-founded criticism among historians. On the one hand, one can rightfully doubt whether any new and surprising insights can be expected from such a perspective. Spurred by fresh scholarly interest in the trajectories of International Law (IL), Human Rights Law (HRL) and Transitional Justice (TJ),[1] numerous monographs and anthologies have informed us about the contentious histories of so-called 'milestone' events like the Versailles Peace Treaty of 1919 and the 1945 International Military Tribunal at Nuremberg.[2] On the other hand, focusing on Germany's role as a subject and catalyst of international humanitarian law seems hopelessly anachronistic at a time when 'de-centring' European history has become the dominant trend in a growing literary corpus on international, transnational and global history.[3] Against this backdrop, one recent strand of historical scholarship has tried to reconstruct international humanitarian law from the margins by recovering the many hidden, lost or untold histories of war crimes tribunals that occurred beyond the shores of the transatlantic world.[4]

In the following chapter, I would like to address why and how twentieth-century Germany became something like a model case and a cautionary tale for international humanitarian law. By discussing selected writings and debates of Anglo-American international lawyers and TJ experts, it will be argued that international humanitarian law was construed discursively by means of a dualistic narrative that distinguished – either synchronically or chronologically – between different 'Germanies' viewed either as outsiders or as constituents of the Western world. While the first part of this chapter covers the debates from the First World War to the post-Second World War era – starting with the example of the Bryce Commission and ending with Allied war crimes policy in occupied Western Germany – the second section takes a big leap into the late

Cold War period by addressing the intellectual and ideological origins of the new sub-discipline TJ. Whereas the astonishing rise of this catch-all concept at the end of the 1980s seems to demonstrate the prevalence of this legalistic variant of liberal internationalism, TJ not only underwent several 'dramatic changes' and 'periodic crises',[5] but was, from the moment of its inception, hotly contested. Finally, a third section will take the example of a recent publication on the Kellogg-Briand Pact to discuss why Germany's role as a *bête noire* of IL has experienced a revival in current Anglophone legal historiography and how this might influence our understanding of international law.

Rather than simply assuming a given causal nexus between German acts of aggression and subsequent international debates about various legal coping strategies, this inquiry starts from a supposition first advanced by Critical Legal Studies and Postcolonial Studies.[6] According to this constructivist approach, IL and its offspring, international humanitarian law, are seen as corollaries of a variant of liberal internationalism and international legalism that evolved during the high times of European pre-eminence, inter-state rivalries and colonial expansionism in the last quarter of the nineteenth century and the first decades of the twentieth century. Though being deeply complicit in the racist ideologies and practices of European imperialism, its followers also promoted a 'progressive' or 'scientific' understanding of law as opposed to politics, and the idea of a 'global humanity' with common moral standards, shared by a transnational community of experts and enlightened citizens.

Due to the various 'cultural turns' in law and political sciences, critical assessment of international law's ideological roots and baggage has become the state of the art in legal historiography. Thanks to the studies of Martti Koskenniemi, Anne Orford, Antony Anghie, Gerry Simpson and Jo-Anne Pemberton, IL is no longer seen as the apogee of a triumphant Western civilisation,[7] but as a medium for re-orientation and re-assertion in times of a cumulative crisis of modernity. Reflecting these inherent tensions, Anne Orford has reminded us that 'international law guards the secret history of a modernity which is itself terrorised by the lack of any sovereign authority to guarantee the law or make sense of death'.[8] Influenced by the recent trend of a new global intellectual history,[9] a couple of works have investigated how different mechanisms of 'othering' were employed in the sphere of European and American international lawyers in order to demarcate the 'West' from the 'rest'. While during the nineteenth century and still in the first half of the twentieth century, a majority of the non-European world was prevented from being an active carrier of 'Christianity', 'humanity' and 'civilisation', countries like Tsarist Russia, the Ottoman Empire and the Wilhelminian Reich were generally perceived as more ambiguous cases.[10]

Though Germany's status as a Western 'civilised' power was only rarely disputed wholeheartedly, events like the Franco-German War of 1870–1 and the subsequent Prussian-led foundation of an empire nurtured a historical-philosophical discourse that accused Prussian authoritarianism of having betrayed Western values of civilisation by conducting 'Eastern barbarianism' into the heart of Europe. As Kim Christian Priemel shows in his *tour d'horizon* on the intellectual foundations of the Nuremberg Military Tribunal, influential voices in France and in the Anglophone world, like Lord Acton or the US naval strategist Alfred Thayer Mahan, popularised a dualistic concept of 'two Germanies' in constant struggle with each other.[11] While Madame de Staël's image of the 'land of poets and philosophers' still remained a persistent archetype for most of the nineteenth century, another distinct and more sinister stereotype took hold in the First World War and revolved around the 'Kaiser, the pan-Germanists and the militarists'.[12] Ironically, these early versions of a negative German 'special path' or *Sonderweg* to modernity were not only based on a specific reading of Kant and Hegel, but were also influenced by the German academic discipline of *Völkerpsychologie*.[13] Because of the rise of social Darwinist patterns of thought, the assumption of inherent national traits became a fashionable tool for rationalising ongoing hierarchies and inequalities in an increasingly globalised and interdependent world.

This inquiry is based on three interconnected conceptual assumptions and arguments. My first point is that the heuristic value of a *longue durée* perspective lies in its capacity to open up new insights about IL's various and complex entanglements with dominant strands of liberal internationalism.[14] A second argument is that it would be reductionist and naive to confine the history of international humanitarian law to a sequential codification of new norms. Instead, a selective analysis of international lawyers' debates proves that law's cultural implications were often more persistent than its legal and socio-political functions. Oscillating between a 'spirit of internationality' and state-based realism, international humanitarian law became the main communicative space where a transnational academic community mapped out for themselves the boundaries of an imagined 'Western civilisation'. This relates to the third argument, which pertains to the peculiar role of Germany in twentieth-century legal discourses. Due to processes of mobilisation and self-mobilisation among transatlantic intellectuals and international lawyers, the framing of Germany as an aggressor state and notorious violator of international rules already started before the century's 'great seminal catastrophe', to use George F. Kennan's famous phrase,[15] which is why the often assumed interdependence between 'ending a war' and 'making law' needs to be strongly relativised. This discourse entailed a dualistic image of 'two Germanies' – one peaceful and civilised, and the other militaristic and expansionist. Focusing on the interconnectedness of legal, political and ideological dimensions not only helps to explain why Germany became first a focal point of international law's discourses and practices, but also why during most of the twentieth century and even in the twenty-first century, punitive international legalism remained imbued with dichotomous notions of German history.

'A guilty despoiler of international law': rights imagination from the First World War to the Second World War

When war broke out in 1914, most internationalists considered this a heavy setback for their ideas and aspirations. Many adherents of IL and 'scientific pacifism' declared their loyalty to the war efforts of their political and military leaderships. But as Glenda Sluga has recently noted, within 'the spate of a year, the conflict's furious and relentless course had revived the relevance of internationalism as a political project'.[16] This was also the case with the related project of liberal legalism, a discipline at the cross-section of traditional diplomacy, legal reasoning and imperial propaganda. Shortly after the German invasion of Belgium, a transatlantic debate emerged that was shaped by the legalistic terminology of the two Hague Conventions of 1899 and 1907 and a moralistic, eschatological rhetoric which blamed the enemy for destroying the foundations of the civilised world.

Paradoxically, it was not the Entente powers, but the German side who first challenged the idea of a unified Western civilisation in its notorious 'Manifesto of the Ninety-Three'.[17] On 4 October 1914, ninety-three German university professors, intellectuals, artists and even eminent liberal legal scholars like Franz von Liszt, Paul Laband and Joseph Kohler issued a public statement in which they declared their allegiance to the Kaiser and his military advisors in the Prussian General Staff. Even more incendiary than the blunt justification of German legal violations as acts of 'self-defence' was that the manifesto to the 'cultured world' blamed the Entente powers for having betrayed the standards and customs of Western civilisation.[18] Since the Allies had concluded a pact 'with Mongols and Negroes' with the aim 'to eradicate the white race from the earth', they forfeited the privilege to act as 'defenders of European civilisation'.[19] While the majority of German legal scholars either supported or endorsed the war positivism of their government, Hans Wehberg belonged to the small circle of legal scholars who refused to sign the declaration. Wehberg first resigned from his position as editor of the *Zeitschrift für Völkerrecht* and later fired a public critique against his peers which also appeared in an English translation in the *American Journal of International Law*.[20]

Because of the persistence of revisionist interpretations in the Anglophone literature, the debate over Germany's war guilt and war crimes during the First World War is often downplayed as a mere 'battle of the manifestos'.[21] But as Benjamin Allen Coates has rightfully shown, especially among circles of British and American legalists, fighting against Germany was ideologically framed as a 'war for law'.[22] The destruction of the University of Louvain's medieval library, the sinking of the passenger liner *Lusitania* in 1915, the aerial bombardments of undefended Western cities by Zeppelins, the first use of poison gas in the attritional war at the Western front, mass executions of Belgian civilians and priests, the deployment of unarmed and therefore vulnerable prisoners of war (POWs) as forced labourers in the battlefield, the practice of unlimited submarine warfare, and the extra-legal executions of the British citizens Edith Cavell and Charles Fryatt formed the long list of incidents which not only incensed the populations in the enemy countries, but also caused moral indignation and strong anti-German sentiments among the neutrals.[23] The fact that these transgressions were perceived as outgrowths of a 'barbarian' mind became one of the catalysts for the implementation of a new mode of forensic historiography that intended to fuse juridical and historiographical methods for the purposes of fact-finding and documentation.

The governmental and non-governmental commissions for the documentation of German atrocities, which were created in France, Britain and Belgium in the first two years of the war, were the continuation of an undertaking that had been started by the Carnegie Foundation for International Peace in a different context.[24] A few weeks prior to the July crisis of 1914, a commission of European and American honoraries had published its final report on atrocities and human rights violations during the Balkan wars of 1912 and 1913. Although the inquiry missed its self-designated aim of providing the European and American public with a more realistic picture of the conflict, it nevertheless established a new and innovative format at the intersections of criminology, investigative journalism and historiography. In particular, the proclaimed mission to lead the semi-civilised people of the Balkans to a higher standard of scientific progress and humanity seemed to have inspired the Western allies in their strategy towards Germany and the neutral countries.

In December 1914, the British government appointed the British historian, jurist, statesman and retired diplomat James Bryce to investigate German transgressions in Belgium. A committee named after him was entrusted with the task of examining reports about military atrocities against Belgian civilians and assessing the veracity of anti-German allegations. Although the Bryce Commission was neither the first nor necessarily the most qualified body to take up the subject of war crimes – ironically, with Sir Frederick Pollock, there was only a distinguished historian of the law, but no international lawyers on board – it nevertheless became a turning point of the Allied propaganda campaign and related legal debates. A decisive factor was Bryce himself, who proved to be an excellent choice for the assignment. His biography as a former student in Heidelberg, an ardent sympathiser of German culture and recipient of the highest German medal seemed to guarantee that he would deliver a carefully weighed judgement on the matter. Even more important was the fact that he had converted from a principled opponent into a supporter of a British war entry. According to his later biographer H. A. L. Fisher, who despite his well-known anti-German attitudes had been included in the commission as well, it had been only the violation of Belgian neutrality which had caused Bryce to endorse the British war involvement and the Allied cause.[25] By this particular action, 'German militarism disclosed itself to him as the enemy of all that he valued most in European civilisation.'[26]

One can assume that these sentiments of deceit and betrayal further intensified when Bryce was confronted with the actual 'evidence', consisting of 1,200 depositions recounting German atrocities against Belgian soldiers and civilians. Most of them were interrogations of Belgian refugees in Britain conducted by British barristers who had been appointed for the purpose, but had been not under oath,[27] and a couple of diaries taken from fallen or captured German officers and soldiers. Although there was growing suspicion in the commission that Scotland Yard had also presented a couple of murky cases to them, Bryce nevertheless followed the recommendation of the Attorney-General and refrained from subjecting the given material to a comprehensive test by interrogating or cross-examining Belgian witnesses. In the end, Bryce seemed to have become a hostage of his self-restraint. According to the Australian historian Trevor Wilson, by accepting the official assignment, Bryce himself seemed to have embraced the same doctrine of state necessity he criticised the Germans for. Despite rising doubts about the validity of the depositions, he eventually decided to rely on the testimonies taken by third parties. Being aware that this method was at odds with his professional ethos as a historian and jurist, he built his judgement on what he considered as the 'larger truth' about German warfare in Belgium. But the epistemology behind this 'larger truth' was actually a subjective one because it did not care very much about the 'truth' and reliability of the individual cases. Instead of validating the concrete allegation of war crimes, Bryce aimed at establishing a metaphysical German 'guilt' for having violated what were considered to be the fundaments of Western civilisation. Like some of his liberally minded peers, Bryce identified the ruthless mentality and backwardness of the Prussian military caste as a universal problem and a major source of interstate conflicts.

Against that negative foil, he juxtaposed the image of the honourable, enlightened, fastidious Englishmen who had to take up the responsibility of eradicating wars.[28]

In May 1915 the commission published its damning and unequivocal verdict. In its final report comprising more than 300 pages and sold for the symbolic price of one penny, it accused the Germans of 'murder, lust, and pillage ... on a scale unparalleled in any war between civilised nations during the last three centuries – deeds committed, not because of in-discipline, but on a system and in pursuance of a set purpose'.[29] In its rhetoric, the report echoed Prime Minister Herbert Asquith's comment on the devastation of Louvain, calling it 'the greatest crime against civilisation and culture since the Thirty Years' War ... a shameless holocaust ... lit up by blind barbarian vengeance'.[30] Bryce's reputations as an esteemed liberal internationalist who had regularly intervened in the humanitarian disasters of the late nineteenth century – one example was his involvement in the investigation of the so-called Bulgarian horrors under Ottoman rule (1876) and another was his unwavering stance against the British scorched-earth policy in the Boer War – gave his judgement additional depth and integrity. Also, the fact that it appeared in the same month in which the *Lusitania* was sunk by German submarines ensured that the report found a receptive audience in the US as well. At least in the view of the British government, the investigation was considered a huge success in terms of winning over the American public. In a letter to Bryce, a British propaganda official exclaimed enthusiastically: 'Your report has swept America. As you probably know even the most skeptical declare themselves converted, just because it is signed by you.'[31]

A different question was what legal consequences would follow or, better, would *not* follow from Bryce's findings. The problem of how to enforce the regulations of the Geneva Conventions from 1864 and 1906 and of the Hague Conventions from 1899 and 1907 had been regularly discussed in the realms of international conferences, diplomatic meetings and legal organisations like the Institut de Droit International/ Institute of International Law (founded in 1873) or the Kriminalistische Vereinigung/International Union of Criminal Law (founded in 1888). The proposal of some cosmopolitan founding fathers to create either an international tribunal or an investigating committee for examining 'war crimes' and other violations of the laws of war had until then received only lukewarm resonance in these circles (the term was first coined in 1872 by the Swiss lawyer Johann Caspar Bluntschli). Due to the almost unchallenged status of the national sovereign state as the cornerstone of the international legal order, not only the law-averse national military elites but also conservative-liberal lawyers like Francis Lieber or John Westlake rejected these ideas as unrealistic, impractical or even dangerous. The

French, who had launched a few trials against German officers and soldiers in August 1914, abandoned this attempt after the German government raised the threat of reprisals against French POWs.[32]

In retrospect, Bryce's report marked a decisive turning point in the debates of international lawyers. Probably its most direct and profound effect was that Elihu Root and Theodore Woolsey, the latter President of the American Society of International Law, put the issue on the agenda of the Society's annual meeting scheduled for December 1915. It was in this milieu that Germany was now depicted as the antithesis of liberal legalism, and where the question of whether an international tribunal should be established to assess the deeds of the German Kaiser and its military caste was first contemplated. On this occasion, Root backed the idea of later punishment with the intriguing argument that 'international laws violated with impunity must soon cease to exist.'[33] At the request of the Scottish steel magnate Andrew Carnegie, Root drafted a resolution, signed by twenty-five trustees of the Carnegie Endowment for International Peace, which demanded international sanctions for violations against the 'rules of national conduct.'[34] It expounded the idea of the Hohenzollern regime as a morally deviant and illegitimate entity that should be excluded from the international system. According to Binoy Kampmark, this was a concept which had first appeared in Hugo Grotius' *Commentary on the Law of Prize and Booty* and was later echoed in John Westlake's 1894 formula that states could be either of 'good' or 'bad breeding.'[35] In 1919, the 'moral' or 'punishment' clauses of the Peace Treaty of Versailles further corroborated the framing of the Wilhelminian Empire as the ultimate 'other'. When the German delegation at the Paris Peace Conference protested against the losses of their former colonial territories by pointing to Weimar's already constrained economy, the Allied powers rebutted this with the argument that Germany as a nation had forfeited its former civilisational status. They called it unthinkable that 'any nation, calling itself civilised' would ever launch a war that was widely considered as 'the greatest crime against humanity and the freedom of peoples.'[36]

While extent to which the American President supported the diplomatic-legal approaches of his legal advisors is still a matter of historiographical dispute, there can be no doubt that his zigzag course did not strengthen, but undermined Allied efforts for the establishment of a coherent legalist international order. Wilson's lack of substantial knowledge of the European political ethnography impaired his policies on nationalities and minority rights, whereas his well-known ambiguity towards Germany and the German people further weakened the American position in the Four Power negotiations.[37] The positivist stance of US Secretary of State Robert Lansing, a representative of the

East Coast establishment and an experienced legal practitioner, played an important role in redirecting Allied discussions from the – presumably less important – matter of international (criminal) law to what he perceived as vital security issues of the Western world. Whereas he fully supported an interventionist course of democracy promotion vis-à-vis the defeated German Empire, he warned the Entente statesmen not to continue with their plans of a tribunal against the German Emperor. Any punitive policy, he exclaimed a few days before Wilhelm's abdication, would be 'foolish', since it would spawn Bolshevism, a more threatening problem than a 'Prussianised' Germany.[38] In the end, the American party endorsed not a juridical, but a political trial. It would personify – and considerably narrow – German 'guilt' by symbolically judging the Kaiser's offences against 'international morality'.[39] Since it was assumed that Germany's abrupt transformation into a democratic republic had demonstrated the superiority of an evolutionary and moderate interventionist approach, the Wilson administration and its conservative legal advisors discarded all schemes for a more expansive and visionary global rights order.

This lack of official American support notwithstanding, international liberal legalism experienced a modest boom in the interwar period. This also occurred because of the formation of pragmatic transnational alliances between Jewish jurists from Eastern Europe and German international lawyers who actively sought to advance minority rights in the context of the League of Nations system.[40] But this honeymoon ended in 1933, when Nazi Germany began to target international law and pan-Germanism revealed its ugly chauvinist and anti-Semitic face. A small group of Jewish émigré lawyers, mostly from Germany and Austria, were the first who would raise the crucial question of what the advent of Nazism would mean for the future of international law. Though the intellectual story of this cohort of legal scholars, who – as disillusioned liberal internationalists – later became adherents of a transformative Cold War realism, has stimulated a wave of biographical scholarship, it still needs to further historicisation.[41] Already in 1938, Hans (John) Herz, a former Kelsen scholar who had followed his mentor from Cologne to Zurich, provided the first in-depth analysis of a Nazified international law and its ramifications for the international order.[42] His book *Die Völkerrechtslehre des Nationalsozialismus*, published under the pseudonym Eduard Bristler, challenged liberal and Marxist rationalisations of German legal thinking under Nazism as the continuation of older, more familiar forms of radical particularism or national legal exceptionalism (*Sonderweg*).[43] Herz also discarded the deterministic belief of his Western peers that the irrational forces within the National Socialist Party would sooner or later yield to the more rational requirements of Germany's diplomatic, legal, scientific and business elites. Referring to Georgi Dimitrov's famous phrase of fascism as the last stage of capitalism, he stated:

> It may be possible to vindicate the thesis that National Socialism qua fascism is the most logical or at least comprehensible political form for a European country having reached late capitalism. It might be also true that the ideological basis of racial thought and its related doctrines could have been a precondition for the Nazi seizure of power. But that does not imply that the particular doctrine which has now become the ruling one could not entail consequences that alter the material fundaments of politics ... If we see things in such a perspective, 'false' terms, myths, and doctrines can shape reality as much as those true factors adapted to conditions and 'circumstances'.[44]

In an early anticipation of an influential International Relations discourse for which Mikkel Vedby Rasmussen retrospectively coined the term 'lessons literature',[45] Herz used the anthropomorphising devices of cognitive psychology in order to paint what he considered a more 'realist' picture of National Socialist understanding of IL. From this perspective, the German discipline *Völkerrecht* was not a contested ground where various individuals and schools competed with each other for assessing the true essence of Nazi foreign policy. Instead, legal thinking under National Socialism was depicted as part of a larger facade that the regime had erected with the support of its national legal elite in order to deceive the international community about its true objectives. It was a 'German' way of legal thinking because it undermined established traditions of reasoning about the stability in international affairs, and it was typically 'National Socialist' because its ultimate aim was that of subterfuge.

Whereas the proto-realist discourses of German-speaking émigré jurists advanced a line of thinking that presented Nazi legal discourses as a prime indicator for the 'fragility of international law and its institutions',[46] the wartime rights talk of American liberal legalists tended to take a more optimistic stance. The fact that this discourse was dominated by renowned and experienced international lawyers like James T. Shotwell and Quincy Wright, who had already served in Wilson's policy advisory group at the 1919 Paris Peace Conference, led to a certain re-evaluation of their former approaches towards Germany and IL.[47] In contrast to earlier discussions during the First World War, Germany's descent into Nazism was no longer blamed on Prussianism, militarism or an innate national character that had alienated Germans from Western values. Instead, spokespersons of America's wartime legal community adopted a popular metaphorical interpretation of contemporary Germany, which equated Nazism with a national disease or infection that had to be eradicated via the means of a globalised human rights system.[48]

In this vein, the Commission to Study the Organisation of the Peace stated in its 1944 report 'how easily' a nation could leap from 'internal oppression to external aggression, from the burning of books and of houses of worship to the burning of cities'. In the same style of stream-of-consciousness prose, it was further claimed that the 'diseased nation' had engaged in 'propaganda campaigns which spread the infection abroad and weaken[ed] the victim nation by germs of religious and racial hatred'. The document concluded with the self-confident diagnosis that 'international concern for individual human rights goes to the heart of realistic measures for wiping out aggressive war'.[49] A slightly different approach was taken by the largest non-Zionist organisation in the US, the American Jewish Committee (AJC). Although it shared the liberal internationalism and the human rights-centredness of Shotwell and other legalists, it was apparently unwilling to let the German people off as mere victims of a pathological leadership. Therefore, the AJC's 'Bill of Rights for All Nations' from November 1944 spoke not only of 'Hitlerism', but also of the 'bigotry and persecution of a barbarous nation' that was pitted against the rest of 'peace-loving nations'.[50]

Despite the efforts of various American legal think tanks and other non-governmental organisations to use the Nazi menace for the advancement of international humanitarian law, it took until the autumn of 1944 for the Roosevelt government to finally pick up the pressing issue of German war crimes. It was not the President himself, but his Secretary of the Treasury Henry Morgenthau, Jr., whose memorandum – later published under the title 'Germany is our problem' – kicked off the debate with a comprehensive post-war retribution scheme that put extra-legal executions over judicial proceedings. Among Morgenthau's co-authors were people like the German émigré jurist and economist Otto Nathan. He invoked the already familiar picture of Germany's fateful path from the Enlightenment to National Socialism ('Fichte, Hegel, Treitschke, and the Kaiser') to justify drastic measures like summary executions, forcible deportations and like the dismantling of industrial infrastructures and the deportation of populations.[51]

Although most members of Washington's political establishment shared Morgenthau's grim outlook, his freewheeling initiative nevertheless attracted harsh criticism. A few months before his departure from office, War Secretary Henry L. Stimson, *éminence grise* of the Republican Party and father of the foreign policy doctrine of non-recognition,[52] asked several members of his senior staff to conceptualise a counter-plan that would be in sync with the norms and customs of IL. In the end, it was not the academic luminaries of American law schools, but a group of Wall Street lawyers and German expatriate jurists who provided the legal and philosophical underpinnings for what later became the International Military Tribunal at Nuremberg. Confronted with the profound scepticism of Anglo-American lawyer-diplomats like Philip Jessup, their strategy was the retrospective 'judicialisation' of the 1928 Kellogg-Briand Pact,[53] in which they sidelined the traditional 'Westphalian' sovereignty doctrine in order to establish individual legal accountability for aggressive wars. In the words of Binoy Kampmark, with such a 'conceptual leap', the 'outlawing of war' was finally synchronised with the 'criminalisation of the warmaker'.[54] This came along with a historical imagination that perceived Hitler and the Japanese general Hideki Tojo as the latest incarnations of a long-held militaristic philosophy that had thrived under the ideological umbrella of IL since the days of European high imperialism. As William Chamberlain Chanler, one of the intellectual pioneers of the Nuremberg indictments, pointed out to the American criminologist Sheldon Glueck, missing the unique possibility to punish 'Hitler and his associates "for the crime of having initiated an unjust war"' would only strengthen the old theory that 'war is a natural and lawful enterprise, provided the rules are observed'.[55]

Whereas Chanler's remarks on the darker aspects of IL revealed an astonishing capacity for critical self-introspection on the victor's side, most Anglo-American prosecutors, judges and journalists at the Nuremburg courtroom refrained from such subtle analysis. Instead, they often preferred a kind of armchair psychology, like that advanced in Sebastian Haffner's book *Germany: Jekyll and Hyde* or in Louis Lochner's characterisation of the Nazis as a gang of bandits.[56] As a vulgarised version of the old *Sonderweg* topos, this psychopathological interpretation also found its way into the American successor trials, better known as the Nuremberg Military Tribunals (NMT). In Case 9 against the *Einsatzgruppen* leader, judge Michael Musmanno applied the Jekyll-Hyde metaphor on SS intellectuals like Otto Ohlendorf, whom he characterised *pars pro toto* as a 'split personality'.[57] After his return from Nuremberg, where he had observed the defendants in Case 1, the American psychiatrist Leo Alexander explained the complicity of his German colleagues with the Hegelian strands in German philosophy. The Germans, he mused in his later writings, had apparently not been able to replace their 'tribal superego' with the 'psychic control mechanism' that other nations had developed.[58] About half a century later, a new corpus of Anglophone TJ scholarship would adopt an inverted version of the negative German *Sonderweg* in order to promote the case of contemporary German history as a universal model for dealing with perpetrators and victims of state-sponsored violence.

The invention of a tradition: Germany in the rights talk of TJ experts

In 1990, shortly after the fall of the Berlin Wall, John Herz – the afore-mentioned eminent IR scholar – meditated on the vagaries of West Germany's *Vergangenheitsbewältigung*.[59] His 'dispassionate inspection',[60] as he called it, appeared in German, in a leading German-Israeli history journal. There he tackled the crucial question of how the Federal Republic of Germany had attempted to cope with the legacies of its Nazi past. The eighty-two-year-old author, now a retired political scientist and jurist, could hardly be called a novice in his field. After his emigration to the US, he had joined an academic group of experts at the Office of Strategic Services (OSS), which provided Washington's war administration with first ad hoc interpretations of the Third Reich. At the end of the war, Herz was temporarily involved in the conceptual preparation of the IMT and the Allied De-Nazification programme. It was also due to his disappointment about the premature abandonment of this policy that he gradually moved away from IL and became a leading expert in the newly emerging discipline of International Relations. After his retirement from City College of New York in 1977, he organised two influential conferences that dealt with the coping processes after the breakdown of several military dictatorships and authoritarian regimes, focusing on post-war Germany and Japan on the one hand, and Southern Europe on the other.[61] About ten years later, Herz reiterated his comparative approach in a paper submitted at the 'Justice and Society' conference of the Aspen Institute. In hindsight, this is often seen as the place where the 'intellectual framework'[62] of what would later become the 'proto science' TJ was crafted.[63]

Only recently have sociologists and historians begun to excavate the ideological origins of TJ. While some speak of an older pattern that emerged with the beginning of international humanitarian law,[64] others focus on the appearance of certain concepts and their subsequent implementation in different post-conflict societies. In her in-depth analysis of the discipline's early conceptual framing processes of the late 1980s and early 1990s, the American historian-activist Paige Arthur makes the point that the Aspen conference apparently structured TJ debates without predetermining them. The terminologies used in these discussions, Arthur maintains, 'were similar because the practical problems faced in various countries were understood in similar ways, and because the legitimate range of responses to those problems was defined similarly. This conceptual structure may have defined the emergence of the field, independent of whether individual participants were aware of it.'[65]

Arthur's observation that TJ experts showed a high degree of convergence and conformity in their normative view of twentieth-century 'transitions to democracy' is accurate and an important point of departure for further historicisation. However, a stronger focus on Western Europe and Germany would have made her argument even more compelling.[66] Contrary to her thesis that the early TJ debates were characterised by the absence of certain specificities of German *Vergangenheitsbewältigung* (like the famous *Historikerstreit* of 1986),[67] I would claim that references to a more or less fictive German 'case' played a pivotal role for the intellectual formation of the new sub-discipline. But what might appear to some as the early Germanisation of TJ[68] was in fact the re-interpretation and re-adaptation of an older, transatlantic model of democracy promotion applied after 1945 in the American Military Occupation zone of West Germany.[69] Its line of thinking sprang from the same US tradition, dating back to the early post-Second World War years that had produced an arsenal of 'civil affairs guides' and 'civil affairs handbooks' as contract research works conceived by the OSS scholars and funded by the Washington bureaucracy. It was with such works that the US military administration and its advisers prepared themselves for the mission of building a stable democracy in their own occupation zone within West Germany. In its close imbrication of scientific expertise with practical implementation of a specific model of political order, American occupation authorities stood out as a conspicuous example of what Lutz Raphael diagnosed as the 'scientification of the social'.[70]

The three volume compendium *Transitional Justice: How Emerging Democracies Reckon with Former Regimes*, edited in 1995 by Neil Kritz, is an illustrative example of how the case of post-war Germany was employed for what Arthur calls the premature 'canonisation' of TJ literature.[71] Of the forty-two texts presented in the first volume under the label *General Considerations*, only a few contributions were authored by German (émigré) authors. However, in the second volume on *Country Studies*, the two sections on Germany's dealing with the National Socialist and communist pasts occupied even more space than all Latin American countries did together. What was further striking about the chapter on post-war Germany (coping with its Nazi past) was how naively it reproduced the epistemic perspectives of the American occupation authorities and their German-American advisors, thereby reflecting a discussion that represented the academic state of the art of the late 1940s. Among the authors were well-known American-European 'democracy doctors' (Nicolas Guilhot) and adherents of Critical Theory like Otto Kirchheimer, Karl Löwenstein, John Dornberg and the already mentioned John Herz.[72] Their early classics about 'De-Nazification' and 'Militant democracy' in post-war Germany were seamlessly incorporated into contemporary TJ narratives as if these were presumably timeless documents without any context or historicity.

It was because of the editorial policy of Kritz & Co. that early TJ literature transmitted a picture of post-war Germany that could be called ambiguous at best. A conspicuous feature of the Kritz compendium and other early TJ reference texts was how they reconciled older and newer meta-narratives about a German *Sonderweg*, a specific Western 'didactic legality'[73] and the implications of the Cold War. In the newly constituted rights talk of TJ specialists, European twentieth-century history was construed in form of a modern morality tale with distinct periodic markers and clear-cut preconceived roles.[74] It was a narration which rejuvenated the image of Germany as the 'problem child' of international law, but one which had experienced multiple transformations under the auspices of Western power politics and the protective shield of a multilateral world order. While the older critical-realist paradigm of a 'De-Nazification fiasco' (John Herz) was conveniently buried under a reductionist interpretation of Cold War power struggles,[75] other episodes, like the premature unwinding of the Allied war crimes programme, the problematic history of West German *Vergangenheitsbewältigung* and the failed attempts of the United Nations' Law Commission in establishing a permanent International Criminal Court, were omitted.

With its emphasis on the forces of progress and moral reckoning, the emerging TJ discourse reflected the reigning *Zeitgeist* of a morally triumphant Western world that presumably could afford to obliterate the past intellectual and ideological antagonisms of the Cold War. Against this backdrop, early TJ literature presented post-war Germany as an exemplary case of successful democratisation via international humanitarian law. Moreover, the country was recommended as a role model for many of its Eastern European neighbours because it had successfully managed to cope with not only one, but two dictatorial pasts. This harmonious note was further complemented by the incorporation of a peculiar aspect of American-German-Jewish intellectual history that had been the cause for strong resentments in the immediate post-war years and in the early Federal Republic. Because American Jewish émigré scholars had been actively involved in the conceptualisation and implementation of the Allied war crimes policy and the De-Nazification programme, many Germans had often dismissed this policy with the contemptuous label of 'Jewish revenge'.[76]

Due to the rediscovery of left German-Jewish thinkers in the context of transnational TJ discourses, these early utterances of a barely hidden anti-Semitism were now veiled behind a depoliticised progressive storyline of a Westernised *Bundesrepublik* that fulfilled what Robert Moeller once poignantly called a 'usable past'.[77] Last but not least, it is plausible to contextualise this optimistic, utterly ahistorical discourse in the post-Cold War project of leading liberal internationalists seeking to amalgamate international law and IR.[78] While on the one hand, the canonisation of the OSS intellectuals in early TJ literature reflected the growing appraisal of American liberals for the 'apostate(s) of international law'[79] and their heritage of 'classical realism' in the age of neo-conservative interventionism, it could be also read as the expression of an epoch that was eager to build its grand moral narratives on the dramatic experiences of those and other victims of manmade twentieth-century disasters.

The German 'rogue' state in current legal histories

On 9 March 1918, a few days after Germany and the Soviet Union had signed their notorious Peace Treaty at Brest-Litovsk, the American magazine the *New Republic* published an article with the title 'The legal status of war'. Its author was Salmon Levinson, a grandson of German Jewish immigrants and successful corporate lawyer from Chicago. The article began with a hypothetical scenario:

> Suppose the world at peace. Abruptly Germany declares war upon France and invades her territories without even disguising the intention of annexation or even of reducing her neighbor to vassalage. What happens legally? What happens as far as international law is concerned? ... The resulting legal situation is in no uncertainty. Immediately the war comes under the sanction of international law. It is henceforth a 'legal war'.[80]

The book *The Internationalists*, written by the two US legal scholars Oona Hathaway and Scott Shapiro, uses the example of Levinson's piece in the *New Republic* to buttress its argument that 'outlawing law' was a decisively American enterprise triggered by a deeply felt moral indignation over German aggression. In their account, Levinson and his fellow legal internationalists are presented as hardworking men and pragmatic centrists 'with neatly trimmed mustaches' and 'wire-rimmed glasses', who lacked any kind of revolutionary fervour or ideological fanaticism.[81] Rather than becoming a part of the broad and heterogeneous American pacifist movement, these men acted alone and on the basis of their individual ethical convictions. In Levinson's case, Hathaway and Shapiro tell us in a chapter in their book, his lobbying for the outlawing of war was preceded by a personal revelation and a subsequent biographical conversion. It was 'the [German] torpedo that destroyed the Lusitania' that would turn the formerly unpolitical man into a committed legal activist.[82] Unsurprisingly, this historical argument is almost congruent with the protagonist's own rationalisations later laid down in his memoirs.

Hathaway and Shapiro's story of the Kellogg-Briand Pact appears to be a struggle of an 'Old World Order', where 'Might was Right', versus a 'New World Order', where aggressive wars eventually become 'illegal'.[83] With its dichotomous structure, the book fits perfectly into an already-established pattern of liberal internationalism that can be traced back to the First World War and the Manichaean style of the Bryce Report. It is a narrative which tends to couch the history of international humanitarian law in the metaphorical language of a biblical epos, thereby replacing the complexities of historical processes with compelling ideas and clear-cut identities.[84] Since the 'extreme' twentieth century has not become known for its stringent adherence to humanitarian ideas, such liberal accounts of IL are usually dependent on the existence of a *bête noire* that sets the forces of progress into motion. As I have argued in this chapter, for the longest time it was the case of twentieth-century Germany which fulfilled the function of a *bête noire* in the discourses of Anglo-American lawyers. Be it 'Prussian Militarism' and its archaic rituals of duelling, the anti-Western salvos of the political theorist Carl Schmitt or the ruthless legal transgressions of the Third Reich, the framing of Germany as the ultimate 'other', the 'great disturber of peace in the world',[85] and the antithesis of international law included a variety of exchangeable topoi which were able to persist independently of any given political context.

But even if we find these liberal accounts to be historically flawed, which they often are, this does not make them invalid or illegitimate. Rather, we might welcome this kind of historiography as a first step towards excavating the forgotten origins of a larger project that has for too long been buried under realist revisionism and the master narratives of the Cold War. However, to my mind, this would entail a blatant disregard of the harmful repercussions of long-term ideological patterns and biases in IL. In other words, it would overlook the extent to which liberal legalism has yet to come to grips with the fact that in most cases its discursive mechanisms of 'othering' had the practical effect of stabilising Great Power relations and the hierarchical 'Old World Order'. Especially in our post 9/11-age, when deformalism and a more robust form of interventionism have become the signature of IL, a new generation of international lawyers need to understand the nuances of a century-old legal discourse that equally served as a smokescreen for pure power interests and as a facilitator for emancipatory mobilisation. Reproducing IL's binary concepts instead of critically analysing them therefore carries the risk of obliterating these idiosyncrasies rather than understanding their continued importance.

Notes

1 While human rights law first emerged in 1945 in reaction to the extreme mass violence committed in the context of the Second World War and the Holocaust, TJ appeared in the late 1980s and early 1990s when, spurred by a series of regime changes in Latin America and Europe, American philanthropic organisations systematically fostered the global intellectual and practical exchange between human rights lawyers and activists in this field.

2 Donald Bloxham was one of the first historians who criticised the often naive assumptions of such 'milestone' historiographies of IL; D. Bloxham, 'Milestones and mythologies: the impact of Nuremberg', in P. Heberer and J. Matthäus (eds), *Atrocities on Trial: Historical Perspectives on the Politics of Prosecuting War Crimes* (London: Lincoln, 2008), pp. 263–82.

3 For an overview on this booming field of literature, see S. Nygard, J. Strang and M. Jalava, 'At the periphery of European intellectual space', in S. Nygard, J. Strang and M. Jalava (eds), *Decentering European Intellectual Space* (London: Brill, 2018), pp. 1–15.

4 K. Heller and G. Simpson (eds), *The Hidden Histories of War Crimes Trials* (Oxford: Oxford University Press, 2013).

5 A. Orford, 'A jurisprudence of the limit', in A. Orford (ed.), *International Law and its Others* (Cambridge: Cambridge University Press, 2009), pp. 1–32, at p. 2.

6 This is also the departure point of my latest monograph which puts Germany and conflicting interpretations of a German history of state-sponsored violence at the centre of a transnational discursive history of twentieth-century international criminal law; A. Weinke, *Gewalt, Geschichte, Gerechtigkeit. Transnationale Debatten über deutsche Staatsverbrechen im 20. Jahrhundert* (Göttingen: Wallstein, 2016) – English edition: A. Weinke, *Law, History, and Justice. Debating German State Crimes in the Long Twentieth Century* (Oxford: Berghahn Books, 2018).

7 J. A. Pemberton, 'Conceptualizing the West in international relations: from Spengler to Said', *Australian Journal of International Affairs*, 58:2 (2004), pp. 301–3.

8 Orford, 'A jurisprudence of the limit', p. 3.

9 S. Moyn and A. Sartori (eds), *Global Intellectual History* (New York: Columbia University Press, 2015).

10 M. Vec, 'Universalization, particularization, and discrimination. European perspectives on a cultural history of 19th century international law', *InterDisciplines*, 3:2 (2012), pp. 79–102; A. Becker Lorca, 'Universal international law: nineteenth-century histories of imposition and appropriation', *Harvard International Law Journal*, 51:2 (2010), pp. 475–552.

11 K. C. Priemel, *The Betrayal: The Nuremberg Trials and German Divergence* (Oxford: Oxford University Press, 2016), pp. 23–35.

12 L. Daudet, 'Contre l'esprit Allemand de Kant à Krupp, Paris 1915', p. 64, in Priemel, *The Betrayal*, p. 26.

13 E. Klautke, *The Mind of the Nation. Völkerpsychologie in Germany, 1851–1955* (New York: Berghahn Books, 2013).

14 G. Sluga, *Internationalism in the Age of Nationalism* (Philadelphia: University of Pennsylvania Press, 2015), pp. 19–44.

15 G. F. Kennan, *The Decline of Bismarck's European Order. Franco-Russian Relations, 1875–1890* (Princeton: Princeton University Press, 1979), p. 28.

16 Sluga, *Internationalism*, p. 32.

17 Professors of Germany, 'To the civilized world', *North American Review* 210:765 (1919), pp. 284–7; see also S. Harden, 'Reply to German professors', in *The American Verdict on the War: A Reply to the Manifesto of the German Professors* (Baltimore: Norman Remington, 1915).

18 This allegation meant the reversal of a statement by nine renowned British scholars who in August 1914 had called the war against Germany a 'sin against civilisation'; 'Scholar's protest against war with Germany', *The Times* (1 August 1914), p. 6.

19 'To the civilized world', 285. For the reactions of British intellectuals on the manifesto, see Leonie Holthaus, Chapter 3 in this volume.

20 See M. M. Payk, *Frieden durch Recht? Der Aufstieg des modernen Völkerrechts und der Friedensschluss nach dem Ersten Weltkrieg* (Berlin: De Gruyter/ Oldenbourg, 2018), p. 124; Wehberg's resignation note was published in *American Journal of International Law*, 9:4 (1915), pp. 924–7.

21 See P. Hoeres, *Krieg der Philosophen. Die deutsche und britische Philosophie im Ersten Weltkrieg* (Paderborn: Schöningh, 2004), pp. 127–9.

22 B. A. Coates, *Legalist Empire: International Law and American Foreign Relations in the Early Twentieth Century* (Oxford: Oxford University Press, 2016), p. 150.

23 I. V. Hull, *A Scrap of Paper: Breaking and Making International Law during the Great War* (Ithaca: Cornell University Press, 2014).

24 S. Troebst and D. Müller (eds), 'Der "Carnegie Report on the Causes and Conduct of the Balkan Wars 1912/13". Wirkungs- und Rezeptionsgeschichte im Völkerrecht und in der Historiographie', Special issue of *Comparativ*, 24:6 (2014); on the issue of war crimes investigations, see also J. Lemnitzer, 'International legal history: from atrocity reports to war crimes tribunals – the roots of modern war crimes investigations in nineteenth-century legal activism and First World War propaganda', in J. Waterlow and J. Schuhmacher (eds), *War Crimes Trials and Investigations: A Multi-disciplinary Introduction* (London: Palgrave Macmillan, 2018), pp. 111–56; A. Weinke, 'Wie neu ist die Suche nach Wahrheit?', in J. Brunner and D. Stahl (eds), *Recht auf Wahrheit. Zur Genese eines neuen Menschenrechts* (Göttingen: Wallstein, 2016), pp. 23–37, at p. 26.

25 T. Wilson, 'Lord Bryce's investigation into alleged German atrocities in Belgium, 1914–15', *Journal of Contemporary History*, 14:3 (1979), pp. 369–83, at p. 371.

26 H. A. L. Fisher, *James Bryce*, 2 vols (London: Macmillan, 1927), I, p. 127.

27 Wilson, 'Lord Bryce's investigation', p. 372.

28 On Bryce's contribution to the emergence of a historical-philosophical discourse on the German 'other', see Leonie Holthaus, Chapter 3 in this volume.

29 Wilson, ,Lord Bryce's investigation', pp. 378–79.

30 Weinke, *Law, History, and Justice*, p. 33.

31 Wilson, 'Lord Bryce's investigation', p. 370.

32 D. M. Segesser, *Recht statt Rache oder Rache durch Recht? Die Ahndung von Kriegsverbrechen in der internationalen wissenschaftlichen Debatte 1872–1945* (Paderborn: Schöningh, 2010), p. 196.

33 Segesser, *Recht statt Rache*, p. 199.

34 Carnegie Endowment for International Peace, 'Resolution of February 16, 1915', in *Carnegie Endowment for International Peace, Yearbook for 1915* (Washington DC: Carnegie Endowment for International Peace, 1915), quoted in B. Kampmark, '"No peace with the Hohenzollerns": American attitudes on political legitimacy towards Hohenzollern Germany, 1917–1918', *Diplomatic History*, 34:5 (2010), pp. 769–91, at p. 775.

35 Kampmark, '"No peace with the Hohenzollerns"'.

36 S. Pedersen, *The Guardians. The League of Nations and the Crisis of Empire* (Oxford: Oxford University Press, 2015), pp. 32–3.

37 M. Mazower, *Governing the World: The History of an Idea* (London: Allen Lane, 2012), p. 127.

38 R. Lansing, 'Memorandum on post-Berlin conditions and Bolshevism, October 28, 1918', cited in Kampmark, '"No peace with the Hohenzollerns"', p. 789.

39 'Outline. Suggested with Regard to Responsibility and Punishment', 9 April 1919, cited in B. Kampmark, 'Sacred sovereigns and punishable war

crimes: the ambivalence of the Wilson administration towards a trial of Kaiser Wilhelm II', *Australian Journal of Politics and History*, 53: 4 (2007), pp. 519–37, at p. 535.

40 J. Loeffler, *Rooted Cosmopolitans: Jews and Human Rights in the Twentieth Century* (New Haven: Yale University Press, 2018), p. 44.

41 See R. N. Lebow, 'German Jews and American realism', in F. Rösch (ed.), *Émigré Scholars and the Genesis of International Relations: A European Discipline in America?* (Basingstoke: Palgrave Macmillan, 2014), pp. 212–43; see also Felix Rösch, Chapter 8 in this volume.

42 P. M. R. Stirk, 'John H. Herz and the international law of the Third Reich', *International Relations*, 22:4 (2008), pp. 427–40; see also C Sylvest, 'Realism and international law: the challenge of John H. Herz', *International Theory*, 2:3 (2010), pp. 410–45.

43 H. Herz (E. Bristler), *Die Völkerrechtslehre des Nationalsozialismus* (Zürich: Europa-Verlag, 1938).

44 Herz (Bristler), *Die Völkerrechtslehre*, p. 191 (my translation).

45 M. V. Rasmussen, 'The history of a lesson: Versailles, Munich and the social construction of the past', *Review of International Studies* 29:4 (2003), pp. 499–519.

46 Lebow, 'German Jews', p. 233.

47 See Kampmark, 'No peace with the Hohenzollerns', 790.

48 See M. P. Bradley, *The World Reimagined: Americans and Human Rights in the Twentieth Century* (Cambridge: Cambridge University Press, 2016), p. 50.

49 Bradley, *The World Reimagined*, p. 49.

50 American Jewish Committee, 'A Bill of Rights for all nations', 19 November 1944; cited in Loeffler, *Rooted Cosmopolitans*, p. 107.

51 Priemel, *The Betrayal*, p. 67.

52 Coates, *Legalist Empire*, 175.

53 For this interpretation of the pact see the letter from Sheldon Glueck to William Chanler, 17 May 1945; printed in J. A. Bush, '"The supreme … crime" and its origins: the lost legislative history of the crime of aggressive war', *Columbia Law Review*, 102 (2002), pp. 2324–424, at p. 2416.

54 B. Kampmark, 'Punishing wars of aggression: conceptualizing Nazi state criminality and the US policy behind shaping the crime against peace, 1943–1945', *War & Society*, 37:1 (2018), pp. 38–56, at p. 42.

55 Chanler to Glueck, December 1944, in Bush, '"The supreme … crime"', p. 2402.

56 Priemel, *The Betrayal*, p. 40.

57 Priemel, *The Betrayal*, p. 299.

58 Priemel, *The Betrayal*, p. 300.

59 J. H. Herz, 'Bürde der Vergangenheit oder: Wie die Deutschen mit der Nazi-Hinterlassenschaft fertig wurden', *Tel Aviver Jahrbuch für Deutsche Geschichte*, 19:1 (1990), pp. 13–32.

60 Herz, 'Bürde der Vergangenheit', p. 14.

61 J. H. Herz (ed.), *From Dictatorship to Democracy: Coping with the Legacies of Authoritarianism and Totalitarianism* (Westport, CT: Greenwood Press, 1982).

62 P. Arthur, 'How "transitions" reshaped human rights: a conceptual history of transitional justice', *Human Rights Quarterly*, 31:2 (2009), pp. 329–30, at p. 327.

63 J. H. Herz, 'An historical perspective', in A. H. Henkin (ed.), *State Crimes: Punishment or Pardon* (Queenstown, MD: Aspen Institute, 1989); S. Lefranc and F. Varire, 'The emergence of transitional justice as a professional practice', in L. Israel and G. Mouralis (eds), *Dealing with Wars and Dictatorships: Legal Concepts and Categories in Action* (The Hague: T.M.C. Asser/Springer, 2014), pp. 235–52, at p. 236.

64 G. J. Bass, *Stay the Hand of Vengeance: The Politics of War Crimes Tribunals* (Princeton: Princeton University Press, 2000).

65 Arthur, 'How "transitions" reshaped human rights', p. 355

66 Arthur's analysis deals mostly with the discussion on Latin American countries.

67 Arthur, 'How "transitions" reshaped human rights', p. 332.

68 In this vein, see G. Mouralis, 'The invention of "transitional justice" in the 1990s', in Israel and Mouralis, *Dealing with Wars*, pp. 83–100, at pp. 96–8.

69 Weinke, *Law, History, and Justice*, pp. 161–162.

70 Weinke, *Law, History, and Justice*, p. 162.

71 Arthur, 'How "transitions" reshaped human rights', pp. 331, 334.

72 N. J. Kritz, 'The dilemmas of transitional justice', in N. J. Kritz (ed.), *Transitional Justice: How Emerging Democracies Reckon with Former Regimes*, vols 1–3 (Washington DC: US Institute of Peace Press, 1995), pp. xix–xxx, at p. xix; N. Guilhot, *Democracy Makers. Human Rights and the Politics of Global Order* (New York: Columbia University Press, 2005).

73 This is a coinage by L. Douglas, *The Memory of Judgement: Making Law and History in the Trials of the Holocaust* (New Haven: Yale University Press, 2000).

74 A critical appraisal of this legalistic version of twentieth-century history is provided in C. S. Maier, 'Consigning the twentieth century to history alternative narratives for the modern era', *American Historical Review*, 105:3 (2000), pp. 807–31.

75 J. H. Herz, 'The fiasco of Denazification in Germany', *Political Science Quarterly*, 63:4 (1948), pp. 569–94.

76 The author of this text has tackled the subject of a Nuremberg-generated anti-Semitism in the context of the study on the West German Foreign Office; E. Conze, N. Frei, P. Hayes and M. Zimmermann, *Das Amt und die Vergangenheit* (Berlin: Blessing, 2010), pp. 421–35.

77 R. G. Moeller, *War Stories: The Search for a Usable Past in the Federal Republic of Germany* (Berkeley: University of California Press, 2003).

78 See P. Akhavan, 'Are international criminal tribunals a disincentive to peace? Reconciling judicial romanticism with political realism', *Human Rights Quarterly*, 31:3 (2009), pp. 624–54; S. Moyn, 'The international law that is America: reflections on the last chapter of *A Gentler Civilizer of Nations*', *Temple International Law & Comparative Law Journal*, 27:2 (2013), pp. 399–415, at p. 407.

79 Moyn, 'The international law that is America', p. 401.

80 S. Levinson, 'The legal status of war', *New Republic* (9 March 1918).
81 O. A. Hathaway and S. J. Shapiro, *The Internationalists: How a Radical Plan to Outlaw War Remade the World* (New York: Simon & Schuster, 2017), p. 108.
82 Hathaway and Shapiro, *The Internationalists*, p. 107.
83 Hathaway and Shapiro, *The Internationalists*, p. xvii.
84 The Canadian legal historian Frédéric Mégret poignantly speaks of a 'summoning history' with respect to recent publications on the history of international criminal law: 'For all our authors, history seems a *passage obligé* in tracing the fortunes of international criminal justice, one that provides the story with both the veneer of age and the character of an epic struggle. Almost all take us through what is by now a fairly familiar routine, from Kaiser Wilhelm (occasionally Napoleon) onwards, to Nuremberg, the Cold War interlude, and the revival of international criminal justice in the 1990s...' F. Mégret, 'The politics of international criminal law', *European Journal of International Criminal Law*, 13:5 (2002), pp. 1261–84, at p. 1265.
85 P. Maguire, *Law and War. An American Story* (New York: Columbia University Press, 2001), p. 69.

8

The silent presence: Germany in American post-war International Relations

Felix Rösch

On 14 February 1966, the *Coburger Tageblatt*, a local newspaper from Coburg in Northern Bavaria, published an article, mentioning the American scholar Hans Morgenthau. The following day, a correction appeared in the *Tageblatt* after a letter had reached the editor, informing the newspaper that Morgenthau was a native of Coburg.[1] This small episode illustrates a wider phenomenon. The German[2] (intellectual) roots of scholars like Morgenthau, who were forced to leave Germany during the 1930s[3] and often found refuge in the US, were no longer noticed after the Second World War to the extent that they became all but forgotten. Their scholarship was no longer situated in the liberal democratic milieu of Weimar Germany that upheld humanistic educational ideals and was sympathetically critical of Marxist thought, but theirs were connected to an American liberalism turned idealism that lacked the intellectual modesty and self-reflexivity that the Weimar version argued for. In short, émigrés had turned into 'hyper-American[s]', as Golo Mann once put it.[4]

The intention of this chapter is to investigate the processes that led to this 'silencing'. How was it possible that their German intellectual socialisation that continued to inform their political thought became overlooked and indeed no longer even realised? It is argued that German émigrés and American International Relations (IR) constitute a case of successful integration. Before this argument is further expounded, it has to be acknowledged that émigré scholars partly caused this silencing themselves. After their forced emigration, they were at pains to adjust their research and teaching to the different intellectual and historical backgrounds of their American colleagues and students. This not only happened in order to find employment in a higher education sector that was under severe financial constraints, but also to avoid being perceived as enemy aliens during the Second World War. Still, while their own silencing contributed to it, it does not provide a fully satisfying answer.

To this end, their integration into American IR has to move into the focus. Already early contributions on émigré scholars, while intending to account for the intellectual loss that Germany suffered from the exodus of numerous scholars and the resultant gain for the American academic world, implicitly engaged with their integration.[5] However, these contributions that Catherine Epstein calls *Beitragsgeschichte* struggled to illuminate their integration much beyond simple dichotomies of loss and gain, and also in later contributions, émigrés were treated in a static way.[6] By using concepts like assimilation,[7] integration was charted as a one-sided effort until émigrés eventually 'had been absorbed into American society'.[8] In this sense, Nicolas Guilhot's reading of émigrés turn to IR theory as a 'realist gambit', highlighting 'a case of intellectual irredentism, resisting its own integration into American social sciences',[9] evokes images of a failed assimilation, as it implies that these scholars, who were critical of American behaviouralism, deliberately withdrew from mainstream academia.

More recent contributions, by contrast, explained the silencing of the German intellectual background of émigré scholars through acculturation,[10] providing a more nuanced, long-term outlook by considering it as an 'interactive process embedded in cultural settings that are themselves fluid enough to change'.[11] This perspective is sustained by considering the private life of émigrés. Even though their impressions of Germany remained 'ambivalent',[12] they often maintained close personal and intellectual ties with Germany and among themselves, as they could 'respond to a quotation from Goethe with a quotation from Heine', as Elisabeth Young-Bruehl[13] put it for the circle around Hannah Arendt. Acculturation even helps to understand Guilhot's claim of a realist gambit, as it was 'at times most successful through opposition to then-current cultural norms' in the US.[14]

However, the conceptual extensiveness of acculturation makes it difficult to chart the integration of émigré scholars. Including cases of (deliberate) separation (and segregation) from the wider society distracts from the often unintentional assemblages of knowledge exchanges, internal and external developments, and personal networks that brought their successful integration about. Before proceeding, two caveats have to be mentioned. First, some émigrés indeed deliberately withdrew from American society and academia, as they could not cope with the changed environment and their changed societal status.[15] Still, a significant amount of émigrés had 'brilliant career[s]'.[16] Second, success is not defined in terms of a linear process, progressing to a predefined, static majoritarian position, as is the case with assimilation. Rather, success implies that all involved groups have the opportunity and the urge to participate in wider societal debates. This might include conflicts and can occasionally entail setbacks, but it does exclude segregation and separation. To capture these constellations, the relations between émigré scholars and American IR have to be seen as a functional integration, as developed amongst others by Richard Münch and recently reconsidered by Philipp Ther.[17] Integration in this sense does not have a normative connotation, but accepts that the arrival of immigrants initiates a messy, partly reversible process, meandering without an absolute end. In this process, functional integration also gradually affects the majoritarian position, moving towards the position of émigrés. This is because integration happens through participation in which immigrants have the opportunity to voice their interests and ideas and have them debated. It also means that they can and have to listen to others' interests and ideas, and debate them with the majoritarian society.

Employing this notion of integration to understand how some émigré scholars could academically excel in the US, while at the same time their German roots were no longer noticed, the rest of the chapter proceeds in three steps. First, the spaces that facilitated the integration between émigrés and their American coevals are being investigated. While there were particular places that gave émigrés and American scholars more opportunities to collaborate, referring to them as spaces of integration acknowledges the role that specific people and institutions played in creating them. Spaces are therefore understood as a 'capacity', highlighting their 'becoming, an emerging property of social relationships'.[18] Second, the importance of language and translation is discussed. In order to integrate, people need to be able to speak to each other. This required from émigrés translating the concepts that informed their political thought into English. The final section investigates the moment when each group's thought started to get affected by the exposure to different kinds of thinking and the multitude of impressions that they made in the process of integration. It highlights how this exposure influenced IR in the US for much of the second half of the twentieth century.

Spaces of integration: New York, Chicago and beyond

Reconsidering the integration of émigré scholars in American IR has to begin at the specific spaces in which these processes took place. This might sound trivial. However, without them, no integration could have taken place. The different groups would have at best lived next to each other, but they would not have been able to establish cohabitation in the sense of creating common life-worlds.

While these spaces are important, they did not exist everywhere. With the exception of cities like Chicago, most émigré scholars lived either on the East Coast or the West Coast, which offered more opportunities for the newly arrived. However, living in the same cities neither meant that they were an intellectually coherent group, nor did it make them into one; rather, they had a range of different experiences and careers in the US. For some like Viennese legal positivists, empirical sociologists and logical empiricists, it was relatively easy to find employment at American universities and attract significant research grants, due to their affinities with American behaviouralism.[19] Others like Arnold Wolfers and Hajo Holborn, the 'Wunderkind'[20] of Weimar history, profited from their prominent position in Germany.[21]

Yet, for most émigrés, starting a new life was difficult. They were at the beginning of their career, had only few contacts in the US and struggled to adjust to a different academic environment. Before finding his first academic position at Brooklyn College, where he had to teach 'just about everything under the sun',[22] Morgenthau worked as an elevator boy.[23] John Herz, Ernst Borinski and Ossip Flechtheim, by contrast, were part of about fifty émigré scholars who initially only found positions at universities for African Americans, again experiencing racism against themselves and their students.[24] When this group of scholars crossed the Atlantic, racial segregation with Jim Crow laws in effect until the 1960s was still common in the US. Hence, most white American scholars would not have considered accepting such positions, as it might have affected their careers negatively. Even Hannah Arendt had a meagre start, initially working for *Aufbau*, the German-language Jewish newspaper in New York, the *Review of Politics*, founded by fellow émigré Waldemar Gurian,[25] and the Jewish Cultural Reconstruction.

One of the reasons why their integration in the US was aggravated was that their arrival coincided with the Great Depression. Unemployment rose to an unprecedented scale, also affecting the university sector. Certainly, with Franklin D. Roosevelt's New Deal, the American government tried to attenuate the effects of the Great Depression through financial reforms, work creation schemes and welfare programmes, of which the Tennessee Valley Authority is perhaps the most famous.[26] However, the university sector, providing employment only to a relatively small group of people, was not the government's priority and given that university budgets were also strained during this time, new faculty openings reduced significantly. Competing with American colleagues for the few available positions, émigrés, by then not yet naturalised citizens, often found themselves to be unsuccessful. For the same reason, philanthropic foundations like Ford, Rockefeller and the Carnegie Corporation of New York were also reluctant to support émigré scholars 'because they represented competition for jobs that young American academics would otherwise fill'.[27]

On top of these financial constraints, émigrés were also affected by anti-Semitism in the US.[28] After 1933, for example, hotels restricted access for Jews, while landlords advertised their apartments with the addition 'no

Jews'.[29] Even at universities, some faculty members would openly voice their convictions and many universities like Columbia, Cornell, Harvard, Johns Hopkins, Princeton and Yale used quota systems to minimise the intake of Jewish students and scholars.[30] In Morgenthau's papers at the Library of Congress, numerous letters with anti-Semitic content are preserved. At one point, he even complained to Walter Lippmann that: 'I receive every day letters with xenophobic … and anti-Semitic attacks, not to speak of anonymous telephone calls … This goes to show how thin the veneer of political civilisation is.'[31] Indeed, for Franz Neumann, who like Morgenthau worked for Hugo Sinzheimer in Frankfurt before his emigration, the US in the 1930s was even more anti-Semitic than Germany.[32]

However, despite these obstacles, many émigré scholars made important contributions to American science, and IR is a particular case in point. Reasons for this, ranging from expert knowledge about Germany otherwise unavailable in the United States to an intellectual open-mindedness, particularly among younger American colleagues at times when the self-understanding of the US was challenged, are further detailed below. At this point, it suffices to reflect on the specific spaces that fostered their integration.

Particularly since the outbreak of the Second World War, expert knowledge that émigré scholars offered came in demand in the US, as the American government could not source it from elsewhere. Providing 'an arsenal of knowledge', as Udi Greenberg calls it,[33] made these scholars sought after employees at newly founded government institutions, such as the Office of War Information, the Experimental Division for the Study of Wartime Communication at the Library of Congress, and the Psychological Warfare Division of the Supreme Headquarters of the Allied Expeditionary Force. Most famous, however, was the Office of Strategic Services (OSS), which was established in 1942. This forerunner of the Central Intelligence Agency (CIA) made ample use of émigrés' expertise, having amongst others Wolfers, Holborn, Herz, Neumann, Ernst Fraenkel and Hans Speier on its payroll.[34] Even Frankfurt School Marxists like Otto Kirchheimer and Herbert Marcuse worked for the OSS. This ideological open-mindedness is remarkable, given that only a few years later, Joseph McCarthy took action against (alleged) communists during the early stages of the Cold War. Even semi-private institutions like the Rand Corporation (initially part of Douglas Aircraft) profited from émigrés. Speier, for example, became the first Director of its Social Science Division in 1948.[35]

Most, however, were appointed to academic positions, particularly at universities in Chicago, New York, Los Angeles and the Bay Area.[36] In New York, the entire political spectrum of émigré scholars was represented, as not only members of the Frankfurt School worked at Columbia University before they moved to California, but also more right-leaning scholars like Ernst Jäckh. Yet perhaps the most well known is the University in Exile at the New School in New York. Indeed, many universities at that time were relieved that the University in Exile had been established, as it provided an 'alibi' for other universities.[37] They could recommend highly qualified émigrés to this institution rather than having them compete with American scholars for the few academic positions available. Its first director, Alvin Johnson, sought opportunities to accommodate émigrés who had reached the US with the help of the Academic Assistance Council and the Rockefeller Foundation.[38] The latter provided the initial funding for the University in Exile and, with Kenneth Thompson later occupying leading positions at the Rockefeller Foundation, it actively encouraged further intellectual exchanges.

Working at the University in Exile provided émigré scholars with the space to engage with like-minded American scholars in collaboration to achieve similar cosmopolitan ambitions.[39] As Ned Lebow remarks and as confirmed by the New School's Graduate Faculty Meeting Records, in contrast to the Francophone members of the *Ecole Libre des Hautes Etudes*, who were also based at the New School, the Germanophone émigrés actively sought this engagement as most of them saw the US as their new permanent home.[40] Consequently, soon after their arrival, academic outlets were established to facilitate intellectual engagement. At the New School, a workshop on intellectual exile was organised as part of its Graduate Faculty's fourth anniversary celebrations and émigré scholars began publishing *Social Research* in 1934.[41] At Notre Dame, as mentioned above, Gurian had founded the *Review of Politics* in 1939, and later *Dissent*, amongst others established by Lewis Coser and Henry Pachter, served a similar purpose.[42] Quickly, these journals turned into mouthpieces for émigré scholars, allowing them to promulgate their ideas among American academics.

Equally, the Charles R. Walgreen Foundation provided space for integration with its lecture series at the University of Chicago between 1937 and 1956. This so far under-researched lecture series was part of a donation, the terms of which stipulated an increasing knowledge of the American way of life among students. Each year, a scholar was invited to give a series of lectures, and what is important for the argument of this chapter is less that it brought forward some of the most remarkable contributions to political theory in the twentieth century, but rather that many émigré scholars were asked to speak about their views on US politics and culture. Eric Voegelin's *The New Science of Politics* (1952), Leo Strauss' *Natural Right and History* (1953), and Arendt's *The Human Condition* (1958) were first drafted for the *Walgreen Foundation Lecture Series*. Other speakers included Hans Simons, the former director of the *Deutsche Hochschule für Politik*, and Karl Löwenstein.[43] However, to what extent émigré scholars supported each other in being given the possibility to speak at this lecture series is a question for further research. Correspondence at the Morgenthau Archive indicates that Morgenthau was involved in suggesting potential speakers, as was Strauss.[44]

Yet, establishing spaces where émigrés and their American peers could meet and exchange their thoughts was just a preliminary step towards integration. As the next section will show, to bring about integration as a mutually relational process, language and translation take centre stage.

Adjusting to American academia: translating German intellectual thought

In order to integrate, people need to be able to talk to each other. To this end, a common language has to be established.[45] As the émigrés arrived in a country where English was the official language, communication required more effort from them. They had to learn the language and ensure the translation of their German political thought.

For many of these scholars, this meant that they had to demonstrate proficiency in a language they had not studied profoundly prior to their emigration. German humanistic secondary education required the study of Latin and ancient Greek, but it did not arrange for the study of English in a way that enabled practical competence. Consequently, many émigrés had to quickly learn English in their late twenties or early thirties and initially faced significant difficulty in making contributions to American intellectual discourses, as confirmed rather polemically by Carl Zuckmayer; while speaking to students at the University of Zurich, Zuckmayer stressed that learning English was the most daunting task to master.[46] Indeed, many of the leading figures in early IR retained a strong accent throughout their lives, although they often achieved a linguistic mastery that surpassed many of their native-speaking peers.[47] Trying to achieve this mastery required significant effort. Voegelin, for example, mentioned that he had to learn to distinguish the 'social stratification of language', meaning that, with the help of American colleagues, he had to acquire the capacity to appropriately address his intended audience by distinguishing different English vernaculars.[48]

However, learning and even mastering a new language is not yet sufficient to establish communication that enhances integration. Rather, people have to align different 'system[s] of intelligibility', meaning that émigré scholars were set with the task of introducing their concepts into a new context and making them common among their American interlocutors.[49] Given that these concepts are defined rigorously and offered intellectual clarity in one linguistic context, attaining a similar stage in a new linguistic context is challenging.[50] However, introducing new concepts does not mean that émigré scholars were forced to shape them into coherence, but it does mean that translation is a 'reciprocal wager'. It rests on the 'desire for meaning as value and a desire to speak across, even under least favourable conditions. The act of translation thus hypothesises an exchange of *equivalent* signs and makes up that *equivalence* where there is none perceived as such'.[51] In doing so, people can experience emotional liberation, as their creativity is being stimulated; they are given the opportunity to critically reflect upon themselves as well as upon their socio-political and cultural backgrounds, thus developing empathy towards others in a new environment.

In their recent delineation of literate ethics, Hartmut Behr and Xander Kirke emphasise the ability to contextualise knowledge in order to avoid misunderstandings or misrepresentations.[52] In other words, contextuality is a first step towards meaningful translations that cannot be accomplished by a simple transliteration or metaphrase.[53] Contextuality requires the translator to have a critical understanding about the cultural memory that contributed to the establishment of knowledge in the original context. This kind of memory is situated in the everyday, as it is objectified in cultural artefacts, for example, texts, rituals and ceremonies that have shaped a community over a long period of time. The resulting 'figures of memory' create a stable, yet gradually changing intellectual horizon to which people refer while creating knowledge. Cultural memory therefore acknowledges the hybridity and multi-dimensionality of intercultural encounters and it also recognises specific spatio-temporal patterns that guide these encounters.[54] Thus, the translation of knowledge into a new context requires its spatio-temporal localisation because a thorough understanding of these figures of memory provides the possibility of a deeper understanding about the historical discourses that have shaped knowledge, as these figures provide the intellectual framework upon which knowledge is being constructed.[55]

Shortly after their arrival in the US, the contextualisation of their knowledge was still unproblematic for émigré scholars. All of them had received an extensive humanistic education, meaning they were well aware of German figures of memory. Still, as Pachter recollected, 'our language froze at the point of emigration, or it even became poorer for want of a dialogue with the people who create and develop speech every day'.[56] It follows that émigré scholars were painfully aware that cultural memory was gradually changing due to the constant reconfigurations of social relationships. In order to retain the ability to contextualise their knowledge, they had to keep engaging with German thought collectives. Substantial engagement with German politics after their emigration is evidenced by many émigré scholars. In addition, many émigré scholars repeatedly returned temporarily to Europe after the end of the Second World War to retain the connection with their former intellectual horizon. Morgenthau was teaching at the Salzburg Seminar in American

Studies from 1950 to 1976 and, with the support of the Rockefeller Foundation, he spent time at its Villa Serbelloni (Bellagio Center) at Lake Como in Italy.[57] Equally, Herz frequently crossed the Atlantic and took up visiting professorships at the University of Marburg and the Free University of Berlin.[58] With the support of the German Academic Exchange Service (*Deutscher Akademischer Austauschdienst*; DAAD), the University of Heidelberg also regularly invited émigré scholars to give lectures. Some such as Voegelin, Fraenkel and Arnold Bergstraesser even returned permanently.[59]

In a second step, this contextualised knowledge needs to be introduced into a new context related to existing knowledge. Relationality requires that an understanding about the constellations of the new societal context needs to be developed because in order for people to make use of new forms of knowledge, they need to be able to relate it to their own cultural memory in order to give it meaning and even consider it for their own life.[60] However, due to its spatio-temporal contextuality, knowledge resists identical transplantation. It is more likely that knowledge is transformed in the process of introducing it into a new context, as people engage with it through different perspectives. In their effort to remove knowledge from its original context, émigré scholars therefore had to demonstrate self-reflexivity and, to paraphrase Brent Steele, contextually reconstruct it by bringing 'it to bear upon … problems [in its new context] or to speak to debates in a scholarly field'.[61] As mentioned above, a metaphrase is not sufficient, as a 'one-to-one' translation does not take the original spatio-temporal context into account. Furthermore, it also lacks the translator's self-reflexivity in terms of the new context, as it does not engage in a contextual reconstruction. As Robbie Shilliam notes, translation is a 'generative act', requiring careful balancing.[62] The constellations of the original context have to be reflected in the translation, while at the same time meaning adjustments have to take place in order to satisfy the demands of the new context. This careful balancing is evidenced in Arendt's work. For the German editions of some of her most well-known books – *Origins of Totalitarianism* (1950), *The Human Condition* (1958) and *On Revolution* (1963) – Arendt neither commissioned a professional translator nor translated it herself; rather, she rewrote them, leading to significant changes. This not only allowed her to clarify some of the unresolved questions in the English editions, but also enabled her to pursue her primary intention of enhancing the books' readability for her German audience, as she rewrote them with a different cultural context in mind.[63]

Certainly, Arendt is an extreme, yet not solitary, example. On the basis of Roger Hart's taxonomy, several linguistic devices can be discerned that were used on a larger scale by émigrés in order to ensure reciprocal wagering. One common method through which German philosophical terms were introduced into American academia is calques.[64] These are 'root-to-root' translations of complex notions. The resulting neologisms are an addition to the existing thesaurus and once they are codified, they lose their direct perceptibility as being loanwords. Calques are evidenced as concepts that enriched intellectual discussions of the Weimar Republic and also guided the ideas of émigré scholars during their careers in the US. Compassion (*Mit-Leiden*), worldview (*Weltanschauung*), thought style (*Denkstil*), and world postulate (*Weltwollung*) are such concepts. The latter three were made popular not least through Mannheim's influential *Ideology and Utopia*, and their calques were used frequently by émigré scholars in their own work.[65] However, as Hart notes, prior to their codification, calques, like metaphrases, require 'lengthy explanations and commentaries' that many émigrés were not prepared or not able to provide.[66] Morgenthau's case, in which he was reminded by Michael Oakeshott about the incommensurability of his concepts – for instance, power, objectivity and rationality – with his Anglophone audience, is illuminating here and so are the well-documented consequences of the resulting misunderstandings.[67]

Despite the lack of explanation and the inability or unwillingness to comment on their meaning, this offers evidence for a second linguistic device that was used more often in their writings. With the help of semantic extensions and, more commonly, synecdoches as semantic reductions, émigrés also aimed to translate their German knowledge into the American context and to propagate it among their interlocutors. With these devices, émigrés made contributions to ongoing discussions in American academia. Arendt frequently made references to the Federalists and even used the example of town-hall meetings in order to visualise her concept of the civic sphere.[68] Even more obvious is the usage of these devices in the writings of Morgenthau. He instructed his assistants in Chicago to search for anglophone examples and references, and substitute them for the existing German ones in order to make his writings more accessible for his American audience.[69] The semantic reduction of *Macht* and *Kraft* or *pouvoir* and *puissance* to power in Morgenthau's American writings can therefore be understood as his acquiescence, as his concept of power became not only an accepted contribution to IR discourses, but also one that still exerts considerable influence today.[70]

German émigrés and American IR: a symbiosis

In this final section, the moment when émigrés' thought started to have an effect on American IR is captured. This section re-assures us that knowledge is conditioned in space and time, as it is formed in social relationships, and the case of émigré scholars and American IR is no exception: their knowledge was sometimes retained, but more often it was re-arranged and altered in processes of collective formation. Eventually, the integration of émigré scholars reached a stage of what has repeatedly been characterised as a symbiosis.[71]

This symbiosis was initiated by the will of most émigrés to make a contribution to American intellectual discourses and society at large because, as mentioned, they considered the US as their new home. Even émigrés like Voegelin, who later returned to Germany, wanted to become Americans, after having 'been thrown out of Austria by the National Socialists'.[72] Certainly, the expert knowledge that many Weimar scholars offered in the first years after their emigration helped in this regard. During the 1930s and 1940s, émigré scholars offered expert insight on the downfall of the Weimar Republic and the rise of Nazism in Germany that became especially sought after when the US entered war in 1941.[73]

Carl Joachim Friedrich and Hannah Arendt are to this day known to a wider public for their work on totalitarianism, not least because it also proved important during the Cold War. Equally, while Neumann and Fraenkel contributed the most insightful elaborations on the NSDAP's infiltration of government institutions, Ernst Cassirer traced the intellectual origins that contributed to the rise of Nazism shortly before his premature death in 1945. Even Hans Kelsen, who in contrast to other émigrés had less of an impact in the US,[74] profited from his knowledge regarding German jurisdiction in his work on communist law. Offering expert knowledge, as mentioned above, was not restricted to the academic realm, as many of the émigrés worked for government institutions like the OSS during the Second World War.

Occasionally, however, their expertise was also rejected. Morgenthau recollected with bitterness that the American government did not call upon him when expertise on Spain was required, although he had close connections to Spanish scholars and politicians since he had worked in Madrid.[75] Still, offering expert knowledge and their expertise on the rise of Nazism in particular proved indispensable for many émigré scholars as it not only helped them to find entry into American academic discourses, but also to find employment. Consequently, '[i]t is no exaggeration to say that at that time we [émigré scholars] needed the Nazis as our raison d'être', as Pachter accentuated.[76]

However, while the offering of expertise can initiate integration, it cannot sustain it. To this end, émigrés' German knowledge had to gain meaning-value, as Lydia Liu calls it, in the American context.[77] Through intercultural interplays of adjustment, this can mean that knowledge remains unaltered, but it is more likely that it will be reduced, enlarged or potentially even changed completely. At this point, it helped that particularly younger American faculty members approached émigrés' German political thought in an open-minded manner, given that the Great Depression and the entry of the US into the two World Wars had challenged their self-understanding.[78] As summed up by Holborn: 'America was in a state of crisis. Would the German immigration have happened ten years earlier, its intellectual outcome would probably have been marginal ... as intellectual questions would not have been of much concern in a prosperous country.'[79] As a consequence, calibrating between external and existing knowledge, American scholars *and* émigrés were encouraged to rethink their commonly accepted knowledge, leading to creative meaning-value reconsiderations. As argued by Paul Tillich, these calibrations, offering 'a common chance',[80] were not free of 'productive misunderstanding[s]'[81] because both sides initially lacked the expertise to contextualise knowledge in its original context. Still, they were productive, as they informed further discourses.

Perhaps the most well known of these misunderstandings is Kenneth Waltz's reading of Morgenthau's contribution to IR. As Waltz stated in the introduction to his article 'Realist thought and neorealist theory', it was the work that originated out of integration spaces of émigré scholars and American IR that stimulated his thought during the beginning of his career.[82] One of these spaces, the Rockefeller-supported 1954 Conference on International Politics had such a significant impact on the discipline's theorising that Guilhot even sees it as the birthplace of IR theory.[83] Indeed, this and related conferences like the Council on Foreign Relations study group on IR theory that met between 1953 and 1954 were major moments in émigré scholars' integration. They provided the space to discuss their views on international politics with American interlocutors who belonged to the discipline's luminaries at that time. Morgenthau and Wolfers participated, as well as Reinhold Niebuhr, Paul Nitze and William Fox.

Furthermore, as recently highlighted by Adam Humphreys, the insights achieved at these conferences incited young scholars like Waltz to voice their criticism of the dominating liberalism in American IR at that time and to further theorise the 'pragmatic sensibility' that informed their thought.[84] However, Waltz's scientism was not free from normative aspirations either, and his reading of Morgenthau was indeed a misunderstanding.[85] Still, it was 'productive' because émigré scholars' knowledge allowed Waltz to question commonly accepted liberal assumptions and, to this day, neorealism has retained a decisive influence on the discipline, at least in the US. Hence, although the example of Waltz demonstrates that the engagement with émigré thought did not establish more creative and humane world politics per se, it did create the space to rethink world politics.

However, the integration of émigrés not only affected American scholarship, but their research also changed. Living in a different continent caused a shift in the topics they were concerned about. Certainly, anti-Semitism, the Holocaust and the worries about democracy remained a constant driver of their thoughts,[86] but their critique of behaviouralism and the unchallenged belief in scientific progress, of which Morgenthau's *Scientific Man vs. Power Politics* (1946) and *Science: Servant or Master?* (1972) are perhaps the most famous examples in IR of their thoughts. However, their critique of behaviouralism only developed in detail after their experience of it in the US.[87] Indeed, many émigrés highlighted that their marginal position helped them to contribute to major American discourses during the mid-twentieth century, as they were able to see the issues at stake from a different perspective.

Yet, being an immigrant also affected the approaches they engaged with. This is most obvious in the case of the *Institut für Sozialforschung*, commonly referred to as the Frankfurt School. Before their emigration and in the years immediately after it, members of the Frankfurt School like Max Horkheimer, Theodor Adorno and Marcuse mainly worked within the tradition of Continental European philosophy, sociology and psychoanalysis.[88] However, partly due to dwindling financial means, gradually its members used methods that were more common in the US, such as survey research. Thomas Wheatland even speaks of a 'marriage of social philosophy and empirical research' in this regard.[89] While Wheatland argues that this happened mainly to 'camouflage' their Critical Theory underpinnings,[90] I am more inclined to follow Eva-Maria Ziege, who showed that the confrontation with American society during their exile in New York and California also led to significant changes in their theorising that opened their work up to methods they would not have considered previously. This is evidenced in some of their major empirical projects during their American years, such as *Antisemitism among American Labor* (1944–5) and *The Authoritarian Personality* (1950) as part of the *Studies in Prejudice* series.[91]

As these examples highlight, the functional integration of émigré scholars into American IR eventually created a symbiosis. Gradually gaining insights into both historical and intellectual horizons allowed them to fuse their experiences, enabling them to make significant contributions to American intellectual discourses.[92] As Johnson put it solemnly in commemorating the twenty-fifth anniversary of the New School, 'it was the purpose of the organisers of the New School to draw together in close relations this body of true Americans and true scholarship, that the Republic might take no permanent injury from the obscurantists and reactionaries.'[93]

To demonstrate this intellectually stimulating and mutually benefiting symbiosis, a case in point is Morgenthau's contribution to the conceptualisation of the national interest, a topic that dominated American foreign policy discourses in the mid-twentieth century. Morgenthau's contribution demonstrates that speaking to an audience does not mean that one has to conform to mainstream assumptions. Rather, an émigré scholar like Morgenthau often contributed to discourses in sympathetic opposition, as he approached intellectual questions with a different epistemological perspective as well as socio-political values and experiences.[94]

Morgenthau understood the national interest as an epistemological tool that could be used to capture the multitude of interests within a political community, which then have to be taken into consideration by political decision-makers in formulating a common good. With his interpretation of the national interest, Morgenthau criticised attempts for reification within American academia and the wider general public. Guilhot's reading of these scholars in taking a gambit and creating IR theory as a 'separatist movement'[95] is therefore too ambitious. Certainly, émigré scholars were critical of American academic discourses, but this did not mean that they were restraining themselves from contributing to these discourses or that they rejected American democracy. On the contrary, with their different perspectives and subsequent oppositional stances, they aimed to reinvigorate these discourses and they focused on the thought collective that was becoming the most important field of American social sciences.[96]

Conclusion

Elsewhere, I have urged to break the silent presence of Germany in American IR and this chapter has investigated this issue in more detail.[97] This silence is curious given that many of the key figures like Morgenthau during the early years of the discipline's institutionalisation in the US were refugees from Germany, but, as this chapter has shown, their successful integration quickly established them as American scholars. Many émigrés had impressive careers and in cooperation with their American peers – sometimes through productive misunderstandings – they were able to influence the discipline's discourses for many years to come. However, it should not be forgotten that productive as their integration may have been, the resulting discourses were often not free of 'ironic, tragic, and [sometimes even] brutal consequences'.[98]

With the recent revival of classical realism and the historiographic turn in IR, the intellectual origins of their work moved into the limelight again.[99] Experiencing the downfall of the Weimar Republic, turning from a liberal democracy that attracted creative intellectuals (*Kulturschaffende*) globally into a brutal totalitarian dictatorship that organised a genocide on an unprecedented scale and set the world on fire within a few years, these changing images of Germany were thoroughly enshrined in the scholarship and political activism of people like Morgenthau, Herz and Arendt in the US to an extent that current IR scholarship finds inspiration in their thought. In the political realities of twenty-first-century international politics, their thoughts on populism,[100] the protection of republican ideals[101] and nuclear deterrence[102] led to important interventions, and even helped cosmopolitan scholarship 'to stay sober'.[103]

Notes

1 Library of Congress, Manuscript Division, Hans J. Morgenthau papers, 1858–1981, Container 185.

2 Referring to the émigrés as Germans does not mean that all of them were born in this country, but they were from Central Europe (*Mitteleuropa*). However, the term 'Germany' has been chosen in accordance with Johan Galtung's notion of a common intellectual style; J. Galtung, 'Structure, culture, and intellectual style: an essay comparing Saxonic, Teutonic, Gallic and Nipponic approaches', *Social Science Information*, 20:6 (1981), 817–56.

3 Reference to the 1930s is important, as it excludes scholars who had arrived earlier in the US like Robert Strausz-Hupé, Carl Joachim Friedrich and Nicolas Spykman. It also excludes 'the second generation' of émigrés like Heinz Eulau, Walter Laqueur and Raul Hilberg; A. W. Daum, H. Lehmann, and J. J. Sheehan (eds), *The Second Generation: Émigrés from Nazi Germany as Historians* (New York: Berghahn Books, 2016).

4 G. Mann in J. Radkau, *Die deutsche Emigration in den USA. Ihr Einfluß auf die amerikanische Europapolitik 1933–1945* (Düsseldorf: Bertelsmann Universitätsverlag, 1971), p. 219; all translations are mine.

5 For example, Radio Bremen, *Auszug des Geistes. Bericht über eine Sendereihe* (Bremen: Heye & Co., 1962); A. Heilbut, *Exiled in Paradise: German Refugee Artists and Intellectuals in America, from the 1930s to the Present* (New York: Viking, 1983); L. Coser, *Refugee Scholars in America: Their Impact and Their Experiences* (New Haven: Yale University Press, 1984).

6 C. Epstein, 'Schicksalsgeschichte: refugee historians in the United States', in H. Lehmann and J. J. Sheehan (eds), *An Interrupted Past: German-Speaking Refugee Historians in the United States after 1933* (Cambridge: Cambridge University Press, 1991), pp. 116–35, at p. 117.

7 For example, H. S. Hughes, *The Sea Change: The Migration of Social Thought, 1930–1965* (New York: Harper & Row, 1975); O. P. Pflanze, 'The Americanization of Hajo Holborn', in Lehmann and Sheehan (eds), *An Interrupted Past*, pp. 107–79; G. Steinmetz, 'Ideas in exile: refugees from Nazi Germany and the failure to transplant historical sociology into the United States', *International Journal of Politics, Culture, and Sociology*, 23:1 (2010), pp. 1–27.

8 Hughes, *The Sea Change*, p. 1.

9 N. Guilhot, 'The realist gambit: postwar American political science and the birth of IR theory', in N. Guilhot (ed.), *The Invention of International Relations Theory: Realism, the Rockefeller Foundation, and the 1954 Conference on Theory* (New York: Columbia University Press, 2011), pp. 128–61, at p. 130.

10 For example, H. A. Strauss, H. P. Kröner, A. Söllner and K. Fischer, 'Wissenschaftstransfer durch Emigration nach 1933', *Historical Social Research*, 13:1 (1988), pp. 111–21, at p. 115; M. Ash and A. Söllner (eds),

Forced Migration and Scientific Change: Émigré German-Speaking Scientists and Scholars after 1933 (Cambridge: Cambridge University Press, 1996); M. Lang, 'Vom Political Scholar zum Global Citizen? Perspektiven der Emigrationsforschung', in F. Schale, E. Thümmler and M. Vollmer (eds), *Intellektuelle Emigration. Zur Aktualität eines historischen Phänomens* (Wiesbaden: Springer VS, 2012), pp. 223–47, at p. 244.

11 M. Ash and A. Söllner, 'Introduction: forced migration and scientific change after 1933', in Ash and Söllner (eds), *Forced Migration and Scientific Change*, pp. 1–20, at p. 12.

12 Library of Congress, Manuscript Division, Hans J. Morgenthau papers, 1858–1981, Container 178.

13 E. Young-Bruehl, *Hannah Arendt: For Love of the World* (New Haven: Yale University Press, 2004), p. xiv.

14 Ash and Söllner, 'Introduction', p. 12.

15 A tragic example is Gustav Ichheiser. Having spent eleven years in a mental hospital, he was 'reduced almost to a vegetable', eventually committing suicide; H. J. Morgenthau, *Political Theory and International Affairs: Hans J. Morgenthau on Aristotle's The Politics* (Westport: Praeger, 2004), p. 41.

16 C. Frei, *Hans J. Morgenthau: An Intellectual Biography* (Baton Rouge: Louisiana State University Press, 2001), p. 74.

17 R. Münch, 'Elemente einer Theorie der Integration moderner Gesellschaften. Eine Bestandsaufnahme', *Berliner Journal für Soziologie*, 5 (1995), pp. 5–24; P. Ther, *Die Außenseiter. Flucht, Flüchtlinge und Integration im modernen Europa* (Berlin: Suhrkamp, 2017). Although David Kettler and Thomas Wheatland do not call their approach 'functional integration', highlighting the continuous transatlantic assemblages speaks the same language as Ther: D. Kettler and T. Wheatland, 'Contested legacies: political theory and the Hitler era', *European Journal of International Political Theory*, 3:2 (2004), pp. 117–20.

18 A. Jiménez, 'On space as a capacity', *Journal of the Royal Anthropological Institute*, 9:1 (2003), pp. 137–53, at p. 140.

19 J. G. Gunnell, *The Descent of Political Theory: The Genealogy of an American Vocation* (Chicago: University of Chicago Press, 1993), p. 183; Hughes, *The Sea Change*, p. 34.

20 A. Vagts in Pflanze, 'The Americanization of Hajo Holborn', p. 171.

21 Both were professors at the Deutsche Hochschule für Politik: G. A. Ritter, *German Refugee Historians and Friedrich Meinecke, 1910–1977: Letters and Documents* (Leiden: Brill, 2010); R. Eisfeld, 'From the Berlin Political Studies Institute to Colombia and Yale: Ernst Jaeckh and Arnold Wolfers', in F. Rösch (ed.), *Émigré Scholars and the Genesis of International Relations: A European Discipline in America?* (Basingstoke: Palgrave Macmillan, 2014), pp. 113–31.

22 H. J. Morgenthau, 'Postscript to the transaction edition: Bernard Johnson's interview with Hans J. Morgenthau', in K. W. Thompson and R. J. Myers (eds), *Truth and Tragedy: A Tribute to Hans J. Morgenthau* (New Brunswick: Transaction Books, 1984), p. 367.

23 R. N. Lebow, *The Tragic Vision of Politics: Ethics, Interests, and Orders* (Cambridge: Cambridge University Press, 2003), p. 219.

24 G. S. Edgomb, *From Swastika to Jim Crow: Refugee Scholars at Black Colleges* (Malabar: Krieger Publishing Company, 1993).

25 E. Thümmler, 'Totalitarian ideology and power conflicts – Waldemar Gurian as international relations analyst after the Second World War', in Rösch (ed.), *Émigré Scholars and the Genesis of International Relations*, pp. 132–53.

26 U. Greenberg, *The Weimar Century: German Émigrés and the Ideological Foundations of the Cold War* (Princeton: Princeton University Press, 2014), p. 51. Helge Pross reports that of the 27,000 scholars working at American universities, 2,000 were made redundant between 1930 and 1933: H. Pross, *Die Deutsche akademische Emigration nach den Vereinigten Staaten 1933– 1941* (Berlin: Duncker & Humblot, 1955), p. 49.

27 C. D. Krohn, *Intellectuals in Exile. Refugee Scholars and the New School for Social Research* (Amherst: University of Massachusetts Press, 1993), p. 78.

28 M. Lamberti, 'The reception of refugee scholars from Nazi Germany in America: philanthropy and social change in higher education', *Jewish Social Studies*, 12:3 (2006), pp. 157–92, at p. 159.

29 E. M. Ziege, *Antisemitismus und Gesellschaftstheorie. Die Frankfurter Schule im amerikanischen Exil* (Frankfurt: Suhrkamp, 2009), p. 57.

30 D. Bessner, '"Rather more than one-third had no Jewish blood": American progressivism and German-Jewish cosmopolitanism at the New School for Social Research, 1933–1939', *Religions*, 3:1 (2012), pp. 99–129, at p. 108.

31 H.J. Morgenthau, 'Letter to Walter Lippmann', 6 May 1965 (Library of Congress, Manuscript Division, Hans J. Morgenthau papers, 1858–1981, Container 36).

32 R.N. Lebow, 'German Jews and American realism', in Rösch (ed.), *Émigré Scholars and the Genesis of International Relations*, pp. 212–43, at p. 221.

33 Greenberg, *The Weimar Century*, p. 93.

34 Lebow, 'German Jews and American realism'; Radkau, *Die deutsche Emigration in den USA*.

35 Krohn, *Intellectuals in Exile*, p. 175; D. Kettler and T. Wheatland, '"Has Germany a political theory? Is Germany a state?" The foreign affairs of nations in the political thought of Franz L. Neumann', in Rösch (ed.), *Émigré Scholars and the Genesis of International Relations*, pp. 103–12, at p. 106.

36 Radio Bremen, *Auszug des Geistes*, p. 88; G. Stourzh, 'Die deutschsprachige Emigration in den Vereinigten Staaten: Geschichtswissenschaft und Politische Wissenschaft', *Jahrbuch für Amerikastudien*, 10 (1965), pp. 59–77, at p. 74; W. Bleek, *Geschichte der Politikwissenschaft in Deutschland* (Munich: C. H. Beck, 2001), p. 251; J. Vecchiarelli Scott, 'Alien nation: Hannah Arendt, the German émigrés and America', *European Journal of Political Theory*, 3:2 (2004), pp. 167–76, at p. 168.

37 Krohn, *Intellectuals in Exile*, p. 76.

38 A. Johnson, 'The intellectual in a time of crisis', *Social Research*, 4:3 (1937), pp. 282–5, at pp. 284–5.

39 Gunnell, *The Descent of Political Theory*, p. 187; Bessner, '"Rather more than one-third had no Jewish blood"', p. 100; W. E. Scheuerman, 'The (classical) realist vision of global reform', *International Theory*, 2:2 (2010), pp. 246–82.

40 Lebow, 'German Jews and American realism', p. 221; The New School Archives, 'Graduate Faculty Minutes', 25 May 1943 (Container 1, The New School Archives, Graduate Faculty Meeting Records, NS.02.11.01).

41 A. Johnson, 'Fourth anniversary: The Graduate Faculty of Political Science and Social Science', *The New School for Social Research Bulletin*, 11 (1937), The New School Archives, NS030102_bd370329.

42 A further example is the short-lived magazine *Measure*, which was published by the Committee on Social Thought at the University of Chicago and edited by the art historian Otto von Simson; Stourzh, 'Die deutschsprachige Emigration in den Vereinigten Staaten', p. 75.

43 Stourzh, 'Die deutschsprachige Emigration in den Vereinigten Staaten', p. 59.

44 Library of Congress, Manuscript Division, Hans J. Morgenthau papers, 1858–1981, Container 178; see also A. Söllner, *Deutsche Politikwissenschaftler in der Emigration: Studien zu ihrer Akkulturation und Wirkungsgeschichte* (Wiesbaden: Westdeutscher Verlag, 1996), p. 19.

45 L. H. Liu, 'Introduction', in L. H. Liu (ed.), *Tokens of Exchange* (Durham, NC: Duke University Press, 2000), pp. 1–12, at p. 1.

46 C. Zuckmayer, 'Amerika ist anders', *Neue Schweizer Rundschau*, 16:8 (1948), pp. 451–74, at p. 455.

47 Lebow, 'German Jews and American realism', p. 179; Lamberti, 'The reception of refugee scholars from Nazi Germany in America', p. 179; Guilhot, 'The realist gambit', p. 130; R. N. Lebow, 'Karl Deutsch and international relations', *International Relations*, 28:3 (2014), pp. 288–95, at p. 288; P. M. Kristensen, 'Revisiting the "American Social Science": mapping the geography of International Relations', *International Studies Perspectives*, 16:3 (2015), pp. 246–69, at p. 248.

48 E. Voegelin, *Autobiographical Reflections* (Columbia: University of Missouri Press, 2011), pp. 86–7. The philosopher Robert Ulich made similar remarks in an interview in 1958: Radio Bremen, *Auszug des Geistes*, p. 42.

49 X. Guillaume, '*Agencement* and traces', in M. Acuto and S. Curtis (eds), *Reassembling International Theory* (Basingstoke: Palgrave Macmillan, 2012), pp. 106–12, at p. 108.

50 D. Jacobi, 'On the "construction" of knowledge and the knowledge of "construction"', *International Political Sociology*, 5:1 (2011), pp. 94–7, at p. 97; S. Guzzini, 'The ends of international relations theory: stages of reflexivity and modes of theorizing', *European Journal of International Relations*, 19:3 (2013), pp. 521–41, at p. 536.

51 L. H. Liu, 'The question of meaning-value in the political economy of the sign', in Liu (ed.), *Tokens of Exchange*, pp. 13–41, at p. 34, emphasis in original.

52 H. Behr and X. Kirke, 'People on the move – ideas on the move: academic cultures and the problematic of translatability', in Rösch (ed.), *European Émigré Scholars and the Genesis of International Relations*, pp. 21–39, at pp. 29–30.

53 Liu, 'The question of meaning-value', pp. 19–20.

54 J. Assmann, 'Collective memory and cultural identity', *New German Critique*, 65 (1995), pp. 125–33, at p. 129.

55 Jacobi, 'On the "construction" of knowledge', pp. 96–7.

56 H. Pachter, 'On being an exile: an old-timer's personal and political memoir', *Salamagundi*, 10–11 (1969–1970), pp. 12–51, at p. 18. Irma Thormann, Morgenthau's wife, made a similar remark after their emigration to the US: 'I have retreated like a hedgehog into myself … having little interest in others. I have

lost the ability to act ... because I cannot put experiences into context anymore ... This ability is rooted in the Fatherland (*Vaterland*) ... the country that gave us culture.' I. Thormann, 'Letter to Unidentified Woman' (Leo Baeck Institute Archives, Hans Morgenthau Collection, AR 4198, Container 2, Folder 9).

57 H. J. Morgenthau, 'Letter to Charles A. McClelland', 16 March 1949 (Library of Congress, Manuscript Division, Hans J. Morgenthau papers, 1858–1981, Container 185).

58 J. H. Herz, *Vom Überleben. Wie ein Weltbild entstand* (Düsseldorf: Droste, 1984), pp. 150–6.

59 S. Liebold, 'Arnold Bergstraesser und Fritz Caspari in Amerika', in Schale, Thümmler and Vollmer (eds), *Intellektuelle Emigration*, pp. 89–110. For a critical reading of Bergstraesser, see R. Eisfeld, *Ausgebürgert und doch angebräunt: Deutsche Politikwissenschaft 1920–1945* (Baden-Baden: Nomos, 1991), p. 79.

60 Jacobi, 'On the "construction" of knowledge', p. 96; Behr and Kirke, 'People on the move – ideas on the move', pp. 32–3.

61 B. Steele, 'Context and appropriation: the risks, benefits and challenges of reinterpretive expression', *International Politics*, 50:6 (2013), pp. 739–52, at p. 741.

62 R. Shilliam, *German Thought and International Relations: The Rise and Fall of a Liberal Project* (Basingstoke: Palgrave Macmillan, 2009), p. 13.

63 V. Jung, 'Writing Germany in exile: the bilingual author as cultural mediator: Klaus Mann, Stefan Heym, Rudolf Arnheim and Hannah Arendt', *Journal of Multilingual and Multicultural Development*, 25:5–6 (2004), pp. 529–46, at p. 532; S. Weigel, 'Sounding through – poetic difference – self-translation: Hannah Arendt's thoughts and writings between different languages, cultures, and fields', in E. Goebel and S. Weigel (eds), *Escape to Life. German Intellectuals in New York: A Compendium on Exile after 1933* (Berlin: De Gruyter, 2012), pp. 55–79, at pp. 71–3. See also H. J. Sigwart, *The Wandering Thought of Hannah Arendt* (London: Palgrave Macmillan, 2016).

64 R. Hart, 'Translating the untranslatable: from copula to incommensurable worlds', in Liu (ed.), *Tokens of Exchange*, pp. 45–73, at pp. 60–1.

65 H. Arendt, *On Revolution* (London: Penguin, 1973), p. 75; E. Voegelin, *Modernity without Restraint* (Columbia: University of Missouri Press, 1999), p. 60; Morgenthau, *Political Theory and International Affairs*, pp. 100–1.

66 Hart, 'Translating the untranslatable', p. 61.

67 H. J. Morgenthau, 'Letter to Michael Oakeshott', 22 May 1948 (Library of Congress, Manuscript Division, Hans J. Morgenthau papers, 1858–1981, Container 44). See also W. Bain, 'Deconfusing Morgenthau: moral inquiry and classical realism reconsidered', *Review of International Studies*, 26:3 (2000), pp. 445–64; H. Behr and A. Heath, 'Misreading in IR theory and ideology critique: Morgenthau, Waltz, and neo-realism', *Review of International Studies*, 35:2 (2009), pp. 327–49; F. Rösch, 'The human condition of politics: considering the legacy of Hans J. Morgenthau for International Relations', *Journal of International Political Theory*, 9:1 (2013), pp. 1–21. For similar experiences of Karl Deutsch, see J. Ruzicka, 'A transformative social scientist: Karl Deutsch and the discipline of international relations', *International Relations*, 28:3 (2014), pp. 277–87.

68 H. Arendt, *Denken ohne Geländer. Texte und Briefe* (Munich: Piper, 2005), pp. 243–5.

69 Frei, *Hans J. Morgenthau*, p. 219; Shilliam, *German Thought and International Relations*, p. 194.

70 For example, R. Schuett, 'Freudian roots of political realism: the importance of Sigmund Freud to Hans J. Morgenthau's theory of international power politics', *History of the Human Sciences*, 20:4 (2007), pp. 53–78; T. Solomon, 'Human nature and the limits of the self: Hans Morgenthau on love and power', *International Studies Review*, 14:2 (2012), pp. 201–24; F. Rösch, 'Pouvoir, puissance, and politics: Hans Morgenthau's dualistic concept of power?', *Review of International Studies*, 40:2 (2014), pp. 349–65; V. Paipais, 'Between politics and the political: reading Hans J. Morgenthau's double critique of depoliticisation', *Millennium: Journal of International Studies*, 42:2 (2014), pp. 354–75. On the rhetoric of realism, see D. J. Levine, 'After tragedy: melodrama and the rhetoric of realism', *Journal of International Political Theory* (advance publication; doi: 10.1177/ 1755088218790987).

71 Greenberg, *The Weimar Century*, pp. 7, 158; Radkau, *Die deutsche Emigration in den USA*, p. 214; Hughes, *The Sea Change*, p. 31. Gerald Stourzh and Carl Mayer called it an 'osmosis'; Stourzh, 'Die deutschsprachige Emigration in den Vereinigten Staaten', p. 61; Radio Bremen, *Auszug des Geistes*, p. 198.

72 Voegelin, *Autobiographical Reflections*, p. 85.

73 Bleek, *Geschichte der Politikwissenschaft in Deutschland*, p. 252.

74 W. E. Scheuerman, 'Professor Kelsen's Amazing Disappearing Act', in Rösch (ed.), *Émigré Scholars and the Genesis of International Relations*, pp. 81–102.

75 Morgenthau, 'Postscript to the transaction edition', pp. 356–7.

76 Pachter, 'On being an exile', p. 18, emphasis in original.

77 Liu, 'The question of meaning-value', pp. 19–20.

78 Stourzh, 'Die deutschsprachige Emigration in den Vereinigten Staaten', pp. 60–1.

79 Radio Bremen, *Auszug des Geistes*, p. 191.

80 Cited in Radkau, *Die deutsche Emigration in den USA*, p. 49.

81 P. Tillich, 'Mind and migration', *Social Research*, 4:3 (1937), pp. 295–305, at p. 303. Stuart Hughes called them a 'creative misinterpretation'; Hughes, *The Sea Change*, p. 31.

82 K. Waltz, 'Realist thought and neorealist theory', *Journal of International Affairs*, 44:1 (1990), pp. 21–37, at p. 21.

83 Guilhot, *The Invention of International Relations Theory*.

84 A. R. C. Humphreys, 'Waltz and the world: neorealism as international political theory?', *International Politics*, 50:6 (2013), pp. 863–79, at p. 863. For a critical account, see Scheuerman, 'The (classical) realist vision of global reform', p. 270.

85 Behr and Heath, 'Misreading in IR theory and ideology critique'.

86 Ziege, *Antisemitismus und Gesellschaftstheorie*; R. Shilliam, 'Morgenthau in context: German backwardness, German intellectuals and the rise and fall of a liberal project', *European Journal of International Relations*, 13:3 (2007),

pp. 299–327; D. Klusmeyer, 'Beyond tragedy: Hannah Arendt and Hans Morgenthau on responsibility, evil and political ethics', *International Studies Review*, 11:2 (2009), pp. 332–51; F. Rösch 'Crisis, values, and the purpose of science: Hans Morgenthau in Europe', *Ethics & International Affairs*, 30:1 (2016), pp. 23–31.

87 H. Behr, 'Scientific man vs. power politics: a pamphlet and its author between two academic cultures', *Ethics & International Affairs*, 30:1 (2016), pp. 33–8.

88 S. Mariotti, 'Damaged life as exuberant vitality in America: Adorno, alienation, and the psychic economy', *Telos*, 149 (2009), pp. 169–90, at p. 169.

89 T. Wheatland, *The Frankfurt School in Exile* (Minneapolis: University of Minnesota Press, 2009), p. 202.

90 Wheatland, *The Frankfurt School in Exile*, p. 206.

91 Ziege, *Antisemitismus und Gesellschaftstheorie*.

92 Vecchiarelli Scott, 'Alien nation', p. 170; Pachter, 'On being an exile', pp. 49–50.

93 A. Johnson, 'Twenty-five years of the New School', *New School Bulletin*, 1, 27 December 1943 (The New School Archives, NS030102_bull0107).

94 K. E. Jørgensen, 'Continental IR theory: the best kept secret', *European Journal of International Relations*, 6:1 (2000), pp. 9–42, at p. 15. On recent debates about the national interest, see M. C. Williams, 'What is the national interest? The neoconservative challenge in IR theory', *European Journal of International Relations*, 11:3 (2005), pp. 307–37.

95 Guilhot, 'The realist gambit', p. 130.

96 V. Schou Tjalve and M. C. Williams, 'Rethinking the logic of security: liberal realism and the recovery of American political thought', *Telos*, 170 (2015), pp. 46–66.

97 F. Rösch, 'Introduction: breaking the silence: European émigré scholars and the genesis of an American discipline', in Rösch (ed.), *Émigré Scholars and the Genesis of International Relations*, pp. 1–18.

98 Greenberg, *The Weimar Century*, p. 5.

99 Many of the émigrés who made their career in American IR had affinities to an intellectual position that is now referred to as classical realism. For this reconsideration, see, for example: C. Rohde, *Hans J. Morgenthau und der weltpolitische Realismus* (Wiesbaden: VS Verlag, 2004); S. Molloy, *The Hidden History of Realism: A Genealogy of Power Politics* (Basingstoke: Palgrave Macmillan, 2006); W. E. Scheuerman, *Hans Morgenthau: Realism and Beyond* (Cambridge: Polity, 2009); O. Juetersonke, *Morgenthau, Law and Realism* (Cambridge: Cambridge University Press, 2010); J. Puglierin, *John H. Herz: Leben und Denken zwischen Idealismus und Realismus, Deutschland und Amerika* (Berlin, Duncker & Humblot, 2011); F. Rösch, *Power, Knowledge, and Dissent in Morgenthau's Worldview* (New York: Palgrave Macmillan, 2015); N. Guilhot, *After the Enlightenment: Political Realism and International Relations in the Mid-twentieth Century* (Cambridge: Cambridge University Press, 2017).

100 H. Behr, 'The populist obstruction of reality: analysis and response', *Global Affairs*, 3:1 (2017), pp. 73–80.

101 V. S. Tjalve, *Realist Strategies of Republican Peace* (New York: Palgrave Macmillan, 2008); V. S. Tjalve, 'Realism, pragmatism and the public sphere: restraining foreign policy in an age of mass politics', *International Politics*, 50:6 (2013), pp. 784–97.

102 R. van Munster and C. Sylvest, 'Reclaiming nuclear politics? Nuclear realism, the H-Bomb and globality', *Security Dialogue*, 45:6 (2014), pp. 530–47.

103 W. E. Scheuerman, *The Realist Case for Global Reform* (Cambridge: Polity, 2011), p. 150.

9

Deutschtum and Americanism: memory and identity in Cold War America

Brian C. Etheridge

One of the remarkable phenomena of the Cold War is the rapid reversal of Germany from enemy to ally in American discourse. Often this reversal has been viewed as a necessary or inevitable expediency of the post-war conflict with the Soviet Union, but this chapter, and the larger work from which it draws, demonstrates that this process was much more complicated, and incomplete, than is typically recognised. Using a framework called memory diplomacy as a unifying analytical concept, this chapter highlights how exploring a diverse range of actors – both American and (West) German, state and non-state, and public and private – involved in the production and reception of images of Germany can illustrate the messy and contentious nature of this process. One part of the story is how different groups fought over the shaping of American understanding of *Deutschtum* (or Germanness) through the mass media. Another, equally important, part is how the fruits of these efforts were interpreted by those Americans who consumed them. When taken together, they illustrate how narratives of Germany were more about the American understanding of self than the American understanding of Germanness.[1]

Unlike some of the other chapters in this book, then, the scope of this inquiry is not focused on or even limited to scholarly writing or rigorous thinking about Germany; instead, it incorporates works of fiction and non-fiction, including films, television shows, novels, journalistic pieces, documentaries and the like. It also ranges beyond the authors themselves, and looks behind the manufacture of these public images for evidence related to the promotion or suppression of certain ideas and narratives. In this sense, it considers the activities of a variety of American and (West) German, state and non-state actors to influence what interpretations are published or circulated (for further images of Germany as a Western ally, see Siegfried Schieder in Chapter 10 of this volume). Finally, it seeks to understand how these public works are received. Rooted in the work of reader-response criticism and reception theory, it incorporates evidence of how these works are understood and received historically. This chapter ultimately argues that the meanings of these cultural products are not immanent – rather, they are contextually determined; they intersect and interact with the presuppositions and prejudices that the readers or consumers bring with them. In making this claim, the chapter argues that these readers or consumers constitute distinct interpretive communities, to use Stanley Fish's term, groups of people stitched together by their shared understanding of a text or image of Germany.[2]

In making some claims about discourses of Germany and Germanness in the post-war period, the chapter therefore looks at three distinct but interrelated levels: the level of the text itself (and its intertextuality – that is, its interactions with other published texts); the level of the politics behind the production or publication of the text (and what counter-texts may have been suppressed); and the level of the reception of the text (which may affirm authorial intent, as derived by either archival evidence of the producer or close textual reading of the piece, or may oppose it, or may do a myriad of things).

In taking this multi-tiered approach, I developed a concept called memory diplomacy. Following the work of Maurice Halbwachs and others, legions of scholars have studied the ways that societies remember and forget their own pasts. Stressing the collective nature of remembrance, these works have shown how societies use rituals, commemorations and other public acts of memory to celebrate and valorise certain narratives while ignoring others. Recent work in the study of electronic media has discussed how these immersive products may enable populations to experience memories to which they have no organic connection. 'Instead of relating to the past through a shared sense of place or ancestry', George Lipsitz argues, 'consumers of electronic mass media can experience a common heritage with a people they have never seen; they can acquire memories of a past to which they have no geographical or biological connection.' Alison Landsberg calls these 'prosthetic memories'. In an age of mass culture, she writes, 'memories of the Holocaust do not belong only to Jews, nor do memories of slavery belong solely to African Americans.'[3]

In this exploration of images of Germany in the US, I found that conceiving of collective memory as prosthetic helped explain how some Americans were engaging with these images. Some Americans identified with German stories and sought to make the German experience their own. Often these Americans saw the German experience as part of a broader Western memory of which they were a part. Others, however, consciously rejected these experiences as 'foreign'. In my archival work in the US and Germany, I saw these as explicit strategies pursued by different actors who hoped to shape American understanding of Germany. In this sense, then, I developed the framework of memory diplomacy to understand how memory activists sought to use narratives of Germany to shape American attitudes and hence American foreign policy towards Germany.[4]

In analysing all these dimensions, I find images of Germany during the post-war period to be a highly contested terrain. I break my analysis of the post-war era into three distinct periods. The first is characterised by a Cold War consensus and runs roughly from 1945 to 1959. The second is shaped by the fracturing of this consensus and lasts from 1959 to 1969. The final period, roughly from 1969 to 1999, shows how the frameworks for understanding Germanness formed during the previous two periods endured throughout the rest of the century in the guise of the sharpened symbols of Berlin and the Holocaust.

I argue that the Cold War consensus – the broadly shared understanding of aims, purpose and raison d'être in the Cold War – is key to understanding the evolution of these narratives, because my ultimate claim is that these images of Germany become constitutive parts of American identity in the Cold War period. It is impossible to understand how Americans interpreted Germannness without understanding how Americans incorporated Germany's story into their own. To that end, the story of how Americans understood themselves and their engagement in the world is completely imbricated with the story of Germany's integration into the Western world. The American efforts to reconcile competing narratives of themselves and their engagement in the world were reflected in the changing ways in which Germany was represented and discussed throughout the latter half of the twentieth century.[5]

Germanness and the Cold War consensus, 1945–59

The first period begins in the last months of the Second World War, as it became clear that Germany would be defeated, and attention in America shifted to a debate about what to do with it after the war is concluded. The period lasts through the occupation of Germany by the US, France, Great Britain and the Soviet Union, and the emergence of the Federal Republic of Germany as a provisionally independent nation and finally as a fully independent nation after 1955. The period ends when the nature of the debate about Germany and its future shifts fundamentally in the context of an emerging counter-culture and critical debate about American society and America's role in the world – essentially when the Cold War consensus begins to break down.[6]

The primary debate of this period can be defined by two competing discourses about Germany and Germanness. The first is a Cold War narrative of Germany. The Cold War narrative of Germany was born out of the evolving context of the emerging Cold War, but it has much deeper roots. During the war, many Americans argued that a notable distinction existed between Nazis and Germans. Following the writing of public intellectuals like Dorothy Thompson, they saw the Nazi Party as a clique that hijacked a nation seduced by Hitler, but they argued that the German people never fully accepted or bought into his murderous plans. As such, they argued for a quick rehabilitation and integration of Germany into the world order. Their narrative involved stressing similarities between Germany and other Western nations, even going so far as to emphasise German contributions to the roots of modern Western society. In this way, they hoped to encourage Americans to adopt prosthetic memories of Germany as part of a much larger Western story. In a sense, their narrative posited that the nations of Western civilisation existed on a continuum of development, with the US existing as the exemplar and model for a fully developed democratic and free market state. Germany, in this narrative, was moving along the continuum towards the US with American help and tutelage. The primary memory activists in support of this narrative were the American government, the new West German government and their employed public relations firms, and lobby organisations such as the American Council on Germany.

By contrast, the World War narrative of Germany was rooted in organic memories of Germany from the war that emphasised collective guilt for the German people. Drawing no distinctions between Nazis and Germans, they argued that Nazism was the logical outgrowth of German society or culture (or both) (for further *Sonderwegstheorien*, see Leonie Holthaus and Annette Weinke in Chapters 3 and 7 in this volume, respectively). Although Germany was facing defeat, they believed that it was laying plans to begin anew an effort for world domination, and so they constantly sounded the alarm about the dangers of a soft peace. Their narrative emphasised Germany as the 'other', and stressed the connected or reciprocal relationship between Nazis and Germans. The primary memory activists associated with this memory narrative were liberal organisations, Jewish organisations and lobby groups like the Society for the Prevention of World War III.

The primary dynamic during this period was the concomitant cultural and social dominance of the American government and the emergence of the Cold War consensus. The Cold War consensus was a broadly held set of assumptions that supported American aims in the emerging Cold War, celebrated American values as superior and deserving of dissemination around the globe, and sought to 'contain' alternative ideologies that challenged the status quo. As such, it created a climate in which criticising American policy or dissenting against American cultural norms was incredibly difficult.

The memory coalition in support of the Cold War narrative deliberately promoted images that stressed the sameness of Americanism and Germanness, and integrated Germany into the larger story of Western society. In its censorship policies on stories coming out of occupied Germany, its information policies through the Public Affairs branch of the State Department, and its relations with mass-media outlets in film and television, the American government deliberately pushed stories that emphasised Germany's emerging role as the frontline of the Western world in its struggle with the communist East. The re-emergence of a West German voice in the US was aided by the employment of an American public relations firm, the Roy Bernard Company, whose explicit strategy was 'Germany belongs in the Western World'. For its client, this firm arranged exchanges of carefully selected Americans and Germans who could promote like-minded thinking, routinely 'planted' stories about German rehabilitation in the American mould and discouraged articles that threatened to dredge up memories of Second World War Germany. In these ways, these government activists promoted images of Germany that stressed the progressive development of German society and culture along American lines.[7]

Both governments were abetted by a private network of scholars and intellectuals on both sides of the Atlantic that echoed these ideas. Helmed by Christopher Emmet, the American Council on Germany was the most prominent of these in the US. Emmet marshalled effective public relations campaigns to counter works that sought to generate concern about Germany, books like T. H. Tetens' *Germany Plots with the Kremlin*. Perhaps his most effective work on behalf of the Cold War narrative was gathering public intellectuals to oppose George Kennan's ideas in 1957 about 'disengaging' American troops from Europe and 'neutralising' Germany. He recruited journalists and scholars like Louis Lochner, James Conant, Robert Strausz-Hupé, Shepard Stone and Jack Jessup behind an effort to combat Kennan's recommendations.[8]

The cultural power of the state in the early Cold War made it difficult for dissenting organisations to support narratives that were critical of American foreign policy or American values. As such, those organisations who sought to promote images of Germany from the Second World War found themselves at a significant disadvantage. A perfect example of the power of the Cold War consensus to influence representations behind the scenes was the internal politics of American Jewish organisations. At the end of the war, virtually all of the major American Jewish organisations worried about the revival of German power, complained about the inadequacy of Denazification efforts and pushed for the punishment of Nazi war criminals. But as the Cold War took shape, and it became evident that the US was pursuing a policy of rehabilitation, Jewish support for a harsh peace splintered, even though most of them continued to receive worrying reports that German society still contained a significant residue from the Nazi period. The American Jewish Committee in particular worried about Jewish inclusion in the emerging Cold War consensus and took pains to ensure that their representatives did not come across as 'vengeful' in their approach to Germany. They chose to work behind the scenes to try and influence American policy, explicitly opposing the more vocal efforts of the American Jewish Congress and other affiliated organisations.[9]

The impact of the Cold War consensus on dissent was even more evident in the marginalisation of organisations such as Progressive Citizens of America (PCA) and the Society for the Prevention of World War III. The emergence of the Cold War split American liberalism, with anti-communist liberals joining organisations like Americans for Democratic Action (ADA), while members of the PCA sought to maintain liberalism's anti-fascist orientation and friendship with the Soviet Union in the face of an increasingly conservative turn. Their champion was Henry Wallace, and his defeat as a third-party candidate in 1948 signalled the end of their influence. This marginalisation was also reflected in the trajectory of the Society for the Prevention of World War III, whose organisational title was explicitly about opposing German rehabilitation. Under the leadership of Rex Stout, the organisation enjoyed influence during the war, with Stout visiting Roosevelt in the White House and Army orientation officers around the country praising his work. But after Roosevelt's death and Truman's firm commitment to a policy of rehabilitation, the Society's influence waned as mainstream liberal and Jewish groups cut ties with it and its strident criticism of the government's foreign policy.[10]

An examination of the impact of these efforts on American public opinion and culture shows that the Cold War consensus played a decisive role in shaping attitudes towards Germany. Thanks to the work of the memory coalition in support of the Cold War narrative, and the power of the American government in generating support and suppressing dissent, Americans spontaneously produced artifacts that echoed the image of Germany as a primary battleground of the Cold War, a place where the struggle between freedom and communism was most manifest. In subscribing to prosthetic memories of Germany, Americans through the lens of totalitarianism saw the Soviet Union as the inheritors of a destructive ideology that threatened the world. The menacing threat of the Soviet Union, coupled with the emerging success story of a rebuilt West Germany in America's image, reinforced the idea that the enemy was an ideology or system of ideas, not a nation or its culture. In the process, the German people became absolved. This process was abetted by images of 'rubble women' in Germany that feminised the nation and made it seem in need of protection. Finally, the dramatic events in Berlin over the course of this period crystallised these interpretations and clarified America's noble purpose in the world.[11]

Germanness and the fracturing of the Cold War consensus: 1959–69

The second period begins with events that started to cast serious doubt in some circles about some of the most importantly held truisms of the Cold War consensus. The publication of William Appleman Williams' *Tragedy of American Diplomacy* in 1959 helped crystallise a nascent critique of American society and American foreign policy. Prioritising economic factors over political ones, Williams argued that the Cold War was not fundamentally about the spread of American freedom, but about the spread of American empire. Blaming the US rather than the Soviet Union for the beginning of the Cold War, Williams contributed to a movement of intellectual thought that condemned American political life as hollow, hypocritical and self-serving. This New American Left celebrated revolutionaries abroad like Fidel Castro and Mao Zedong. Drawing strength and insight from the American civil rights movement, student organisations like the Students for a Democratic Society (SDS) questioned the Cold War consensus that assumed the superiority of American civilisation.

This period also witnessed a number of events that suggested that Germany had not made as much progress as previously believed. In 1959, Germany experienced an epidemic of swastika daubings and anti-Semitic manifestations, and even more disturbingly, the US experienced copycat episodes the following year. In 1960–1, the State of Israel put the captured Adolf Eichmann on trial in what became a highly publicised, worldwide media event that re-awakened fears of anti-Semitism. In 1965, there was a bruising debate over extending the statutes for war crimes in Germany, and the following year the National Democratic Party (NPD) enjoyed surprising electoral success. All of these events reinforced the need to re-examine some of the easy ways in which Germanness had been incorporated in Americanism.[12]

Indeed, the fracturing of the Cold War consensus was the dominant factor in shaping images of Germany in the US. Unlike the earlier period, in which the primary debate was between the Cold War narrative and the World War narrative, the chief debate during this second period concerned the nature of the Cold War narrative and the consensus that it buttressed. Largely discredited in the previous era, the World War narrative as a means of emphasising difference or Germany as the 'other' did not resurface, even though a number of cultural products dealing with Germany during the Second World War were disseminated. Instead,

these products circulated in a milieu in which the aforementioned continuum for Western national development remained (in which America
had previously been held as the exemplar for democratic growth); the
difference now was that, instead of Americans judging how Germany had
progressed, many of them worried that America was slipping towards
Nazi Germany. In that sense, the strategy of memory activists in support
of the Cold War narrative to encourage Americans to adopt prosthetic
memories of Germany by emphasising sameness worked, but with unintended or unanticipated effects.

Two developments enabled this re-orientation. The first was that
the American government subtly shifted away from Germany. Perhaps
channelling some of the disaffection in the general population, Kennedy
and later Johnson distanced themselves somewhat from the close identification between the US and Germany that Truman and Eisenhower
had forged. This meant that the American government no longer
actively and directly addressed images of Germany, as it had under
previous administrations. In the process, it created permissive space
for images more critical of Germany, although no major mainstream
memory activists defected from the coalition in support of the Cold War
narrative. The second, and perhaps more important, development was
that the legitimacy of the American government itself came under serious question in an era of protest and rebellion. In that regard, dissenting
organisations felt more comfortable – and some even viewed it as essential – to resist the influence of the state.[13]

The Federal Republic failed to realise these larger shifts in its pan-
icked reaction to what it called 'die antideutsche Welle' (the anti-German
wave). Beginning with the publication of William Shirer's blockbuster
in 1960, West German officials feared the return of the World War
narrative through an increase in the amount of anti-German cultural
products in circulation in the US. Previously hopeful that wartime
images of Germany would fade over time, they were alarmed to see them
re-appear in a new guise. Officials noted with disdain the distribution
of films like *Battle of the Bulge, Ship of Fools, Blue Max* and, worst of all,
Judgment at Nuremberg. They also worried about the impact of new television shows like *Rat Patrol, Combat!* and *Hogan's Heroes* on America's
impressionable youth.

West German officials pursued a number of means to counter these
narratives. They lobbied media-makers directly. They considered economic retaliation against firms that sponsored anti-German products.
Most importantly, they founded the German Information Center (GIC)
to provide a more robust presence in the American mass-media landscape. Taking over many of the functions previously handled by the
Roy Bernard Company, the GIC served as a clearing house of information about Germany. It also endeavoured to place articles in major

periodicals, although not quite with the same effectiveness as the Roy Bernard Company.[14]

As in the previous period, West German officials enjoyed the support of the private network of pro-German supporters, organised around the American Council on Germany. In addition to co-sponsoring a highly visible series of conferences beginning in 1959, the American Council on Germany fought against the perceived anti-German wave. Emmet rallied a response to senator Claiborne Pell's 1963 proposal to normalise relations by recognising East Germany (at the Oder-Neisse line) by soliciting responses by senators like Jacob Javits and coordinating efforts with West German officials like Egon Bahr. More significantly, he galvanised public intellectuals like William Chamberlain, Norbert Muhlen and George Shuster to address and discredit elements of the anti-German wave like *Judgment at Nuremberg* and T. H. Tetens' *The New Germany and the Old Nazis*. These allies claimed that anti-German products were inspired by communists seeking to drive a wedge in the Western world. Put off by the frequently histrionic responses by Emmet and his friends, Jewish groups began to distance themselves from Emmet's work.[15]

Indeed, in this new permissive space American Jewish organisations demonstrated a willingness to vocalise more critical views of Germany. Most of the groups thought this necessary because the strategy of 'going along to get along' had not worked. The American response to the swastika epidemic in Germany, as well as to the copycat incidents in the US and the Eichmann trial the following year, convinced these groups that they needed to take a more activist approach to educating Americans about the Holocaust. They also felt more comfortable engaging directly in issues that worried them in Germany, such as the rise of the NPD and the election of Kurt Georg Kiesinger as Chancellor. Still despite these emboldened efforts, Jewish groups refused an open break with the American and West German governments, reasoning that they stood to gain more by collaborating with government officials.[16]

Although many of these memory activists believed that the conflict over German images was a continuation of sorts of the conflict that had existed in the 1950s, the evidence related to American reception of these events suggests otherwise. The evidence suggests that Americans understood these German images, especially the critical ones, through the prism of the Cold War narrative. Again, the Cold War narrative posited that the US and Germany were essentially the same, just that the US was further along in its development as a democratic, free-market society. During the previous period, America was framed as a positive destination for Germany's future development. But if we look at how Americans responded to these ostensibly anti-German images of the 1960s, it becomes clear that they were interpreting them in the context of the state of affairs in America. And as that understanding of America fractured in the 1960s, different interpretive communities responded to German representations that circulated in the American media in different ways.

Mainstream media spontaneously echoed traditional Cold War narratives. Although German officials worried about products like *Combat!* and *Hogan's Heroes*, a thorough examination of the shows and the responses to them demonstrates that they were more about re-affirming traditional American values. The longest-running Second World War drama in television history, *Combat!* featured American troops fighting for American values in Europe. The series re-affirmed the superiority of American values in the struggle against totalitarianism, while reifying distinctions between bad Nazis (the SS officers) and good Germans (infantry troops). The other major Second World War-era show of the 1960s, *Hogan's Heroes*, make fun of the Nazi ecosystem. Set in a German prisoner-of-war camp behind enemy lines, the big joke of the show lay in drawing distinctions between the superiority of American values, as exemplified by Hogan, and the murderous, dysfunctional ethos of the totalitarian camp in which they were held captive. A running gag, and the greatest source of leverage for Hogan, was the fear of Klink and Schultz (the two prominent German administrators of the camp) that they would be sent to the Russian front – which was tantamount to death. In these ways, mainstream culture products sought to shore up familiar uses of German images.[17]

Liberals, on the other hand, used images of Nazi Germany to challenge notions of American superiority. In *The Feminine Mystique*, Betty Friedan compared American suburban domesticity to German concentration camps in one of the last chapters entitled 'Progressive dehumanisation: the comfortable concentration camp'. In his famous experiments on obedience, psychologist Stanley Milgram started out trying to understand why Nazi guards would support genocide. After his first experiment at Yale, he reported to the National Science Foundation that he 'once wondered whether in all of the United States a vicious government could find enough moral imbeciles to meet the personnel requirements of a national system of death camps of the sort maintained in Germany. I am beginning to think that the full complement could be recruited in New Haven'. Mainstream publications shared his results with provocative titles such as: 'Could we be Nazi followers?' and 'You might do Eichmann's job'. Finally, liberal filmmakers like Abby Mann and Stanley Kramer made message films like *Judgment at Nuremberg* and *Ship of Fools* that used Germany as a metaphor for critiquing American society and foreign policy. Worried that America was sliding down the continuum towards totalitarianism, these liberals sought to point out similarities between Nazi Germany and the US in an effort to mobilise support for reform.[18]

The New Left took this line of critique event further. With no living memory of the Second World War, these student radicals saw the US, with its repression against peaceful protestors and dissenters at home and its prosecution of an unjust war abroad, and not the Soviet Union as the true heir to Nazi Germany. To use one of the popular metaphors of the day, these radicals refused to be 'good Germans' who were silently complicit to the evils that they saw committed by the state in their name. The most radical manifestation of this approach was the Weather Underground, which carried out a bombing campaign against the 'Nazi state' of the US in the late 1960s and early 1970s.[19]

Finally, conservatives and white supremacist organisations also used images of Germany as a means of critiquing contemporary American society. Beginning with William F. Buckley and reaching maturity with Barry Goldwater's presidential campaign in 1964, the emerging conservative movement decried the growth of the welfare state, seeing its trajectory leading towards totalitarianism and a 'police state'. White supremacists, on the other hand, capitalised on the atomising effects of post-war society to recruit disaffected young men. In the aftermath of the swastika epidemic of 1960–1, concerned Jewish groups found in studies that young white men were drawn to images of Nazis because they projected strength and unity. George Lincoln Rockwell's American Nazi Party emerged as the most prominent symbol of this movement. Rockwell's vision lay in the mass extermination of Jews, the deportation of African-Americans to Africa and the relocation of other undesirables to relocation centres in desolate parts of the US. For white supremacists like Rockwell, images of Germany provided a blueprint for solving America's social ills.[20]

The continuing debate: 1969–99

The third era lasts from the conclusion of the 1960s to the end of the millennium, although one may argue that it continued until the most recent wave of xenophobia and nationalism, signified most powerfully by Donald Trump's election as President of the United States. This period is marked by the continued use of Germany and Germanness as a metaphor and a lens for understanding America and Americanism. The language for understanding is very much framed by the previous period. Despite efforts by some marginal groups to re-introduce Germany as 'other' through the World War narrative, most narratives of Germany during this period focused their discussion of images of Germany as a way of understanding progress in American society. The most significant development of the period is the emergence of two symbols that simplified the German metaphor for America. One was unambiguously positive and celebratory of American virtues – the Berlin Wall. The second was the Holocaust. Representations of the Holocaust in the 1970s and 1980s were mired in greater complexity, but by the 1990s had emerged as more triumphal of American values.[21]

Although divided Berlin had been a potent symbol of the Cold War narrative of Germany since the emergence of the rivalry between the Soviet Union and the US, its power for symbolising the superiority of American civilisation increased dramatically after the wall was built in the late summer of 1961. The Berlin Wall visually split the city in two, offering a compelling contrast between democratic, capitalist West Berlin and communist East Berlin. The fact that the German Democratic Republic had to build a wall to keep its most talented citizens from leaving was a visceral demonstration of the bankruptcy of the communist system, a perspective that scores of American politicians and observers shared. Because of its powerful message, Berlin's meaning remained more durable; for example, it resisted efforts by the Nixon and Carter administrations to remake it as a symbol of East–West reconciliation and détente. Harsher rhetoric during the Reagan administration helped amplify it, but Americans still resisted a return to the simplicity of the early Cold War. When Reagan delivered his now-famous 'Tear down this wall' speech in 1987, for example, it received a mixed reception in the US. For their part, many West Germans at the time worried that it would inflame tensions and draw protesters. Even the breach in the wall in 1989 was not seen at the time as victory in the Cold War; rather, it was seen more as a sign of the permissiveness of the Gorbachev regime. However, the manner in which the Cold War ended strengthened the symbolism of Berlin and the Berlin Wall, and by the end of the century, the fall of the Wall became shorthand for the end of the Cold War.[22]

Representations of the Holocaust followed a similar pattern. By the 1970s, the Holocaust had emerged as the most visible symbol of the evils of the Third Reich. NBC's miniseries *Holocaust* was a massive hit in the US, as Jewish groups and other interested groups initiated a major campaign to get people to watch it. By and large, many Americans interpreted the mini-series from a perspective of universalisation, seeing in the Holocaust a cautionary lesson for all civilisations. However, by the 1990s, a more conservative and more traditional approach towards Nazi Germany re-emerged with reactions to Steven Spielberg's *Schindler's List*. Mainstream audiences gravitated to Spielberg's simple morality tale, while academics flinched at his efforts to make the Holocaust an uplifting tale of the human spirit. A similar dichotomy emerged over responses to Goldhagen's very popular *Hitler's Willing Executioners*. Mainstream readers gravitated towards its clear explication of eliminationist anti-Semitism, while academic scholars railed against its efforts to represent the Holocaust as a German flaw. Omer Bartov put it this way: 'The argument that after the fall of Nazism the Germans became "just like us" and that they are as unlikely to perpetrate a genocide as "we" are can produce an excessive sense of complacency not merely about postwar Germany but about the rest of "us". Finally, the construction of the US Holocaust Memorial

Museum offered a highly visible monument to America's interpretation of the Holocaust. Visitors to the museum are introduced to the Holocaust through the perspective of liberating Americans. As the director of the museum put it, the museum seeks to 'translate an American experience into an American idiom'[23] In all of these ways, the Holocaust, like the Berlin Wall, came to symbolise the triumph of Americanism, even though a significant interpretive community continued to caution Americans against their easy appropriation of images of Germany for these purposes.

Conclusion

American narratives of Germans and Germanness during and after the Cold War are crucial to understanding the construction of American self-conceptualisation and identity after the Second World War. American images of other nation-states during this time also played an important role; a number of good works have illustrated the influence that images of Japan had in America during the second half of the twentieth century, for example.[24] But in the case of Japan, so much of this discourse was racialised that it made it difficult for Americans to centre Japan's story as much as Germany's in America's narrative about itself. The story of Germany, from the outbreak of the Cold War and the division of Germany and Berlin through to the fall of the Berlin Wall and the dissolution of the Soviet Union four decades later, mirrored and reinforced domestic narratives about the US and its role in the world.

And as this high-level overview demonstrates, American engagement with Germanness during the Cold War was far more complex than most accounts suggest. Different actors sought to shape American understanding of Germany for various reasons, but American support for its former enemy can ultimately be traced to how narratives of Germany intersected with American stories about themselves. Skilful actors realised the role that images of Germany played in buttressing positive American portrayals and acted accordingly. Even seeming anti-German narratives were often understood in an American context, in which post-war Germany's story, for good or for ill, was seen as a chapter in America's Cold War.

Notes

1 The arguments in this chapter are fleshed out in my book *Enemies to Allies: Cold War Germany and American Memory* (Lexington: University Press of Kentucky, 2016).

2 S. Fish, *Is There a Text in this Class?: The Authority of Interpretive Communities* (Cambridge, MA: Harvard University Press, 1980).

3 M. Halbwachs, *On Collective Memory*, ed. and trans. by L. A. Coser (Chicago: University of Chicago Press, 1992); G. Lipsitz, *Time Passages: Collective Memory and American Popular Culture* (Minneapolis: University of Minnesota Press, 1990), p. 5; A. Landsberg, *Prosthetic Memory: The Transformation of American Remembrance in the Age of Mass Culture* (New York: Columbia University Press, 2004), p. 8.

4 Useful works on public diplomacy, past and present, include W. L. Hixson, *Parting the Curtain: Propaganda, Culture, and the Cold War, 1945–1961* (New York: St Martin's Press, 1997); R. H. Pells, *Not Like Us: How Europeans Have Loved, Hated, and Transformed American Culture since World War II* (New York: Basic Books, 1997); R. Wagnleitner, *Coca-colonization and the Cold War: The Cultural Mission of the United States in Austria after the Second World War* (Chapel Hill: University of North Carolina Press, 1994); J. C. E. Gienow-Hecht, *Transmission Impossible: American Journalism as Cultural Diplomacy in Postwar Germany, 1945–1955* (Baton Rouge: Louisiana State University Press, 1999); J.C. Parker, *Hearts, Minds, and Voices: US Cold War Public Diplomacy and the Formation of the Third World* (New York: Oxford University Press, 2016); K. A. Osgood, *Total Cold War: Eisenhower's Secret Propaganda Battle at Home and Abroad* (Lawrence: University Press of Kansas, 2006); P. M. Taylor, *British Propaganda in the 20th Century: Selling Democracy* (Edinburgh: Edinburgh University Press, 1999); J. Eder, *Holocaust Angst: The Federal Republic of Germany and American Holocaust Memory since the 1970s* (New York: Oxford University Press, 2016); and M.T. Bennett, 'The spirits of '76: diplomacy commemorating the U.S. Bicentennial in 1976', *Diplomatic History*, 40:4 (2016), pp. 695–721.

5 On the Cold War consensus, see W. Wall, *Inventing the American Way: The Politics of Consensus from the New Deal to the Civil Rights Movement* (New York: Oxford University Press, 2008); S. J. Whitfield, *The Culture of the Cold War* (Baltimore: Johns Hopkins University Press, 1996); M. Peacock, *Innocent Weapons: The Soviet and American Politics of Childhood in the Cold War* (Chapel Hill: University of North Carolina Press, 2014); M. A. Henriksen, *Dr. Strangelove's America: Society and Culture in the Atomic Age* (Berkeley: University of California Press, 1997); and P. J. Kuznick and J. B. Gilbert (eds), *Rethinking Cold War Culture* (Washington DC: Smithsonian Books, 2001).

6 See Etheridge, *Enemies to Allies*, pp. 55–160.

7 See for example, Huebner to War Department, 12 April 1947, Central Decimal Files, Record Group (RG) 319, National Archives II (NA), College Park, Maryland, US; Television Broadcast on 20 August, 1950, Television Broadcasts, Miscellaneous German Files, 1943–54, Records of the Office of Western European Affairs, 1941–54, RG 59, NA; John J. McCloy, 'Assisting Germany to become a peaceful democracy', *Department of State Bulletin*, 9 July 1951, p. 63; Simon to Breen, 21 November 1949, Chief of Information, Central Decimal Files, RG 59, NA; Breen to Carl Humelsine, 23 November 1949, Central Decimal Files, RG 59, NA; Aufzeichnung, 18 July 1951, Band (B) 90/71, Politisches Archiv des Auswärtigen Amts (PAAA), Berlin, Germany; Krekeler to AA, 20 August 1951, B 145/775, Bundesarchiv, Koblenz (BAK), Germany; German Embassy to AA, 28 January 1951, B 11/298, AA; Auszug aus

dem Zwischenbericht der Firma Roy Bernard an Dr Heinz Krekeler, 16 April 1952, B 145/775, BAK; Report, Blumenthal to Gong, 9 June 1952, B 145/775, BAK; Report on Roy Bernard, 19 July 1954, B 145/775, BAK.

8 Report on the Activities of the American Council on Germany, 15 October 1953, American Council on Germany – Reports of Activities, Box 4, C. T. Emmet, HIA; Report on Activities of the American Council on Germany, Inc., 1 January 1954, American Council on Germany – Reports of Activities, Box 4, C. T. Emmet Papers, Hoover Institution Archives (HIA), Stanford, CA, US; Secretary's Annual Report of Activities, 1955, American Council on Germany – Reports of Activities, Box 4, C. T. Emmet, HIA.; Chris Emmet to Louis P. Lochner, 2 May 1956, American Council on Germany, 1952–61, Box 1, Louis Lochner Papers, Wisconsin Historical Society (WHS), Madison, WI, US.

9 S. Shafir, *Ambiguous Relations: The American Jewish Community and Germany since 1945* (Detroit: Wayne State University Press, 1999), pp. 87–104; P. Novick, *The Holocaust in American Life* (Boston: Houghton Mifflin Company, 1999), pp. 90–7. The positions of different organisations were laid out in Memorandum, 14 June 1949, Activities-Denazification, Box 68, National Jewish Community Relations Council (NJCRAC), American Jewish Historical Society Archives (AJHSA), Center for Jewish History, New York, NY, US; Samuel Spiegler to NCRAC agencies, 8 August 1949, Folder 9, Box 56, Cincinnnati, Ohio-Jewish Community Relations Council (CO-JCRC), American Jewish Archives, Cincinnati, Ohio (AJA).

10 S. M. Gillon, *Politics and Vision: The ADA and American Liberalism, 1947–1985* (New York: Oxford University Press, 1987), pp. 13–21; M. L. Kleinman, *A World of Hope, a World of Fear: Henry A. Wallace, Reinhold Niebuhr, and American Liberalism* (Columbus: Ohio State University Press, 2000), pp. 222–34; 'Statement of policy of the Society for the Prevention of World War III', *Prevent World War III*, June–July 1944, inside cover; J. McAleer, *Rex Stout: A Majesty's Life* (Rockville, MD: James A. Rock & Company, 2002), pp. 265–321; S. Casey, 'The campaign to sell a harsh peace for Germany to the American public, 1944–1948', *History*, 90:1 (2005), pp. 62–92; Allan J. Winter to Donald Steven, 13 May 1944, 1, Society for the Prevention of World War III (hereinafter SPWWIII), Rare Book and Manuscript Library, Columbia University, New York, US (RBML/CU).

11 A. Gleason, *Totalitarianism: The Inner History of the Cold War* (New York: Oxford University Press, 1995); L. K. Adler and T. G. Paterson, 'Red fascism: the merger of Nazi Germany and Soviet Russia in the American image of totalitarianism, 1930s–1950s', *American Historical Review*, 75:4 (1970), pp. 1046–64; Novick, *The Holocaust in American Life*, pp. 86–7; P. Goedde, *GIs and Germans: Culture, Gender and Foreign Relations, 1945–1949* (New Haven: Yale University Press, 2003), pp. 81, 101–8; J. O'Donnell, 'Russian zone: a German Lenin in Berlin', *Newsweek*, 3 June 1946, p. 36; E. Hughes, 'Berlin under siege', *Life*, 19 July 1948, pp. 25–7; 'Two Berlins: photographs', *New York Times Magazine*, 12 June 1949, pp. 8–9; 'Journey to the West', *Time*, 23 May 1949, p. 25.

12 For more on this process, see Etheridge, *Enemies to Allies*, pp. 161–254.

13 On changes in the American position vis-à-vis Germany, see F. A. Mayer, *Adenauer and Kennedy: A Study in German-American Relations, 1961–1963*

(New York: Palgrave Macmillan, 1996); and T. A. Schwartz, *Lyndon Johnson and Europe: In the Shadow of Vietnam* (Cambridge, MA: Harvard University Press, 2003).

14 Aufzeichnung, Bauer to Thomas, 15 October 1965, B 145/2873, BAK; Graf Schweinitz to von Lilienfeld, 1 December 1965, B 145/2873, BAK; Aufzeichnung, NYT article 'German Americans provoked by portrayal of Germans on TV', 25 February 1968, B 145/3005, BA; Thomas to Leonard H. Goldenson; Thomas to Hedda Hopper, 19 November 1965, B 145/2140, BA; Graf Schweinitz to Sellier, 18 January 1966, B 145/2873, BAK; 11 June 1959, B 145/1304, BAK; Von Eckardt to AA, 3 August 1960, B 145/1304, BAK; Grewe to AA, 21 October 1960, B 145/1304, BAK; News release: 'Germany opens information center in New York City', 6 May 1961, B 145/3255, BAK; Botschaft to AA, 2 February 1962, B 145/3255, BAK; Fehr to Diehl, 23 November 1965, B 145/2873, BAK; Auszug aus einem Brief von Michael Fehr, Salem, MA, US, 26 October 1965, B 145/2873, BAK.

15 W. H. Chamberlin, 'The revival of anti-Germanism', *Modern Age*, Summer 1962, p. 277; C. Emmet and N. Muhlen, *The Vanishing Swastika: Facts and Figures on Nazism in West Germany* (Chicago: H. Regnery1961), p. 54; Report on Activities, 1960–61, 1961, American Council on Germany-Reports of Activities, Box 4, C. T. Emmet, HIA; Simon Segal to Irving Engel, 1961, Education-American Council on Germany, 23, AJC FAD-1, YIVO.

16 The German Dilemma, 1959, Folder 2, Box H140, WJCC, AJA; Shafir, *Ambiguous Relations*, pp. 206, 232; Dear Colleague, 27 January 1960, Folder 19, Box H343, WJCC, AJA; George Kellman to John Slawson, 21 October 1960, Swastika Epidemic-AJC Reports, Box 10, AJC FAD-1, YIVO; Effect of Publicity on Vandalism, 13 January 1960, Swastika Epidemic–Mass Media, Box 10, AJC FAD-1, YIVO; Report by Dr Joachim Prinz in CIA Perspectives, n.d., Folder 19, Box 270, American Jewish Congress, AJHSA; Press Release, 1966, Folder 2, Box 64, WJCC, AJA.

17 J. Davidsmeyer, *Combat!: A Viewer's Companion to the WWII TV Series*, revised ed. (Tallevast, FL: Strange New World, 2002); 'The duel', in *Combat!* (1964); 'A rare vintage', in *Combat!* (1964); 'The masquers', in *Combat!* (1967); B. Scott Royce, *Hogan's Heroes: A Comprehensive Reference to the 1965–1971 Television Comedy Series with Cast Biographies and an Episode Guide* (Jefferson, NC: McFarland & Co Inc., 1993); 'The battle of Stalag 13', in *Hogan's Heroes* (1966); 'Praise the Fuhrer and pass the ammunition', in *Hogan's Heroes* (1967); 'Heil Klink', in *Hogan's Heroes* (1967).

18 K. L. Fermaglich, *American Dreams and Nazi Nightmares: Early Holocaust Consciousness and Liberal America, 1957–1965* (Waltham, MA: University Press of New England, 2006), pp. 58–123 (quote on p . 88); Souvenir Program from Berlin Premiere, 1961, Berlin, 'Judgment at Nuremberg' Clippings File, Margaret Herrick Library (MHL), Beverly Hills, CA, US; Abby Mann, 'Judgment at Nuremberg', 1961, Stanley Kramer Papers, UCLA, Los Angeles, CA, US.

19 T. Gitlin, *The Sixties: Years of Hope, Days of Rage* (New York: Bantam Books, 1993); T. Windt, *Presidents and Protesters: Political Rhetoric in the 1960s* (Tuscaloosa: University of Alabama, 1990); R. Lieberman, *Prairie Power: Voices of 1960s Midwestern Student Protest* (Columbia: University of

Missouri Press, 2004), p. 71; S. Stern, *With the Weathermen: The Personal Journal of a Revolutionary Woman* (New York: Rutgers University Press, 1975); J. Varon, *Bringing the War Home: The Weather Underground, the Red Army Faction, and Revolutionary Violence in the Sixties and Seventies* (Berkeley: University of California Press, 2004).

20 J. A. Andrew, *The Other Side of the Sixties: Young Americans for Freedom and the Rise of Conservative Politics* (New Brunswick, NJ: Rutgers University Press, 1997), pp. 18, 42; B. Goldwater, *Conscience of a Conservative* (Princeton: Princeton University Press, 2007 [1960]), p. 8; The 1960 Swastika-Smearings: Analysis of the Apprehended Youth, 1962, Folder 2, 17, WJCC, AJA; F. J. Simonelli, *American Fuehrer: George Lincoln Rockwell and the American Nazi Party* (Urbana: University of Illinois Press, 1999).

21 For more on this period, see Etheridge, *Enemies to Allies*, pp. 255–78.

22 R. Mason, *Richard Nixon and the Quest for a New Majority* (Chapel Hill: University of North Carolina Press, 2004), pp. 138–9; M. Brennan, *Turning Right in the Sixties: The Conservative Capture of the GOP* (Chapel Hill: University of North Carolina Press, 1997), pp. 135–7; W. Tuohy, '6 Germans reportedly killed in bizarre attempt to flee to West', *Los Angeles Times*, 3 July 1986, p. 15; 'Tear down Berlin Wall, Reagan asks; challenge issued to Soviet leader in divided city', *Los Angeles Times*, 13 June 1987, p. 1. The letters to the editor in the *Los Angeles Times* were all critical of Reagan's speech, with most viewing it as a cynical public relations ploy.

23 J. Shandler, *While America Watches: Televising the Holocaust* (Oxford: Oxford University Press, 1999), pp. 155–78; T. Cole, *Selling the Holocaust: From Auschwitz to Schindler; How History is Bought, Packaged, and Sold* (New York: Routledge, 1999); O. Bartov, 'Reception and perception: Goldhagen's Holocaust and the world', in G. Eley (ed.), *The 'Goldhagen' Effect* (Ann Arbor: University of Michigan Press, 2000), p. 43; Remarks by Dr Michael Berenbaum, Content Committee – 20 January1988 – joint Dev. Meeting, Box 1, Michael Berenbaum's Committee Memoranda and Reports, United States Holocaust Memorial and Museum Institutional Archives, Washington DC (USHMMIA).

24 C. Klein, *Cold War Orientalism: Asia in the Middlebrow Imagination, 1945–1961* (Berkeley: University of California Press, 2003); N. Shibusawa, *America's Geisha Ally* (Cambridge, MA: Harvard University Press, 2009); A. C. McKevitt, *Consuming Japan: Popular Culture and the Globalizing of 1980s America* (Chapel Hill: University of North Carolina Press, 2017).

10

'Civilian power' seen from abroad: the external image of Germany's foreign policy

Siegfried Schieder

> The second German republic is the best Germany ever: liberal, stable, prepared to balance out social differences and with citizens actively engaged in public life. How did this career from the ugly German to moral superpower come about?[1]

It is common to use the term 'civilian power' to describe Germany's conception of its role in the world after the Second World War. Since its beginning in 1949, the foreign policy of the Federal Republic of Germany (FRG) has been driven by its rejection of Germany's militarist past and its integration into the liberal international order in Europe and the US. The catastrophic consequences of Nazism, the Second World War and the Holocaust led to a fundamental recasting of Germany's identity in the world. (West) Germany adopted a different approach to foreign policy, underpinned by democratic values as well as new foreign policy practices, such as multilateralism, European integration and military restraint. The resulting strategic culture of the country's foreign policy role is built around three central tenets: 'never again', 'never alone' and 'politics before force'.[2] According to this self-perception, Germany is not just a power, but also a profoundly 'tamed' and 'civilian' one.

The self-perception as a 'civilian power' has fundamentally influenced Germany's behaviour in Europe and the world, which has simultaneously affected the process of identity-building at home. However, the idea of Germany as a 'civilian power' suffers from two key shortcomings: it is German-centric and deeply permeated by the assumption that being 'civilian' means being a 'better' power. One reason that Germany has been able to remain a 'civilian power' for the past seventy years is that other countries – notably the US – have served as international military powers. While the US, Great Britain and France took on the tasks of fighting global communism, Germany was free to concentrate on its own domestic parochial interests in a stable liberal international order.[3]

However, after the end of the Cold War and the re-unification of Germany in 1990, Germany's partners' expectations about the country's engagement in global politics changed. Many foreign policy analysts began to ask whether the new German foreign policy was becoming more 'normal' – that is, more like that of established nation-states such as France, Great Britain and the US.[4] In an attempt to further examine this question, scholars have assessed whether Germany's foreign policy is still that of a 'civilian power', as is so often claimed. Berlin's increasing engagement in international crises and its role in crisis-ridden Europe have proven key factors in leading some foreign policy observers to doubt whether Germany is still a 'civilian power'.[5] In particular, the eurozone crisis has pushed the German government into the disagreeable role of Europe's leading or 'hegemonic power'.[6]

Nevertheless, these studies are limited to analysing the impact of German foreign policies and fail to capture how Germany's foreign policy is perceived from the outside. The dynamics generated by the 'image' that nation-states hold of each other has major implications for what German foreign policy can realistically achieve in world politics. Despite the importance of these dynamics, the literature has failed to scrutinise the external image of Germany's foreign policy in detail. Given the importance of the debate on German power in Europe and the wider world, this chapter explores how Germany's foreign policy is seen from the outside. In order to answer this question, I draw on insights from academic literature, recent surveys and public opinion concerning Germany's role in the world, particularly as it relates to international influence and responsibility. In addition, I also evaluate statements by leading German decision-makers, including speeches by Germany's most important allies and partners.

The goal of this chapter is threefold. It begins by setting out briefly the main reasons why the analysis of the external image of Germany's foreign policy can contribute to our overall understanding of Germany's role in world politics. Since external images are a powerful influence on policy, studying how other countries view German foreign policy can contribute to International Relations (IR) theory by giving us a broader understanding of how formerly conquering states can break with the past and replace their image as a 'military power' with one centred on the conquered realm of 'civilian' capabilities. Second, the chapter reconstructs the main features of Germany's conception of its foreign policy role during the so-called 'Bonn Republic'. In light of the changes in German foreign policy both domestically and internationally over the last few decades, I discuss the extent to which we can still justifiably refer to Germany as a 'civilian power'. Third and above all, the chapter explores whether Germany is still seen as a 'civilian power' from the outside. It contends that there is a growing gulf between the expectations of Germany's allies and partners on the one hand, who would like to see Germany take a greater and more active role in global politics, and the country's still-dominant self-perception as a 'civilian power' on the other hand, which is backed by German public opinion. This backing reveals a marked dissonance between Germany's self-perception and others' perceptions, which has been increasingly generating unease and criticism among Germany's partners and within Germany itself. I conclude by summarising the main empirical findings and outlining discrepancies between domestic and external images of Germany.

Why study the external image of Germany's foreign policy?

The external image of Germany's foreign policy – that is, how the country's global stance is seen from outside – is an often-neglected field in foreign policy analysis (FPA). To be sure, there is a well-established literature on image and perception that examines the origins and consequences of how nation-states see each other.[7] In the same vein, foreign policy role theoreticians focus on the co-constitution of 'ego' (self) and 'alter' (other) expectations in an interstate relationship.[8] There is also an abundant literature by academic scholars who continue to debate whether Germany is a 'civilian power',[9] a 'power state',[10] a 'trading state',[11] a 'geo-economic power'[12] or a 'shaper nation'.[13] In 2016, German Foreign Minister Frank-Walter Steinmeier portrayed Germany as a 'reflective power'.[14] There is also a growing literature on Germany's foreign image policy and public diplomacy'.[15]

However, there is a lack of research on the external image and perception of Germany's foreign policy. This is a major shortcoming since 'the credibility of a state in world politics' is often based 'on a state's image in the eyes of others'.[16] National images or stereotypes are relevant in foreign policy as they serve to justify a state's treatment of another state. Glen Fisher has underlined the importance of perceptions, emphasising that 'international relations revolve around an interplay of images'.[17] This 'interplay of images' not only explains relations among states; it can also be an important factor in determining whether or not a state can achieve its foreign policy goals. As Robert Jervis pointed out:

> [A] desired image can often be of greater use than a significant increment of military and economic power. An undesired image involves costs for which almost no amount of the usual kinds of power can compensate and can be a handicap almost impossible to overcome.[18]

This means that conquering hearts and minds is more important than conquering territory and people. Therefore, the purpose of diplomacy as an instrument of foreign policy is to construct a 'desired image' abroad.

This may be why nations that aspire to be credible and recognised in the world work to enhance their image in foreign countries. In other words, the goal of a foreign image policy is:

> to create an image of the nation in the minds of foreigners. A positive image will make foreigners want to support our policies, visit (or emigrate) to our country, invest in our industries or buy our goods and services. There is also sometimes a deeper idea at work that if we can show what our country is really like then we will remove misunderstanding and produce an improvement in political relations.[19]

In this sense, analysing the image of Germany's foreign policy from abroad not only has the potential to reveal gaps between how Germany perceives itself and how it is perceived by other countries' governmental elites, civil society groups and the media, but it may also tell us whether there is widespread acknowledgement of Germany's distinctiveness as a 'civilian power'. If leading German decision-makers have a limited understanding of what the rest of the world 'thinks' of the country, this may have a negative effect on its external relations and the impact of its policies.

How the idea of Germany as a 'civilian power' became a reality

History – and the foreign policy norms it has helped create – continues to play a critical role in understanding contemporary German foreign policy.[20] For a long time, Germany's role in Europe was synonymous with *Realpolitik* – a term often applied to the 'power politics' of Otto von Bismarck's chancellorship.[21] As American journalist G. A. Schreiner argues in his book *The Craft Sinister*, the prevalent opinion was to contrast the German *Realpolitik* with an avowedly moral form of British *Idealpolitik*.[22] Germany's defeat in the Second World War represented a major turning point for Germany's foreign policy, whereas the country's subsequent division into a Western Federal Republic and an Eastern Democratic Republic after 1949 represented a major trauma.

Traditional German foreign policy norms developed as a reaction to Nazism and the Second World War. In particular, domestic and European developments set specific parameters for the symbiotic relationship between Germany and Europe. European integration replaced the idea of a 'relationship between Germany and Europe' with a conception best described as 'Germany in Europe'.[23] The innate advantages of the Western liberal order in terms of individual freedom and material prosperity allowed (West) Germany to develop an 'extraordinarily successful foreign policy'.[24] In order to do so, it first had to accept the external constraints imposed by the Cold War and Germany's historical and geopolitical position, and then find ways to turn these constraints into assets. As a consequence of the successful foreign policy strategy developed by (West) Germany as a 'semi-sovereign state',[25] Germany's foreign policy has long been shaped by its self-perception as a 'civilian power'.

The term 'civilian power', which is both descriptive and normative as an ideal-type role concept,[26] dates back in the early 1970s and to François Duchêne, who sought to describe the role of former European Community (EC) in IR.[27] As a key adviser to Jean Monnet and Director of the London-based International Institute for Strategic Studies (IISS), Duchêne (who worked with Monnet first as spokesman for US and British interests in the High Authority of the European Coal and Steel Community from 1952 to 1953, and later as his Chef de Cabinet at the Action Committee for the United States of Europe from 1958 to 1963) shared Monnet's vision of European unity. If Monnet was the 'First Statesman of Interdependence', as Duchêne[28] emphasised in his seminal biography of the principal architect of European integration, Duchêne was probably 'one of the foremost political thinkers and analysts of the "méthode Monnet"'.[29]

In his application of the concept of 'civilian power' to the Western Europe of the early 1970s, Duchêne argued that the EC 'must be a force for the international diffusion of civilian and democratic standards' and 'must promote values that belong to its inner characteristics', such as equality, solidarity and justice.[30] This new approach reflected the new civilisational realities of globalisation, which created the capacity 'to transform international politics from their traditional, inter-state focus towards a law-centred and participatory approach which characterised politics within Western democracies'.[31] In Duchêne's words, European integration had shown that this transformation was possible and that interstate relations could be 'domesticated' neither by incrementalism nor by social revolution, but rather by 'that rarest of all phenomena in history, a change in political civilisation'.[32]

During the 1980s, leading realist scholars questioned the term 'civilian power' as a valid description of the EC's external posture. One of the first academics who criticised the notion of Europe as a 'civilian power' was Hedley Bull. Bull argued that Europe needed to be more self-sufficient in defence and security.[33] His solution was to turn the EC into a military power as a prerequisite for being taken seriously as an actor in global politics. Although Duchêne's original idea of 'civilian power Europe' was considered vague and sharply criticised as 'a contradiction in terms',[34] this notion or overlapping concepts such as 'normative power Europe' have dominated the debate on Europe's role in the world since the 2000s.[35] Whereas a 'civilian power' need not necessarily be guided by norms, 'normative power Europe' emphasises the 'ability to shape conceptions of "normal" in international relations'.[36]

While Duchêne's main contribution was to provide an academic focus on what Europe is or should be, by the end of the Cold War, the term 'civilian power' was used to describe Germany's and Japan's post-war foreign policy trajectory. Writing in 1990, Hanns W. Maull observed that Germany and Japan had not only tied themselves to the US-led liberal international order, but had also actively civilised their foreign policy through integration and legalisation, both internationally and domestically.[37] As a former IISS research fellow – it was at this time that he became familiar with Duchêne's thinking – and European Secretary of the Trilateral Commission from 1976 to 1979, Maull has popularised the concept of 'civilian power' within the FPA community. The concept as such derives from research carried out by the German sociologist Norbert Elias (1897–1990) on the evolution of civilisation. Elias' main argument was that the evolution of modern society had been accompanied by the substitution of violent forms of conflict management by the state's monopoly of force as well as by the internalisation of inhibitions to using force. As Elias himself argued that these findings could be applied in social contexts of larger dimensions, it is hence reasonable to assume that Elias' insights can also be found in the realm of foreign policy.

The role concept of 'civilian power' describes a foreign policy orientation that aims to civilise politics in IR. The term 'power' in this context explicitly describes states as actors, the will to exercise influence (i.e. a willingness to pursue and realise these objectives, even against opposition) and the means through which 'civilian powers' pursue their objectives (i.e. specific strategies and instruments of foreign policy). According to Maull, Germany and Japan became 'prototypes' of 'a new type of international power' that – more by necessity than choice – had accepted to cooperate in the pursuit of international objectives.[38] Although the term 'civilian power' was first used to describe German foreign policy at the end of the Cold War in 1989, the FRG found itself on this path from its inception. Key foreign policy decision-makers of the new German Federal Republic – and particularly its first Chancellor, Konrad Adenauer – supported this re-orientation of German foreign policy.[39] In contrast to other role concepts, such as those of the superpowers (i.e. the US and Soviet Union during the Cold War) or great powers (i.e. China, France and Great Britain), Germany's grand strategy was built around three foreign policy principles:

> 'never again' was (West) Germany to fall back into the clutches of totalitarianism (which included not only Nazi fascism, but also communism) and military expansionism; in its foreign policy (West) Germany should act 'never alone', but only in closest coordination above all with its Western allies; and there should be 'politics before force' – Germany should keep its distance, as far as possible, from

military force, which had brought so much destruction not only to Germany itself, but to the whole of Europe during two world wars.[40]

The first principle 'never again' was about regaining recognition as a power in world affairs and a strong commitment to pacifism and democracy.[41] One special expression of this precept has been the FRG's 'special relationship' with the State of Israel.[42] Protecting Israel's security is still part of Germany's 'reason of state'. 'Never again' also explains why the *Grundgesetz* integrates international law in the German legal system and underpins Germany's vocal support for human rights and the rule of law through its foreign policy. During the war in Kosovo in 1999, German Foreign Minister Joschka Fischer changed 'the formula from "never again war" to "never again Auschwitz"' in order to morally justify Germany's first participation in a war since the end of the Second World War in humanitarian terms.[43]

Second, a 'civilian power' is characterised by a strong multilateral orientation, an emphasis on international institutions and a preference for diplomatic means. This rejection of unilateral positions was confirmed by Germany's continued preference for 'embedded' multilateralism and 'coalition-building'.[44] 'Never alone' provided the foundations of (West) Germany's multilateralist foreign, security and defence policies, built around membership of the North Atlantic Treaty Organization (NATO) and the European Union (EU). These binding institutions increased the FRG's 'margin of political manoeuvrability' while allowing 'its partners to maintain soft control over Germany'.[45] International institutions and multilateralism also constituted key aspects of the liberal international economic order designed by the US after 1945. (West) Germany thus became a 'trading state'[46] that was fortunate enough to operate in a multilateral economic order.

Finally, 'politics before force' or 'never be revisionist'[47] stressed a sceptical attitude towards the use of military power (which must only ever be a last resort) and a preference for diplomacy. Before 1945, Germany was the European power most prone to changing the European order.[48] After 1945, although (West) Germany would probably have preferred to remain unarmed, this was impossible in the context of the Cold War. Rearmament was the price that had to be paid for the security guarantees provided by the US, eventually through extended nuclear deterrence.[49] Nevertheless, scepticism concerning the use of force and the deployment of German soldiers in combat remain deeply ingrained within the German politic to this day.

The end of the Cold War eliminated many of the external constraints that had hedged in German foreign policy during the Cold War era. At the same time, re-unification increased Germany's already-substantial power base. In light of these changed geopolitical circumstances, it is no surprise that there has been a re-orientation of German foreign policy behaviour towards less multilateralism, less European vocation and a greater role for power politics.[50] Germany's increasing engagement in international crisis management operations has led foreign policy observers to conclude that Germany is no longer a 'civilian power'. Indeed, in the mid-2000s, there were roughly 10,000 German soldiers deployed abroad, whereas in the early 1990s, Germany had confined itself to 'cheque-book diplomacy'.[51]

However, Berlin's assumption of greater responsibility for international security (which explains Germany's increasing engagement in international crisis management since the 1990s) in no way amounts to a departure from a 'civilian' foreign policy. This would be a misinterpretation of the changes in Germany's foreign policy because these changes reflect its responsibility to protect human rights in Kosovo, Afghanistan and elsewhere according to the 'never ever' principle.[52] Moreover, the German armed forces are sent abroad only within a multilateral institution as a result of Germany's maxim 'never alone again'. Thus, despite Germany's changing foreign policy, such as its first participation in a combat mission in Kosovo in 1999 and then in Afghanistan from 2001 onwards, these norms remain important.[53]

Recent studies have mostly confirmed that Germany still adheres to its central maxims, which are based on its self-understanding as a 'civilian power'.[54] For example, Germany has been widely criticised by its EU and NATO partners for its half-hearted commitment to the war in Afghanistan and its failure to support its allies in Libya.[55] The German government's refusal to join its key NATO allies in enforcing UN Security Council resolutions on Libya in 2011 as well as its unwillingness to help solve the problem of Syria's chemical weapons are foreign policy decisions that have been viewed with growing irritation. Germany prides itself on being a civiliser, set apart from other Western powers, but when Bashar al-Assad's government carried out a chlorine-gas attack, 'the United States, France, and Britain responded'.[56] It seems that Germany is 'reverting to its old "Bonn Republic" mentality of caution, restraint, and reserve in foreign and security policy'.[57] The same is true when it comes to the EU's foreign policy towards Russia in the Ukraine crisis. As Beverly Crawford has rightly pointed out, 'the civilian strategy that is slowly succeeding [there] is essentially a German-led EU strategy'.[58]

While Germany was reviled by Greece as a 'reluctant hegemon' during the eurozone crisis, it has been praised as a 'moral leader' in the refugee crisis. Although this crisis is still evolving, Germany has followed its familiar pattern. Again, Germany's response to the refugee crisis mirrors its view of itself as a 'civilian power'.[59] To be sure, this 'civilian power' has some difficult challenges to overcome, prompting some scholars to conclude that the '"sleep-walking giant" has woken up'.[60] However, in comparing different interpretations of German foreign policy over the last few years, 'we find that the old, originally West German role concept of "civilian power" still corresponds rather well to the foreign policies that Germany has pursued since 2013.'[61]

Germany's changing foreign policy from the outside-in

If the ideal type of 'civilian power' still offers the best way of understanding German foreign policy, how is Germany's new global role seen from the outside? I begin by briefly reconstructing how Germany has succeeded in transforming its international image from that of an 'enemy state' to one of the most popular countries in the world. I then elaborate the most common 'images' of German foreign policy in Europe and among important allies and partners, comparing them with Germany's self-perception.

From 'unloved people number one' to the world's most admired country

Although the early Bonn Republic's foreign policy was long shaped by its strong commitment to multilateralism, European integration and military restraint, Germany suffered from an extremely negative image abroad for many years.[62] After 1945, the Germans were seen as 'unloved people number one'.[63] The legacy of the Third Reich has etched itself deeply into the psyche of Germans themselves and that of their international partners. As scholars have noted, 'Germany's rich cultural history and her spectacular rise from ruins during the post-war period rarely figure in foreigners' perception of modern-day Germany.'[64] Given Germany's traumatic past, it had much to gain from crafting a positive image rather than one stuck in the stereotypes established during two world wars.[65]

The production of a positive post-war German image was an intergenerational process; therefore, the transformation from a 'stigmatised' state – that is, one subject to stereotyping and discrimination – to an admirable member of the international community of states took place slowly. As Rebecca Adler-Nissen has claimed, how Germany 'handled its controversial past' is an 'archetypical example of stigma recognition' in IR.[66] At the same time, (West) Germany's attempt to transform its stigma through recognition and moral renewal after the Second World War was also a 'pioneering example of "nation branding"'.[67] While the first phase was characterised by the country's reconstruction within the multilateral framework of the EC and NATO, a process that 'expressed a liberal-democratic ethos', a second phase began 'as the 1960s social revolution gathered momentum'.[68] A third phase dates from the mid-1970s when (West) Germany's image abroad was more positive. Moreover, the FRG became both a 'model democracy' and an 'economic giant' of Western Europe, but was still a 'political dwarf', and 'buying peace' became the basis for its foreign policy. A fourth phase began after the end of the Cold War. Although the notion of a 'European Germany' did not allay all suspicions about the country, after re-unification in the 1990s, Germans displayed the 'normal pathology of modern life in all its variety'.[69]

Nevertheless, much of Germany's status as a state admired across the world is due to a fifth phase in the development of its post-war image. Since about 2000, the country's successful stigma management and image politics have shifted the focus away from history to its ability to shape international relations.[70] On the one hand, changes have been made to Germany's 'foreign image policy'. Until the mid-1990s, the German government cared about its foreign image mostly for security reasons and used traditional instruments of foreign cultural policy for its image projection. Since the mid-1990s, as Hülsse pointed out, 'its image policy has pursued commercial goals – promoting the *Standort* – and for this purpose relies on public relations and marketing instruments such as the "Land of Ideas" nation-branding campaign'. The German *Kulturnation* has become what Hülsse calls a 'catwalk power'.[71]

On the other hand, hosting the 2006 Football World Cup led to an upward trajectory in Germany's image abroad. That football has the capacity to rebrand a nation is part of the official *Deutschlandbild*. For example, the 'Miracle of Bern' – when (West) Germany won the FIFA World Cup for the first time in 1954 – facilitated 'Germany's return to the international community'.[72] In a similar vein, the so-called *Sommermärchen* in 2006 improved the country's image (critics would argue that the 'summer's tale' is the beginning of a new German nationalism) and appeal worldwide. According to Jonathan Grix, 'there is little evidence of any other event or reason that helps explain this turnaround in international image other than the sports mega event of 2006'.[73] Germany topped the so-called 'Nation Brands Index' (NBI) for the first time in 2007, beating the US, the UK and France to the title of the world's most-admired country. In 2014 and 2017, Germany again replaced the US as the country with the best global image, after reaching second place in 2015 and 2016 and between 2010 and 2013.[74]

Public opinion and other surveys show similar trends. In 2018, Gallup recorded 84 per cent of people having a 'very' or 'mostly favourable' opinion of Germany. These scores confirm 'a consistent trend back to 2000, increasing in the "very favourable" component from 2011'.[75] In BBC World Service Polls, which have been tracking opinions about countries' influence in nineteen countries, Germany has been seen

Table 10.1 Views of Germany's influence in selected countries

Country	2017 +	2017 -	2014 +	2014 -	2013 +	2013 -	2012 +	2012 -	2011 +	2011 -	2010 +	2010 -	2008 +	2008 -
Canada	73	15	77	10	69	13	75	15	69	12	64	7	68	10
US	70	17	73	13	71	13	68	14	76	11	65	10	n/a	n/a
Brazil	63	18	66	21	53	15	48	30	64	14	70	15	44	23
Chile	n/a	n/a	47	18	58	14	48	12	54	19	66	11	53	15
Peru	45	28	44	22	43	20	35	15	40	18	n/a	n/a	n/a	n/a
Mexico	54	25	43	24	54	24	41	21	45	27	44	17	43	18
UK	84	14	86	9	78	12	70	21	77	10	63	8	62	20
France	79	17	83	11	81	11	80	13	84	9	84	9	74	9
Germany	71	2	68	19	64	8	67	6	82	4	79	8	75	10
Spain	56	26	44	40	68	13	60	27	74	12	74	8	77	6
Italy	n/a	n/a	n/a	n/a	n/a	n/a	n/a	n/a	89	4	77	8	82	7
Greece	29	50	n/a	n/a	n/a	n/a	n/a	n/a	n/a	n/a	n/a	n/a	n/a	n/a
Russia	31	29	57	12	55	10	62	4	68	5	61	11	61	9
Turkey	36	45	47	24	46	28	n/a	n/a	53	28	30	33	37	47
Israel	n/a	n/a	25	38	n/a	n/a	n/a	n/a	n/a	n/a	n/a	n/a	65	19
Ghana	n/a	n/a	72	13	84	6	56	6	70	5	65	10	59	10
Nigeria	71	16	63	23	69	18	80	13	73	8	61	27	66	15
Kenya	64	19	58	15	52	14	61	18	58	21	75	12	73	17
Egypt	n/a	n/a	n/a	n/a	43	21	47	25	46	12	50	13	36	43
South Africa	n/a	n/a	n/a	n/a	n/a	n/a	n/a	n/a	49	16	n/a	n/a	n/a	n/a
Australia	79	10	86	7	76	10	79	8	77	9	65	8	71	12
South Korea	n/a	n/a	84	6	76	8	75	12	82	10	82	12	71	18
Indonesia	48	20	53	28	60	21	56	13	65	17	55	19	48	27
Japan	n/a	n/a	46	3	47	3	38	2	37	4	40	3	45	4
China	84	13	42	22	48	23	53	24	50	39	62	15	58	16
Pakistan	21	20	35	27	29	26	21	26	22	19	13	18	n/a	n/a
India	40	17	32	26	27	14	29	20	37	19	22	19	19	14

Source: BBC World Service Polls 2009–18 (author's own compilation)
Legend: + = 'mostly positive'; − = 'mostly negative'

(with the exception of 2017) as the country with the most positive influence in the world since 2009. On average, 60 per cent of people rated Germany 'mostly positive' in this regard, whereas only between 15 and 21 per cent viewed the country's influence as 'mainly negative' (see Table 10.1).

Compared to 2014, when the BBC Poll was last conducted, the strongest support comes from Britain (84–86 per cent) and France (79–83 per cent). The picture becomes even more impressive if we look beyond Europe. In Canada and the US, positive attitudes towards Germany's influence in the world continue to be very stable at over 70 per cent. Feelings towards Germany are also positive in African countries (from 64 per cent in Kenya to 71 per cent in Nigeria) and in Central and South America (Brazil 63 per cent, Mexico 54 per cent and Peru

45 per cent). The results in Asia and Oceania are more mixed. A large majority of Australians (79 per cent) and South Koreans (84 per cent in 2014) and many Japanese (46 per cent) hold positive views, while Indians (the highest level since 2009) and Indonesians also continue to express generally positive views. Opinion in Pakistan has deteriorated, shifting from narrowly positive in 2014 (35 per cent) to divided in 2017 (21 per cent positive vs. 20 per cent negative).

In contrast to this very positive global trend, perceptions of German influence have taken a negative turn in Russia (32 per cent positive vs. 29 per cent negative) and Turkey (36 per cent positive vs. 45 per cent negative) since 2014, when opinion was positive (57 per cent in Russia and 47 per cent in Turkey). This is the least favourable view of Germany that Russia has held since polls began in 2008. German positive influence has also deteriorated in Israel (from 65 in 2008 to 24 per cent in 2014). The largest increase in favourable views of Germany is seen in China, where the proportion of respondents with a positive opinion has doubled since 2014 to 84 per cent.

While NBI, the BBC and Gallup are designed to provide quantitative information in the form of rankings and percentages, qualitative surveys largely confirm their findings. For the third time since 2011, the *Gesellschaft für Internationale Zusammenarbeit* has interviewed representatives from the worlds of politics, business, science and research in five continents to find out about their perceptions of Germany.[76] The findings revealed that the overall image of contemporary Germany abroad is positive and Germany's history is now increasingly seen as a less legitimate reason for German foreign policy restraint.[77] Another indicator is Germany's ability to attract foreign students or facilitate academic exchanges. In 2016/17, nearly 360,000 of the 2.85 million students enrolled at German universities came from abroad, making Germany one of the most popular international destinations for higher education.[78] Widely recognised and respected cultural and educational organisations, such as the German Academic Exchange Service and the Goethe Institute, add further value to what scholars famously called 'soft power'.[79]

Two recent developments – Germany's role during the eurozone and migration crises – seem to have confirmed the country's positive image abroad. Surveys conducted in eight EU countries and the US during the sovereign debt crisis in Europe established that Germany is the most admired Member State in the EU.[80] Roughly eight in ten people in France (84 per cent), the Czech Republic (80 per cent) and Poland (78 per cent) hold a favourable view of Germany. Significantly lower scores were recorded in Spain (57 per cent), Italy (67 per cent) and Greece (21 per cent). These responses, like the response of Greece in the 2017 BBC Poll, reflect popular discontent with Chancellor Merkel's handling of the sovereign debt crisis in the countries of Southern Europe. Nevertheless,

Merkel is widely seen as the most effective national leader when it comes to dealing with European crises and fostering Europe's longer-term stability.

Germany's treatment of refugees from September 2015 onwards is another factor that has earned respect abroad. While Merkel's refugee policy still has the potential to divide Europe and has been challenging internally, 'it has certainly done no damage to its reputation in the wider world. Quite the opposite is true'.[81] According to an Amnesty International survey on attitudes towards those fleeing war and persecution, Germany is one of most welcoming countries in the world for refugees.[82] While Germany's 'Willkommenskultur' was lauded worldwide,[83] the European reaction has been more sceptical. The Visegrád group – the Czech Republic, Hungary, Poland and Slovakia – in particular strongly oppose Merkel's open-door policy on migrants, accusing her of 'moral imperialism'.[84] Subsequently, the appreciation felt for 'the much-acclaimed *Willkommenskultur* reduced' and many members of the German public, neighbouring states and other observers 'questioned Merkel's decision-making'.[85] Nevertheless, Germany's treatment of refugees has softened 'the image of the typical German as hard-working and efficient, and added a new characteristic – that of a global citizen with humanitarian principles'.[86]

To sum up, the available data support the argument that after 2000, Germany's global image was very positive, apart from situational declines attributable to controversies such as the 2003 Iraq War.[87] The country's foreign image was further enhanced from 2006 onwards, despite its abstention in the UN Security Council vote on Libya in 2011 (pitting Germany against the US, France and the UK), the embrace of austerity during the eurozone crisis, the struggle to deal with the refugee challenge and, recently, the 'Dieselgate' scandal involving German car-makers. After Donald Trump was elected President of the United States, Chancellor Merkel was even considered (misleadingly, in my opinion) the new 'leader of the Free World'.[88] Germany's strong reputation in surveys and rankings was repeatedly monitored by leading German decision-makers. Frank-Walter Steinmeier was delighted that 'Germany enjoys such a good reputation in the world'.[89] His successor in the Foreign Office, Sigmar Gabriel, emphasised that 'Germany's image hasn't simply been based on our economic clout'; instead, people think 'we're capable of doing a lot in the world'.[90] Meanwhile, Heiko Maas, the new Foreign Minister, warned that 'the increasing number of racist attacks against migrants and Jews create a shameful situation and damage the international reputation of Germany'.[91] In other words: 'The Germans have reason to be proud of this shift from ugly German to moral superpower.'[92]

The widening gap between expectations of German foreign policy from inside and outside

Germany's stigma and image management after the Second World War has certainly done no damage to its reputation in the broader foreign policy field. Maull rightly claimed that anything more successful than the foreign policy of the FRG since 1949 is hardly imaginable.[93] In 1985, Hans-Peter Schwarz argued that during the twentieth century, Germany's foreign policy shifted '[v]on der Machtbesessenheit zur Machtvergessenheit' ('from obsession with power to oblivion with power'),[94] yet Maull has always insisted that (West) Germany has enjoyed considerable power and has used it very intelligently to achieve influence. Since 'power', as a phenomenon, 'is closely related to causality, it seems obvious that the success of West German foreign policy reflected the exercise of power' – namely that exercised by Germany as a 'civilian power'.[95]

After 1945, Germany's self-perception as a 'civilian power' long remained broadly consistent with the view from outside. However, within the German post-unification foreign policy debate since the late 1990s, for the first time a gap has opened between foreign policy perspectives within Germany and growing international demands on German foreign policy. Most recently, studies conducted under the heading *Germany in the Eyes of the World* highlight a development of which Germans themselves are probably not yet fully aware:

> In 2011/2012, Germany was being cordially invited to show greater confidence. By contrast, in 2014/2015, the dominant perception was that Germany had no choice but to step up and get more involved in the wake of the financial crisis and the Greek debt crisis. Now ... a loud chorus of interviewees worried about global turmoil and urging Europe and Germany to act as guardians of Western values and stand up for the common good of as many people as possible, especially as a counterweight to the USA, Russia and China.[96]

The ongoing eurozone crisis, the conflicts in Syria and Ukraine, the migration crisis as well as the uncertain development of European integration and transatlantic relations after 'Brexit' and the Trump presidency have pushed 'German foreign policy into an international leadership role', although Germany had not 'actively sought such a role'.[97] Germany did not seek 'greater responsibility in Europe after reunification'; rather, it emerged as a central player 'by remaining stable as the world around it changed'.[98] However, the growing international demands on German foreign policy are only mirrored by domestic expectations to a limited degree, despite the fact that the term 'responsibility' – as a post-war leitmotif of German foreign policy first articulated by Foreign Minister

Hans-Dietrich Genscher in 1975 – again became in vogue in the foreign policy public discourse.[99]

The recent debate around Germany's responsibilities on the international stage was initiated by speeches during the Munich Security Conference in 2014 by former German President Joachim Gauck, former Foreign Minister Frank-Walter Steinmeier and former Defence Minister Ursula von der Leyen. Gauck[100] argued that politicians should stop using Germany's 'historic guilt' as an excuse to 'look away' from global problems. Six months before, to mark the Holiday of German Unity on 3 October 2013, Gauck had asked whether Germany's 'international engagement was on a par with the weight that our country carries'.[101] His call for a new sense of responsibility was followed by speeches in a similar vein by Steinmeier and von der Leyen. 'Having the resources and abilities means we also have the responsibility to engage', von der Leyen insisted,[102] while Steinmeier contended: 'Germany is really too big to merely sit on the sidelines and comment on world politics'.[103]

In order to generate an open dialogue about Germany's responsibilities in Europe and beyond, in December 2013 Steinmeier initiated a process of reflection on the future prospects of German foreign policy. The so-called *Review 2014 – Außenpolitik weiter denken* adopted a three-pronged approach, which not only involved discussions with the German public and debate among Federal Foreign Office staff but also asked international experts for their views on German foreign policy.[104] While from the inside-out German voters continued to expect that 'our habitual, familiar procedures in international politics' would remain effective, from the outside-in, the review documented a broad consensus in favour of a more active German foreign policy.[105] Nearly all external experts emphasise 'the underdeveloped international conscience of Germany's decision-makers' and express 'their regret and inability to understand the fact that Germany is behaving too hesitantly and is underestimating her potential'.[106]

However, in contrast to the consensus among foreign policy elites and experts, the German public wants Germany to act with restraint on the international stage. In opinion polls conducted by the Körber Foundation, only 40 per cent of respondents agreed that Germany should accept more responsibilities in international crises, while 60 per cent believe that, given its history, the country should 'continue to demonstrate restraint'. A more robust military posture was only approved by 13 per cent of respondents. The German public remains particularly sceptical about foreign deployments of the *Bundeswehr*, with 82 per cent of Germans wanting to see them reduced in 2014. In contrast, majorities support a stronger civilian engagement of Germany in global politics in the form of humanitarian aid or diplomatic assistance. What is most surprising is not the lack of support for engagement, but that these figures virtually reverse those recorded in 1994.[107]

German foreign policy and the view from the US and France

As we have seen, there is a growing gap between the foreign policy views of leading decision-makers and the German public on the one hand, and the expectations held by Germany's allies and partners on the other. In terms of Germany's role conception as a 'civilian power', the most significant others ('alters') are the US and France. Since Germany's re-unification in 1990, the German–American relationship has become the pivot in the larger transatlantic partnership 'due to an increase in [Germany's] power as well as the decline of France and Britain as European powers'.[108] However, the inauguration of US President Trump in January 2017 showed how fragile German–American relations are.[109]

When former US President George H. W. Bush was still hoping that a unified Germany would be a strong international partner in the Persian Gulf War (1990–1), the US learned to accept German 'cheque-book diplomacy', in other words funding rather than active participation in war. A few years later, Germany came out of its post-war 'pacifist shell', undertaking its first post-war military engagements in Bosnia and Kosovo.[110] Chancellor Gerhard Schröder's commitment of 'unlimited solidarity' with the US after the '9/11' attacks and the deployment of up to 7,000 German forces in Afghanistan were the high points in this 'partnership in leadership', to be followed by the schism that emerged between Germany and the US over the Iraq War in 2003. Although the coming to power of the grand coalition in 2005 led by Chancellor Merkel raised hopes that the partnership would be reinvigorated, 'German policy remained restrained with Merkel's refusal to commit German forces to NATO operations in Libya' and continuing 'German-American disagreements over financial management of the Eurozone crisis'.[111]

The enhanced alliance between the two countries resulting from strong US support for German re-unification did not prevent the US from viewing Germany as a 'free rider' that takes advantage of a stable international order. 'Free riders aggravate me', US President Barack Obama told Jeffrey Goldberg in an interview for *The Atlantic*,[112] while former Defence Secretary Robert Gates warned:

> The blunt reality is that there will be dwindling appetite and patience in the U.S. Congress – and in the American body politic writ large – to expend increasingly precious funds on behalf of nations that are apparently unwilling to devote the necessary resources or make the necessary changes to be serious and capable partners in their own defense.[113]

The grand coalition governments led by Chancellor Merkel pledged to boost the *Bundeswehr* through higher defence spending; nevertheless, the allocation of public expenditure has shifted decisively away from foreign affairs towards domestic spending since the 1990s.[114] In the 1980s, on average Germany spent about 2.3 per cent of its GDP on defence and the *Bundeswehr* had the largest European armed forces in NATO, with more than 400,000 soldiers. Today, Germany only commits 1.2 per cent of GDP. The Trump administration has harshly criticised Germany for failing to meet the NATO target of spending 2 per cent of GDP on defence and has questioned continuing the US commitment to the alliance's Article 5 collective defence provision. Other criticisms from the Trump administration relate to Germany's trade surplus, which hurts US interests, or Germany's alleged status as a 'captive of Moscow' because it imports so much gas from Russia.[115]

To be sure, whatever Trump says and does, Germany and the US will remain connected through shared interests and values. A Pew Research Center survey in 2015 found – despite disagreements at the time over the Iraq War and the NSA surveillance controversy – that 72 per cent of Americans see Germany as a reliable ally. Roughly four in ten Americans (38 per cent) approve of how Merkel is handling bilateral ties, while fewer (27 per cent) disapprove. When it comes to Germany's reluctant approach to foreign affairs, more than half (54 per cent) of Americans think Berlin should play a more active military role in global politics.[116] In a survey conducted in 2018, 45 per cent of Americans say Germany should spend more on national defence and only 12 per cent mention Germany (behind the UK, China and Israel) as one of America's top foreign policy partners.[117]

The US is not the only important ally and partner to take Germany to task. In his speech at the Charlemagne Prize award ceremony in Aachen, French President Emmanuel Macron said Berlin should desist from 'constantly fetishising budget and trade surpluses: they always arise at the expense of others'.[118] In the past Germany and France evolved strong mutual expectations of cooperative behaviour and each assumed that the other held the status of 'essential partner' in Europe.[119] In recent years, however, the two countries are widely perceived to have struggled to cope with each other's expectations:

> France, proud of its seat at the UN Security Council, its operation-ready army, of its nuclear strength and its influence, because of its language and its history, as the nation of the Enlightenment, Revolution and Human Rights, maintains its sight set on the wide world, with privileged zones of influence in the South, especially in Africa. Germany, proud of its economic power and the quality of its products, is reticent about military interventions, has its sight on its continent and especially on Central and Eastern Europe, where its main interests lie, and acts as one of the world's leading export powers.[120]

While France and Germany 'constitute the inner circle of EU coalition-building' in various policy fields,[121] both countries slowly moved away from their close relationship during the multiple crises in Europe. During the financial crisis of 2008, French readiness to support the banks as soon as the financial crisis broke out came up against initial German caution. In a similar vein, the German government was very reluctant to deal with the eurozone crisis and for a while resisted a rescue package for Greece in 2009, while France was inclined to help Greece from the beginning.[122] In the case of Europe's banking union, France and Germany turned out to be the main antagonists.[123] Although the new German grand coalition agreed to enter into a meaningful dialogue with the French President on reform of the eurozone, Germany is frustrating Macron's grand ambitions because Berlin does not want an enlarged European Stability Mechanism, the rescue umbrella or a single eurozone budget. By contrast, France considered Germany overly generous in its willingness to admit refugees during the migration crisis.[124]

When it comes to security and defence issues, mutual expectations of a rejuvenated form of Franco-German co-leadership is becoming more visible. The permanent structured cooperation (PESCO) initiative was launched in December 2017 by 25 EU Member States, along with the French-led push to establish a European intervention initiative in June 2018. They are intended to foster a common strategic culture and are real steps forward for European defence, but they do 'not tally with the French goal of creating a hard European core that is capable of operational combat deployments. It is the German vision that has prevailed in the drafting of the PESCO, which includes nearly all of the Union's Member States, i.e. that of a joint development of military capabilities, but without any operational target'.[125]

The French view of Germany has traditionally been based on the notion of rough equality between both countries. Until the 1980s, (West) Germany's economy and population were only slightly larger and French economic growth exceeded that of its neighbour. Only three decades later, this equality between Paris and Berlin no longer exists because Germany's population and economy have expanded and the likelihood of 'German hegemony' in the post-Brexit EU is being discussed as a possible future scenario.[126] The political and economic decoupling of Germany and France is accompanied by a growing gap in German and French public opinion. A 2013 Pew survey found that:

> French attitudes have sharply diverged from German public opinion on a range of issues since the beginning of the euro crisis. Differences in opinion across the Rhine have long existed. But the French public mood is now looking less like that in Germany and more like that in the southern peripheral nations of Spain, Italy and Greece.[127]

With Macron's new reform agenda, a 'dyspeptic France' may soon be a thing of the past. Moreover, in order to rejuvenate the 'Joint Declaration of Franco-German Friendship' signed in 1963, France and Germany signed a new 'Elysée Treaty' on 22 January 2019 that is designed to deepen the Franco-German friendship. However, the long 'Franco-German honeymoon' seems to be over and 'Paris and Berlin are no longer natural allies'.[128] Although a poll commissioned by the German embassy in Paris in 2017 found that a large majority of the French have a positive image of Germany, in recent years the German–French friendship has deteriorated.[129] Germany is a source of admiration when it comes to its economic (80 per cent) and political power (62 per cent), but only 41 per cent agree with Germany's handling of the refugee crisis and just 4 per cent appreciate Germany as an ally. The painful history is a thing of the past for the French; what matters above all is Germany's attachment to the EU. Put differently, the Franco-German tandem might be a 'solid couple', but the French see Germany merely as 'partner' and no longer as 'friend'.

Conclusion

This chapter has assessed how Germany's foreign policy role as a 'civilian power' is seen from the outside. Studying the external image of Germany's foreign policy, widely ignored in FPA, contributes not only to our understanding of Germany's changing role; the dynamics generated by the 'image' nation-states hold of each other could have major implications for what Germany can realistically achieve in foreign policy. Although German foreign policy has changed over the years, most political observers would subscribe to the view that the old, originally (West) German role concept of 'civilian power' still describes rather well the foreign policies Germany has pursued since the 1990s. The 'civilian power' paradigm portrays Germany after the Second World War as a 'different' kind of international actor, one committed to economic rather than military power, with a strong preference for multilateralism and a desire to 'civilise' world politics trough international law. Germany's status as a 'civilian power' and its post-war attempt to gain international acceptance have reinforced each other in such a way that Germany is now among those countries with the best international image. To be sure, Germany's conception of its role as a civilian power has been modified. Hanns W. Maull, who adapted the term on the basis of Duchêne's 'civilian power Europe' to convey Germany's post-Second World War foreign policy trajectory, has recently referred to 'civilian power 2.0' to indicate that Germany is formulating its new ambition in foreign policy more in global than European terms.[130] Nevertheless, its role as a 'civilian power' is uncontested domestically, despite far-reaching changes in the international environment.

Yet Germany's traditional and still-dominant self-image as a 'civilian power' at home is producing unease and criticism abroad, especially among its most important partners and allies. Paradoxically, Germany's successful transformation of its international image from that of a 'stigmatised state' to one of the most-admired countries in the world – which has certainly reinforced its reputation as a 'civilian power' – is now coming under pressure because of the growing sense of a European and international leadership vacuum, which German foreign policy was expected to fill. German governments have responded with a foreign policy review and a declared willingness to assume greater international responsibility. More recently, with the arrival of President Trump, Merkel has acknowledged that Germany will increasingly have to 'take its fate into its own hands', and Foreign Minister Maas is working to build a global alliance of 'like-minded middle powers'.[131] But if the country wants to be taken seriously by the US and trusted in the EU, its leading decision-makers also need to deal seriously with the mismatch between domestic and international expectations of German foreign policy. The present analysis contends that there is a growing gulf between an emerging international consensus that Germany should play a greater military role in world politics and the country's still-dominant self-perception as a 'civilian power'. This tension between international and domestic expectations has played out differently across the various crises (i.e. the eurozone crisis and the migration crisis) and with respect to different allies (i.e. the US and France) and has increased rather than diminished during Merkel's chancellorship.[132]

Navigating the growing gulf between domestic and international expectations is thus the real challenge in present-day German foreign policy – both domestically and internationally. At the domestic level, when it comes to foreign policy, the German government has made significant efforts to mobilise domestic political support in the context of the 'Review 2014' and there are signs that the leading decision-makers have now recognised the need to correct the long-standing financial neglect of the *Bundeswehr*. But will Germans really support these new ambitions for Germany's foreign policy when the bills come in? Through a slow learning process, since the 1990s German society has come to accept multilateral combat missions under certain circumstances. After a highly contested German debate about the use of force and a landmark ruling of the Constitutional Court in 1994 permitting German soldiers to be deployed in NATO's 'out-of-area' missions, a large German majority supported the idea of more military engagement. However, in light of the *Bundeswehr* experience in Afghanistan, this lesson has been unlearned. Once again there is a need to reverse public opinion and develop a new narrative about how, where and when members of the German armed forces might participate militarily in international missions.

Turning to the international arena and the view from outside, a growing mismatch between domestic and international expectations might be a major problem for Germany and might result in what scholars have called foreign policy 'autism'.[133] Furthermore, the gulf between expectations from outside on the one hand and an inward-looking electorate that favours restraint on the other hand reveals a marked dissonance between Germany's self-perception as a 'civilian power' and others' perceptions. In the long run, such 'cognitive dissonance' vis-à-vis the rest of the international community may undermine the credibility of Germany's foreign policy both abroad and at home. It would be deeply ironic if Germany's extraordinarily successful foreign policy during the last seventy years should become a serious problem for its allies and partners at the beginning of the new century!

Notes

1 J. Joffe, *Der gute Deutsche. Die Karriere einer moralischen Supermacht* (Gütersloh: C. Bertelsmann, 2018), p. 2.

2 H. W. Maull, 'Germany and Japan: the new civilian powers', *Foreign Affairs*, 69:5 (1990), pp. 91–106; H. W. Maull, 'From "civilian power" to "trading state"?', in S. Colvin (ed.), *Routledge Handbook of German Politics and Culture* (London: Routledge, 2014), pp. 409–24.

3 P. H. Gordon, 'Berlin's difficulties: the normalization of German foreign policy', *Orbis*, 38:2 (1994), pp. 225–43, at p. 225.

4 K. Brummer and K. Oppermann, *Germany's Foreign Policy after the End of the Cold War: 'Becoming Normal'?* (Oxford: Oxford University Press, 2016).

5 G. Hellmann, D. Jacobi and U. Stark Urrestarazu (eds), 'Früher, entschiedener und substantieller? Die neue Debatte über Deutschlands Außenpolitik', *Zeitschrift für Außen- und Sicherheitspolitik, Sonderheft*, 6 (Wiesbaden: Springer VS, 2015); M. Matthijs, 'The three faces of German leadership', *Survival*, 58:2 (2016), pp. 135–54.

6 B. Crawford and K. B. Olsen, 'The puzzle of persistence and power: explaining Germany's normative foreign policy', *German Politics*, 26:4 (2017), pp. 591–608; H. Kundnani, *The Paradox of German Power* (Oxford: Oxford University Press, 2015); S. Schieder, 'Zwischen Führungsanspruch und Wirklichkeit: Deutschlands Rolle in der Eurozone', *Leviathan*, 42:3 (2014), pp. 363–97; S. Bulmer and W. E. Paterson, 'Germany as the EU's reluctant hegemon? Of economic strength and political constraints', *Journal of European Public Policy*, 20:10 (2013), pp. 1387–405.

7 See R. Jervis, *Perception and Misperception in International Relations* (Princeton: Princeton University Press, 2017); R. K. Herrmann, 'Image theory and strategic interaction in international relations', in D. O. Sears, L. Huddy and R. Jervis (eds), *The Oxford Handbook of Political Psychology* (Oxford: Oxford University Press, 2003), pp. 285–314.

8 S. Harnisch, C. Frank and H. W. Maull (eds), *Role Theory in International Relations: Contemporary Approaches and Analyses* (New York: Routledge, 2011).

9 Maull, 'Germany and Japan'.

10 H. P. Schwarz, *Die Zentralmacht Europas: Deutschlands Rückkehr auf die Weltbühne* (Berlin: Siedler Verlag, 1994).

11 M. Staack, *Handelsstaat Deutschland. Deutsche Außenpolitik in einem neuen internationalen System* (Paderborn: Schöningh, 2000).

12 H. Kundnani, 'Germany as a geo-economic power', *Washington Quarterly*, 34:3 (2011), pp. 31–45; S. F. Szabo, *Germany, Russia, and the Rise of Geo-economics* (New York: Bloomsbury, 2014).

13 C. Stelzenmüller, 'Germany, between power and responsibility', in W. A. Hitchcock et al. (eds), *Shaper Nations: Strategies for a Changing World* (Cambridge, MA: Harvard University Press, 2016), pp. 53–69.

14 F. W. Steinmeier, 'Germany's new global role – Berlin steps up', *Foreign Affairs*, 95:4 (2016), pp. 106–13.

15 R. Hülsse, 'The catwalk power: Germany's new foreign image policy', *Journal of International Relations and Development*, 12:3 (2009), pp. 293–316; S. Wood, 'Rebranding the nation: Germany's image politics', *International Politics*, 54:2 (2017), pp. 161–81; S. Wood, 'Das Deutschlandbild: national image, reputation and interests in post-war Germany', *Contemporary European History*, 27:4 (2018), 651–73.

16 S. Smolnikov, *Great Power Conduct and Credibility in World Politics* (London: Palgrave Macmillan, 2018), p. 193.

17 G. Fisher, *Mindsets: The Role of Culture and Perception in International Relations* (Yarmouth: Intercultural Press, 1997), p. 4.

18 R. Jervis, *The Logic of Images in International Relations* (Princeton: Princeton University Press, 1970), p. 6.

19 R. Brown, 'Four paradigms of public diplomacy' (paper presented at the ISA Annual Convention, San Diego, 2012), p. 5.

20 H. A. Winkler, *Der lange Weg nach Westen II: Deutsche Geschichte vom 'Dritten Reich' zur Wiedervereinigung* (Munich: C. H. Beck, 2000).

21 J. Bew, *Realpolitik: A History* (Oxford: Oxford University Press, 2016).

22 G. A. Schreiner, *The Craft Sinister* (New York: G. A. Geyer, 1920), p. 270.

23 P. J. Katzenstein, 'United Germany in an integrating Europe', in P. J. Katzenstein (ed.), *Tamed Power: Germany in Europe* (Ithaca, NY: Cornell University Press, 1997), pp. 1–47, at p. 19.

24 H. W. Maull, 'Reflective, hegemonic, geo-economic, civilian …? The puzzle of German power', *German Politics*, 27:4 (2018), pp. 460–78, at p. 467.

25 P. J. Katzenstein, *Policy and Politics in West Germany: The Growth of the Semi-sovereign Polity* (Philadelphia: Temple University Press, 1987).

26 K. Kirste and H. W. Maull, 'Zivilmacht und Rollentheorie', *Zeitschrift für Internationale Beziehungen*, 3:2 (1996), pp. 283–312.

27 F. Duchêne, 'Europe's role in world peace', in R. J. Mayne (ed.), *Europe Tomorrow: Sixteen Europeans Look Ahead* (London: Collins, 1972), pp. 32–47.

28 F. Duchêne, 'The European Community and the uncertainties of interdependence', in M. Kohnstamm and W. Hager (eds), *A Nation Writ Large? Foreign*

Policy Problems before the European Community (London: Macmillan, 1973), pp. 1–21.

29 H. W. Maull, 'Francois Duchêne: political thinker and analyst', *The Independent* (25 July 2005), www.independent.co.uk/news/obituaries/francois-duchene-301409.html.

30 Duchêne, 'The European Community', p. 20.

31 Maull, 'Francois Duchene'.

32 Duchêne, 'The European Community', p. 20.

33 H. Bull, 'Civilian power Europe: a contradiction in terms?', *Journal of Common Market Studies*, 12:2 (1982), pp. 149–64

34 Bull, 'Civilian power Europe'.

35 J. Orbie, 'Review essay: civilian power Europe', *Cooperation and Conflict*, 41:1 2006), pp. 123–8.

36 I. Manners, 'Normative power Europe: a contradiction in terms?', *Journal of Common Market Studies*, 40:2 (2002), pp. 232–58, at p. 239.

37 Maull, 'Germany and Japan'.

38 Maull, 'Germany and Japan'.

39 See H. Haftendorn, *Coming of Age: German Foreign Policy since 1945* (Lanham, MD: Rowman & Littlefield, 2006).

40 Maull, 'From "civilian power" to "trading state"?', p. 410.

41 Winkler, *Der lange Weg nach Westen II*.

42 L. Gardner Feldman, *The Special Relationship between West Germany and Israel* (Boston: Allen & Unwin, 1984).

43 P. Daehnhardt, 'German foreign policy, the Ukraine crisis and the Euro-Atlantic order: assessing the dynamics of change', *German Politics*, 26:4 (2018), pp. 1–23, at p. 3.

44 S. Bulmer and W. E. Paterson, 'Germany and the European Union: from "tamed power" to normalized power?', *International Affairs*, 8:5 (2010), pp. 1051–73; H. W. Maull, 'Germany and the art of coalition building', *Journal of European Integration*, 30:1 (2008), pp. 131–52.

45 Daehnhardt, 'German foreign policy', p. 3.

46 R. Rosecrance, *The Rise of the Trading State: Commerce and Conquest in the Modern World* (New York: Basic Books, 1986).

47 Daehnhardt, 'German foreign policy', p. 3.

48 C. Clark, *The Sleepwalkers: How Europe went to War in 1914* (New York: Harper, 2014).

49 Maull, 'From "civilian power" to "trading state"?', p. 412.

50 Bulmer and Paterson, 'Germany and the European Union'.

51 G. Hellmann, 'Goodbye Bismarck? The foreign policy of contemporary Germany', *Mershon International Studies Review*, 40:1 (1996), pp. 1–39.

52 H. W. Maull, 'Germany and the use of force: still a "civilian power"?', *Survival*, 42:2 (2000), pp. 56–80.

53 A. Geis, 2005. 'Die Zivilmacht Deutschland und die Enttabuisierung des Militärischen', in *Standpunkte. Beiträge zum Demokratischen Frieden*, 2 (Frankfurt am Main: HSFK, 2005).

54 S. Harnisch and J. Schild (eds), *Deutsche Außenpolitik und internationale Führung. Ressourcen, Praktiken und Politiken in einer veränderten Europäischen Union* (Baden-Baden: Nomos, 2014).

55 C. Hacke, 'Deutschland und der Libyen-Konflikt: Zivilmacht ohne Zivilcourage?', *Aus Politik und Zeitgeschichte*, 61:39 (2011), pp. 50–3; A. Miskimmon, 'German foreign policy and the Libya crisis', *German Politics*, 21:4 (2012), pp. 392–410.

56 J. Dempsey, 'Germany's no-go foreign policy', *Carnegie Europe* (2018), www.carnegieeurope.eu/strategiceurope/76091.

57 A. Hyde-Price, 'The "sleep-walking giant" awakes: resetting German foreign and security policy', *European Security*, 24:4 (2015), pp. 600–16, at p. 601.

58 B. Crawford, *'Moral leadership or moral hazard? Germany's response to the refugee crisis and its impact on European solidarity'* (Berkeley: University of California Memo, 2016), p. 4, https://migrationcluster.ucdavis.edu/sites/g/files/dgvnsk821/files/inline-files/paper_crawford_germany-response-to-refugee.pdf.

59 Crawford and Olsen, 'The puzzle of persistence and power'.

60 Hyde-Price, 'The "sleep-walking giant" awakes', p. 601.

61 Maull, 'Reflective, hegemonic, geo-economic, civilian …?', p. 474.

62 G. Paschalidis, 'Cultural outreach: overcoming the past?', in S. Colvin (ed.), *Routledge Handbook of German Politics and Culture* (London: Routledge, 2014), pp. 457–71.

63 E. Friedlaender, 'Deutschland: Unbeliebtes Volk Nr.1', *Die Zeit* (13 January 1949), https://www.zeit.de/1949/02/deutschland-unbeliebtes-volk-nr-1.

64 J. Grix, and C. Lacroix, 'Constructing Germany's image in the British press: an empirical analysis of stereotypical reporting on Germany', *Journal of Contemporary European Studies* 14:3 (2006), pp. 373–92, at p. 373.

65 Wood, 'Das Deutschlandbild', p. 3.

66 R. Adler-Nissen, 'Stigma management in international relations: transgressive identities, norms, and order in international society', *International Organization*, 68:1 (2014), pp. 143–76, at p. 156.

67 Wood, 'Rebranding the nation', p. 161.

68 Wood, 'Rebranding the nation', p. 164.

69 Wood, 'Rebranding the nation', p. 165.

70 Gesellschaft für Internationale Zusammenarbeit (GIZ) (ed.), *Germany in the Eyes of the World: Key Findings of the GIZ Survey* (Bonn: GIZ, 2012); Stiftung Wissenschaft und Politik and German Marshall Fund, *New Power, New Responsibility: Elements of a German Foreign and Security Policy for a Changing World* (Berlin: SWP and GMF, 2013).

71 Hülsse, 'The catwalk power', p. 293.

72 H. Dichter, 'Kicking around international sport: West Germany's return to the international community through football', *International Journal of the History of Sport*, 30:17 (2013), pp. 2031–51.

73 J. Grix, 'Sport politics', in: S. Colvin (ed.), *Routledge Handbook of German Politics and Culture* (London: Routledge, 2014), pp. 441–56, at p. 452.

74 S. Anholt, 'Germany reclaims top "nation brand" ranking, with USA dropping to sixth place', *Growth from Knowledge* (15 November 2017), https://www.prnewswire.com/news-releases/germany-reclaims-top-nation-brand-ranking-with-usa-dropping-to-sixth-place-in-anholt-gfk-nation-brands-index-2017-657884033.html.

75 Wood, 'Rebranding the nation', p. 170.

76 GIZ, *Germany in the Eyes of the World 2012* (Bonn: GIZ, 2012).

77 GIZ, *Germany in the Eyes of the World: Key Findings of the Second GIZ Survey* (Bonn: GIZ, 2015), p. 80; GIZ, *Germany in the Eyes of the World: Findings of the 2017/2018 GIZ Survey* (Bonn: GIZ, 2018), p. 100.

78 Deutscher Akademischer Austausch Dienst, 'Germany surpasses international student target three years early' (2018), www.thepienews.com/news/germany-surpasses-international-student-target-three-years-early.

79 J. S. Nye, 'Public diplomacy and soft power', *Annals of the American Academy of Political and Social Science*, 616:1 (2008), pp. 94–109.

80 Pew Research Center, '*European unity on the rocks: Greeks and Germans at polar opposites*' (2012), www.pewresearch.org/wp-content/uploads/sites/2/2012/05/Pew-Global-Attitudes-Project-European-Crisis-Report-FINAL-FOR-PRINT-May-29–2012.pdf, pp. 35–40.

81 GIZ, *Germany in the Eyes of the World* (2018), p. 3.

82 Amnesty International, '*The Global Refugee Crisis in 2015*' (2015), https://www.amnesty.org/en/latest/news/2015/12/global-refugee-crisis-2015-gallery.

83 N. Kristof, 'Compassion for refugees isn't enough', *New York Times* (20 September 2015).

84 A. Meiritz, 'How Germany became Europe's moral leader on the refugee crisis', *Vox* (11 September 2015), www.vox.com/2015/9/11/9307209/q-a-germanys-leadership-role-in-the-european-migrant-crisis.

85 Wood, 'Rebranding the nation', p. 162.

86 GIZ, *Germany in the Eyes of the World* (2018), p. 3.

87 Wood, 'Rebranding the nation'.

88 J. Kirchick, 'Verteidigung des Westens: Warum Deutschland die Freie Welt nicht anführen kann', *Frankfurter Allgemeine Zeitung* (17 July 2017), www.faz.net/aktuell/politik/ausland/warum-deutschland-freie-welt-im-westen-nicht-anfuehren-kann-15109703.html?printPagedArticle=true#pageIndex_0.

89 F. W. Steinmeier, 'Rede von Außenminister Frank-Walter Steinmeier anlässlich der 50. *Münchener Sicherheitskonferen*' (1 February 2014), www.auswaertiges-amt.de/en/newsroom/news/140201-bm-muesiko/259556.

90 S. Gabriel, 'Germany tops the Nation Brands Index', Federal Foreign Office press release (16 November 2017), www.auswaertiges-amt.de/en.

91 A. Sauerbrey, 'A new face in German diplomacy', *New York Times* (22 May 2018).

92 Joffe, *Der gute Deutsche*, p. 2.

93 Maull, 'Reflective, hegemonic, geo-economic, civilian ...?'.

94 H. P. Schwarz, *Die gezähmten Deutschen. Von der Machtbesessenheit zur Machtvergessenheit* (Stuttgart: DVA, 1985).

95 Maull, 'Reflective, hegemonic, geo-economic, civilian ...?', p. 468.

96 GIZ, *Germany in the Eyes of the World* (2018), pp. 2–3.

97 K. Oppermann, 'Between a rock and a hard place? Navigating domestic and international expectations on German foreign policy', *German Politics*, DOI: 10.1080/09644008.2018.1481208, p. 3.

98 Steinmeier, 'Germany's new global role', p. 106.

99 K. A. Crossley-Frolick, 'Revisiting and reimagining the notion of responsibility in German foreign policy', *International Studies Perspectives*, 18:4 (2016), pp. 443–64.

100 J. Gauck, Opening Speech to 50th Munich Security Conference, 31 January 2014, https://www.bundespraesident.de/SharedDocs/Reden/EN/JoachimGauck/Reden/2014/140131-Munich-Security-Conference.html.

101 J. Gauck, Speech to Mark the Day of German Unity, 3 October 2013, https://www.bundespraesident.de/SharedDocs/Reden/EN/JoachimGauck/Reden/2013/131003-Day-of-German-Unity.html.

102 U. von der Leyen, Speech by the Federal Minister of Defense at the 50th Munich Security Conference (31 January 2014), https://www.securityconference.de/fileadmin/MSC_/2014/Reden/2014-01-31-Speech-MinDef_von_der_Leyen-MuSeCo.pdf.

103 Steinmeier, 'Rede von Außenminister Frank-Walter Steinmeier anlässlich der 50. Münchener Sicherheitskonferen'.

104 Auswärtiges Amt, *Review 2014 – Außenpolitik weiter denken: Krise, Ordnung, Europa* (Berlin, 2014).

105 Auswärtiges Amt, *Review 2014*, pp. 24–5.

106 A. Bendiek, *The 2014 Review: Understanding the Pillars of German Foreign Policy and the Expectations of the Rest of the World* (Berlin: Stiftung Wissenschaft und Politik, 2015), p. 3.

107 N. Müller and C. Blume (eds), *Involvement or Restraint? Findings of a Representative Survey Conducted by TNS Infratest Policy Research on German Attitudes to Foreign Policy* (Berlin: Körber-Stiftung, 2014), pp. 2–5.

108 S.F. Szabo, 'Partners in leadership? American views of the new German role', *German Politics* (2018), https://doi.org/10.1080/09644008.2018. 1460661, p. 1.

109 K. Larres and R. Wittlinger, 'A fragile friendship: German–American relations in the twenty-first century', *German Politics*, 27:2 (2018), pp. 152–7.

110 Szabo, 'Partners in leadership?', p. 3.

111 Szabo, 'Partners in leadership?', p. 2.

112 J. Goldberg, 'The Obama doctrine', *The Atlantic* (4 April 2016).

113 R. Gates, 'On NATO's future', *Wall Street Journal* (10 June 2011).

114 G. Hellmann, 'Germany's world: power and followership in a crisis-ridden Europe', *Global Affairs*, 2:1 (2016), pp. 3–20.

115 G. Chazan, 'How Germany became Donald Trump's European punchbag', *Financial Times* (2 August 2018), p. 7.

116 Pew Research Center, '*Germany and the United States: reliable allies;* (2015), https://www.pewresearch.org/global/2015/05/07/germany-and-the-united-states-reliable-allies.

117 Pew Research Center, '*Americans say US-German Relations are in good shape, but Germans disagree*' (2018), https://www.pewresearch.org/global/2018/02/28/americans-say-u-s-german-relations-are-in-good-shape-but-germans-disagree.

118 E. Macron, 'The International Charlemagne Prize of Aachen. For the unity of Europe' (2018), www.elysee.fr/declarations/article/speech-by-m-emmanuel-macron-president-of-the-republic-on-receiving-the-charlemagne-prize.

119 U. Krotz and J. Schild, *Shaping Europe. France, Germany, and Embedded Bilateralism from the Élysée Treaty to Twenty-First Century Politics* (Oxford: Oxford University Press, 2013).

120 C. Schott, 'An analysis of Franco-German relations in the political context following the most recent elections', *European Issues* No. 464 (Paris: Foundation Robert Schuman, 2018), p. 1.

121 U. Krotz and J. Schild, 'Back to the future? Franco-German bilateralism in Europe's post-Brexit union', *Journal of European Public Policy*, 25:8 (2018), pp. 1174–93, at p. 1178.

122 Schieder, 'Zwischen Führungsanspruch und Wirklichkeit'.

123 J. Schild, 'Germany and France at cross purposes: the case of Banking Union', *Journal of Economic Policy Reform* 21:2 (2018), pp. 102–17.

124 W. Münchau, 'Germany is frustrating Emmanuel Macron's grand ambitions', *Financial Times* (15 April 2018), p. 5.

125 Schott, 'An analysis of Franco-German relations', p. 5.

126 Krotz and Schild, 'Back to the future?', p. 1177.

127 Pew Research Center, 'The new Sick Man of Europe: the European Union' (2013), https://www.pewresearch.org/global/2013/05/13/the-new-sick-man-of-europe-the-european-union.

128 Münchau, 'Germany is frustrating Emmanuel Macron's grand ambitions'.

129 Embassy of Germany in Paris, 'France-Allemagne, un partenariat de raison ?' (2017), https://allemagneenfrance.diplo.de/blob/1407976/c889851c9024b22353ad34e597d1aefb/2017-sondage-csa-datei-data.pdf.

130 H. W. Maull, 'Deutsche Außenpolitik nach der 'Review 2014': Zivilmacht 2.0?', *Zeitschrift für Politik*, 62:3 (2015), pp. 323–41.

131 H. Maas, 'Speech by Minister for Foreign Affairs at the National Graduate Institute for Policy Studies in Tokyo' (25 July 2018), www.auswaertiges-amt.de/en/newsroom/news/maas-japan/2121846.

132 Oppermann, 'Between a rock and a hard place?'.

133 Maull, 'Reflective, hegemonic, geo-economic, civilian …?', p. 474.

11

Conclusion: International Relations theory and Germany

Richard Ned Lebow

A well-known neo-realist repeatedly told his students that they did not have to leave Ohio to understand International Relations (IR). IR theorists know better. They are a well-travelled lot, mostly as a matter of choice, but sometimes not; in the 1930s, many important theorists had no choice but to flee their homelands. From the early years of the discipline, the interchange of IR scholars between the Anglosphere and the *deutsche Sprachraum* (countries in which German is spoken) has been nearly continuous and important for the intellectual growth of those involved, the development of the discipline and the view of Germany in the discipline. The contributors to this volume extend this tradition; they have studied, researched or taught outside their home countries. They are particularly sensitive to the perception others – most notably Americans – have of Germany and how these understandings reflect both historical developments in which Germany played a central role but also ongoing controversies and political projects in these other countries.

In this final chapter I focus on Germany and IR theory. There is widespread recognition that nineteenth- and twentieth-century German scholars have played an important role in the development of IR theory. This is most evident in the case of the realist paradigm, but equally applicable to constructivism and critical theory. Lucian M. Ashworth's chapter documents how German scholars were also central to the emergence and popularity in the first half of the twentieth century of the geopolitics paradigm. Discredited by two world wars, it is now undergoing a revival, especially in Eastern and Southern Europe.[1] Beginning in the Cold War, but even more in its aftermath, German scholars are once again playing an important role in IR theory.

Paul Petzschmann shows how the American study of Weimar and its Constitution was motivated by growing concerns about America's

Constitution. Leonie Holthaus argues that the construction of Germany as a 'negative other' was instrumental in the development of liberalism and the liberal paradigm of IR. Andreas Osiander analyses shifting conceptions of power in Germany. Annette Weinke shows how for much of the twentieth century, Germany fulfilled the function of a *bête noire* in the discourses of Anglo-American lawyers. Jens Steffek and Tobias Heinze explore a neglected aspect of German influence on the development of American realism. They document how reactionary Americans and German revisionists, and legal scholars in particular, deployed realist arguments to discredit the League of Nations, the Kellogg-Briand Pact and the Versailles peace settlement. Felix Rösch examines how these German refugee scholars were largely ignored in post-war Germany and, if commented on, dismissed as 'hyper-Americans'. Brian C. Etheridge explores the 'messy' and conflict-prone evolution of Cold War American understandings of 'Germanness' and how they were often used to glorify 'Americanism', but also to strengthen support for the ideals associated with it. Siegfried Schieder documents the contrasting perspectives of contemporary Germans and foreigners on the country's proper role in the world, and how this dissonance reflects different priorities and historical experiences.

I follow the lead of the previous chapters in exploring the way in which Germany was understood by others, but with a focus on IR theory. These understandings stimulated the development and relative appeal of different paradigms and they in turn provided frames of reference for understanding Germany and its foreign policy. There has been an iterative recursive relationship between national images and theory. Germany is, of course, only one of several countries whose domestic and foreign policies have stimulated the development of IR theory. The core focus of this concluding chapter is on Germany's relative standing as a role model and source of evidence for theorists. I suggest that in the post-war era, Germany has been the most frequent national role model for IR theorists and used in diverse ways by different paradigms.

There are probably several explanations for these phenomena. The most important may be the political fact that there have been multiple Germanies: pre-unification, Wilhelminian, Weimar, National Socialist, *Bundesrepublik* and DDR, and today's reunified, Germany. No other great power has gone through so many political and territorial changes in the course of the last 150 years. As a consequence, Germany went from being a playground for other powers to the dominant continental power, a pariah, a great power intent on revenge and world conquest, a country divided between opposing power blocs, middle-range power and economic powerhouse. Wilhelminian Germany was a positive role model for American public administration scholars, but after 1914 a negative role model for IR scholars. Nazi Germany was viewed even more negatively and was foundational for post-war realist balance of power and deterrence theories. It also figured prominently in the thinking of critical theorists.[2] The *Bundesrepublik* has been a positive role model for liberals and constructivists, but has been criticised by offensive realists for allegedly neglecting its defence. Germany is a laboratory in its own right given the many comparisons that can be made across its multiple iterations and identities.

Cases, learning, bias

The practice and theory of IR is very case-dependent. Throughout the ages, those who have practised or written about foreign policy or patterns of foreign relations have acted or generalised on the basis of their readings of recent history. This is, of course, unavoidable, but also problematic, as it encourages several kinds of conceptual errors and, moreover, errors that may to lead to misguided foreign policies.[3]

The first and perhaps most significant problem is that many generalisations based on recent history and countries tend to ignore historical context and may miss the conditions responsible for particular kinds of foreign policies or their consequences. They also risk mistaking the unusual for the general. Sometimes, generalisations have wider import, as is certainly true for Thucydides and Machiavelli. More often they are misleading, as is arguably true of so many realist and liberal claims made during the Cold War. The so-called 'Long Peace' between the superpowers seemed like an anomaly that required an extraordinary explanation primarily because of the analogies between Hitler and Stalin and the use of the lens of the 1930s to analyse the Cold War of the 1950s, 1960s and even 1970s. Consider too the assertions of Hans Morgenthau (until late in his life), Kenneth Waltz and John Mearsheimer that IR is unchanging and that there is no way to escape anarchy and its consequences, the imposition of hegemony aside.

Second, all such generalisations rely on interpretations of the recent events that are deemed important. As a general rule, close-to-the-event readings of history rarely stand up over time. They are formulated in the absence of adequate documentation and, more often than not, play fast and loose with what evidence is available as they are intended to advance contemporary political agendas. The origins of the First World War offer a striking example. Early accounts made use of selectively released documents in selective ways to try to establish the responsibility of adversaries for war, and slightly later revisionist accounts did the same in reverse.[4] The first unbiased and truly scholarly account of the origins of the First World War was that of Luigi Albertini, written in the 1940s but not published until the 1950s.[5] German revisionism, triggered by Fritz Fischer's *Griff nach der Weltmacht*, published in 1961, and the release of additional documents in the aftermath of the Cold War and re-unification of Germany prompted more refined interpretations.[6] Interpretation is also ongoing because the war guilt question has receded in importance, to be replaced by other research foci deemed more relevant to present-day concerns.[7]

Third, generalisations about past events encourage superficial comparisons between them and the present. Once patterns are established in our mind, we are primed to impose on them on the information we receive and also to look for information that confirms it. We are correspondingly less open to contradictory information and interpretations. For this reason, close-to-the event interpretations of history and the putative lessons based on them are likely to have a longer shelf life than they might otherwise.[8] Belief in the efficacy of deterrence is a case in point. Without a shred of evidence, American scholars and policy-makers came to believe that the Second World War in Europe could have been prevented if France and Britain had resisted by force, if necessary, Hitler's efforts to overturn the territorial settlement of the Treaty of Versailles. Deterrence was accordingly made the cornerstone of American national security policy in the Cold War and confirmed tautology. Leaders and scholars alike remained blind to its counterproductive consequences and dismissed out-of-hand arguments that deterrence, as practised by both superpowers, had been the principal cause of the Cuban missile crisis.[9]

Fourth, rereading debates about Germany – or any country or case – reveals how specific historical interpretations and their lessons are to the perceived problems and aspirations of the moment. Max Weber was right on target in insisting that the research questions we pose, and often the answers we find to them, are influenced, if not determined, by our worldview, position in society and moment in history.[10] They may tell us more about these attributes than the subject of the research. This problem cannot readily be circumvented by extending our reach back to earlier cases and periods of history because they too will be selected and interpreted on the basis of our current concerns.

There are thus close links across countries, cases, lessons and theory. Transformative events generate research questions, and answers to them most often depend on our reading of recent history. These readings generate associated lessons which may become the basis or justification for foreign policies. These readings and lessons in turn shape worldviews of policy-makers and theorists, making them more sensitive to information that might confirm these views and much less so to that which appears to contradict it. Looking at the treatment of Germany in temporal perspective offers some insights into this process. Several contributors to this volume shed light on pieces of this process. In the section that follows,

I analyse Germany in comparative perspective and assess its relative importance as an inspiration and role model for theory, source of evidence in support of or against particular theories and, perhaps most importantly, of the questions that drive the development of theory.

Quantitative comparisons

As noted above, Germany is not the only country central to the development of IR theory in the twentieth century. To get some rough idea of how important respective countries might be for IR theory, I conducted a simple quantitative analysis. I constructed a sample of twenty-one well-known theory books, representative of diverse traditions in the field. The first of these books (see the list below) was published in 1948 and the most recent in 2012. There is at least one book in the sample from every decade. I deliberately avoided books that tried to develop theory on the basis of a one- or two-country study in favour of those that developed theories that they illustrated with numerous short examples.

There are twenty-one books and twenty-three authors because two of the books are co-authored. The Deutsch book has seven co-authors, but one senior author. These books are representative of Anglo-American

Table 11.1 Authors and books

E. H. Carr, *The Twenty Years' Crisis* (1939)
Hans J. Morgenthau, *Politics among Nations* (1948)
Karl W. Deutsch et al., *Political Community and the North Atlantic Area* (1957)
Thomas Schelling, *The Strategy of Conflict* (1964)
Hedley Bull, *The Anarchical Society* (1977)
Robert Jervis, *Perception and Misperception in International Relations* (1979)
Kenneth Waltz, *Theory of International Politics* (1979)
Bruce Bueno de Mesquita, *The War Trap* (1981)
Robert Gilpin, *War and Change in World Politics* (1981)
Robert Keohane, *After Hegemony* (1984)
Gordon Craig and Alexander George, *Force and Statecraft* (1985)
Nicholas Onuf, *A World of Our Making* (1989)
Friedrich Kratochwil, *Rules, Norms, and Decisions* (1989)
Cynthia Enloe, *Bananas, Beaches, and Bases* (1990)
Alexander Wendt, *Social Theory of International Politics* (1999)
John Mearsheimer, *The Tragedy of Great Power Politics* (2001)
Barry Buzan and Ole Weaver, *Regions and Powers* (2003)
Kenneth Booth, *Critical Security Studies and World Politics* (2005)
Richard Little, *The Balance of Power* (2007).
Richard Ned Lebow, *A Cultural Theory of International Relations* (2008)
Daniel Levine, *Recovering International Relations* (2012)

IR. Sixteen of the authors are Americans or worked in the US when their books were published. Two of these were German by origin and one of them Czech. Six are British or worked in Britain. One of the co-authors is Danish. One of the British authors is Australian by nationality and five of the American authors were born in Europe. All the books were written in English.

The books and their authors represent a wide range of approaches to IR. Five of the authors – Carr, Morgenthau, Waltz, Gilpin and Mearsheimer – are realists, but represent different traditions within that paradigm. Three are liberals – Deutsch, Keohane and Wendt – but here too there is diversity. There are three constructivists (Kratochwil, Onuf and Lebow), two representatives of the Copenhagen School (Buzan and Waever), two of the English School (Bull and Little), one feminist (Enloe), one rationalist (Bueno de Mesquita) and one critical theorist (Levine). Four authors – Schelling, Jervis, Craig and George – are difficult to classify because they work in different traditions or bridge them. A case could nevertheless be made for counting Jervis, Craig and George among the realists. There are no poststructuralists represented.

To construct my data set, I used the indexes to each of the selected books to determine how much attention was devoted to any country. I counted pages for any country for which there were two or more page references. I summed page numbers for each book and for the totals across the twenty volumes. Indexes vary in quality and there is no good way of controlling for this other than random checks and re-indexing of books whose indexes are shown to be wanting. I made random checks in volumes that looked slim in their indexing to see if any countries were excluded that would otherwise have been included in my totals. I did not find any. I had to take into account that countries sometimes have multiple names in the same book. The UK is indexed differently in different books, and sometimes, in books that draw examples from a longer span of history, there are separate references for England, Scotland and Ireland. There is also true for other countries, among them Germany and Russia. In the latter case there are sometimes separate headings for Russia and the Soviet Union. I also had to control for references to prominent leaders of countries. Hitler and Stalin have numerous citations in some books on pages not listed under Germany or the Soviet Union. I included Scandinavia and the European Union (EU) as regional actors because they are treated as such by some authors and are central to their theorising. I did not create separate categories for Europe, Africa, Latin America or the Middle East, even though there are frequent references to them. They are treated by authors who cite them as regions, not as regional actors.

Good indexes indicate the frequency with which countries are cited, but say nothing about the purposes for which they are mentioned. One of the most important dimensions in this regard is agency. There is a big difference between discussing a country because of its domestic structure or foreign policies or because it is the focus of attention of other actors. In the 1930s, Germany was most frequently cited for its domestic politics and foreign policy, but during the Cold War because it was a site of contestation between the superpowers. More recently, Afghanistan and Iraq feature prominently for this reason. For much of its history as a unified country, Germany was an important actor on the world stage, but before national unification and later as a divided nationfor five decades of the post-war era, it was a zone of competition by greater powers. The Berlin crises, in which it was a largely passive actor, get much play in some books, but the Germany of Wilhelm and Hitler, and the *Bundesrepublik* receive the most theoretical attention.

Even controlling for active and passive references to countries, raw frequency in indexes is not necessarily a good measure of a country's importance for IR theory. Another important consideration is the nature of the event in connection with which a country is cited. Some events are considered more important than others by many theorists, as are the origins of the two World Wars and the beginning and end of the Cold War. Also important are 'dogs that do not bark', among which are no world revolution following the Bolshevik success in Russia, no World War III arising from the Cold War and no triumph of liberal democracy in the aftermath of that conflict and the break-up of the Soviet Union. Only particular combinations of countries and events – or non-events – have importance for IR theorists. Their judgements are paradigm-driven or theory-driven and there is considerable variation across paradigms and approaches nested in them. They determine which events or countries receive attention and act as spurs to theory development or evidence in support of or against particular theories.

My data indicate that not all paradigms have an equal interest in the empirical world. Realists, liberals and constructivists are very interested in history. They refer extensively to countries and events mostly, but by no means exclusively, from 1914 up to the present day. The Western world gets more attention than the non-West. Some realists and constructivists engage early modern Europe or the ancient world. Liberals understandably have little interest in the pre-industrial and pre-democratic era. Interestingly, the level of empirical engagement differs less across these three paradigms than within them. Some authors – Carr (a realist), Deutsch (a liberal), Buzan and Waever (of the Copenhagen School) and Lebow (a constructivist) – have many more country citations than other scholars in their respective paradigms. Keohane (a liberal), Kratochwil (a constructivist) and Jervis (difficult to classify) cite far fewer countries. The constructivist Onuf and the structural liberal Wendt have no country cites.

Rationalists and feminists – there is one book of each on the list – engage the historical world and here too variation seems greater within than across paradigms. Critical theorists are the least interested in the empirical world and the one book in my sample – Levine – has only two country references. To be fair, Levine has engaged the empirical world in other writings.

Differences arise across paradigms because of their different assumptions, interests and questions. Many realists – Morgenthau is a major exception – work at the system level and treat all states as interchangeable units. They are primarily interested in great powers, although Mearsheimer has multiple references to other states. Liberals, constructivists and the Copenhagen School are the most concerned with states that do not qualify as great powers. Lebow indexes twenty-nine countries, Buzan and Waever sixty-eight countries. Realists E. H. Carr and Mearsheimer refer to thirty-five and thirty-one countries, respectively, but most in a passive manner. See the appendix to this chapter for the full list of authors, books and countries.

As we might expect, the great powers are the most frequently indexed countries. Figure 11.1 below lists all the countries that were great powers from 1900 up to the present day. Their combined citation is 4,837, which means that 9 out of 102 international actors account for 72 per cent of the total citations. The EU comes next with 119 cites, and there is a significant drop from it to the next countries on the list: Poland (72) and Cuba (67). Forty countries are cited 10 or fewer times.

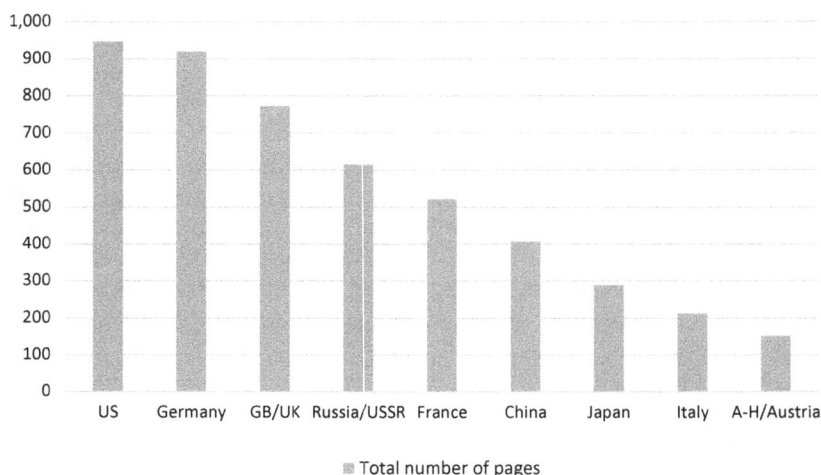

Figure 11.1 Total index pages of the top nine countries

Not surprisingly, the US, a great power up to 1945 and a superpower since, is first with 947 citations. It is also the home country or professional residence of 16 of our 23 authors. The decade in which it received no cites – the 1960s – is an artifact of the data set. There is one book in this decade – Schelling's *Arms and Influence* – and it is badly indexed. There is no index citation for the US, although it is central to the book and would have close to 100 cites. I have accordingly left this decade blank as re-indexing Schelling would have required similar indexing of other books to avoid bias.

Germany, with 920 entries, comes second, and I will discuss it momentarily. Great Britain/UK is third with 773 cites. This is clearly a sign of its central role in IR, even in the post-war era, but also the fact that five of the authors are British and one, an Australian, spent much of his career in that country. The rankings of Russia (615), France (521), Japan (289), Italy (213) and Austria-Hungary/Austria (152) reflect their rankings as great powers for much of the twentieth century. Italy and Austria-Hungary were among the weakest of the powers, and the latter ceased to exist in 1918, which may account for why they are at the bottom of the top nine. China (407) ranks sixth, but has attracted more attention in recent decades as it has become more powerful (see Table 11.2 below). It is highly likely that China citations will grow absolutely and relatively in the decade ahead.

Germany, number two on the index list, has 920 index entries, only 27 citations fewer than the US – although the gap between the two countries would have been larger if Schelling's book had been indexed properly. The high German score is really quite striking as Germany has not been a great power since 1945. It is nevertheless of interest to IR scholars in every decade (see Table 11.2 below) and across paradigms.

For many realists, Germany is the negative 'other', the aggressive state against which status quo powers must balance. Realist analyses of the

Table 11.2 Number and percentage of index entries per country

US	947	13.90%
Germany	920	13.51%
GB/UK	773	11.35%
Russia/USSR	615	9.03%
France	521	7.65%
China	407	5.97%
Japan	289	4.24%
Italy	213	3.13%
Austria-Hungary/Austria	152	2.23%
Top 9	**4,837**	**71.01%**

origins of the two World Wars analyse them in terms of power. Realists ask why the balance of power failed in 1914 and did not form prior to 1939. In our sample, realists E. H. Carr, Hans Morgenthau, Kenneth Waltz, and John Mearsheimer make these questions central to their theories. Other realists not included in my sample – this includes power transition theorists – use Germany in similar ways. The biggest difference among them is the extent to which their analyses are based on the relative capability of great powers in 1914 and 1939, their leaders' perceptions of likely changes in these capabilities, and their respective goals (expansion vs. defence of the status quo). Some of these theorists do not see Germany as exceptional in any way in comparison to other great powers, but those who stress leader goals do.

Critical theorists are polar opposites of realists in many ways. For a start, they focus more on state and society than the system level. While most realists are concerned about preserving the territorial status quo, most critical theorists favour dramatic, even revolutionary change and transformation, of units and the society in which they function and study. Many critical theorists – and this includes most members of the Frankfurt School – make no distinction among capitalist states. Horkheimer, Adorno and Marcuse – not in our sample – treat them as more or less interchangeable, even though they felt the need to flee for their lives from one capitalist state to another. Germany was only of interest to them because it was one of the most advanced capitalist economies. Some critical theorists, including Erich Fromm and Dan Levine – the last author in my sample – are very much interested in differences among states. For Fromm, Germany is more different in degree than in kind from other developed countries and of interest because of the intolerable angst freedom can create for people.

Liberals are drawn to Germany for negative and positive reasons. The country has progressed from negative role model to positive exemplar of the values of capitalism and democracy. Joseph Schumpeter typifies the former. Writing in the immediate aftermath of the First World War, he attributed that conflict to the atavistic survival of an aristocracy, whose claim to power in Germany, Austria-Hungary and Russia was based on their military prowess. He argued that they went to war to preserve their political authority and honour. Like earlier British liberals, John Bright and Richard Cobden, he expected a world of democratic, capitalist states to be a peaceful one. For liberal theorists, Nazi Germany was the ultimate negative 'other', although after 1945 the Soviet Union would assume this role. Both countries were perceived as existential threats to the survival of liberal, democratic values. The *Bundesrepublik*, by contrast, was cited as proof of the virtues of democratic capitalism, and so too is the collapse of the Soviet Union, East Germany and the communist regimes of Eastern Europe. Self-congratulation reached its apotheosis in Francis

Fukuyama's famous, if erroneous, claim that these events had brought about an end to history.[11]

Constructivists are more eclectic in their choice of countries. Germany is at the top of the list for Lebow, but *Cultural Theory of International Relations* is not typical of the paradigm. The English School, represented by Hedley Bull, focuses largely on the great powers. Bull is atypical because of his disproportionate number of references to China. Feminism may be the most eclectic of paradigms and Cynthia Enloe's book represents it well. There are as many references to non-Western and developing countries as there are to Western ones. Germany is treated as merely one more Western power. The Copenhagen School and post-colonial scholars follow feminists in having a more global than European outlook. Germany accordingly recedes in importance as non-Western countries receive more attention.

Conclusion

Germany's central role in IR is, in my judgement, attributable to several reinforcing factors. First and foremost is its role in world affairs in the first half of the twentieth century. Germany was Europe's dominant power from 1870 to 1945 and for much of that period sought to advance its perceived interests through the exercise of military and economic power, often at the expense of the European community. Its foreign policy did not justify *Realpolitik*, but to many students of IR, made it appear the almost inevitable *modus operandi* of great and dominant powers. During this era and its immediate aftermath, the realist paradigm took shape. It was hardly surprising that Germany provided positive and negative role models for theorists.

Next in importance is the partially German roots of the realist paradigm. Thucydides, Machiavelli and Hobbes are generally described by Anglo-Americans as the fathers of this paradigm, but so too are Ranke, Treitschke, Weber and Meinecke. Writing in the shadow of Hegel's philosophy and Germany unification, they stressed the moral and political centrality of the state. Influenced as well by Darwin, Treitschke and Weber depicted IR as a no-holds-barred struggle for survival and greatness.[12] First-generation realists Hans Morgenthau, Nicholas Spykman, George Liska and Arnold Wolfers were steeped in this intellectual tradition. So too was John Herz, although he, more than the others, was also influenced by liberal and legal traditions.

It is also significant that many first-generation realist scholars emigrated from continental Europe to the US. The US emerged as the dominant power in the post-Second World War era, very much in need of theoretical foundations for its foreign policy, and these theorists hastened to fill the need. Given the country's importance, wealth and expanding university population, their writings found ready audiences. They benefited from still-rampant American cultural and intellectual insecurity that valued European thinkers, artists and performers more than their native-born counterparts. The thick accents of Hans Morgenthau and Henry Kissinger were an advantage, not a detriment. While their thinking was initially European, it gradually took on American overtones. This was particularly evident in the intellectual development of Hans Morgenthau, who was very much influenced by American political traditions and writings, and increasingly liberal in his take on international relations. First-generation realists and, even more, their successors could credibly describe themselves as Americans and be accepted as such by other Americans.

These transplanted Germans and other Europeans became the dominant voice in IR theory. Through them, German thinking about international affairs entered American discourse, although over time it assumed an increasingly American flavour. So too did the centrality of Germany for IR theory, as it was foundational to their personal and intellectual development. In recent decades, American interests have become increasingly focused on Asia. Theory has also begun to move in this direction, as my study of indexes suggests. This shift reflects the growing importance of the Pacific Rim for American trade, investment and security, but also the passing from the scene of European émigré and European-trained American scholars of IR. It may be a manifestation of a broader phenomenon. In history and language, attention and student interest has shifted away from Europe towards the Middle East and Asia.

Finally, the discipline is more highly fragmented than it was in the 1940s, 1950s or 1960s. In those decades, realists and liberals, and their respective variants and syntheses, dominated the scholarly discourse. Germany was central to both paradigms for reasons I have already described. With the rise of other paradigms, Germany declined in relative importance and is likely to continue to do so.

Forecasting is notoriously problematic, but I will attempt this with regard to Germany and IR theory. My look ahead is based on the proposition that two factors above all others determine a country's importance for IR theory. The first is the distribution of paradigms and the second is the role of a country for these paradigms. I noted the increasing fragmentation of the field and think it is highly unlikely that any one paradigm will become dominant any time soon. In the US, rationalism is on the rise, but so are constructivism, feminism and critical theory. In Britain and Europe, diversity is equally great, but the distribution is different. Realism and liberalism find much less resonance, and constructivism, the English School, critical theory, poststructuralism, postcolonialism and Marxism correspondingly more.

Realism and rationalism focus on the great powers and are focused more than anything else on the origins and outcomes of wars. Rationalists are almost entirely concerned with the great powers, as is true of Bueno de Mesquita, their representative in my index sample. Germany is of less interest to contemporary realists and rationalists because it is no longer a world-class power, like the US or China, or perceived to be an aggressive one, like Russia. It appears most often in their writings when they use one or both World Wars as illustrative cases. Even without another great power war, references to Germany are likely to decline, those to the US remain about the same, and those to China, and perhaps India, increase.

Another reason for Germany's decline in interest to IR theory has to do with documentation about the policies of Germany and other great powers in the run-up to both World Wars. Documents emerged in dribs and drabs during and after both wars. When new documents appeared, they served as catalysts for new historical writing, which in turn was picked up by IR scholars and used to sustain or attack theories and theoretical claims. With the collapse of the GDR, the last major treasure trove of documents about Germany became available to scholars. It influenced the raft of books that appeared on the one-hundredth anniversary of the First World War. These works have stimulated new debates in IR theory. This cycle of new documents, new histories and new theories has, I think, all but run its course.

For all other paradigms, Germany, as noted above, is one of many countries, and idiosyncratic perhaps, but not special. I do not expect this to change. My forecast rests on my second consideration: the centrality of a country to a paradigm. Germany has been of great interest to realists and rationalists because of its perceived role as an initiator of two world wars. For liberals, Germany morphed from a negative to a positive role model, and the unification of Germany under Western aegis provided more evidence of their claim that capitalist democracy is the only rational response to the modern world.

Today, Germany is of most interest to scholars who study the EU, NATO, the ways in which political and economic influence is exercised without force or threats of force, and the shifting nature of, and conflict about, national identities. These foci cut across paradigms and methods. The EU is almost certain to remain a subject of great interest to IR scholars, regardless of whether the European project falters or remains robust. Germany's role in it will continue to remain central, and even more so if Brexit takes the UK out of the EU.

As noted, one of the several reasons why German was central in the development of IR between the wars and for several decades afterwards was the prominence of Germans in the profession. Germany may now be getting another boost for the same reason. It has produced a large number of IR scholars in the last two decades, many of them working in

Britain and the US, and almost all of them are writing in English. They are becoming increasingly prominent and helping to shape the IR agenda. Many of them draw on Germany, or Germany and other countries, for empirical evidence.

Notes

1 S. Guzzini (ed.), *The Return of Geopolitics in Europe? Social Mechanisms and Foreign Policy Identity Crises* (Cambridge: Cambridge University Press, 2012).
2 E. Fromm, *Escape from Freedom* (New York: Holt, Rinehart & Winston, 1941); M. Horkheimer, *Critique of Instrumental Reason; Lectures and Essays since the End of World War II* (New York: Seabury Press, 1974); T. W. Adorno, *The Authoritarian Personality* (New York: Harper, 1950).
3 I. Lustick, 'History, historiography, and political science: multiple historical records and the problem of selection bias', *American Political Science Review*, 90:3 (1996), pp. 605–18.
4 H. H. Herwig, 'Clio deceived: patriotic self-censorship in Germany after the Great War', *International Security*, 12:2 (1987), pp. 5–44.
5 L. Albertini, *The Origins of the War of 1914*, 3 vols, trans. I. M. Massey (Oxford: Oxford University Press, 1952–6).
6 F. Fischer, *Griff nach der Weltmacht: Die Kriegszielpolitik des kaiserlichen Deutschland 1914–18* (Düsseldorf: Droste Verlag, 1961); H. Pogge von Strandtmann, 'The political and historical significance of the Fischer controversy', *Journal of Contemporary History*, 48:2 (2014), pp. 251–70; A. Mombauer, 'The Fischer controversy, documents and the "truth" about the origins of the First World War', *Journal of Contemporary History*, 48:2 (2014), pp. 290–314.
7 W. Mulligan, 'The trial continues: new directives in the study of the origins of the First World War', *English Historical Review*, 129:538 (2014), pp. 639–66; R. J. Evans, 'The road to slaughter', *New Republic* (5 December 2011), www.newrepublic.com/book/review/the-road-slaughter; R. N. Lebow, 'What can international relations theory learn from the origins of World War I?' *International Relations*, 28: 4 (2014), pp. 387–411; R. N. Lebow, 'World War I: recent historical scholarship and IR theory?', *International Relations*, 28:2 (2014), pp. 245–50. For recent accounts, see S. Schmidt, *Frankreichs Außenpolitik in der Julikrise 1914* (Munich: Oldenbourg, 2009); H. Strachan, *The First World War: To Arms* (Oxford: Oxford University Press, 2013); T. G. Otte, *July Crisis: The World's Descent into War, Summer 1914* (Cambridge: Cambridge University Press, 2014), pp. 518–19; M. MacMillan, *The War That Ended Peace: How Europe Abandoned Peace for the First World War* (London: Profile, 2013); G. Kronenbitter, *Krieg im Frieden: Die Führung der k.u.k. Armee und die Grossmachtpolitik Österreich-Ungarns 1906–1914* (Munich: Oldenbourg, 2003); C. Clark, *The Sleepwalkers. How Europe Went to War in 1914* (London: Allen Lane, 2012); M. Rauchensteiner, *Der erste Weltkrieg und das Ende der Habsburger-Monarchie* (Vienna: Böhlau Verlag, 2013).
8 R. Jervis, *Perception and Misperception in International Relations* (Princeton: Princeton University Press, 1979), pp. 239–48; R. N. Lebow, 'Generational learning and foreign policy', *International Journal*, 40:4 (1985), pp. 555–85.

9 R. N. Lebow and J. Gross Stein, *We All Lost the Cold War* (Princeton: Princeton University Press, 1994), chs. 2–4, 13–15; R. N. Lebow, *Avoiding War, Making Peace* (London: Palgrave Macmillan, 2017), ch. 2.

10 M. Weber, *Protestant Ethic and the Spirit of Capitalism*, trans. S. Kalberg (Oxford: Oxford University Press, 2011), pp. 83, 98. R. N. Lebow, 'Weber's search for knowledge', in R. N. Lebow (ed.), *Max Weber and International Relations* (Cambridge: Cambridge University Press, 2017), pp. 70–88.

11 F. Fukuyama, *The End of History and the Last Man* (New York: Free Press, 1992).

12 R. N. Lebow, 'Max Weber and international relations', in Lebow (ed.), *Max Weber and International Relations*, pp. 10–39.

Select bibliography

Adler-Nissen, R., 'Are we all "lazy Greeks" or "Nazi Germans"? Negotiating international hierarchies in the Euro crisis', in A. Zarakol (ed.), *Hierarchies in World Politics* (Cambridge: Cambridge University Press, 2017), pp. 198–218.

Angell, N., *Prussianism and its Destruction* (London: William Heinemann, 1914).

Ash, M. and Söllner, A. (eds), *Forced Migration and Scientific Change: Émigré German-Speaking Scientists and Scholars after 1933* (Cambridge: Cambridge University Press, 1996).

Baldwin, A. R., 'British Opinion on the German Constitution, 1918–1934' (PhD dissertation, Oxford University, 2008).

Banchoff, T., *The German Problem Transformed: Institutions, Politics and Foreign Policy, 1945–1995* (Ann Arbor: University of Michigan Press, 1999).

Baumann, R. and Hellmann, G. 'Germany and the use of military force: "total war", the "culture of restraint" and the quest for normality', *German Politics*, 10:1, pp. 61–82.

Baumann, R., Rittberger, V. and Wagner, W., 'Macht und Machtpolitik. Neorealistische Außenpolitiktheorie und Prognosen über die deutsche Außenpolitik nach der Vereinigung', *Zeitschrift für Internationale Beziehungen*, 6:2 (1999), pp. 245–86.

Bavaj, R. and Steber, M. (eds), *Germany and 'the West': A History of a Modern Concept* (New York: Berghahn Books, 2015).

Berman, S. E., 'Modernization in historical perspective: the case of imperial Germany', *World Politics*, 53:3 (2001), pp. 431–62.

Boulding, K. E., 'National images and international systems', *Journal of Conflict Resolution*, 3:2 (1959), pp. 120–31.

Bracher, K. D., *Deutscher Sonderweg – Mythos oder Realität?* (Munich: Oldenbourg, 1982).

Bradley, M. P., *The World Reimagined. Americans and Human Rights in the Twentieth Century* (Cambridge: Cambridge University Press, 2016).

Brockmeier, S., 'Germany and the intervention in Libya', *Survival*, 55:6 (2013), pp. 63–90.

Bucher, J. et al., 'Domestic politics, news media and humanitarian intervention: why France and Germany diverged over Libya', *European Security*, 22:4
(2013), pp. 524–39.

Bulmer, S. and Paterson, W. E., 'Germany as the EU's reluctant hegemon? Of
economic strength and political constraints', *Journal of European Public Policy*,
20:10 (2013), pp. 1387–405.

Bulmer, S. and Paterson, W. E., 'Germany in the European Union: gentle giant or
emergent leader?', *International Affairs*, 72:1 (1996), pp. 9–32.

Coser, L., *Refugee Scholars in America: Their Impact and Their Experiences* (New
Haven: Yale University Press, 1984).

Douglas, L., *The Memory of Judgement: Making Law and History in the Trials of
the Holocaust* (New Haven: Yale University Press, 2000).

Duffield, J. S., 'Political culture and state behaviour: why Germany confounds
neorealism', *International Organization*, 53:4 (1999), pp. 765–803.

Duffield, J.S., *World Power Forsaken: Political Culture, International Institutions
and German Security Policy after Unification* (Stanford: Stanford University
Press, 1999).

Eley, G., *The Pecularities of German History: Bourgeois Society and Politics in
Nineteenth-Century Germany* (Oxford: Oxford University Press, 1984).

Ellis, H. and Kirchberger, U. (eds), *Anglo-German Scholary Networks in the Long
Nineteenth Century* (Leiden: Brill, 2014).

Etheridge, B. C., *Enemies to Allies: Cold War Germany and American Memory*
(Lexington: University Press of Kentucky, 2016).

Fermaglich, K. L., *American Dreams and Nazi Nightmares: Early Holocaust
Consciousness and Liberal America, 1957–1965* (Waltham, MA: University
Press of New England, 2006).

Germann, J., 'Beyond "geo-economics": advanced unevenness and the anatomy
of German austerity', *European Journal of International Relations*, 24:3 (2018),
pp. 590–613.

Gienow-Hecht, J. C. E., *Transmission Impossible: American Journalism as
Cultural Diplomacy in Postwar Germany, 1945–1955* (Baton Rouge: Louisiana
State University Press, 1999).

Greenberg, U., *The Weimar Century: German Émigrés and the Ideological
Foundations of the Cold War* (Princeton: Princeton University Press, 2014).

Haftendorn, H., *Deutsche Außenpolitik zwischen Selbstbeschränkung und
Selbstbehauptung 1945–2000* (Stuttgart: Deutsche Verlagsanstalt, 2001).

Harnisch, S., 'Change and continuity in post-unification German foreign policy',
German Politics, 10:1 (2001), pp. 35–60.

Harnisch, S. and Maull, H. W. (eds), *Germany as a Civilian Power? The
Foreign Policy of the Berlin Republic* (Manchester: Manchester University
Press, 2001).

Hellmann, G., 'Fatal attraction? German foreign policy and IR/foreign policy
theory', *Journal of International Relations and Development*, 12:3 (2009),
pp. 257–92.

Hellmann, G., 'Deutsche Rollen in der Weltpolitik. Eine Kritik der IB-
Rollentheorie', in K. Brunner and F. Kießling (eds), *Von der Zivilmacht zum*

europäischen Hegemon? Bundesdeutsche außenpolitische Rollen aus geschichts-und politikwissenschaftlichen Perspektiven (Baden-Baden: Nomos, 2019).

Herbst, J., *The German Historical School in American Scholarship: A Study in the Transfer of Culture* (Ithaca: Cornell University Press, 1965).

Herz, J. H. (ed.), *From Dictatorship to Democracy: Coping with the Legacies of Authoritarianism and Totalitarianism* (Westport, CT: Greenwood Press, 1982).

Holthaus, L., *Pluralist Democracy in International Relations: L.T. Hobhouse, G.D.H. Cole and David Mitrany* (New York: Palgrave Macmillan, 2018).

Jervis, R., *The Logic of Images in International Relations* (Princeton: Princeton University Press, 1970).

Joffe, J., *Der gute Deutsche. Die Karriere einer moralischen Supermacht* (Gütersloh: C. Bertelsmann, 2018).

Junker, D. (ed.), *Transatlantic Images and Perceptions: Germany and America since 1776* (Cambridge: Cambridge University Press, 1997).

Jütersonke, O., *Morgenthau, Law and Realism* (Cambridge: Cambridge University Press, 2010).

Kaelberer, K., 'Hegemony, dominance or leadership? Explaining Germany's role in European monetary cooperation', *European Journal of International Relations*, 3:1 (1997), pp. 35–60.

Katzenstein, P. J., *Policy and Politics in West Germany: The Growth of a Semi-sovereign State* (Philadelphia: Temple University Press, 1987).

Katzenstein, P. J. (ed.), *Tamed Power: Germany in Europe* (Ithaca: Cornell University Press, 1997).

Katzenstein, P. J., 'Same war, different views: Germany, Japan, and the war on terrorism', *Current History*, 101:659 (2002), pp. 427–35.

Kennedy, P. M., *The Rise of Anglo-German Antagonism 1860–1914* (London: George Allen & Unwin, 1980).

Khong, Y. F., *Analogies at War: Korea, Munich, Dien Bien Phu, and the Vietnam Decisions of 1965* (Princeton: Princeton University Press, 1992).

Lebow, R. N., 'German Jews and American realism', *Constellations*, 18:4 (2011), pp. 545–66.

Lebow, R. N. (ed.), *Max Weber and International Relations* (Cambridge: Cambridge University Press, 2017).

Létourneau, P. and Räkel, M. E., 'Germany: to be or not be normal?', in P. G. Le Prestre (ed.), *Role Quests in the Post-Cold War Era: Foreign Policies in Transition* (Montreal: McGill-Queen's University Press, 1997), pp. 111–30.

Matthijs, M., 'The three faces of German leadership', *Survival*, 58:2 (2016), pp. 135–54.

Maull, H. W., 'Germany and Japan: the new civilian powers', *Foreign Affairs*, 69 (1990), pp. 91–106.

Maull, H. W. and Kirste, K., 'Zivilmacht und Rollentheorie', *Zeitschrift für Internationale Beziehungen*, 3:2 (1996), pp. 283–312.

Moeller, R. G., *War Stories: The Search for a Usable Past in the Federal Republic of Germany* (Berkeley: University of California Press, 2003).

Oppermann, K., 'National role conceptions, domestic constraints and the new "normalcy" in German foreign policy: the Eurozone crisis, Libya and beyond', *German Politics*, 21:4 (2012), pp. 502–19.

Paterson, W. E., 'Beyond semi-sovereignty: the new Germany in the new Europe', *German Politics*, 5:2 (1996), pp. 167–84.

Payne, J. L., 'Did the United States create democracy in Germany?', *The Independent Review*, 11:2 (2006), pp. 209–21.

Record, J., *The Specter of Munich: Reconsidering the Lessons of Appeasing Hitler* (Washington DC: Potomac Books, 2006).

Rösch, F. (ed.), *Émigré Scholars and the Genesis of International Relations: A European Discipline in America?* (Basingstoke: Palgrave Macmillan, 2014).

Schmidt, B. and Guilhot, N. (eds), *Historiographical Investigations in International Relations* (London: Palgrave Macmillan, 2018).

Schneider, C. J. and Slantchev, B. L., 'The domestic politics of international cooperation: Germany and the European debt crisis', *International Organization*, 72:1 (2017), pp. 1–31.

Schwarz, H. P., *Die gezähmten Deutschen. Von der Machtbesessenheit zur Machtvergessenheit* (Stuttgart: Deutsche Verlagsanstalt, 1985).

Scully, R., *British Images of Germany: Admiration, Antagonism, and Ambivalence 1860–1914* (New York: Palgrave Macmillan, 2012).

Shafir, S., *Ambiguous Relations: The American Jewish Community and Germany since 1945* (Detroit: Wayne State University Press, 1999).

Shilliam, R., *German Thought and International Relations: The Rise and Fall of a Liberal Project* (Basingstoke: Palgrave Macmillan, 2009).

Smith, H. W., 'When the Sonderweg debate left us', *German Studies Review*, 31:2 (2008), pp. 225–40.

Söllner, A., 'German conservatism in America: Morgenthau's political realism', *Telos*, 72 (1987), pp. 161–72.

Söllner, A., *Deutsche Politikwissenschaftler in der Emigration: Studien zu ihrer Akkulturation und Wirkungsgeschichte* (Wiesbaden: Westdeutscher Verlag, 1996).

Steinmetz, G., 'Ideas in exile: refugees from Nazi Germany and the failure to transplant historical sociology into the United States', *International Journal of Politics, Culture, and Sociology*, 23:1 (2010), pp. 1–27.

Sternberg, C., Gartzou-Katsouyanni, K. and Nicolaïdis, K., *The Greco-German Affair in the Euro-crisis: Mutual Recognition Lost?* (London: Palgrave Macmillan, 2017).

Storer, C., *Britain and the Weimar Republic: The History of a Cultural Relationship* (London: I. B. Tauris, 2010).

Sylvest, C., 'British liberal historians and the primacy of internationalism', in W. Mulligan and B. Simms (eds), *The Primacy of Foreign Policy in British History, 1660–2000: How Strategic Concerns Shaped Modern Britain* (Basingstoke: Palgrave Macmillan, 2010), pp. 214–31.

Taylor, A. J. P., *The Course of German History: A Survey of the Development of Germany since 1815* (London: Hamish Hamilton, 1945).

Teitel, R. 'Nuremberg and its legacy, fifty years later', in B. Cooper (ed.), *War Crimes: The Legacy of Nuremberg* (New York: TV Books, 1999), pp. 44–54.

Tewes, H., 'Das Zivilmachtkonzept in der Theorie der Internationalen Beziehungen. Anmerkungen zu K. Kirste und H. W. Maull', *Zeitschrift für Internationale Beziehungen*, 4:2 (1997), pp. 347–59.

Tewes, H., *Germany, Civilian Power and the New Europe: Enlarging NATO and the European Union* (Basingstoke: Palgrave Macmillan, 2002).

Volkmann, H. E. (ed.), *Ende des Dritten Reiches – Ende des zweiten Weltkriegs. Eine perspektivische Rückschau* (Munich: Piper, 1995).

Wallace, S., *War and the Image of Germany: British Academics 1914–1918* (Edinburgh: John Donald Publishers, 1988).

Weinke, A., *Gewalt, Geschichte, Gerechtigkeit. Transnationale Debatten über deutsche Staatsverbrechen im 20. Jahrhundert* (Göttingen: Wallstein, 2016).

Wolff, J., 'Democracy promotion and civilian power: the example of Germany's "value-oriented" foreign policy', *German Politics*, 22:4 (2013), pp. 477–93.

Index

Academy of International Law (The Hague) 102
Adenauer, Konrad 33, 189
Adorno, Theodor xi, 157, 232
Afghanistan 18, 191, 199, 203, 217
al-Assad, Bashar 191
Albertini, Luigi 213
al-Gaddafi, Muammar 4
Alsace 26–7
American Civil War *see* United States of America
American Council on Germany 170–1, 175
American Jewish Committee 133, 172
American Society of International Law 130
anarchy 52, 57, 85, 95, 107, 213
Angell, Norman 46, 48–50, 52
Anne of Bohemia and Hungary 21
anti-Semitism 77, 103, 137, 148, 157, 173, 178
appeasement 3, 50, 105, 115
Arab Spring 4
arbitration 21–2, 102, 105, 108–9
Arendt, Hannah viii, x, 146, 148, 150, 153–5, 158
arms export 4, 110
Arthur, Paige 135–6
Asquith, Herbert 129
austerity (regime) 4, 196
Australia 194–5
Austria-Hungary 219–20
autocracy 1, 49, 53

balance of power 101, 106, 115, 213, 215, 220
Barnes, Harry Elmer 101, 109, 114
Beard, Charles 101, 103–4, 114–15
Belgium 6, 25, 31, 48, 71, 126–8
Bentham, Jeremy 44
Berber, Friedrich J. (Fritz) 102, 111
Bergstraesser, Arnold 153
Berlin 27, 86, 102, 110, 111–12, 169, 173, 114
    crises (1948–49, 1958–59, 1961) 3, 172–3, 217
    University of 102–3, 153
    Wall viii, 9, 134, 177–9
Bernhardi, Friedrich von 49–50
Bilfinger, Carl 102, 104, 113
Bill of Rights 133
Bismarck, Otto von 27, 31, 37n20, 45, 51, 55, 64, 187
Bluntschli, Johann Caspar 129
Boer War 129
Borchard, Edwin M. 100–1
    approach to IR 104–8
    biography of 102–4
    reception of 111–14
    relations with Germany 108–11
Boulding, Kenneth E. 5
Bourbon dynasty 26
Bowman, Isaiah 8, 64–5, 68–72, 74, 76–7
Brandenburg Gate 5
Brandt, Willy 33
Brexit 197, 201, 223

Brigham, Albert Perry 67
Bright, John 220
British Empire 43, 45, 75, 93
Bruns, Viktor 102–3
Bryce Commission 123, 127
Bryce, James 48, 127–30, 138
Bulgaria 129
Bull, Hedley 188, 215–16, 221
Bülow, Bernhard von 30, 51
Bülow, Dietrich Heinrich von 73
Bundeswehr 198–203
Burgess, John 83, 89–92, 96, 98n36
Bush, George H. W. 199

Carnegie, Andrew 127, 130, 148
Carnegie Corporation 148
    Endowment for International
        Peace 130
    Foundation for International
        Peace 127
Carolingian dynasty 20
Carr, Edward Hallett 2, 105, 115,
    215–18, 220
Cassirer, Ernst 155
Catherine II, Empress of Russia 23
Cavell, Edith 127
Central Intelligence Agency (CIA) 149
Charlemagne Prize 200
Charles R. Walgreen Foundation 150
Chicago School of Political
    Science 101
China 4, 189, 194–5, 197, 200,
    218–19, 221, 223
Christendom 24, 26
civilian power *see* Zivilmacht
civilisation 6, 43, 47, 53, 69, 89–90,
    100, 129, 130, 149, 178, 188–9
    Western (liberal) 6, 7, 41, 47, 50–1,
        57, 124–6, 128, 170, 173, 178
Clark, Charles E. 104
Clemenceau, Georges 31
coalition government 4, 199
Coalition of the Willing (US-led) 4
Coates, Benjamin Allen 127
Cobden, Richard 220
Cold War viii, ix, 3, 10, 34, 73, 86, 105,
    124, 131, 136–7, 139, 144n84,
    149, 155, 167–76, 178–9, 185,
    187, 189–90, 193, 211–14, 217
    consensus 169–73, 180n5

collective security 9, 111, 114
    practice of 108, 115
    system of 101, 105, 107, 115
colonial administration 43–4
Columbia University 102, 149
Commission to Study the
    Organisation of the Peace 132–3
concentration camp 5, 45, 176
concert of powers (Europe) 101
Congress (United States) 112, 199
Congress of Vienna 17, 28
constructivism 211, 222
contextuality 152–3
Coser, Lewis 150
Council on Foreign Relations 69,
    80n26, 156
critical theory xi, 211, 222
Cuban missile crisis 214
culture, political 1, 14n18, 19, 32,
    39n32, 72, 83–5, 172, 184, 201

Dahrendorf, Ralf 56
Dalton, Hugh 69
Daniel, prophecy of 20
Darwin, Charles 221
Darwinism 106
de-Nazification 135–7
de Staël, Madame Germaine 125
decision-making 5, 13n11, 17, 32, 196
decolonialisation 3
democracy 13, 41–2, 44, 52, 83–4, 86
    American 1, 85, 92, 112, 158
    liberal 1, 42–3, 51, 158, 217, 223
    militant 54–5, 136
    promotion of 3, 5, 41, 52–3,
        131, 135–6
    Western 46, 53, 136
Denmark 29
deterrence 213–14
    nuclear 3, 159, 190
Deutsch, Karl W. x, 215–17
Deutsche Hochschule für Politik 103,
    150, 160n21
Deutscher Akademischer
    Austauschdienst (DAAD) 153
Deutsches Institut für außenpolitische
    Forschung 111
development, economic viii, x, 35, 41,
    83–4, 110
Dewey, John 46, 48–52, 55

Dickinson, G. Lowes 55, 107
Dieselgate scandal 196
Dimitrov, Georgi 132
diplomacy 106, 126, 190
    check book 191, 199
    public 10, 167–9, 180n4, 186–7
disarmament 110
Dornberg, John 136
Dorpalen, Andreas 64, 75
Duchêne, François 188–9, 202

Ebert, Friedrich 85, 92
Elias, Norbert 189
Elysée Treaty 202
Emerson, Rupert 8, 95
emigration 135, 145, 149–57
emigre scholars viii, x, 2, 10, 94, 100,
    137, 145, 146–59
Emperor (of the Holy Roman Empire)
    19, 21–6, 28, 36n8
English School (IR theory) 216, 221–2
Eulau, Heinz 159n3
Eurocentrism 53
Europe 4, 11, 17–28, 31–4, 44, 54, 73,
    75, 84–5, 101, 109, 124, 126–7,
    137, 222
    Christian 26
    Eastern 125, 131, 137, 200,
        211, 220–1
    integration of viii, x, 1, 3, 77, 184,
        187–93, 197–9, 201, 221, 223
    Southern 4, 135, 196, 211
European Community (EC) 188,
    192, 221
European Union (EU) 190–1, 216
Eurozone 195–6, 201

Fairgreve, James 76
fascism 50, 78, 84, 108, 132, 189
federalism 8, 88, 92–6
feminism x, 45, 216, 221–2
Ferdinand I (emperor) 21
Fichte, Johann Gottlieb 49–50, 52,
    74, 133
financial crisis (2008–09) 4, 11 185,
    191, 195–7, 199, 201–3
First World War 30, 32, 41–2, 46, 57,
    65, 66, 69, 71
Fischer, Fritz 32–3, 214
Fischer, Joschka 190

Fisher, Herbert A. L. 128
Flechtheim, Ossip K. 148
Football World Cup (2006) 193
Ford Foundation 148
foreign policy
    analysis of 105, 157, 169, 171, 173,
        184–204, 212–13, 221
    Prussian 1–2, 11, 30, 38n21, 45, 49
'Fourth Reich' 34
Fox, William T. R. 18, 156
Fraenkel, Ernst 149, 153, 155
France 3, 6, 18, 25–31, 46, 52, 69,
    90–1, 109, 125, 127, 138, 169,
    185, 193–6, 199–203, 214, 219
Franco-German War 125
Frankfurt School 149, 157, 220
Friedrich II, German Emperor 23–4
Friedrich, Carl Joachim 49, 82, 87,
    94, 155
Friedrich Wilhelm I, King of
    Prussia 23–4
Fryatt, Charles 127

Gabriel, Sigmar 196
Galtung, Johan 159n2
Gates, Robert 199
Gauck, Joachim 34–5, 198
GDR *see* German Democratic Republic
Geneva Conventions 129
genocide viii, 1, 115, 158, 176, 178
Genscher, Hans-Dietrich 33, 198
geopolitics *see* Geopolitik
Geopolitik 2, 8, 64–5, 71–8, 105, 211
George, Alexander 215–16
German Academic Exchange Service
    see Deutscher Akademischer
    Austauschdienst (DAAD)
German Democratic Republic 175,
    178, 220, 223
Germanness (Deutschtum) ix, 10,
    167–9, 171, 173–7, 179
Germany
    Empire of 1, 7–8, 16n32, 17, 19–20,
        30, 89, 131
    Federal Republic of 19, 33
    National Socialist 17, 20, 32, 34,
        71, 105, 110, 115, 174, 176–8,
        212–13, 220
    re-armament of 110, 114
    reunified ix, 20, 34, 197, 212

Germany (*cont.*)
  reunification 20, 34
  Weimar 8, 41, 56, 76–7, 82–96, 130,
    145, 148, 154–8, 211–12
  Wilhelminian 124, 130, 212
Gesellschaft für Internationale
  Zusammenarbeit (GIZ) 195
Gierke, Otto von 55
Gilpin, Robert 216
globalisation 6, 125, 132, 188
Glueck, Sheldon 134
Goebbels, Joseph 5, 113
Goethe Institute 195
Great Britain *see* United Kingdom
great powers 2–3, 17–18, 28, 34–5, 75,
  189, 212, 218–21, 223
Grotius, Hugo 130
Grundgesetz 190
Gurian, Waldemar 76, 148, 150

Habsburg (dynasty) 19, 21, 24–8
Haffner, Sebastian 134
Hague Conventions 126, 129
Hanover (electorate) 21–2
Haushofer, Albrecht 77
Haushofer, Karl 8, 64–5, 71, 74–7
Hegel, Georg Friedrich Wilhelm xi, 45,
  47–8, 50, 52, 55, 74, 125, 133, 221
hegemony 4, 26–31, 201, 213
Herz, John H. (Hans-Hermann) x, 76,
  100–1, 103, 115, 131–2, 134–7,
  148–9, 153, 158, 221
Hess, Rudolf 64, 74, 77
High Authority (European Coal and
  Steel Community) 188
Hilberg, Raul 159n3
Hindenburg, Paul von 32, 85–7
Historikerstreit 135
historiography 6, 100, 114, 124, 127,
  130, 139
Hitler, Adolf 1, 5, 49–50, 73, 77, 82,
  87, 100, 103, 108–10, 113, 134,
  170, 178, 213–14, 216–17
Hobbes, Thomas 104, 221
Hobhouse, Emily 45
Hobhouse, L. T. 7, 41, 45–7, 49–57
Hobson, John A. 45–6, 52, 57
Holborn, Hajo (Hans Joachim)
  148–9, 156

Holocaust viii, xi, 103, 111, 157,
  168–9, 175, 177–9, 184
  TV series 178
Holy Roman Empire 19–20, 22,
  24–6, 36n6
  character of imperial dignity 19, 20,
    24–5, 26
  public law in 21
  supreme courts of 21, 23
Horkheimer, Max xi, 157, 220
human rights law 9–10, 123–5, 127,
  132–3, 135, 137–8, 139n1, 190–1
humanitarian intervention 4, 15n22,
  35, 139, 159, 200–1
humanitarianism 41, 43, 47, 50,
  196, 198
humanity 5, 34, 43, 72, 78, 124,
  127, 130
Hungary 21, 196, 219–20
Huntington, Ellsworth 8, 68

Ichheiser, Gustav 160n15
idealism 51, 69–71, 83, 96, 104
Idealpolitik 187
ideology 43, 46, 54, 57, 114, 154, 172
Imperial Aulic Council 23
Imperial Germany *see* Germany
imperialism 30, 43, 45–6, 52, 124,
  134, 196
  British 45–6
industrial revolution 4, 16n32,
  28, 43, 73
Institut de Droit International /
  Institute of International Law 129
integration 41, 145–51, 155–6, 158,
  169–70, 184, 187–9
  functional 147, 157, 160n17
interdependence 106, 125, 188
intergovernmentalism 106
International Criminal Court
  (ICC) 137
International Institute for Strategic
  Studies (IISS) 188–9
international law 101, 103, 113,
  123–4, 132
  breach of 2, 9, 48, 102, 110, 114, 126
  compliance with 190, 202, 111
  conception of 91, 95, 109, 111, 123
  equality of states under 103, 131

enforcement of 125–6, 130
obligations under 113, 138
rules of 43, 113
status of 9, 54, 95
International Military Tribunal 123,
125, 129, 130, 133–4
international organisations 77, 101,
108, 113–15
International Political Geography
(IPG) 64–5, 67, 69, 71–4, 76–8
International Relations (IR) viii–xi,
1–4, 6–11, 41–2, 45, 50, 54–5,
57, 65, 68–9, 77–8, 82, 95, 100–2,
104, 106–9, 114–15, 132, 134–5,
137, 145–7, 149, 151, 154, 156–8,
185–6, 188–9, 192–3, 211–13,
215–17, 219, 221–4
Iraq 4, 18, 196, 199–200, 217
Ireland 216
isolationism 83, 101, 114–15
Israel 3, 6, 18, 105, 135, 173, 190,
194–5, 200
Italy 20–1, 25, 36n8, 36n10, 115, 153,
194–5, 201, 218–19

Jäckh, Ernst 150
Japan 3, 75, 77, 84, 103, 115, 134–5,
179, 189, 194–5, 218–19
Jervis, Robert 5, 186, 215–17, 224
Jessup, Philip 133, 171
Jews 100–3, 115, 131, 133, 137–8,
148–9, 168, 170–2, 175, 177–8,
196
Joanna of Aragon 21
Johnson, Alvin 150, 157, 174

Kaiser Wilhelm Society 103
Kaiser-Wilhelm-Institut für
ausländisches öffentliches Recht
und Völkerrecht 102–4, 112
Kampmark, Binoy 130, 134
Kant, Immanuel viii, x, 49–50,
73–4, 125
Kellogg-Briand Pact 100–1, 105,
112–14, 124, 133, 138, 212
Kelsen, Hans 131, 155
Kennan, George F. 105, 125, 171
Keohane, Robert O. 215–17
Kirchheimer, Otto 136, 149

Kissinger, Henry x, 222
Kjellén, Rudolph 74–5
Kohl, Helmut 3
Köhler, Horst 4, 34
Kohler, Joseph 126
Kriminalistische Vereinigung /
International Union of Criminal
Law 129
Kritz, Neil 136
Kulturnation 193

Laband, Paul 126
Lansing, Robert 130
Laqeur, Walter 159n3
Latin America 68, 102, 136, 139n1,
143n66, 216
league of democracies 52–3
League of Nations 48, 100–1, 113,
115, 131, 212
Covenant 108
foundation of 105
legalism 9, 124, 126, 130–1, 139
Levinson, Salmon 138
liberal internationalism xi, 7, 40, 42–6,
53, 56–7, 104, 124–5, 133, 138
liberalism 40–6, 52, 56–7, 145, 156,
172, 212, 222
Wilsonian 106, 114
Library of Congress 102, 149
Libya 4, 18, 191, 196, 199
Lieber, Francis 129
Lippmann, Walter 149
List, Friedrich 73
Liszt, Franz von 126
Lochner, Louis 134, 171
Lord Acton, John E. 125
Lorraine 27
Löwenstein, Karl 87, 150
Ludendorff, Erich 32

Maas, Heiko 196, 203
Machiavelli, Niccolò 105, 108,
213, 221
Mackinder, Halford 8, 65, 69–74, 76
Macron, Emmanuel 200–2
Mahan, Alfred Thayer 125
Manchester Guardian 45–6
Manifesto of the Ninety-Three
46–7, 126–7

Mann, Golo (Angelus Gottfried Thomas) 145
Mannheim, Karl 154
Marcuse, Herbert 149, 157, 220
Marxism 131, 145, 149, 222
Maull, Hanns W. 189, 197
Maull, Otto 71
Max-Planck-Institut für ausländisches öffentliches Recht und Völkerrecht 104
Mazzini, Giuseppe 44, 56
McCarthy, Joseph 149
Mearsheimer, John 105, 213, 216, 218, 220
Mein Kampf (Adolf Hitler) 77, 113
media 10, 34, 167–8, 171, 173–4, 176, 187
mediation 105, 108, 113
Meinecke, Friedrich 221
memory activism 169–71, 174–5
memory diplomacy 10, 167–9
Merkel, Angela 1, 4, 195–6, 199–200, 203
Mesquita, Bruce Bueno de 216, 223
metaphrase *see* translation
Middle East 216, 222
militarism x, 1, 7, 17, 32, 35, 42, 47, 51–2, 55, 105, 128, 132, 139
Mill, John Stuart 40, 42–4
Miracle of Bern (football) 193
Mitrany, David 52
Mixed Claims Commission 109
modernity, industrial 4, 43
modernisation, economic 7, 41
Monnet, Jean 188
Moore, John Basset 105–6, 114
Morgenthau, Hans J. viii, x, 9–10, 76, 82, 96, 100–1, 103, 105, 115, 145, 148–9, 151–2, 154–8, 162n56
  on the national interest 157–8
Morgenthau, Henry 133
Moroccan Crises (1905–11) 30, 46
Moscow Declarations 113
multilateralism 1–2, 184, 190–2, 202
Munich Security Conference 198
Murray, Gilbert 47

Napoleon Bonaparte 22, 27
narrative ix, 5, 45, 51–2, 56, 74, 76, 106, 123, 138, 170–5, 178–204

national interest 14n18, 34, 114
  see also Morgenthau, Hans J.
National Socialism viii, x, 4, 7, 32, 34, 111, 132–3, 155, 170–1, 176, 184, 187
  collaboration with 64, 71, 75–6, 88, 108, 110, 155, 174, 176
  party (NSDAP) 77, 103, 111, 113, 155, 170
nationalism ix–x, 8, 32, 41–2, 44–5, 47–9, 51, 53, 55–7, 89, 96, 177, 193
NATO *see* North Atlantic Treaty Organization
Naval Defence Act (Britain) 30
Nazism *see* National Socialism
negotiation 28, 55, 108, 130
neorealism (IR theory) 156
Netherlands, The 18
Neumann, Franz L. 82, 96, 149, 155
neutrality (international law) 104–6, 108, 110–12, 114, 128
New Deal 148
New School (university) 150, 157
New York Times 1, 36n4
Niebuhr, Reinhold 101, 156
Nietzsche, Friedrich xi, 49–50, 64
Nitze, Paul 156
non-intervention (legal doctrine) 105, 108
North Atlantic Treaty Organization (NATO) 190–2, 199–200, 223
  Article 5 200
NSA surveillance controversy 200
NSDAP *see* National Socialism
Nuremberg
  party rally (NSDAP) 5
  trials viii, 3, 123, 125, 133–4, 143n73, 174–6

Oakeshott, Michael 154
Obama, Barack H. 199
Office of Strategic Services (OSS) 135–7, 149, 155
Ohlendorf, Otto 134
Oppenheim, Lassa 40
Orford, Anne 124
Ostpolitik 33
Ottoman Empire 26, 53, 124, 129

pacifism 47, 126, 138, 190, 199
Palatinate 26
Paris Peace Conference (1919) 31, 69, 130, 132
peace 9, 17, 25, 27, 29, 37n11, 37n16, 42, 44–5, 49, 51–4, 57, 69, 71, 100–2, 106–7, 110, 112, 115, 123, 127, 130, 132–3, 138–9, 170–1, 193, 212–13
Pearl Harbor 103–4
Permanent Court of International Justice 105
Peter III, Emperor of Russia 23
Philip of Habsburg 210
philosophy 42–3, 47–50, 52, 54–5, 69, 73, 119n57, 134, 157, 221
Plan for Destruction (1943) 64, 71, 75
pluralism 86, 92, 94
Poincaré, Raymond 33
Poland 3, 6, 18, 33, 195–6, 218
   partitions of 24
Pollock, Sir Frederick 128
populism 1, 34, 159
Portugal 18, 25
post-colonialism 124, 221–2
post-structuralism xi, 222
power
   naval 43, 75
   transition 87, 220
Priemel, Kim Christian 125
progress 6, 40, 88, 90, 100, 127, 137, 139, 157, 173, 177
Progressivism 85
projections 193
Prussia 18–19, 21, 23–4, 26–9, 35, 54, 56, 88, 93
   militarism 7, 17, 35, 105, 139
Prussianism 41, 48, 50, 132
public intellectuals 6, 170–7, 175
public opinion 6, 51, 112, 172, 185, 186, 193, 201, 203
public relations firms 170–1

Rand Corporation 149
Ranke, Leopold von 45, 221
Rasmussen, Mikkel Vedby 132
rationalism 85, 222–3
Ratzel, Friedrich x, 8, 64–8, 74–6, 78
realism 125, 223

American x, 9, 100–1, 104–5, 107, 111, 113–15, 137, 212
   canon of 105
   classical 2, 10, 76–7
   epistemology of 105–6
Realpolitik 28, 45, 78, 105, 187, 221
recognition (international law) 108, 133
refugee crisis 191, 202
Reichstag (1871, German Empire) 30
Reinhard, Rudolf 71
Reinsch, Paul 68
Reiswitz, Georg Leopold von 66
relativism (law) 107, 111, 119n59
reparations 84, 101, 109–10
representation 43
   mental 5
   narrative 6
re-unification *see* Germany
revanchism 2, 109
revisionism 3, 9, 114, 139, 213
Ribbentrop, Joachim von 111
Ritter, Karl 73
Rockefeller Foundation 150, 153
rogue state 2–3, 6, 138
Roman Empire 20
Roosevelt, Franklin D. 103, 112, 133, 148, 172
Root, Elihu 49, 53–4, 130
Rousseau, Jean-Jacques 105
Russel, Bertrand 49–50
Russia 4, 6, 18, 23, 77, 86, 124, 191, 194–5, 197, 200, 216–20, 223
   revolutionary 53

Saar area 26
sacro egoismo 33
Saudi Arabia 18
Saxony 28–9, 37n20
Schelling, Thomas 215–16, 219
Schlüter, Ferdinand 112
Schmitt, Carl x, 3, 82, 88, 93–4, 100, 113, 139
Schröder, Gerhard 4, 199
Schuman, Frederick L. 101, 108, 115
Schumpeter, Joseph 220
Schwarzenberger, Georg 76
Scotland 216
Scott, Charles. P. 46, 53

Second World War viii, x, 1, 3, 7, 9, 11,
   19, 33, 49, 65, 71–2, 83–4, 103,
   110–11, 113–15, 123, 126, 136,
   139, 145, 149, 152, 155, 169, 171,
   173, 176, 179, 184, 187, 190, 192,
   197, 202, 214, 221
self-determination 44, 53
self-interest 19, 108
self-restraint (foreign policy
   doctrine) 106–7
Semple, Ellen Churchill 8, 66–8,
   72–4, 76, 78
Senate (United States) 112–13
Serbia 33
Seven Years War 37n11
Shotwell, James T. 132–3
Sidgwick, Henry 40
Sinzheimer, Hugo 149
socialisation 4, 10, 145
Society for the Prevention of World
   War III 170, 172
sociology 3, 46, 100, 157
Sommermärchen *see* Football World
   Cup 2006
Sonderweg 8, 16n32, 50–1, 56
South African Wars 45–6
sovereignty 3, 8–9, 82–3, 85, 87,
   89–96, 105, 113, 133
   juristic theory of 90–2, 94
Soviet Union (USSR) x, 10, 18, 77,
   105, 138, 167, 169, 172–3, 177–9,
   189, 216–17, 220
Spain 18, 21, 25, 155, 194–5, 201
Spanish Succession, War of the 17, 26
Speier, Hans 149
Spencer, Herbert 43–5, 47
Sportpalast speech 5
Spykman, Nicholas 75, 101, 159, 221
Stalin, Joseph 213, 216
State Department (United States)
   110, 171
States General, Dutch 25
Steinmeier, Frank-Walter 186,
   196, 198
Stimson, Henry L. 133
Strauss, Leo 150–1
Strausz-Hupé, Robert 64, 72–6, 171
Stresemann, Gustav 77
Stuart dynasty 22
Suganami, Hidemi 100

superpower x, 18, 36n4, 184,
   196, 219
Sweden 18, 25
Switzerland 21
symbolism 178
synecdoche *see* translation
Syria 18, 197

Third Reich *see* National Socialism
Thirty Years War 25, 37n11,
   38n26, 129
Thormann, Irma 162n56
Thucydides 105, 213, 221
Tillich, Paul 156
Tirpitz, Alfred von 30
total war 5
Toynbee, Arnold 47–8
traditionalism (international law)
   105
transatlantic partnership 199
Transitional Justice viii, 3, 9, 123, 136
translation
   as calque 154
   as metaphrase 152–3
   as synecdoche 154
Treaty of Berlin 110
Treaty of Brest-Litovsk 138
Treaty of Versailles 72, 77, 86, 100–3,
   105, 108–11, 113–14, 120n78,
   123, 130, 212, 214
   as Diktat 111, 113
   and disarmament 110
   legitimacy of 102
   peace settlement 9, 100–2, 212
   resistance against 2
   sanctions under 101
Treitschke, Heinrich von 45, 50,
   133, 221
Trilateral Commission 189
Trump, Donald J. 1, 18, 177, 196–7,
   199–200, 203

Ukraine crisis 191
United Kingdom 6, 7, 18, 21, 30,
   40–9, 51–7, 65–6, 69–71, 84, 86,
   112–15, 127–8, 169, 184–5, 189,
   191–9, 214–19, 222, 224
United Nations 106, 108, 113
   Law Commission 137
   Security Council 4, 191, 196, 200

United States of America
  Civil War 9, 88, 93–4, 96
  federal courts 104
  foreign policy x, 104–5, 157, 169,
    171, 173
  legislation 104, 106, 112
  neutrality 105–6, 108, 110–12, 114
University in Exile *see* New School
US *see* United States of America
utopianism 104

Vergangenheitsbewältigung x, 134–5,
    137
Versailles Treaty *see* Treaty of
    Versailles
Vienna
  Congress of 17–18, 28
  siege of 26
Vietnam War 105
Visegrád group 196
Voegelin, Eric 150–5
Vogel, Walter 71
Völkerpsychologie 125
von der Leyen, Ursula 198

Walsh, Edmund A. 75
Walt, Stephen 105
Waltz, Kenneth 156, 213, 216, 220
Wanklyn, Harriet 65
war
  American participation in 111–12
  causes of 8, 46, 107, 114, 214
  continuation of 109, 117, 175
  and human nature 107–8
war guilt (*Kriegsschuld*) 41, 49, 55, 57,
    127, 214
War of the Spanish Succession 17, 26
Weber, Max 3, 100, 214, 221
Wehberg, Hans 126

Weigert, Hans 64, 75
Weimar Constitution 8, 82, 84–5,
    87–9, 92, 95–6
  Article 48 86–7
  emergency powers 86
Weimar Republic 8, 41, 56, 76, 82–5,
    96, 100, 154–5, 158
West Germany *see* Germany
West, the 2–3, 33–4, 53, 65, 77, 84, 147
Westlake, John 129–30
Westphalia 28
  Peace of 25
Whittlesey, Derwent 8, 64, 68,
    72–4, 76, 78
Wilhelm II, German Emperor 30, 32,
    46, 131, 217
Willkommenskultur 196
Wilson, Andrew 70–1
Wilson, Trevor 128
Wilson, Woodrow 68, 131
Wolfers, Arnold 100, 148–9, 156, 221
Woolf, Leonard 54
Woolsey, Theodore 130
working class 44
World War I *see* First World War
World War II *see* Second World War
Wright, Quincy 132

Yale University 101
Young Turk Revolution 53

Zeitschrift für ausländisches
    öffentliches Recht und
    Völkerrecht (ZAÖRV) 103, 111
Zeitschrift für Geopolitik 64, 76–7
Zimmern, Alfred 41, 46, 51–2, 57
Zivilmacht 1, 3–4, 10–11, 14n18, 34,
    184–92, 197, 199, 202–4
Zuckmayer, Carl 151

EU authorised representative for GPSR:
Easy Access System Europe, Mustamäe tee 50,
10621 Tallinn, Estonia
gpsr.requests@easproject.com

www.ingramcontent.com/pod-product-compliance
Lightning Source LLC
Chambersburg PA
CBHW052000270326
41929CB00015B/2729